CONTEMPLATIVE BEHOLDING
A WAY OF LIFE AND LOVE

CONTEMPLATIVE BEHOLDING

A Way of Life and Love

Joel M. Upton

Lindisfarne Books | 2025

2025
Lindisfarne Books
Steinerbooks / Anthroposophic Press, Inc.
834 Main Street, PO Box 358
Spencertown, New York 12165
www.steinerbooks.org

Library of Congress Control Number: 2023931632

ISBN: 978-1-58420-901-0

Printed in the United States of America by Versa Press

To my wife Sara, the very embodiment of love,
into whose eternal thrall I fell during the first moment of our meeting
and without whom this book would not exist

The Cairn

A heap of stones makes a place
where nobody would think of stopping.
All there is to see is the gradual drop away
to some lost brook perhaps, and silence.
Yet you stand here miles from anywhere
Staring at the stones as if they could speak.
And what would they say but that here
is where to stay a while and listen.

Henry Lyman
Northampton, Massachusetts

CONTENTS

IV: VIA AMORIS

FOREWORD

Arthur Zajonc

IN A LETTER to his wife on October 10, 1907, Rainer Maria Rilke wrote concerning his struggles to understand the paintings of Cezanne on display at a Paris exhibition. Hour after hour Rilke stood before Cezanne's paintings, seeking but not seeing. He wrote to his wife, "For a long time nothing, and suddenly one has the right eyes."

How many times have you, like me, stood before a work of art without truly seeing the "art" of the painting or sculpture? We lack the right eyes required to see it. As Rilke describes, for a long time it seems that we are blind to it, but then quite suddenly we have the eyes to see it. The same experience is had by scientists when they stand before the data of an experiment seeking to see the law of nature that remains hidden in the data before them. Finally, the patient and fortunate researcher has the right eyes and sees deeply into what was always there.

In this remarkable book, my dear friend and colleague Joel Upton shares his practice of contemplative beholding, which is a journey from separation and loss to the intimation of reconciliation. It is a journey I have been privileged to share with him over many years, and I am delighted that he shares it now with any and all who wish to join him in the practice of contemplative beholding through the arts. His is a trustworthy path toward cultivating the "right eyes" to see deeply into humanity's great works of art, which is simultaneously a seeing into the human condition and to a "more human love."

A Beholder's Guide to This Book and Its Companion Website

I HAVE constructed this book and its companion website (amherst.edu/go/contemplative-beholding) as a guide to an art and practice of contemplative beholding. On the website you will find images that provide focused occasions for beholding with the art of works of art, including painting, sculpture, and architecture. The book and website together offer a resource for embracing multiple ways of knowing; of engaging with the world, with nature, and with each other.

I intend the combined act of reading the book and beholding with the images to initiate a contemplative process of change, growth, and transformation, a journey leading us to a point of renewal—a threshold of love—in our turbulent world.

Each time you prepare to read, please be ready to open the website and access the images; when you visit for the first time, click on "BEGIN" to access the Welcome page; thereafter you can go directly to Contents.

The images are keyed to prompts in the book that identify them by chapter and image number (for example, the first image in the first chapter is numbered 1.1). With the image open on the screen, you may shift your focus back and forth between it and the book, taking as much time as you need to read and behold with the image before moving on. (To enhance these contemplative beholding occasions, enter "full screen" view when engaging with the images.) **An "Advance screen" prompt** in the book will be your signal to clear the image from the screen and continue reading until prompted to access the next image in that chapter. At the end of each chapter, the "Advance screen" prompt will direct you to a slide allowing you to "Exit Images." Clicking on the X in the upper right corner will return you to the image index for that chapter; scrolling to the bottom of the image index will allow you to link back to the contents or proceed to the next chapter.

Although in this dual format contemplative beholding with the art of works of art is deliberately separated from the act of reading, it is neither detached nor isolated. At times, the experience of determined contemplative beholding will reach beyond the limits of more familiar verbal description, analysis, interpretation, and reflection to open moments of poetic insight and enduring wisdom.

To help guide these contemplative beholding occasions, I offer opportunities for you to reflect and meditate on passages that I have offset from the main text (like these two paragraphs). They also provide clarification or gentle instruction on how to proceed.

I intend the path of *Contemplative Beholding* to be flexible, with freedom to move at a comfortable pace or repeat a section before proceeding. Our journey has already begun with Henry Lyman's poem, "The Cairn," to set the tone: "... here / is where to stay a while and listen." From there the journey continues through part I, "Preparation," as the following summaries describe:

- Arthur Zajonc's foreword focuses our sights on cultivating the "right eyes" to look deeply into "humanity's great works of art, which is simultaneously a seeing into the human condition" and to Rainer Maria Rilke's vision of a "more human love."
- "Thoughts About Word and Image" describes how the two parts of this process (verbal and visual knowing; discursive and contemplative engagement) work together.
- "An Opening Invitation to Behold" offers an occasion to engage contemplative beholding directly with a particularly vivid work of art whose very "art" appears to be contemplative beholding itself. In the text, word and a printed image are purposefully set side-by-side.
- In the introduction I share the circumstances of my own arrival in a threshold of contemplative beholding, and then set out the itinerary that *Contemplative Beholding* will follow.
- Chapter 1, "Beginning: In Silence and Solitude," encourages us to depart from the familiar consciousness of our ordinary realities, to leave behind all we think we know—all our already-thought thoughts, expectations, and preconceptions—and prepare for a quiet perception to emerge: the threshold of a new way of being.

- Chapter 2, "Reconciliatory Longing: A Condition of Our Human Being" leads us to recognize that from our unalterable condition of limitation comes our endless search for wholeness—as in thirst needing water, fear seeking courage, confusion striving for clarity, fatigue needing rest, ordinary loneliness looking for the embrace of another lonely being, and grief seeking solace. As we pursue tangible realizations of reconciliatory longing in the act of contemplative beholding through poetry, art, and love, our goal is to experience evermore completely our fullest being.

These first few steps, along what may be an unfamiliar path for many, provide the context and preparation for anyone willing to engage in deliberate contemplative beholding.

As *Contemplative Beholding: A Way of Life and Love* continues with part II, "Setting Out," through part IV, "Via Amoris," you can engage sequentially with chapter 3 and the remaining chapters (through 11). Or you may choose an alternate order depending on your individual preferences for painting, sculpture, or architecture. From 3 to 11, each chapter is a self-sufficient exemplar, comprising individual opportunities for contemplative beholding, which like all art, beauty, and most certainly Rilke's "more human love"—humanity—are simultaneously unique and universal.

In the coda, another purposeful placement of words and image signals an occasion for beholding with Rembrandt's *Return of the Prodigal Son.* I hope that this experience will resonate with T. S. Eliot's promise in "Little Gidding": that "the end of all our exploring will be to arrive where we started and know the place for the first time."

Thus the images on the website may become a path to the *art*, *beauty*, and *love* embodied by works of art.

Thoughts About Word and Image

MY APPROACH shares explicitly the well-known Buddhist reminder that the finger pointing to the moon is not itself the moon. While reading, the very process of turning to the images may serve as a meditative act that will allow the text to give way to an ever-increasing capacity for vision beyond words, objects, and the inevitable limitations we all know. Similarly, this format may recall "reading" a Book of Hours from an earlier time, when concentration on the written word—prayer—was followed by reorientation toward an image, which in turn reached outward beyond immediate realities to elusive, larger matters of consequence.

Of course, *Contemplative Beholding* is not a Book of Hours. Yet its format may provide some degree of purposeful adjustment to the reading and beholding experience it offers. To begin and end our journey in this book, I have included two images, Katsushika Hokusai's *Boy Viewing Mount Fuji* (on the page adjacent to "An Opening Invitation to Behold") and Rembrandt van Rijn's *Return of the Prodigal Son* (in the coda) as vivid exemplars of these artists' own contemplative beholding.

> *Before reading further, please open the website and click on the link to "Thoughts About Word and Image." We begin with Jan van Eyck's* Madonna of Chancellor Rolin.

The chancellor looks up from his Book of Hours toward a vision of the Madonna and Child that has appeared before him—inspired, we may imagine by his prayerful reading. As contemplative beholders ourselves, we may now turn from our text to this image of a work of art in search of its *art*. Note: the angel tilts Mary's crown slightly toward you.

> *Allow Arleen Auger's rendition of Stephen Foster's "Why, No One to Love?" to set us on our way.*

(Advance screen)

Katsushika Hokusai (1760–1849), *Boy Viewing Mount Fuji*, ca. 1839
(Freer Gallery of Art and Arthur M. Sackler Gallery, Washington, DC)

(Advance screen)

An Opening Invitation to Behold

Listening in silence
  opens a fresh awareness of being at peace
    with ambiguity and contradiction:
      a way of art, beauty, and love.

The soft sound of a flute fills the air around you,
  becoming a "cairn" of discovery.

In Hokusai's painting a young boy is poised
  within a series of visual and conceptual oppositions
    in an image suspended within a framing scroll.

The boy occupies the elusive middle ground
  between foreground and background.
    He is the focused center of visual asymmetry . . . longing . . .

The composition rises chiasmally from the lower left and right.

The calligraphy records the presence of the artist,
  who in approaching his ninth decade
    bravely joins both youth and aging
      in the relation of pictorial surface with illusory space.

The visible weave of the silk fabric embraces the space of the landscape.

The remote sky lies beyond the contour of the mountain
  where the darkest dark measures the lightest light.

So too, the green branches of the willow define the interval of space
  between the actual upper pictorial border
    and the illusory distance of the mountain they touch.

Red complements green,
  yellow complements violet.

The hanging basket is weightless.

As the river flows forward past an awakened viewer
  white spots of watery foam, floating like cherry blossoms,
    still the sound and movement of rushing thoughts
      releasing the music . . . listen . . .

(Advance screen)

Introduction: Contemplative Beholding with the *Art* of Works of Art

This is an art which does mend Nature, change it rather, but the art itself is Nature.
—William Shakespeare, *The Winter's Tale,* act 4, scene 4

IN THIS BOOK, I present neither argument nor theory. Instead, I invite you to accompany me on a path of encounter, engagement, and reflection. On this journey, whose Holy Grail is an art and practice of contemplative beholding, we will search for ways to focus, intensify, and deepen our shared capacity for beholding, not only with works of art, but as a way of life, a way of being and knowing—a way of loving.

Such a journey has informed my life as a teacher of the history of art for nearly fifty years. Moreover, it reflects my experience of studying, of feeling a close kinship with nature and my fellow human beings, of my being a son and brother, a husband, a father and grandfather, and much else not usually included in an academic curriculum vitae. In a word, I have learned from the many "beholding" moments my life has brought and continues to bring me. They remain in me as a sacred endowment.

I recall vividly one moment during a conference on contemplative knowing at Amherst College organized by my colleague Arthur Zajonc, a professor of physics. When a visiting Tibetan monk recounted his ten thousand hours of meditation as the foundation of his approach to "wisdom," my first response was, "Oh well, I could never accomplish that." Then I thought, "Wait, I have spent countless hours returning again and again to behold with works of art from museum to museum, country to country: how many miles, how many hours." This sustained act of beholding has been my adult life in and out of the classroom.

May I now say that you too have probably been "beholding" all your life and may not have known it?

For me "beholding" began as an intuitive awareness and over time an increasingly lucid awakening that brought me to a threshold where I could consider what the *art* of works of art might be. Let me explain what I mean by that phrase, "the *art* of works of art." Normally in English "art" is understood as the object of a process or a skill, rather than the act (*techne*) itself and its effect (*poesis*) on the beholder. Here, with the word *art* in italics, I emphasize its meaning as both verb and noun.[1] The phrase, then, defines *art* as the deliberate act of constructing *intimations of reconciliation between and among all manner of contradictory realities.* Such intimations—whether we call them hints, subtle suggestions, or indirect indications—define both the essence of works of art and the very basis of interacting with them. They shape an art and practice of contemplative beholding, as contrasted with observation from a distance.

Although no less real than reasoned resolution, intimations of reconciliation are as fragile and ephemeral as a rainbow. They engage with contradiction in an embrace of suspended disbelief; they exist as a "bridge state" that reunites even as they preserve contending realities. They are "peace" rather than the mere absence of war. They are trans-rational rather than irrational. They are elusive affect rather than hardened causal effect; productive ambiguity rather than impacted certainty. They are like the unutterable moment of becoming aware that one is falling in love.

We experience intimations of reconciliation as being similar to inklings: a kind of intuition-seeking embodiment; healing rather than curing. Intimations of reconciliation result in a sense of undefined, and yet intensely felt, wellbeing. They move us toward a larger reality within an unending process of change, growth, and transformation. The apostle Paul considered such steps in his personal journey to be an evolutionary "straining forward" (Philippians 3:13), but they also require holding on and letting go. They embody past and future in a fully awakened present moment. Intimations of reconciliation are related, at least tangentially, to the Romantic poet John Keats's "negative capability," namely, the capacity "of being in uncertainties, mysteries, doubts, without any irritable reaching after fact and reason."[2]

In *Contemplative Beholding* I set out to articulate and trace the act that this "negative capability" enables, in part because our rational discomfort with the irreconcilable contradiction of consciousness itself is the very origin of the *art* of works of art. From this perspective *art* originates in our recognition, acknowledgment, and embrace of contradiction. We will follow this embrace with a deliberate effort to construct intimations of reconciliation, allowing the contradiction to remain. The *artist* then, is one who commits these acts by which others, when they behold, will be *artists* themselves.[3]

Artistic intimations of reconciliation are both literal and metaphorical. They exist along a spectrum of contradiction, ranging from formal-structural (part-whole, horizontal-vertical, light-dark, for example) and iconographic (real-ideal, human-divine presence—Mary as human mother and celestial queen, let's say), to psychological (I-You) and metaphysical (humanity-divinity, sound-silence, visible-invisible, finite-infinite). In this understanding the word *art*, thus animated, directly relates to several other common words—*love, beauty, beholding*—as questions worthy of continued reflection.

No less importantly, this awakening assumes ever more compellingly a spiritual dimension that I have come to accept as the way toward an active love seeking wholeness—love the noun—beyond all limitation and longing. An art and practice of contemplative beholding—as imagined here in both attitude and action—constitutes the source *and hence the threshold* of this animated love.

> *If you are willing, may we now set out together toward this threshold of love?*

This threshold will bring us to a Via Amoris, a way of love where love itself is the means. Walking on this path, each individual and hard-won act of love will then radiate as a luminous manifestation of human longing from the irreducible core of our begotten conscious being. The consequences are manifold. Indeed, if epistemology is ethics, as Parker Palmer has suggested, this way of being and knowing, in the inexorable passage of time and space, will determine how we act in this world we inhabit together.[4] It may even slowly but surely replace violence of every kind—rejection or disparagement of *other* by any means—with countless intimations of reconciliation. The direction and guiding light of this Via Amoris is both faith in and hope for human evolution toward the inherent *beauty* of conflict resolution, realized by a love in which "the art itself is Nature."[5]

Finding a Path to a Via Amoris

My first remembered awakening to the experience of intimated reconciliation occurred when, as a young boy, I became infatuated with the luminous paintings of the American artist John Marin. Whether he was present in lower Manhattan or Maine, his artistic work suspended "pure mark" and "pure image" by embracing simultaneously both the material fabric and the image of an object known as a "painting." His manipulation of pictorial surface, edge, color, illusory and actual space, including real and imagined frames, gave me a sense of true well-being. Without any analytical understanding of what I was witnessing, this early, utterly innocent, first encounter with John Marin during a brief museum visit with my parents led to a child-like attempt to make "paintings" of my own that would resemble Marin's.

At one point my father matted and framed one of my "Marin paintings" as a gift to my fifth-grade teacher, who had encouraged me in my first steps. But my education proceeded along a distinctly nonartistic path. Only much later, beginning my career as a teacher of the history of art at Amherst College, did I rediscover my youthful enthusiasm in a more deliberate effort to define and articulate what over time would emerge explicitly as the attitude and process of contemplative beholding. Since then, the reconciliatory act present as the art of works of art, which resonated with my discovery of Rainer Maria Rilke's "more human love," has marked the evolutionary trajectory and the north star of my adult life. As we proceed, I hope Rilke's "more human love" will resonate for you as it has for me.

My undergraduate experience at Rutgers University informed the next steps of my journey. Although I had scored high on a math placement exam in my first year, a yearlong advanced calculus class turned out to be a colossal intellectual and emotional disappointment. With some help I was able to survive the first semester, taking away little more than a transactional acquaintance with the mathematical realities of calculus and certainly no affection for its poetry. The second semester began on a particularly cold Saturday in January when, in an early morning class, the essentially nonverbal instructor scribbled an extensive sequence of numbers and symbols from the upper left to the lower right side of a large chalkboard and concluded by simply muttering, "The answer is: more marks. Class dismissed." I left the room, never to return, and accepted the personal pain and educational disruption of a failing grade. By comparison with other considerably more rewarding classroom experiences, this sad encounter left a hole in my academic experience that most likely obscured and slowed my own growth. But in retrospect it led directly to my subsequent artistic journey toward contemplative beholding. French language and literature soon filled the gap, offering the chance to write several mediocre but strongly felt short stories in another language.

A summer spent traveling in France with French-speaking companions opened wide the threshold of unfamiliar and difficult, but inviting, possibilities. Two courses in art history—a general survey and later a limited enrollment seminar on Mesopotamian art and architecture—offered another vivid sense of joy and accomplishment. My first assignment for the survey course was to write ten pages on a single painting without reference to any external comment. With no place to hide, this effort returned me unknowingly to my youthful encounter with John Marin. Now, obliged to move past obvious and fairly superficial observations of subject matter, I entered step by step deeper into formal relationships and their integration with the particularities of Giotto's Arena Chapel *Lamentation*, only to discover that same sense of awakened pleasure I had known as a child. For despite the ostensible content of death and mourning revealed by the rising diagonal of intimated resurrection, the art of this work of art possessed a beauty of lived compassion no less real than that embodied by the grieving figures and weeping angels. I left this encounter with a palpable but as yet undefined memory of the wellbeing I had felt with Marin's paintings. I know now that these experiences were essentially spiritual openings to the relationship of art and the love that has come to define my life.

Another classroom art historical assignment led to an invitation by the teacher to visit the Morgan Library in New York. There we would engage directly with several masterpieces of medieval manuscript illumination. I spent several hours with this congenial guide responding to the gentle questions *What do you see? What do you see now?* Again and again we moved from color to color, line to line, shape to shape, to format, scale, to actual and illusory space. Finally we came to the artistic function of pictorially embodied prayer brought home by the light of gold leaf borders reflected into our eyes and the shadowed space of the museum gallery. The unexplained mystery and joy of Marin's watercolors now extended beyond my childhood into my emerging though still youthful enchantment with the artistic presence of intimated reconciliation.

Following service as an officer in the US Air Force assigned to Fontainebleau, France, I applied to Bryn Mawr College for graduate study in art history. The lingering memory of the artistic revelations of my college experience—combined with an invitation to apply for a Woodrow Wilson Fellowship, which required choosing an area of study—sparked thoughts of leaving a rewarding military career. Having spent many hours visiting the Cathedral of Chartres—a short, beautiful drive from Fontainebleau—my decision was not just easy; it seemed fated. As I look back on the time spent at Chartres, my hours of "pure" beholding uninformed by art history were comparable perhaps to Johannes Wolfgang von Goethe's ecstatic experience as a young student in Strasbourg.[6] Certainly, those hours not only amplified the sense of wellbeing that has accompanied me since my first awakening to the art of John Marin, but they also encouraged me to pursue a sustained effort to embrace and be embraced by an underlying, though still inchoate, reality at the center of my life.

My graduate program focused on the discipline of art history: on iconographic identification and analysis. Formal questions beyond simple location of figures, objects, and settings played little or no part in our work. Actual encounter with works of art gave way exclusively to subject matter, textual identification, supporting visual comparisons, and photographic representation, preferably black and white to avoid the confusion of color. As a reaction to this iconographic exclusivity, my dissertation sought to rediscover the particular art of a fifteenth-century Flemish artist who existing scholarship had reduced to being nothing more than a disciple or doppelgänger of greater talents, primarily Jan van Eyck.[7] To my eye, Petrus Christus had sought in his work to elicit a direct, virtually embodied response from those who would "behold with" his paintings rather than observe them from an objectifying distance. His accomplishment included many instances of the intimated reconciliation of material substance and image that had already become familiar to me and would presumably embrace the spiritual purpose he sought to serve.[8]

The irony of this personal account of my journey into an art and practice of contemplative beholding may simply be that it has slowly, fitfully, redeemed my failure to respond to the exquisite beauty and precision of the calculus, to articulate with the same precision another means of intimating reconciliation of contradictory realities, and to experience its art. My undergraduate limitation is clearly at fault, but so too is the disembodied abstraction that dominated the classroom of young students.

I began my career at Amherst College by teaching courses in medieval art from the Fall of Rome through the beginning of the Italian Renaissance; I was determined to avoid as much as possible the artistic alienation of the distant and hierarchical assessment that results from dismembering form and content in the discipline of art history. No less problematic was the chronological, "evolutionary" periodization—the so-called boxcar theory of art history—that all too often obscures the timeless human character of the art that informs works of art. The history of art from antiquity to the present had become for me an occasion of unifying wholeness and aspiration. This I hoped to bring into my classroom. What great good fortune, then, to begin my teaching career in a Department of Fine Arts—so named to raise it above the expectations of academic entertainment to a level comparable with the serious purpose of courses in history, English, and above all the natural sciences. In that department a purposeful and dedicated academic tradition of integrating the studio practice of art with the discipline of art history already existed.

The Mead Art Museum was once the home of the Department of Fine Arts at Amherst. It included a studio wing, along with a library and classroom wing flanking centralized spaces dedicated to the presentation of works of art that served as the conceptual and actual bridge between *ars* and *scientia*. These were understood as complementary practices: no practice without theory and, conversely, no theory without practice.[9] At the time, all students wishing to "major" in the Fine Arts were encouraged and then required to include at least three courses in each area to develop a degree of awareness and skill, if not mastery, of the two pillars of artistic knowing. The art historical argument for studio was to know the language of form so as to achieve independence from inadequate "translations" by unknowing practitioners. The complementary argument by practicing artists was to approach a knowledge of the complexity of art's long history as something greater than a superficial naming of a few great masters. For many years, this program witnessed the remarkable result that the best student "artists" in the department were often the best student "art historians" and the reverse. My own involvement in this program led me to pursue painting with an artist colleague for some twenty years and to welcome artists into my class to demonstrate firsthand the reality of artistic creation.

One such demonstration included a series of steps employed in the indirect oil technique used by Rembrandt, in which layers of transparent paint allowed light to penetrate inward only to be redirected outward, resulting in the particular luminosity we associate with him. The artist I invited began by placing a dirty automobile carburetor on a table in the front of the classroom. From an initial sketch, with broad light and dark strokes that established the underlying composition, subsequent panels revealed the emerging image. With a concluding gesture, the artist removed a cloth that covered the completed painting. He had transformed the ostensible subject of this work of art—that greasy old carburetor—into a shining cosmos of light and dark, suffused with saturated color. Everyone in the class enthusiastically responded to something like an epiphany: a higher order of experience now resided in our relationship with the painting compared with the lingering presence of the old carburetor on the nearby table. Unaware of precisely what had happened at the time, my determined effort since has been to find my way back home to this art that had there, before our very eyes, so transformed ordinary reality into something extraordinary.

Sadly, in time, the willingness of new colleagues to venture beyond the limitations of their training and experience in either studio practice or art history led to the complete disintegration of the department. The resulting fragmentation further isolated and estranged *ars* and *scientia*. Reacting to the loss of the Department of Fine Arts—now called the Department of Art and the History of Art—I redoubled my efforts to define, design, and present courses that would open a way into an art and practice of contemplative beholding. In those courses I would seek to embrace contradictory realities—not only the academic challenges of the practice of art and art history, but universally those of our conscious sense of separation and longing—and then hold them in the suspension of intimated reconciliation. In sum, my goal was first to find the threshold into the syzygetic wholeness—the dynamic yoking together, like the gravitational pull of the sun, moon, and earth during a solar or lunar eclipse—that our universal "wandering mourning" (in Rilke's words) so desperately needs. And second, to assert the experience of oneness in the art of all works of art, the multiple beauties they embody, as well as the love animated by them. This way of love, a Via Amoris, is the ultimate subject of this book; its trajectory might lead in time to that state of being St. Augustine envisioned, "where there will be such poise, such grace, such beauty as become a place where nothing unbecoming can be found."[10]

Beyond the Classroom

My experience has been in extended contemplation with the *art* of works of art in situ. This experience has flowed into and informed my teaching through personal encounter, oral presentation, conversation, and quiet shared viewing in the darkened sanctuary of my classroom. The chapters that follow and the accompanying platform of digital images seek to translate my life of contemplative beholding for others to share. Like all translations, this one cannot be finite or literal. The spoken word with its full range of expressiveness and voice, including theatrical moments of drama, both planned and unplanned, must change in order to address you, a solitary reader in your own silent space and circumstances. No less obviously, the digital images on your screen are not the equivalent of large (sometimes larger than life) images projected in the classroom. Of course, neither these images nor the classroom experience can approach the actual reality of engaging works of art face to face. Nevertheless, from the beginning, I imagined class time as an occasion to experience as completely as possible what an informed attempt to be in thrall to the art of multiple works of art could offer a willing pilgrim. Consequently, I don't consider the images that complement this text as illustrations of this or that historical or artistic idea. Rather, I invite you to attend to them as you will, to observe slowly, to reflect, and perhaps, with the help of my guidance, to meditate with the particular intimation of reconciliation embodied by the given work of art they represent. Thus we may set a goal to behold through contemplative intimacy—rather than distanced observation—the hard-won art-love offered by artists willing to share our deepest human aspirations to wholeness from an acknowledged condition of mortal limitation.

As with all human encounter, contemplative beholding with the art of works of art requires developing particular skills of informed observation and reflection. We will need to allow for an ontological perspective—namely, an awareness of the experienced condition of our human being. But more than any other single preparation, profoundest humility—rather than our habit of aggressive, often noisy, "authoritative" control—will sustain our necessary vulnerability to the art with which we would behold, and at the same time provide for the silence necessary to listen for its intimated wisdom.

The impetus to write this book—to describe my journey along a Via Amoris—takes its inspiration and particular form from several years of experience teaching the seminar "Eros and Insight" at Amherst College with Arthur Zajonc. The singular purpose of this seminar for first year college students was to pose the question: "What would it be like to encounter yourself, those around you, and the world through deliberate and disciplined contemplation?"[11] We aimed to construct with our students a *sacral* place of change, growth, and transformation that in this book I call the "threshold of love."[12] As Arthur and I proceeded, we often interrupted the discursive flow of information and explanation to allow the full force of an image to be present in silence. At times, the sound of a bell focused our contemplative beholding. Music, likewise, offered parallel openings into felt moments of artistic epiphany. Within these pages I allow for similar moments of contemplative reflection. Aside from sharing my contribution to this seminar with anyone who may be interested, my purpose is to extend the classroom, not only to other educators, but also to those seeking a contemplative approach to works of art. My hope is to affirm an art and practice of contemplative beholding as a valuable form of "open" higher learning—by which I mean: available to all and capable of a wider range of understanding than is commonly present in the American academic community.[13]

More generally, I've written this book for anyone interested in discovering or rediscovering those enduring joys that will redeem the inevitable occasions of sadness in our lives. I offer it simply to people of good will and the desire to engage. Although from the perspective of this book such joys take particular shape in works of pictorial, sculptural, and architectural art, they are available in countless other forms to any of us who would reflect on our universal condition of human being. Whether our art and practice of contemplative beholding emerges in gardening, mechanical engineering, caring and healing of all kinds, politics, business, the law, academic research and teaching, or just determined friendship, the resulting renewal, purpose, and joy remain the same. Grounded in contemplative beholding, our efforts to reconcile the contradictory realities that conscious existence entails will empower endless evolution toward beauty beyond all calculation and limitation.

In teaching courses in the history of art I always aimed to respond openly to the friendly skepticism that even the very best students conveyed when presented with a work of art: that unspoken, but nonetheless vivid, question "So what? What's that got to do with me?" I could understand the impatience of my students with the ever-increasing art historical specificity, complexity, and apparent clarity concerning the narrative, pictorial, and contextual circumstances of a given object, but I also sensed in them a shared lingering desire to connect with an unarguable artistic authenticity. In fact, that desire never failed to animate the classroom.

This is why, in my teaching, I sought to foster in my students an awareness that art not only exists naturally in the conscious condition of our being but also resides deep in the very physiology of our bodies—and indeed, in nature. From this perspective, art emerges across time and space, and spans the intellectual, social, physical, and metaphysical realities by which a particular work of art emerges into the light. By tracing a path that can return us to the thrall of art, my aim is to approach a heightened awareness in which *art,* before it is the familiar noun, will be an active verb. On that path, along with acts of love, art will become a synonymous effort to envision the elusive reality of peace revealed in the face of an infinite beloved. Here, and throughout this book, as the word *beloved* becomes integral to our journey toward the threshold of love, I use it in an expansive context to describe wholeness beyond all rational calculation.

My aspiration in and out of the classroom has been always to address a fundamental crisis in the quality of our lives: namely, our estrangement from ourselves, from each other, and from the world and the infinite wholeness we share. The impoverishment we experience as a result often extends to our habitually distanced observation of works of art, resulting in endless information about them with little or no engagement with their art or even much curiosity concerning what art, in general, might be. Over the years, I have tried to offer a way back from potential alienation. This journey, as I see it, will move us toward some form of relational wholeness as we realize in art an intimation of reconciliation animated by deliberate and disciplined acts of beholding. By any other name, this wholeness is the love we so desperately seek. Were such an art of beholding (both the act and its product) allowed to reach beyond the exemplary encounter with works of art—were it to include our awareness of ourselves as human beings in endlessly expanding relation—the degradation and selfish contraction caused by estrangement might be diminished, if not eliminated. On this path of beholding, unbecoming acts of any kind would be literally unimaginable, and the meanness that weighs so heavily upon us all will have become a distant memory.

By *beholding*, I mean here a quite particular kind of active-receptive seeing. Henry David Thoreau, a favorite guide, whether to nature or art, provides a clue to our goal when he writes: "Wisdom does not inspect, but behold. We must look a long time before we see."[14] But there is more to it. *Beholding* requires more than just looking, however attentively. In place of objective observation of the world, we learn through practice to behold *with* it, *with* works of art, including visions beyond our normal immediate grasp and, most importantly, *with* another human being in a reciprocal act of reunion. In the chapters that follow I pursue this contemplative beholding as a deliberate effort to hold multiple, discontinuous, and contradictory realities in relation. The experience of such expanded seeing granted by the liminal in-between state of love's threshold will offer us moments of fleeting and enduring well-being. Since none of this, of course, comes without effort, along the way I will invite you to practice such contemplative beholding in direct encounter *with* works of art.

You might ask: What happened to an art of beholding, once a shared, skillful act of silent wonder that for millennia offered this way of seeing each time as though for the first time? Such beholding provided an opening into a diverse world, one that is still and forever unfolding. In ancient Greece, for instance, *techne* and *theoria* amounted to an art of beholding as contemplative seeing in an act of reciprocal encounter.[15] What changed?

Reclaiming Contemplative Practice

Two statements on the nature of our collective potential for beholding, the first by Martin Luther in 1525 and the second by Václav Havel in 1994, may serve to bracket an era in which the discipline of art history evolved in tandem with modern technology.

> I approached the task of destroying images by first tearing them out of the heart through God's Word and making them worthless and despised. . . . For when they are no longer in the heart, they can do no harm when seen with the eyes.[16]

> Man as an observer is becoming completely alienated from himself as a being.[17]

Today, instruments of observation have made more art of more varied means, forms, and styles accessible to more people in more places than at any time in history; contemporary textbooks, countless illustrated publications, and now rapidly expanding digital resources continue to multiply the number of images on demand. Anyone of us, for instance, with little effort, can download more of Rembrandt van Rijn's oeuvre in a single moment and place than any one of his contemporaries could have hoped to see in a lifetime. This calling forth of works of art of every medium and date from around the globe can be repeated endlessly, even as many of us may find ourselves remarkably empty before actual works of art. To fill the void, we grasp for more and still more information about, and the "official" interpreted meaning of, an endless array of objects rather than simply contemplating with the human significance embodied in them. Missing from this vast second-hand, nearly obsessive relationship with objects of art is an accompanying means of experiencing much of anything beyond the surface of transitory realities. Having thus been torn from the heart and moved into the museums and scholarly disciplines of objective observation, art that might have been the realization of our immanent wholeness has become little more than a momentary distraction from lingering despair.

As an art historian concerned not only with art's long and varied past, but also with the living presence of that art, I have turned increasingly to contemplative practice for two reasons. First, disciplined contemplation provides the most effective calming and focusing preparation for any full encounter with complex works of art. Second, the very act of contemplating informs art within a genuine, abundant awareness of wholeness beyond limitation. From this perspective, contemplative practice amounts to a radical reclaiming of art at its human core.

In this act of beholding, contemplative practice serves as a quieting and focusing complement to substantive learning. But it may also become the very basis of an active way of knowing that will reveal cognitive possibilities otherwise obscured by the conventions of "scientific" scholarship. This contemplative beholding offers a new (or very old!) perceptual threshold in which the art of art might emerge. Rather than define art exclusively as an object that one would seek to possess by way of ownership, interpretation, or even analytical understanding, this "way" of beholding imagines art, like love, to be an act of aspiration. Drawing on a fundamental psychological impulse we all share, but may have forgotten, this embodied and deliberate beholding challenges the potentially estranged voyeurism of merely looking at or objectively measuring works of art, and it resists our habitual stance of neutral, disembodied, and essentially iconoclastic observation. In the recognition and acceptance of a paradoxical tension between self-conscious separation and dynamic involvement in the world, we might rediscover within ourselves precisely that profound reconciliatory longing—or eros—we possess at least from birth, if not before. Such longing animates artistic imagination and action, even as it informs our capacity for enduring insight.

As we learn how to engage this artistic impulse—both in ourselves and as it is embodied in a given work of art—we may find that a disciplined and particularized attitude and approach can rediscover a living art that will revive the embalmed objects of a museum-deadened world. Such contemplative return to a place and presence within the thrall of an artwork's art might then actually allow us once again to encounter and to construct for ourselves those intimations of reconciliation that will rekindle meaning in our lives and *bridge* the infinite chasm of solitude with compassion.

With *Contemplative Beholding* I explicitly aim to reanimate our experience with works of art. But implicitly I hope to reclaim contemplative knowing itself as a secular and yet fully spiritual act of love, one that might recharge our human aspiration to know wholeness from an acknowledged condition of unalterable fragmentation and limitation. I see this contemplative knowing as more than just another cognitive tool in an otherwise unchanged academic enterprise. Embedded in an art of beholding, contemplative knowing might offer some small measure of artistic reintegration and reunion in a world of loneliness, and perhaps even a fleeting vision of peace in the face of irreconcilable contradiction, conflict, and mortality. As an instrument of psychological (if not also social, political, and certainly scientific) reality, this contemplatively based beholding might open a way to approach an elusive blending of self and transcendence, as Havel himself dreamed. If nothing else, contemplative beholding—as a deliberate, but gentle, mechanism for seeking out and realizing ways to approach our lives overall—might allow us to recover some sense of belonging with each other, the world, and the universal mystery of our being: hence *art... compassion... love... the beloved.*

From Engagement and Encounter to Life and Art

As I guide you through this book, we will explore how involvement with the art of works of art entails direct engagement between people. For us to imagine that an artist is not a special kind of person, but that each of us is, or ought to be, a special kind of artist, we must encounter ourselves, those around us, and the world through purposeful and disciplined artistic contemplation.[18] In this sense, there is no real distinction between art and life. Therefore the threshold of love and the particular Via Amoris it leads to are open to any and all of us who would engage contemplative knowing as it evolves beyond the habitual, exclusive confidence in information and learning that in our world today serves a presumed need for unrelenting power, control, and authority.[19] Thus stated, this "way of love" may recall for some Martin Buber's challenge in his 1923 book *I and Thou*: to approach life through mutual and reciprocal dialogue and encounter—with each other, with the natural world, or with God—as contrasted with pursuing relationships of separateness and estrangement.[20] For others, Thoreau's artistic manifesto may be helpful:

> It is something to be able to paint a particular picture, or to carve a statue, and so to make a few objects beautiful; but it is far more glorious to carve and paint the very atmosphere and medium through which we look, which morally we can do. To affect the quality of the day, that is the highest of arts.[21]

In his recent book, *Meditation as Contemplative Inquiry*, Arthur Zajonc articulated an "epistemology of love" in which he defined and portrayed a theory and practice of contemplative cognition.[22] Within that framework, we can begin to identify a threshold of love in every human encounter that might foster an art of beholding. From this vantage point, we may reformulate Martin Heidegger's radical observation, that "the essence of technology is by no means anything technological" and say instead that *the essence of epistemology is by no means anything epistemological.*[23] Both technology and epistemology are modes of revealing; both are expressive of human longing. As we acknowledge and honor multiple modes of inquiry on our journey, their fruition in every instance will become a way of knowing and being—and of revealing being—that always seeks to embrace and reconcile the very contradictoriness of contending ways. In place of the opposition of art and science, for example, or religion and science—an opposition that results in separation, isolation, and then alienation or hierarchical privilege (science and all the rest)—we may begin to envision an alternative path to joy and the reduction of ignorance and suffering.

In *Contemplative Beholding* we will leave behind rational and adversarial exclusivity of all kinds and move toward an art of harmony, rhythm, proportion, and deepest existential humility. I propose that we foster the realization of countless human works of art: individual *beauties*, independent of the divisive categories of art and science or religion. Despite all their differences, they aspire to *beauty* beyond contradiction as exemplified in Johannes Kepler's scientific poetry of "sacred ecstasy," or in Goethe's poetic science of the *apercu*, "experiences of a higher kind."[24]

I now invite you to pause here, and turn to the image platform . . .

(0.1) Two water lily blossoms, Ryoan-ji, Kyoto, Japan

(0.2) Bamboo path, Kyoto, Japan

The water lily blossoms resonate in a reciprocal relationship to suggest a goal of mutuality: following a path from here to there, not unlike a path through a bamboo forest, both closed and open, with neither a fixed beginning nor a definitive end. So too, the flowering plants not only border each other, they reach upward into the light and downward to unknown depths.

(Advance screen)

Toward a Lived Reality

My ultimate goal, then, is to open a way into a lived reality, suspended somewhere between two poles of non-conscious being: it imagines our finite existence to be suffused with a discontinuous, infinite wholeness to which we belong and within which we reside—*and of which we may find ourselves oblivious*. In a graduation speech for undergraduates, David Foster Wallace evoked something similar with his disarming story about two young fish: when asked by an older fish, "How's the water?" they swam on for a bit before one asked the other, "What the hell is water?"[25]

For the physicists among us, "energy" may be the equivalent of an intimated reconciliation of contradictory realities in which the "speed of light," calculated as 186,000 miles per second squared, serves to approximate infinity in relation with finite mass. In this context, the iconic equation $E = mc^2$ is also an image of intimated wholeness, with which we might behold, even as infinite white light is artistically incarnated as color. Although seemingly utterly incompatible, both scientific and artistic imaginations emerge within the same humbly perceived condition of our conscious human being. From this singular, universal, and unmediated awakened reality, any one or many multiple and conflicting ways of knowing and acting—rationally objective to mystically religious, profane to sacred—will radiate outward to animate our common human presence along an endlessly evolving Via Amoris.

Although our progress toward a Via Amoris is made in solitude, we are not alone. Many, not to say countless, others are there with us and have been all along. Listen again to Thoreau, whose "voice" we will encounter often along our path. In a talk on "Walking" offered to his neighbors in Concord, Thoreau invented an etymology for the word *saunter*, suggesting its origin in medieval pilgrimages to "*Sainte Terre*" (the Holy Land) and those who journeyed there (the "Sainte-Terrers" or "Santerers").[26] In Thoreau's neologism, to *saunter* meant to walk reflectively toward a place of simultaneous earthbound and transcendent reality. Perhaps in these pages you will realize something of Thoreau's *sauntering* as contrasted with our habitual hurried and often thoughtless—or worse, merely instrumental—movement from here to there.

I encourage you to literally stop reading from time to time, shift focus, and meditate with the works of art in various forms that you will encounter. Engage with the artistic circumstance of the moment. The visual, verbal, and musical works of art available on the website that accompanies this book are the "cairns" that mark the path the text seeks to follow. With self-sustaining purpose, they invite contemplative release. They are comparable perhaps to the epiphany provided by painted illuminations of transcendent reality that sought to merge the sound of words spoken in prayer with vision beyond sight, as we might discover them in precious Books of Hours from an earlier era.[27]

Thoreau's own visually and poetically potent words, which conclude his lecture "Walking," may set the tone for what follows in *Contemplative Beholding*:

> We had a remarkable sunset one day last November. I was walking in a meadow, the source of a small brook, when the sun at last, just before setting, after a cold, grey day, reached a clear stratum in the horizon, and the softest, brightest morning sun-light fell on the dry grass and on the stems of the trees in the opposite horizon and on the leaves of the shrub-oaks on the hillside, while our shadows stretched long over the meadow eastward, as if we were the only motes in its beams. It was such a light as we could not have imagined a moment before, and the air also was so warm and serene that nothing was wanting to make a paradise of that meadow. When we reflected that this was not a solitary phenomenon, never to happen again, but that it would happen forever and ever, an infinite number of evenings, and cheer and reassure the latest child that walked there, it was more glorious still.
>
> The sun sets on some retired meadow, where no house is visible, with all the glory and splendor that it lavishes on cities, and perchance, as it has never set before—where there is but a solitary marsh hawk to have his wings gilded by it, or only a musquash looks out from his cabin, and there is some little black-veined brook in the midst of the marsh, just beginning to meander, winding slowly round a decaying stump. We walked in so pure and bright a light, gilding the withered grass and leaves, so softly and serenely bright, I thought I had never bathed in such a golden flood, without a ripple or a murmur to it. The west side of every wood and rising ground gleamed like the boundary of Elysium, and the sun on our backs seemed like a gentle herdsman, driving us home at evening.
>
> So we saunter toward the Holy Land, till one day the sun shall shine more brightly than ever he has done, shall perchance shine into our minds and hearts, and light up our whole lives with a great awakening light, as warm and serene and golden as on a bank-side in autumn.[28]

(0.3) Milo Kalambokis, *Autumn Light*, 2020

(Advance screen)

As we saunter along a path of ongoing change, growth, and transformation, a Via Amoris is accessible to any one of us who would enter our own threshold of love only to discover that this *sacral* place exists within each of us or not at all. And were we to rediscover our own threshold of love, our most inconspicuous acts would slowly but inexorably and radically alter the way we live and relate with one another and the world.

Our Itinerary

> *In this book I guide you along three interrelated paths in the first three parts of the book: "Preparation," "Setting Out," and "Heading Home." Together they prepare for an opportunity in the fourth part to engage with your own Via Amoris by relating artistically focused contemplative beholding to the particular disciplines of your life, whether they involve the work of your hands, mind, heart, or soul.*

In this introduction and the rest of part I, "Preparation," we take several short steps to orient ourselves in what may be unfamiliar territory. (Think of Thoreau leaving his familiar and habitual Concord for the new awakening experience in the woods at Walden Pond.) With chapter 1, titled "Beginning," we look back at the early 1900s and Rainer Maria Rilke, one of the greatest lyric poets of his day: we accept his embrace of purest *solitude* freed of gender bias and paired with his vision of an emergent "more human love . . . which we are preparing with struggle and toil." And we heed his haunting reminder, from *Sonnets to Orpheus*, that "*killing is a form of our wandering mourning*." This engagement with Rilke and these ideas can guide us now at the beginning of a new and especially noisy, violent, and divisive century. On our path toward a threshold of love, we look to the wise counsel of T. S. Eliot's "Little Gidding," especially its message "to arrive where we started / And know the place for the first time." With the images that accompany chapter 1, of a Zen Buddhist temple in Kyoto, leading from the outer gate, along a curving path, and to an "ancient" pond, I hope to offer a moment of quiet reflection in solitude.

I begin the second chapter, "Reconciliatory Longing," with two stories from my own life that convey "turning around"—the change of heart and mind, the sudden reversal of consciousness, in how we see, understand, and respond to the world and other human beings. One tells of a perfectly ordinary but transformative experience hiking on the slopes of Cadillac

Mountain in Maine. The other, which I call "Milo's lament," involves an inconsolable moment in my infant grandson's life when my wife and I were caring for him in his mother's absence. Milo's mournful sobbing allowed me to formulate my own language for the universal reality we had just witnessed—*to be is to be separate . . . and being separate, we long to be whole.* I also draw on several exemplary voices, such as the apostle Paul, Simone Weil, and Wallace Stevens; they help us to consider how we might pursue tangible realizations of this bodily reconciliatory longing in the act of contemplative beholding through poetry, art, and love as we acknowledge our goal to seek intimations of reconciliation in our own lives.

Moving into part II, "Setting Out," I provide several occasions for deliberate and focused meditation guided by widely divergent artistic exemplars, beginning in chapter 3 with Rembrandt van Rijn and his explicitly contemplative painting called *Aristotle with a Bust of Homer*. Following this, in chapter 4, we join the youthful Johann Wolfgang von Goethe at the very moment of his artistic and spiritual awakening as he approached the Cathedral of Strasbourg. Guided by the opening images that accompany this chapter, we too will approach this Gothic structure as Goethe did until we are confronted by its full form. Once there we may begin to understand his embrace of obverse realities—the cathedral's soaring vertical movement and the repeated, grounding, horizontal platforms of its towers—by reflecting on a singular monument of classical vision: the Parthenon in the sanctuary of the Acropolis, placed high above the city of ancient Athens. In chapter 5, with the pictorial transformation of visible "landscape" into the invisible presence of cosmic dreaming and light beyond light, Piet Mondrian leads us to the unsuspected but nonetheless real cognitive possibilities he embeds within his own serene embrace of obverse realities. Then, in chapter 6, drawing on several extended trips to Japan that carried me beyond my own habitual "Western" understanding, I offer a personal equivalent of Thoreau's unfamiliar "woods" in a spatial construction named *ai-no-ma*. Quiet entry into this unfamiliar place as we reflect will invite us to break the all too familiar "law of the excluded middle" that disallows the very intervals love and solitude demand.

In part III, titled "Heading Home," I offer extended meditations about eros (our fullest sensual awareness) and insight (our heightened intuitive perception and understanding), as animating partners of our universally human capacity for love and contemplative beholding. Chapter 7 brings us to medieval Europe, where an influential and creative feminine culture of "refined" or "purified" love (*fin'amor*) emerged to challenge the ruling masculine paradigm of raw power. We imagine visiting Marguerite Porete in Flanders, where she lived "cloistered" among other Béguine mystics, to listen carefully to the passionate interior dialogue between Reason and Lady Love preserved in her book *The Mirror of Simple Souls*. In one such conversation, as Reason struggles to understand "amazing things about the Soul," Lady Love makes clear that only by transcending Reason (and letting go of "virtues" we have been taught) can another kind of understanding arise, one sustained by an ability to embrace the ever-recurring presence of opposites, contraries, and contradictory truths. I offer a meditation like the one Marguerite Porete presented to her readers: by attempting to let go of what we think we have learned, we come to understand the reality that she lived, and within which her vision of love emerged.

Marguerite's courageous embodiment of love leads us to consider the poet Jaufré Rudel's "love from faraway" (*amour de loin*), then to revisit Rilke's "more human love" and his thoughts on solitude, which in turn lead us back to Thoreau. In this chapter we reflect on Aphrodite, at once completely physical and ephemeral to experience what love itself once looked like in the Greek imagination. Images of the goddess (and those inspired by her) from the fifteenth to the twentieth centuries—by Masaccio, Titian, Rembrandt, and Degas, contrasted with photographs from the popular magazines *Cosmopolitan* and *GQ*—will help us to consider what I see as a contemporary pictorial impoverishment of embodied love. Then, in chapter 8, with the images of humbling doubt offered by the three greatest masters of the Renaissance Dream of Reason—Michelangelo, Dürer, and Leonardo—we may rediscover the soft light of the forgotten *fin'amor* to guide our movement toward the threshold of love.

In chapter 9, "Circles of Affection," we accept an invitation to talk all night long as if we were guests at the famous symposium on love, which in Plato's telling of it remains timeless. When nearly everyone has fallen asleep and the sun rises on a new day, we will hear Socrates quietly challenge the two playwrights in attendance to embrace both tragedy and comedy. This brief moment, in which he implicitly acknowledges the irreducible contradictions of our mortal existence, brings us once again face to face with a "more human love."

We can then imagine attending a dramatic presentation in the ancient theater at Epidaurus. Greek theaters were in actual effect the training ground of love and its vital embrace of contradiction artistically embodied for everyone to see, hear, and live. As those who would embody love, we too, like the theater at Epidaurus, are all center and all periphery. We too move inward and outward. Having at last entered into this threshold of love, we might rediscover or reawaken to a "higher life" that will slowly animate and integrate our shared human Via Amoris. Along this path there will be uncounted occasions to come face to face with another human being who is truly and vividly—as Thoreau expressed our fullest human potential—"quite awake."

Although part IV, "Via Amoris," suggests the destination of our journey, I intend it instead as a welcoming place of arrival and potential renewal. For this reason I title chapter 10 "Homecoming and Departure." Echoes of Thoreau's sauntering "toward the Holy Land" and aspiring to the "poetic or divine life" set our pace on the pathway to the Cathedral of Chartres. Once there, we pause several times as this architectural conflation of solid stone, structural weight, and artistic suspension emerges in our experience so that we may embrace it and allow it to embrace us. As we behold with the intimacy of monumental transcendence embodied by the cathedral, it gives way to the monumental transcendence of intimacy itself in one rapidly sketched drawing by Rembrandt van Rijn, *Two Women Teaching a Child to Walk.*

To foster both self *and* transcendence along an emerging Via Amoris, not as a Greek, Roman, Medieval, Renaissance, European, or even Western reality, but as a primal human aspiration, I begin chapter 11, "A Point of Renewal," with a return to Japan and a visit to Hiroshima with my class, where we hear from Miyoko Matsubara, an A-bomb survivor. Her words of affection (even for those who destroyed her home), contrasted with her startlingly honest admission, "If we had invented the bomb first, we would have used it," bring us full circle to a call—a need—for a "more human love."

I then offer a chance for us, together, to imagine and reflect: Might it all have been otherwise? To enhance that imagining, a series of "ground zero" images, pre- and post-bombing, guides us through an extended meditation, where we may reconsider the fateful decision to drop the first atomic bomb. The pilot of the Enola Gay and its crew approaching Hiroshima, being members of a military structure, had already (implicitly) chosen. But *we*, now more than seventy-five years later, can consider how the spatial reality of *ai-no-ma* we discovered in chapter 6 might have changed the events that led to the bombing. Failing this, we may turn to the science of nuclear physics to provide fresh insight in a renewed search for a "more human love." In place of the material force of $E = mc^2$ which when unleashed or uncontained has caused unfathomable destruction, imagine a poetic (*artistic*) energy reaching for the relativity of finiteness and infinite wholeness.

When we revisit Kyoto, a blossoming cherry tree, dazzling even in the shadow of the setting sun, evokes a place of mysterious meeting between night and day as well as the promise of renewal. Like our visit in chapter 10 to the Phoenix Hall at the Buddhist temple named Byōdō-in, the light of this tree leads us to experience the plausibility of a self-generating Via Amoris as vivid as the rising sun each morning—even as the setting sun anticipates the next inexorable cosmic rotation.

Regardless of our age, work, or cultural origin, any act born of a primal impulse to reach out in the purposeful realization of a "more human love" will approach that infinite wholeness our conscious awakening has revealed. The result of this individual and collective transformation will be the rippling effect of endlessly expanding circles of affection.

In the coda I invite you to behold with Rembrandt van Rijn's *Return of the Prodigal Son* and the art of this work of art, which offers an unexpected and possibly life-changing moment of awakening. I hope that this experience will allow us all as *beholders* to realize a moment comparable to what T. S. Eliot promised in "Little Gidding": that "the end of all our exploring will be to arrive where we started and know the place for the first time."

(Advance screen)

I

PREPARATION

CHAPTER 1

Beginning: In Silence and Solitude

Killing is a form of our wandering mourning...
—Rainer Maria Rilke, *Sonnets to Orpheus*

CONSIDER the phenomenon of silence, both inner and outer. Silence is not diminished noise, whether within our surroundings or in our heads. Think of it as the infinite presence of a wholeness that hears nothing and sees nothing and knows nothing. From this point of view, silence summons us home into the condition of our human being. In such silence, love is born. We begin then with silence, and with solitude, its close companion.

Awakening

Rainer Maria Rilke's challenge of "solitude" marks the start of our journey toward beholding. The observation he shared with an aspiring young poet will serve here as a declaration of liberation from the "noise" of lingering patriarchal dependence on exclusive power, control, and authority. This liberation will open our path to a free relationship with our solitude within which love will thrive.

> Someday there will be girls and women whose name will no longer signify merely as opposite of the masculine, but something in itself, something that makes one think, not of any complement and limit, but only of life and existence: the feminine human being. This advance will (at first much against the will of the outstripped men) change the love-experience, which is now full of error, will alter it from the ground up, reshape it into a relation that is meant to be one human being to another, no longer of man to woman. And this more human love (that will fulfill itself, infinitely considerate and gentle, and kind and clear in binding and releasing) will resemble that which we are preparing with struggle and toil, the love that consists in this, that two solitudes protect and border and salute each other.[1]

What might the words "protect and border and salute"—written by an established poet at the very beginning of the twentieth century to a young person seeking advice on how to become a poet—mean for us today on the path to a threshold of love? How might they guide us now at the beginning of a new and especially noisy century? Why do they still sound so urgent, so startling and incomprehensible? Could they perhaps invoke the infinite silence of the solitude in which a "more human love" might transform our separation and estrangement into an embrace of eros and insight, yearning and knowing, at once sensory and cerebral? But we may still wonder: Why *solitude*?

Our path begins with Rilke's insistence on the bond between solitude and love precisely because there is clear cause for misunderstanding. Given the chaotic and often devastating events, both natural and human, that surround us, a response based on love might well strike many people as a romantic diversion from reality: at best, a quaint curiosity, but essentially irresponsible in the face of unspeakable suffering; or perhaps even a childish fantasy, as if love could make all the pain go away and leave us certain and secure again—like little children. For those of us who think this way, any talk of love will seem an empty retreat from the true task at hand. Given this compelling present moment of palpable distress, confusion, and violence manifest everywhere in the world—if not in each one of us—we might even imagine that any effort begun by invoking love distracts us from what should be our actual approach to purposeful living: that to be truly caring, we must be practical and act to counter the distress. In which case, to talk of love when real service is needed, will appear to avoid the urgency of the moment, to look away selfishly. Worse still, how could an arcane confrontation of eros and insight be anything other than a self-indulgent distraction from the pressing realities of the world: a kind of esoteric entertainment, escape, or aesthetic and academic banality, when what is most required is robust action?

Let me stress at the beginning of this effort that our goal is not to escape reality or cloud it in passive sentimentality. Rather, it is to move willfully toward the very heart of what might be called a "higher education" to which all are called and admitted. Rilke's challenge to approach with "struggle and toil" a "more human love" does not exist in a vacuum. We can apply his haunting insight from *Sonnets to Orpheus* (no. 11, in Book II), that "*killing is a form of our wandering mourning*," to all acts, however seemingly innocuous, that would disparage *other*.[2] But can't also love be a "form of our wandering mourning"?

Here we might recall the biblical account of Adam and Eve's first two sons, Cain and Abel (Genesis 4:1–10). In that ancient, archetypal story, Cain (who works the soil) shares with his brother Abel (who tends flocks) his idea to make an offering to the Lord. When God inexplicably rejects Cain's gift (freshly harvested wheat) but accepts what Abel offers (the first-born lamb), Cain is confused and angry—and so too might we all be, had the thought of making the gift been ours. But how do we respond when we learn that Cain then murders his brother? What about when God asks where Abel is, and Cain responds defensively, "Am I my brother's keeper?"

The gifts themselves, the wheat and the lamb, were both apparently worthy. Where then lay the difference? Was it the disposition with which each brother made his offering? Might we imagine that Cain's was transactional, constrained by selfishness, a means to an end, while Abel's was utterly open and vulnerable to the infinite mystery of otherness? According to the popular medieval legend, Seth, the third son born to Adam and Eve, was ordered by his aged father to return to Paradise through the gate of humanity's expulsion to recover a branch from the Tree of Life. Entering Paradise, Seth saw two trees, not only the Tree of Life, but also the Tree of Knowledge. Beneath the Tree of Knowledge, among its roots, he saw a child, and in its withered, dry branches another child. The guardian angel of the Garden of Paradise explained these figures. He said that the child beneath the tree, in its roots, was Abel, while the child in the branches was Christ, whose birth to a Virgin and ultimate sacrifice would provide the True Oil of Mercy and redeem the sins of Cain and his parents.[3] Drawing on this primal opposition of killing and loving, we may begin to chart the direction of our Via Amoris.

In this sense, to move toward love rather than killing as a form of our universal and unalterable "wandering mourning"—and let me emphasize again that I refer to "killing" even in its most metaphorical use—calls us to rediscover what love truly entails by returning to the beginning: a time before the complexities of life had generated discontent and a pervasive, habitual meanness of intent, if not action. For so long as killing or love remain equally available choices, killing will prevail. The wolf and the lamb will lie down together only until dinnertime. Not until love evolves as the sole impulse to act will the extinction of all forms of killing finally occur "and the wolf will dwell with the lamb" (Isaiah 11:6).

The most pervasive and obvious presence of such "*killing [as] a form of our wandering mourning*" in the contemporary United States reaches beyond the injustice of racism (not to exclude every other "ism" that enslaves us) to embrace sheer brutality in the irreducible inhumanity of disembodiment and the essentializing objectification of physical characteristics. Ta-Nehisi Coates echoes James Baldwin's clarion observation that some "have brought humanity to the edge of oblivion because they think they are white," rather than simply human. Coates's urgent and timely "Letter to My Son" reveals the unarguable irony that those who would honor (and practice) an unrelenting agenda of exclusive power, control, and authority have diminished their own unalterable mortal humanity in word and deed.[4] Coates's moment of awakening is stark. He writes to his son: "Part of me thinks that your very vulnerability brings you close to the meaning of life, just as for others, the quest to believe oneself white divides them from it. The fact is that despite their dream, their lives are also not inviolable."

By this fact—and forced by abstraction from reality always and everywhere to struggle simply to be human beings—African Americans, as well as every person of color, thus become the very vessel of ontological humility into which the grace of being human would flow. Coates's concluding words in this most poignant letter might direct this reality to us all: "The people who must believe they are white can never be your measuring stick. I would not have you descend into your own dream. I would have you be a conscious citizen of this terrible and beautiful world." This warning from father to son—*do not make the fatal mistake of believing you are "black" as a way of overcoming the pain of "whiteness" that surrounds you*—will remind us of the sense, universally experienced, that beneath even the deepest held belief we are all vulnerable.

"*Killing [as] a form of our wandering mourning*" thus emerges as one result of this need to defend against existential limitation. We respond by any means, ranging from seemingly trivial but nonetheless harmful banter at another's expense up to self-elevation by violent assault, culminating, in extreme cases, even in actual killing. To put it bluntly, it is precisely the radical transformation of an epistemology of *killing* to one of *loving* that we are challenged to embrace. In an exemplary way, therefore, Ta-Nehesi Coates provides wise and vital counsel to guide us on our journey. He points us away from all forms of killing and orients us toward a threshold of love and a true Via Amoris.[5]

> *Be still, silent. Soften your eyes, your body. Let the noise around you subside. Be present, here . . . now . . .*
>
> *Reflect on the possibility of a new beginning: anxious, exciting, and as yet unknown and unknowable—as though perhaps you*

were about to fall in love for the first time. Embrace the utter simplicity of the moment, the joy of a new beginning.

As for beginning, T. S. Eliot's well-known lines from "Little Gidding," the concluding work of his *Four Quartets*, provide perhaps the wisest counsel:

> We shall not cease from exploration
> And the end of all our exploring
> Will be to arrive where we started
> And know the place for the first time.
> Through the unknown, remembered gate
> When the last of earth left to discover
> Is that which was the beginning;
> At the source of the longest river
> The voice of the hidden waterfall
> And the children in the apple-tree
> Not known, because not looked for
> But heard, half heard, in the stillness
> Between the two waves of the sea.
> Quick, now, here, now, always—
> A condition of complete simplicity
> (Costing not less than everything)
> And all shall be well and
> All manner of things shall be well
> When the tongues of flame are in-folded
> Into the crowned knot of fire
> And the fire and the rose are one.[6]

Thoreau, too, speaks to such a second beginning in the account of his sojourn at Walden Pond:

> Little is to be expected of that day, if it can be called a day, to which we are not awakened by our Genius, but by the mechanical nudging of some servitor, are not awakened by our own newly acquired force and aspirations from within, accompanied by the undulations of celestial music, instead of factory bells, and a fragrance filling the air—to a higher life than we fell asleep from; and thus the darkness bear its fruit, and prove itself to be good, no less than the light.[7]

To characterize the hard reality of this auroral awakening, Thoreau challenges us with a remarkable mathematical metaphor of aspiration to our highest human potential:

> The millions are awake enough for physical labor; but only one in a million is awake enough for effective intellectual exertion, only one in a hundred millions to a poetic or divine life. To be awake is to be alive. I have never yet seen a man who was quite awake. How could I have looked him in the face?[8]

This quantum leap from "the millions" and "one in a million" to "one in a hundred millions" invites us to reach beyond quantitative change to qualitative transformation. The shift from the constraints of ordinary scale and expectation to the dazzling radiance of "a poetic or divine life" is difficult—not to say impossible—to imagine; nevertheless, it is the elusive goal to which we are all called as potentially fully awake human beings. Thoreau acknowledges that were we actually to come upon such an infinitely awakened soul, the brilliance would be too much to bear. This aspiration to wholeness, as contrasted with the false promise of finite acquisition, draws us on within the mortal reality of our "wandering mourning." So too, in the plaintive poetic words "Love—Thou art high—I cannot climb thee," written by Emily Dickinson, Thoreau's contemporary in Amherst, this shared vision of aspiration to wholeness from our unalterable condition of mortal limitation locates the threshold of love squarely within the miraculous daily tapestry of life itself. Taking possession of his own awakening, Thoreau famously affirms:

> I went to the woods because I wished to live deliberately, to front only the essential facts of life, and see if I could learn what it had to teach, and not, when I came to die, discover that I had not lived.[9]

In this spirit, leaving his familiar home and habitual life in Concord, Thoreau ventured to woods barely two miles from town. Was his purpose an abstraction: to find the randomness of "wilderness" as compared to "civilized" order? Or were his intentions and choice far more urgent and much more immediate? Certainly he broke with the life he had known, departing from his "unconscious" life to live deliberately. He separated himself from the known to push against the unknown and perhaps unknowable, wishing to see if something might stir within him. He carried out his controlled "experiment" by identifying the contradictory realities that compelled him to measure the "essential" facts of life against the inessential, the deep against the superficial, and the enduring against the transitory. Embracing the contradiction of Concord and Walden, "city" and "woods," he abandoned neither, but held both close to him in daily experience. To move beyond a life taken for granted, he acknowledged mortal life, in order, as he put it, to "see if I could learn what it had to teach, and not, when I came to die, discover that I had not lived." This sober awakening was his (and perhaps our) second birth, and he shared it with us directly:

> We must learn to reawaken and keep ourselves awake, not by mechanical aids, but by an infinite expectation of the dawn, which does not forsake us in our soundest sleep.[10]

This dawn is our permanent awakening. It is the repeated beginning of our continuing birth, the great silence that is too quickly lost in the noise of the day that deafens those sweet sounds of our most alert, enduring, and confident being.

> *Pause again to be silent for a moment. Hear the sound of silence in the quiet beating of your heart and in the opened space of the alternating asymmetrical rhythm of your breathing out and breathing in, like waves of the sea that empty and refill you as light dispels the night.*
>
> *Lower the artificial lights around you, soften your eyes. Depart your familiar consciousness, but remain open, aware, awake in readiness for a fleeting moment of clarity, understanding, and enlightenment beyond words or thought. Enter a momentary threshold of shadowed connection.*
>
> *Allow for quiet perception embedded in ordinary familiar existence—and yet felt as a new awareness of something that had always been there, but now might become truly present in you: an emergent recognition; your vital presence summoned forth . . .*

Moments of awakening are never what we expect, nor do they necessarily occur when we most expect them. Most often they manifest in moments of silence, of pause, of emptiness, within the radical reality of simply living and being; our hearts quietly beating, our breathing calmly alternating . . . in, out, in, out. Departing the familiar consciousness of our ordinary realities, leaving behind all we think we know—all our already-thought thoughts, expectations, and preconceptions—moments of awakening come to pass with the suddenness of a lightening flash or the touch of someone's hand. A quiet perception emerges: a momentary threshold of a new way of being.

I offer the following photographs as an invitation for quiet reflection. The first two bring us to the outer gate of Ryoan-ji, a Zen Buddhist temple in Kyoto, Japan. This gate might serve as our first step: let it welcome our entry as if into Thoreau's "woods." The third image leads us along a curving path that extends beyond our sight to the outer border of the temple. The fourth image, heading to the East Gate of Ryoan-ji and through the imperial wall, brings us to the inner space of the temple grounds. The fifth image reveals the pond that lies just beyond the East Gate; the sixth shows two rocks protruding through the surface of the water.

> *Experience these images as a brief occasion of calm, beholding meditation. Imagine approaching step by step the awakening reality of Ryoan-ji. Let us approach slowly, deliberately, each at our own pace.*

(1.1) Outer Gate I
(1.2) Outer Gate II
(1.3) Curving path
(1.4) East Gate
(1.5) Pond with moored boat
(1.6) Pond with two rocks

> *Now, allow images 1.7 and 1.8 to introduce a threshold experience animated by the poetic insight of Matsuo Bashō in image 1.9.*[11]

(1.7) Pond with two rocks and still water
(1.8) Pond with ripples
(1.9) Matsuo Bashō, text, "Breaking the silence . . . "

(Advance screen)

The Embodied Embrace of All Contradiction

Our goal is not to invoke an innocuous, abstract love as the solution to the reality of killing—an obviously empty and futile gesture—but to engage with the question of what a "more human love" might actually be in daily practice. In other words: how to approach and then to enter into the threshold of that love where, from that embodied vantage point, we become free to embrace the specificity of love and thereby experience an ever-diminished need to "kill." With our heightened alertness to the human capacity each of these now-special words evokes, we may reconsider Rilke's stark observation. Might "*killing is a form of our wandering mourning*" in turn give way to a deeply animated "more human love," not as a remote abstraction but as a vital life-affirming impulse to act?

On the first page of the section in *Walden* titled "Where I Lived, And What I Lived For," Thoreau affirmed his experiential, physical, and metaphorical center by declaring that "wherever I sat, there might I live, and the landscape radiated from me accordingly."[12] Although Thoreau went to the "woods" for his epiphanous awakening, it might have been the reverse. He might as well have gone from the "woods" to Concord, from "wilderness" to "civilization." His goal, it seems, was not to escape into "nature" or even to deny the values of the "town." His intention was the disruption of the ordinary, unmindful ways of his being that had presumably become habit. His move to Walden Pond was therefore a willful and active break with Concord (and even Ralph Waldo Emerson, his transcendentalist mentor and patron). He hoped it would open in him a threshold of awakening to a "higher life than we fell asleep from," even the night before in Concord. Though *Walden* is most often assumed to be a naturalist's manifesto disconnected from Concord, we might reimagine here the complementary obverse to our own "Concord"—in other words, our own "Walden Pond." Such a change of direction would allow us to find the centripetal core of our own life to see what it might have to teach—and to prevent us from discovering, when we come to die, that we had not lived.

In this spirit I offer to guide us on a likely unfamiliar journey toward a form of contemplative beholding (or knowing). Along the way we may find an opening—a place to reawaken to the nearly invisible realities that exist in even the most familiar aspects of our lives—where we can generate some measure of change, growth, and transformation. In this way, we could begin the work of replacing our all too familiar "killing" with a revitalized "more human love" whose radiance would illuminate the world.

The "poetic or divine life" Thoreau imagined breaks free not only from habit but also transcends the necessary incremental realities of "physical labor" that "the millions" are capable of. Such labor includes even "intellectual exertion," which only "one in a million" can manage. In his poetic ascent to "one in a hundred millions," Thoreau aspired to discontinuous realities, inaccessible to mere arithmetic, or to causal or instrumental calculation. The contemplative beholding that will animate the threshold of love requires a comparable ascent beyond exclusively rational limitations to a sublimated alchemy, in which eros and insight emerge together—like "the fire and the rose" in Eliot's poem—to become the luminous components of that "more human love" we are seeking. And if we are to find it, "more human love" will be both earthbound and celestial—at once fully physically grounded and of the stars—profane and sacred. In sum: *the embodied embrace of all contradiction.*

The twelfth-century monk and priest Abbot Suger, who restored the royal mortuary Basilica of St. Denis just north of Paris, experienced one form of this "more human love" during his meditation within the thrall of his new sanctuary:

> It seems to me that I see myself dwelling, as it were, in some strange region of the universe which neither exists entirely in the slime of the earth nor entirely in the purity of Heaven; and that, by the grace of God, I can be transported from this inferior to that higher world in an anagogical manner.[13]

The pathway into this elusive, virtually suspended and dreamlike (but always poetic) reality is simultaneously experiential and spatial as well as cognitive and analytical. To move into the threshold of love will thus entail our simultaneously careful and disciplined attentiveness to material presence, our willing openness to immaterial awareness and, most especially, our devoted act of identifying and sustaining with Abbot Suger this and every other contradiction. This deliberate act of contemplative beholding will also occasionally reveal glimpses of a wholeness in every way greater by a factor of infinity than any sum of its parts. Indeed, the act of love, reaching for the beloved beyond our grasp, may well intimate that face Thoreau imagined to be so dazzling that he could not look at it. Or, perhaps our experience of this shining face will open the way to an artistic beholding that would seize without touching that precious *amour de loin* (love at a distance) that the troubadours and poets of *fin'amor* (purified love) once knew. Our final step, as awakened beholders at the journey's end, will then be to approach this face as the very art—the *art* of art—embodied by works of art. By this means, the threshold of love will emerge in us as the place and attitude of our being where our beloved will appear.

(Advance screen)

CHAPTER 2

Reconciliatory Longing: A Condition of Our Human Being

The demonstrable correlation of opposites is an image of the transcendental correlation of contradictories.

—Simone Weil, *Gravity and Grace*

THE PROCESS of "awakening" often begins with a metanoia, or change of heart and mind: that is, a sudden reversal of consciousness in the way we see and understand the world and other human beings. We may call these "turning around" experiences "initiatory," but that doesn't mean they are in any sense esoteric. In some sense, they are extraordinary "ordinary" moments. They can transform us. Often, if we are awake, or grace is with us, they can and do occur in the course of daily life. They are equally likely to occur in a conversation with a friend, or in nature, or when a painting stops us in our tracks. They are moments that change us and also teach us, if we are able to learn from them—in which case, our awakening deepens and becomes a continuing experience. They are always unexpected, unanticipated, and unplanned.

Turning Around

My own adult awakening occurred on Mt. Desert Island off the coast of Maine during a family trip to Acadia National Park.

Having pitched our tent in one of the remarkably civilized areas of this "wilderness" park, outfitted with picnic tables, fireplaces, and a washroom—the camping version of "Concord" perhaps—we drove to the nearby summit of Cadillac Mountain. It was a beautiful day. The blue sky was cloudless, and the smoky-green spruce and pine forest opened outward to the 360-degree horizon, from land to ocean. On all sides, the rolling slopes rose gently up to our empowered vantage point, as though we had achieved panopticon-like authority over all we surveyed.

We had a plan in place: I would guide our two young daughters down the mountain through the woods along a marked hiking trail to our campsite, where my wife would meet us with a well-deserved open-fire dinner. Anticipating all manner of wildlife and alpine flora to entertain us on our easy descent, we set out with joyful expectation. The hike was to be our great adventure. In no time at all we located the entrance to the trail leading down the mountain. My wife drove off past the ranger's hut at the summit, waving an optimistic good-bye. My daughters and I walked into the forest in high spirits to find the first stone cairn that identified the trail. We soon found another cairn, and then another. As the woods grew thicker, finding the cairns became the game of the moment. Each of the little girls took turns as the trailblazer, running ahead to show me the way, gaining in confidence with each new cairn. What a joy! The plan made complete sense: healthy exercise, family bonding, a perfect learning experience for the children (and not bad for me). All that was required to retrieve our ultimate reward—a promised wild blueberry pie—was a short walk downhill.

After about a half hour, our younger daughter, who was then seven, ran back to tell me that she was having trouble finding the next cairn. No problem, I thought. Her older sister would step up to become the teacher. She would guide us safely to the next closest marker and we could then pick up our trail. We walked on ten yards, then another ten and a few more until we began to feel a bit disoriented. Unable to find the next cairn, we turned around to get a fresh start by returning to the last cairn. To my rising concern, we could not find that reassuring little pile of rocks (or any other marker) on what I now began to suspect was an abandoned trail. By this time the exhilarating view from the summit, descending gently to the invisible but easily imagined campsite nestled in the woods below, had completely disappeared. We saw nothing but random trees, alpine flowers, and rocks, which in the circumstances of the moment appeared randomly arranged as if to challenge our confidence. All too quickly I realized that we were utterly lost, surrounded by a rather dense forest that extended outward for dozens of uninhabited square miles.

Without warning, the bright weather changed to rain and the air turned colder by the moment. Continuing seemed impossible. Trying hard not to show my own considerable distress, I proposed changing our game. Instead of looking for cairns, we would now see how fast we could return to the summit. I took the lead, and the girls, thrilled with the new challenge, bobbed along behind as I ran upward, always *upward*, as fast as I could, to reach the mountaintop. Eventually we found ourselves at the ranger's hut. We telephoned the park office and were soon driving down the macadam road to our comfortable campsite. Adventure over. I learned later that my wife had spent a terrified hour at the end of the trail waiting for us, asking hopefully of all the other happy hikers if they had seen a man and two little girls along the trail. They, of course, had not.

This family story is surely unexceptional, but its implications for the path toward the threshold of love are important. Certainly, for me, and my own professional life, this brief walk in the woods of Acadia National Park was a transformative event. To understand how, and in what sense, this occurred, we must turn our imagination back to the moment when the game changed. Not only did it dawn on me that we were lost and that the situation could quickly get much worse, but we were also becoming dangerously wet and cold with little hope of being found any time soon as the evening sun began to fade.

My real awakening occurred, however, when I realized that this beautiful forest had no concern for us whatsoever. It did not matter to the trees, the flowers, and the rocks whether we lived or died. That we were decent, worthy people enjoying a pleasant afternoon was existentially irrelevant. This humbling recognition separated me from all the caring support I knew, including my wife—painfully close-by but helpless—the park rangers, and the remote possibility of other random hikers. We were lost and alone. For the first time in my life, I felt the presence of an infinite solitude I had previously never known. The confident panoramic survey I had experienced at the summit had been reversed.

Without in any way anticipating it, without fanfare, I had come to experience the life-altering reality of felt human frailty in the face of a vast otherness, a wholeness beyond my imagining and beyond my control. My life had changed: to live now meant to accept this condition. Without alarming the children, my thoughts had turned to the uncaring mountain and the need to allow it to be our only cairn; I sensed that no other agency than deliberate collaboration with this mountain would save us.

In this state of consciousness, turning to climb back to the summit, I became attentive in a new way to every shift in the terrain, assuming that "up" would mean movement toward it. Each detail of the mountain's contour became another natural cairn guiding us home. I followed where they led, never knowing where we were, but clear about where we were going. During those frantic moments, although unaware of what was happening to me as I ran, I now know that I transformed an essentially voyeuristic relationship with the mountain into a literally life-saving partnership, accepting gratefully that it did not care what happened to us on that or any other day. In retrospect, it was like being in the thrall of a new reality that would transform my encounter with art, teaching, and, in truth, life—not to say love.

Was this awakening my "Saul moment"? (Think here of how the anti-Christian zealot was struck blind on the road to Damascus upon hearing Jesus say, "Saul, Saul, why do you betray me?"—only to be baptized as Paul three days later *and regain his sight.*)[1] Perhaps in an inconspicuous way it was, as all such awakenings are. It certainly opened me to the fathomless reality within which I exist. But another comparison seems closer—to me at least. The art historian Meyer Schapiro once accounted for the stark simplification of color and the oddly reversed spatial perspective that inform Vincent van Gogh's *Wheatfield with Crows.* He suggested that the artist had, in this painting, retreated from unmanageable complexity, as if he had returned from an incomprehensible number to start all over again at the beginning, counting from zero . . . one . . . two . . . three . . .[2]

(2.1) Vincent van Gogh, *Wheatfield with Crows,* 1890

(Advance screen)

My experience that summer day amounted to my own circumstance-enforced reversal from complexity to utter simplicity. Turning away from the rapidly expanding complications of being lost in a vast forest toward the movement back to an origin—if not zero, at least a fresh beginning—required humble recognition, but also a change of perspective that would bring me and two little girls home to a virtually sacral meal shared as a family.

Could it be, then, that this perfectly ordinary but transformative experience on the slopes of Cadillac Mountain was a first walking step on one path toward the threshold of love?

Milo's Lament

Let me tell another family story, a second experience that set me on the way toward my own threshold of love. I call this next step "Milo's lament."

One of our daughters is now the mother of a son who, at the moment I recall here, was five months and ten days old. Having been inseparable from her infant son since he was born, our daughter one day asked my wife and me to care for him while she enjoyed a night out—her first since giving birth—with old friends. Certain that our own experience with infant babies was adequate, we agreed. Milo was clean, fed, and fast asleep in an upstairs bedroom with a state-of-the-art digital color monitor watching his every move and listening for the slightest rustle.

After an hour or so, we heard a very gentle cry, a whimpering, but without urgency. When the crying continued, my wife went to investigate. I could hear her singing softly to him. Soon enough I too went to Milo's room to help comfort him. To my dismay, Milo's crying turned into a more distinct sobbing. He was, despite all our efforts, inconsolable. Then I noticed that Milo's eyes were tightly shut. Though visibly upset, he was still fast asleep. I offered to hold him and walked downstairs to our living room, where he continued to sob. As I sat down, trying to make him comfortable in my arms, Milo opened wide his large brown eyes and looked around the room. He smiled his crooked baby smile and woke up. My wife brought him warmed formula. Although normally restless when he ate, this time Milo inhaled his complete bottle. He turned, smiled again, and went peacefully back to sleep. What had happened?

With no confirming "scientific" evidence, I am convinced that we witnessed something extraordinary. Is it possible that Milo at five months and ten days of age experienced the primal human moment of "conscious" separation from wholeness? He remained fast asleep but nonetheless, while in this condition, he became aware of himself *in relation*.

Might I convince you to revisit this experience with me once again, so you too can understand how my dismay at Milo's distress turned into wonder? Nothing, as I said, appeared to be the evident cause of his discomfort. He did not wake up looking for his absent mother. He was not wet, cold, or even obviously hungry. He was asleep, and yet disconsolate. When he did wake up, he was perfectly happy, took his formula without his usual fuss—and then slept again calmly through the rest of the night.

Although Milo cannot tell us about his "awakening" in the night, or provide a first-person account of what had happened to cause him to cry so mournfully, might we imagine that his sobbing by any other name was a primordial human lamentation caused by his emergent though infant self? Did he—without a waking understanding—enter the conscious reality of the universal human separation from the infinite wholeness of which he was an inseparable part? Did we witness Milo at the very onset of his life's "wandering mourning"?

I have devised my own language for the ontological reality of Milo's lament: *to be is to be separate... and being separate, we long to be whole.*[3] Each side of this existential paradox (separation and wholeness) is vibrantly alive at the same time. Martin Buber's beautiful image comparing conscious life to a child's long periods of sleeping, followed by moments of waking, followed again by long periods of sleeping, captures the temporal condition of our human existence.[4] Milo's lament reveals, I believe, this irreducible and insatiable yearning.[5]

For those who are no longer infants, Milo's "awakening," even as he slept, may be as obvious and simple as our endless physiological hunger for food and our thirsting for water. So too, when we are cold, we seek warmth and when too hot, we seek to be cool. These longings are our "wandering mourning." They drive our endless search for wholeness from our unalterable condition of limitation—as do fear seeking courage, confusion striving for clarity, fatigue needing rest, ordinary loneliness looking for the embrace of another lonely being and, of course, grief seeking solace.

An Operatic Interlude

> *Pause here with me for several minutes. Listen to Renée Fleming sing "Marietta's Song" (from Erich Korngold's opera* Die tote Stadt*) and let the sound of inconsolable mourning surround you.*

(Advance screen)

*** Erich Wolfgang Korngold (1897–1957), "Marietta's Song"**

Korngold's opera portrays the haunted dream-like longing of a widower named Paul who grieves for his wife Marie. His desperate efforts to recapture his lost love for her are animated by his "wandering mourning" through the streets of Bruges, where he meets a beautiful young woman named Marietta, a dead ringer for Marie. When Paul invites Marietta to his home, she performs a song and tries to seduce him with a dance. Conflicted by feelings of loyalty to his wife and his desire to feel whole again, he eventually comes to see the emptiness of his false affection for Marietta. Sunk despairingly into a chair in front of his wife's portrait, which he's kept hidden in a secret chamber called the "Shrine to the Past," he begins to hallucinate. In a rage of disappointment mirroring his nostalgia for Bruges and its once luminous past, he imagines strangling Marietta with his wife's golden braid—and further fantasizes that participants in the city's annual religious procession, which is actually taking place outside his window, have invaded the room. When Marietta next comes to Paul's home, ostensibly to retrieve a forgotten umbrella that she sees as an omen to bring them together, Paul refuses to have anything more to do with her: his dream of strangling her—the "reality" of it—has destroyed his fantasy and allows him to leave Bruges behind, as well. The song Marietta sings to Paul before she performs her seductive dance is called "Glück, das mir verlieb" (Joy, that near to me remains). It ironically and passionately intimates the true character of a love that would, in the last word of the song, "resurrect" the *fin'amor* of his dearest Marie, if not the glory of medieval Bruges.[6]

> *Pause to reflect on Renée Fleming singing "Marietta's Song." Her voice will pierce even the hardest of hearts with the gentle hope of enduring love.*
>
> *Now, shift from the implications of the widower Paul's "awakening" and return to the paradoxical moment of Milo's profoundest transformation from unconscious to conscious being.*

(Advance screen)

Imagining Our "Second Birth"

Certainly, my wife and I were unusually privileged to have witnessed such a moment. Although Milo could not yet imagine the implications of his "awakening," we around him could. Think here of Thoreau's ironic account of true awakening to a "higher life than we fell asleep from," where in our ordinary waking and working days we likely forget the very wholeness from which our consciousness separates us. But what if, as he suggests, our "Genius," and the "undulations of celestial music," and "a fragrance filling the air" are what awaken us instead of "factory bells"?[7] Might we then remember our fullest condition of simultaneously being separate and longing to be whole?

I could look for an exemplar of comparable unity within the monastic tradition that conflates work and prayer, but for me the Irish poet John O'Donohue offers the gentlest articulation of this wholeness by imagining an infant even younger than Milo. In a blessing titled "As a Child Enters the World," the poet speaks in the voice of the "awakened" infant:

> May my eyes never lose sight
> Of why I have come here,

That I never be claimed
By the falsity of fear
Or eat the bread of bitterness.

In everything I do, think,
Feel, and say,
May I allow the light
Of the World I am leaving
To shine through and carry me home.[8]

Might we then imagine our "second birth" as an endless awakening to the reality of our true being—so that as Thoreau suggested, *when we come to die, we will not discover that we had not lived*? Think of the apostle Peter's moral awakening to the sound of crowing: upon remembering the words of Jesus—*before the rooster crows you will deny me three times*—his remorse causes him to weep bitterly (Matthew 26:34, 26:75).

We can now begin to consider, in Rilke's "*wandering mourning*," how *love* might replace *killing*. Martin Heidegger asserts, somewhat abstractly, that "questioning is the piety of thought," but for Rilke, questioning is a way of being itself, as he implores his young poet-correspondent to understand:

> I tell you that I have a long way to go before I am—where one begins.
>
> You are so young, so before all beginning, and I want to beg you, as much as I can, to be patient toward all that is unsolved in your heart and try to *love the questions themselves* like locked rooms and like books that are written in a very foreign tongue.
>
> Do not now seek the answers, which cannot be given you because you would not be able to live them. And the point is, to live everything. *Live* the questions now. Perhaps you will then gradually, without noticing it, live along some distant day into the answer.[9]

Love, twinned with living, thus becomes the question we would live. And living it, the question would move us ever closer to the threshold we seek to approach. Does loving "the questions themselves" mean avoiding the clarity of answers, which is our habit? If life at its irreducible core is the very contradiction Milo now knows, living the questions does not mean avoiding questions with answers. It means, above all, avoiding the mistake of assuming that any answer, however simple, complicated, or materially and logically demonstrated it may be, is ever the same as the misty wholeness from which our conscious waking has separated us. The Buddhist might say the finger pointing to the moon is not the moon. Milo simply wept.

Loving the questions themselves might mean living patiently, as Rilke advised the young poet to do. But accepting the mystery of an answer into which, with care, we might one day live, we may need a working strategy through which we seek a sacral place between the finite part that we are and the elusive, infinite whole that we aspire to—including the very contradictoriness of this and every other discontinuous reality. The clearer the answer, the clearer the contradiction, and the greater the unending need of intimated reconciliation—the poetry or, by any other name, *love*—that would comfort us in our "wandering mourning."

In his well-known and cherished first letter to the citizens of ancient Corinth, the apostle Paul raised love as the highest of these comforts:

> For we know only in part, and we prophesy only in part; but when the complete comes, the partial will come to an end. When I was a child, I spoke like a child, I thought like a child, I reasoned like a child; when I became an adult, I put an end to childish ways. For now we see in a mirror, dimly, but then we will see face to face. Now I know only in part; then I will know fully, even as I have been fully known. And now faith, hope, and love abide, these three; and the greatest of these is love. (1 Corinthians 13:9–13, New Revised Standard Version)[10]

Although the eschatological reference in Paul's construction of the human condition—"when the complete comes . . . "—may be too theological for many of us, its vivid existential presence remains compelling. To leave behind "childish ways" is to acknowledge Milo's lament as our own—thus to accept our condition of separation and longing—and to embrace our longing for wholeness from this irremediable condition of limitation. We are hungry, thirsty, cold, hot, afraid, confused, lonely, and lost. Consequently, invoking the apostle's words once more, we leave behind "childish ways" when we identify counterfeit abundance of all kinds—think here perhaps of the widower Paul in *Die tote Stadt*—and wait patiently to be in the presence of true abundance beyond all grasping, not in the distant future, but now, in this life and in this body.

As we accept separation and longing as a condition of our existence we may turn to the cardinal virtues from Plato and Cicero—prudence, courage, justice, and temperance—and the complementary theological virtues of the apostle Paul: "faith, hope, love, these three; but the greatest of these is love." Together, these seven canonical virtues sustain our "wandering mourning" in their very embodiment of the discontinuity between finite and infinite realities. So also do the seven liberal arts—the *trivium* (arithmetic, music, geometry) and the *quadrivium* (astronomy, grammar, rhetoric, logic)—with which, like the builders of the great cathedrals, we too may construct the transformative cathedrals of our endless longing.[11]

Conscious Awareness *in Relation with* Infinite Wholeness

Before we can begin to imagine building our own "cathedrals" as we approach contemplative beholding and the threshold of love, let's try to visualize our universal condition of conscious human being. Here we start with a schematic representation of conscious awareness.

(2.2) Conscious Awareness *in Relation with* Infinite Wholeness I

The large random shape in this image represents infinite wholeness—silence. The dotted border of this shape suggests that there is neither outside nor inside, neither beginning nor ending. Let this amorphous shape be infinity beyond all calculation and knowing.

Now imagine that a child emerges physically into this reality and yet remains unconsciously indistinguishable from this wholeness, as though still enveloped in amniotic fluid within the mother's womb.

At some moment, following the physical separation from the mother, a primal awakening occurs, as in the moment of Milo's lament. The child now lives as a consciously "separate" entity within this infinite wholeness, animating the irreducible contradiction of our being: *to be is to be separate . . . and being separate, we long to be whole*. We are paradoxically separate even as we long not to be separate: not one condition and then the other, but both simultaneously; "quick, now, here, now, always," as Eliot reminds us in "Little Gidding." In our schematic rendering the child has become an "I" within the open circle of self-recognition while remaining part of infinite wholeness.

Simone Weil—a thinker of remarkable range who established a reputation as a philosopher of margins and paradoxes, and who pursued inquiries of truth and justice as an activist, mystic, and seeker of spiritual solitude—poetically illuminates this existential contradiction of our being in her account of human incarnation:

> All the *natural movements* of the soul are controlled by laws analogous to those of physical gravity.[12]

That is, in our ordinary physical experience, the cardinal virtues—prudence, courage, justice, and temperance—prevail. Weil then goes on to add:

> Grace is the only exception.... Grace fills empty spaces but it can only enter where there is a void to receive it, and it is grace itself, which makes this void.[13]

In the schematic image the diminutive (but otherwise identical) random shape represents this void. The blue line reaches out from the separated "I" through the void to infinite wholeness and back, in essence to "shine through" the separated "I" and "carry me home," as O'Donohue would put it.

Imagine now that this smaller shape also might hold the theological virtues (in both active and passive forms) of faith, hope, and love. They reach out and they receive. They are the *vita activa* and the *vita contemplativa*—the active life and the contemplative life—united as one in our aspiration to fullest human being. We are separate, governed by gravity even as we long through grace to be whole. The smaller of the two random shapes also represents the realization of our deliberate efforts to know, or to construct, intimations of reconciliation of the contradictory realities that all conscious being entails.

This void into and from which grace will flow is the elusive sacral bridge with wholeness. In its identity with the larger random form, we may imagine it also to be our infinite solitude, and the solitude of another "I" that Rilke hoped we would "protect and border and salute." This animated shape is, therefore, love *as a verb*. It is perhaps Rilke's "more human love...which we are preparing with struggle and toil."

The bridge (or interval) between finite and discontinuous, infinite realities accounts for the metaphorical leap that "connects" existential scarcity of all kinds with absolute abundance. Within this interval, grace renders palpable all attempts toward infinite wholeness. Milo's lament was his sad and joyful entry into this reality, the source of his lifelong capacity to *love* and be *loved*, should he elect to choose this path. To wake up is merely to be conscious. But to awaken is to enter the threshold where our "wandering mourning" will find solace in the *love* that needs no *killing*. To recognize this means to leave behind "childish ways" and begin an artistic life that knows no end other than animated love—accomplished by an art and practice of contemplative beholding, resulting in the art of works of art, beauty, and love.

(Advance screen)

Reconciliatory Longing

The *art* of works of art is the fragile offspring of this delicate moment of profoundest awareness, born in the recognition and acceptance of our condition of human being. Charles Baudelaire's famous assertion that the artist is an "eternal convalescent" suggests an art of enduring recovery from this awakening into mortal reality. The art of contemplative beholding, in its turn, will embody meaning within us so that all our living will be an endless act of becoming whole or "well" again, a movement toward ever fuller consciousness as in the continuous gestation of a child.[14] To approach this homecoming, each one of us is born with a biologically immanent potential for a capacity I call *reconciliatory longing*. Although our emergence as a person follows a slow evolution from one tense "embeddedness" to another, this potential is constant. It will be the source of rebirth again and again, in the midst of constant change and transformation.

In the beginning then, we are "embedded" within the physiology of our mother's body, sensually alive and alert to our mother's world—her voice, the rhythms of her very being, and the sounds surrounding her—but utterly unaware. Upon our "first" birth we are separated from our mother (from that biological paradise, we might say). Yet we remain "embedded" and unaware of any distinctions between ourselves, our mother, and the world. All three, despite physical separation, remain experientially one. Preconsciously (or precognitively), even during the first moments out of the womb, we have the capacity to know. We are hungry until fed. We are cold unless made warm. Furthermore, as a surprisingly critical requirement of physiological survival, we are lonely until we are held. Indeed, if we are isolated as infants, our very lives are potentially threatened, unless through nurturing attachment we are united with another living being.

Each of these circumstances within our second "embeddedness" may be taken as biological instances of separation, lack, loss, and scarcity seeking redress, fulfillment, and true abundance. This longing for wholeness from a condition of biological limitation recapitulates the microbiological reality of conception and prenatal growth. During the months of our existence following birth, an emerging "consciousness" evolves until the moment of our second "birth," which occurs in the awareness of the separation from our mother, and hence the world. At this profoundest of all moments—Milo's lament—we are delivered into solitude: that contradictory condition (affliction) of our conscious existence within the interval (the *void*) between finite and infinite being. Listen once more to Rilke:

> And to speak of solitude again, it becomes always clearer that this is at bottom not something that one can take or leave. We are *solitary*. We may delude ourselves and act as though this were not so. That is all. But how much better it is to realize that we are so, yes, even to begin by assuming it?[15]

This cosmic yearning rising from within our solitude is the engine of our being. Beginning with conception, this irrepressible reconciliatory longing will redeem the pain of separation. Whether it takes biological, psychological, intellectual, artistic, or spiritual form, this reconciliatory longing is the core of our living and dying. For death only transmits this vital dynamic process back to the world. Our inborn capacities for accommodating to the paradoxical reality of separation and longing (reconciliatory longing) will naturally develop into ever more complicated means of "reunion." But this won't happen if we remain enclosed in "egocentric" alienation (separation without hope of reunion) or, unless fostered by fear, power, and an unwarranted need for control, we opt for the enticements of counterfeit abundance. (Among these enticements I include exclusive rational knowing and finite, tangible certainty, as well as other enticements I introduce in succeeding chapters.)

Reconciliatory longing exists in each one of us: in order even to exist, we must seek nourishment, warmth, attachment. Hence, in order simply to be, each one of us is called to become the special kind of artist that each unique one of us is. From an ontological perspective, then, the word *artist* identifies any person who would recognize this reality and deliberately act from within their solitude, as an artist.

The art of reconciliatory longing is no mere epiphenomenon. Although causally dependent, it is not limited to the material/biochemical functioning of the body/brain.[16] This reconciliatory longing is the conscious equivalent of the very "life" of the human soul, including what Simone Weil spoke of as *gravity* and *grace*. For the poet Wallace Stevens, reconciliatory longing might be what he called the "necessary angel of earth," namely, the presence of "imagination" in all of its forms.[17] Stevens's self-reflective poem "The

Final Soliloquy of the Interior Paramour" finds reconciliatory longing in the interior dialogue with our most intimate muse:

> Light the first light of evening
> In which we rest and, for small reason, think
> The world imagined is the ultimate good.
> This is, therefore, the intensest rendezvous.
> It is in that thought that we collect ourselves,
> Out of all the indifferences, into one thing:
>
> Within a single thing, a single shawl
> Wrapped tightly round us, since we are poor, a warmth,
> A light, a power, the miraculous influence.
>
> Here, now, we forget each other and ourselves.
> We feel the obscurity of an order, a whole,
> A knowledge, that which arranged the rendezvous.
>
> Within its vital boundary, in the mind.
> We say God and the imagination are one...
> How high that highest candle lights the dark.
>
> Out of this same light, out of the central mind,
> We make a dwelling in the evening air,
> In which being there together is enough.[18]

As we pursue tangible realizations of reconciliatory longing in the act of contemplative beholding through poetry, art, and love, our goal is to experience evermore completely our fullest being. We can look back in history to Western and Eastern cultures for their insights and traditions. The ancient Greeks, for instance, had no word for art as such. They understood this reconciliatory act as the twin faces of *theoria* (contemplative seeing, with wondrous eyes, of a beautiful or divine object) and *techne* (applying or practicing a skill, craft, or art with, as the ancients made clear, the intention of making it visible).[19] Thus, we may say that art then was a kind of contemplative "beholding-revealing," offering intimations of immortal realities. The Japanese, whose word for art (*bijutsu*) did not exist before the nineteenth century, sought in the medieval literary tradition of "linked verse" (*renga*) to produce collaborative poems that join otherwise incommensurate realities. The Japanese phrase *ai-no-ma,* which I associate in chapter 6 with Heian-court love poetry, names a place of mysterious meeting, as in the fateful encounter of lovers. In the Yoruba tradition of Africa, the seventeenth Odu, Osun (Our Lady of Charity, or Love) was the female divinity—distinct from the sixteen male divinities—whose powers of reunion were to be invoked on any occasion when art and the deepest human healing were required.[20]

In his book *I and Thou*, Martin Buber envisioned a "return" from objectified estrangement to an immanent capacity for reconciliation with ourselves, each other, the world, and, above all, infinite wholeness. In his translation of Buber, Walter Kaufmann explained his use of "You" rather than "Thou" as a way of focusing the intimate subjective vitality—"spontaneous and unpretentious"—of human dialogue and understanding.[21] In this view, we may imagine that the beholding inherent in a reciprocal "I and You" is the moral purpose of our being. Here I invoke Martin Heidegger to take this idea further: we will build buildings and all manner of things, but this beholding will allow us to envision those cathedrals that help us to dwell within the "four-fold earth and sky, divinities and mortals" alike, and guide us home.[22] And once more, I bring us back to Thoreau, who wrote:

> It is something to be able to paint a particular picture, or carve a statue, and so to make a few objects beautiful; but it is far more glorious to carve and paint the very atmosphere and medium through which we look, which morally we can do. To affect the quality of the day, that is the highest of arts.[23]

Beholding actually avoids the spiritual pathology of being confined by our bodies and estranged from our souls. In other words, it can free us from living as if material factors alone determine our social, political, psychological, and moral choices. At the same time, this beholding is not an exercise in parapsychology. Neither do we seek material manifestations of inaccessible psychic realities. Nor is this beholding a way to externalize our subconscious being. Beholding from the ontological perspective, as I guide you through this book, is a physical, intellectual, and finally spiritual act, anchored to our immanent reconciliatory longing that is accessible when we make a conscious choice to accept "loving" as the form of our "wandering mourning." The "unconscious" in this view is no longer the dreaded invisible yet driving reality of our conscious lives.[24] Our being is now, directly and openly, the result of an increasingly aware conscious self as experienced in relation to the world from which that very consciousness "separates" us. Recall again Thoreau's section of *Walden* titled "Where I Lived, And What I Lived For":

> Wherever I sat, there might I live, and the landscape radiated from me accordingly.[25]

As some of us come to understand through our meditative practices, we are not prisoners of our thoughts. Thoughts come and go, but we exist as embodied beings of reconciliatory longing who, as artists, are able to choose the means we use to embrace contradiction. We are not "driven" unless, in a failure of imagination, we allow ourselves to be driven. By acknowledging and accepting the condition of our being, we free ourselves from childish "embeddedness." For St. Augustine and Marguerite Porete, as we will discover in chapter 7, this freedom will empower *love* as both verb and noun, articulated succinctly as the challenge (in Porete's vision) to "love Love, and do as you will."[26]

First Perception

As artists then, endowed with reconciliatory longing, let us imagine our first perception as it occurs in the crib. We see inchoate movement. Each raw, sensory potential flows into and through another. Light and dark appear, along with an optical awareness of warm and cool stimuli, but without form. As instances of precognitive knowing or pre-reflective being, this "pure experience" is consistently random, swirling, and dynamic.[27] All is chaos—a "formless void," like the earth in Genesis 1:2. Slowly, repeated occurrences take shape as form and color. Soon, we begin to "measure" warm to cool perceptions, until "red" becomes "known" by the relative presence and absence of its retinal complement "green." Other "colors" soon provide further "order" to stabilize our perceiving "experience." According to their degree of warm stimuli, "red" becomes "orange" and then "yellow;" cool stimuli move from "green" to "blue" and then on to warmer "violet" and back to "red." In every case, each color possesses both its complementary hue and temperature. Cool "reds" exist with warm "greens."

Of course, *all these "colors" exist in our experience independent of their names*. As Milo became increasingly verbal at about age three, his willingness to assign any color name to particular colors, calling a red toy green or blue, may confirm the learned verbal component of our encounter with color. When we would say that he "was learning his colors," we'd mean he was learning *our* names for particular sensory experiences. To reaffirm this infantile memory, we need only stare at a starkly "red" shape for a minute and then close our eyes and wait quietly, confidently. Soon enough we'll see a faint but real and glowing green shape that will resist naming. Similarly, if the red shape was closed, the green image will be open or the reverse. (In chapter 5, I explain the glee of a student in my class who had this experience.)

As our perception develops further, formal distinctions then begin to appear; curvature measures straightness; convex pushes against concave; verticality pulls away from the horizontal; near and far tug at each other, and so on. Gradually, a coherent world of opposition, rhythm, harmony . . . and finally, shape, space, and time stands forth before us. In this way, we experience the ongoing dynamic dance between being and nonbeing, form and nonform, as they arise between the asymmetry of sensory "experience" and the relatively stilled symmetries of repeatable and enduring conceptual "order." This dance occurs on the potentially ever-expanding continuum of our perceptual interaction with the world (including not only sight, but all of the senses).[28]

Tentatively stable "order" reifies constantly shifting "experience." Like our conscious awareness of separation and longing, this unfolding animation is no less paradoxical. Just as experience and order are irreconcilably contradictory, so too the very *redness* of red denies the *orangeness* and *yellowness* of its immediate neighbors and the *greenness* of its opposing complement. Similarly, the standing vertical repudiates the slumbering horizontal, and round alters straight. Contradiction drives cognition.

Now our rapidly emerging incarnate awareness occupies a place between the contradictory possibilities of "pure experience" and "pure order," perceived and abstracted as subjectivity and objectivity, movement and permanence. An *immortal*, disembodied world now shares our conscious being with a mortal, embodied one of artistic reconciliatory longing.

Since infants cannot relate their experience to researchers, scientific studies about how we first perceive anything in the world risk being limited by after-the-fact projections of adult verbalization. For example, because we see "red," researchers will ask: Does the child see "red?" Any apparent distinction the infant might make only confirms our adult conceptual notion of "red" rather than allowing for the warm or cool sensations of the preverbal child. We may doubt William James's description of infantile perceptual chaos: "the baby assailed by eyes, ears, nose, skin, and entrails at once feels it all as one great blooming, buzzing confusion."[29] But it is plausible and likely that the infant's rudimentary physical and cognitive capacities would naturally first respond to the more primal, irreducible warm and cool, which only later become "red" and "green." From the vantage point of our first perceptions in the world within the crib of our infancy, we might well imagine a dynamic interaction between sensory experience and conceptual order from the very beginning. And, without assuming developmental superiority of one over the other, discover that our earliest awareness entails both together, as the complementary pillars of our emerging capacity for cognition.

If we were to visit the incomparably rich cognitive construction known as the Cathedral of Our Lady, in Chartres, France, our continuing embodiment of this reality might return us to the threshold of Milo's lament. Approaching the extraordinary stained-glass windows facing each other in the north and south transepts, for instance, we experience a complicated arrangement of colors that in the shifting light of day ranges between the relatively *cool* "blueness" of the north—the "mother's" portal—and the *warm* "redness" of the south: the "son's" portal.

(2.3) Cathedral of Chartres, France, 12th–16th century:
a. north transept windows (13th century)
b. south transept windows (13th century)

May we now imagine that our direct, unmediated physical presence between these two windows will bring us close to the precognitive white wholeness? Indeed, arriving at the "crossing" (the intersection of nave and transept) within the precisely organized space of this cathedral, we will have come to a "sacred place" where we may experience how our habitual and limited finite cognitive perception of "colors" and ecclesiastical iconography is now just one infinitesimal step removed from a "return" to infinite wholeness. If we find ourselves standing or kneeling in this space, T.S. Eliot's urgent words, "quick, now, here, now, always," will become palpably meaningful. The path to wholeness is, perhaps, back through primal realities whether in the once high-tech world of Gothic stained glass or in our own era of Kasimir Malevich's *White on White*, in which nearly irreducible neutral warm and cool colors emerge:

(2.4) Kasimir Malevich, *Suprematist Composition: White on White,* 1918

(Advance screen)

Color and Value

To escape unconscious habit, Henry David Thoreau went to the actual "woods" surrounding Walden Pond. We might consider an alternate route to reengage with our earliest perceptions from the crib by constructing a black and white value chart and a red and green neutral color chart. The particular materials and steps for actually doing such an exercise will vary, but we can approach it instead as a thought experiment.

Let me guide your imagination here: Between black and white, construct seven incremental steps. Beginning from either black or white, vary each step so that your movement from one value to the next is precise. To do this you will need to judge the shift of each step relative to the immediately adjacent steps and all of the remaining steps. You will need to pay attention to both the particular part and the whole. To simplify your seven "measurements," you can narrow the optical reach by halving the distance, beginning at the center and continuing to the left and right. Or you may proceed step-by step while keeping an eye on the larger whole. Either way you will have simultaneously used experiential and conceptual measurement.

In both cases the dynamic relation between the immediate sensory "experience" and conceptual "order" of your first emerging perceptions from the crib will have evolved into something remarkably like "prescientific" notions of *ars* (sensory experience, observation, practice, craft) and *scientia* (cerebral reflection, theory, conceptual order) that apparently informed medieval cathedral builders: both approaches required overlapping direct practice or craft and rationalized theory grounded in tradition, with neither dominating.[30]

This exercise of constructing a simple value chart is admittedly rudimentary. Its implications are not. Although the theoretical number of steps between black and white is infinite, let the seven steps in this exercise represent our ordinary perception. This physiological limitation within an infinite continuum offers us another awakening moment. Once again, the finite part cannot exist independent of an elusive infinite whole—in this case the interval between black and white. Making a value chart will bring us surprisingly quickly to an embodied experience of reconciliatory longing, if not Milo's lament, in which his sobbing will have become our adult frustration.

Watching students who do this exercise in a group I have experienced the unarguable and vividly felt presence of multiple unique solitudes. Even though the simple directions for this exercise are identical for everyone—seven value steps between black and white—no two handmade value charts are alike. They are as different as the people who make them. Some choose to arrange the steps horizontally, others vertically, or in a circle. Some use round shapes for the steps. Others construct little squares placed within a grid. Some measure out the task geometrically and then fill in the steps while others "eyeball" their progress from one value to the next. Some smooth their brushstrokes to leave an untouched impression. Others leave behind rough and palpable marks. Some "paint" within neat boundaries. Others feel little or no border constraint. Some position their steps on the page thoughtfully to relate "figure" and "ground" in subtle compositions. Others just mark the page more or less randomly, ignoring any deliberate relation between their value steps and the edges and center of the page.

In every case, however, each of us doing this exercise out of the classroom will have entered into the same interval of multiple contradictory possibilities. Completing this exercise requires a conscious or unconscious recognition of our need to embrace contradiction and to proceed by precise juggling: either deliberately—mindfully—or mindlessly, like the startled Monsieur Jourdain in Molière's *Le Bourgeois Gentilhomme*, who discovers he has been speaking prose his whole life without realizing what prose is.

We may extend the awakening reality contained in this value exercise by creating a neutral color chart. To do this, we move in incremental steps toward a center point between "red" and "green," progressively mixing each color with its complement. The central step in this exercise, neither "red" nor "green," will be chromatically neutral and either warm or cool, depending on the proportion of each color in the final mixture. The tonality of this neutralized color might recall how from the crib we first perceived existing warm and cool equally, as they waited to stand forth as colors to be named. Again, the actual results of this exercise will vary for each of us. For Carl N. Schmalz, a teacher making a color value chart to use in the classroom, the results might look like this.

(2.5) A teacher's color value chart, after Carl N. Schmalz

Some results will almost resemble the "Abstract Expressionist" subjectivity of a Hans Hofmann. Others will recall Giorgio Morandi, whose art lives in deliberate chromatic "neutrality." Piet Mondrian, as we will discover in chapter 5, actively embraced the entire continuum from the frailest color neutrality to the fullest chroma of primary red, yellow, and blue. Mark Rothko reached out to the full range of neutral and saturated color to create chromatically charged constructions of juxtaposed, overlapping, or transforming color in which red and green might occasionally reverse warm and cool tonality.

(2.6) a. Hans Hofmann, *Sommernachstraum*, 1957
b. Mark Rothko, *No. 1*, 1961; c. Giorgio Morandi, *Still Life*, ca. 1955

(Advance screen)

Opening and Closing the Panels of Bosch's Garden of Earthly Delights

The vast scholarship attempting to interpret the iconography of Hieronymous Bosch's *Garden of Earthly Delights* often overshadows our approach to the triptych as a simple realization of color.[31] Bosch painted the enclosing exterior panels of this famous work, now at Madrid's Prado, to represent the first days of divine creation. He portrayed the cosmic separation of light and dark, land and water, in the subtlest possible merging of warm and cool neutrality, nearly but not quite ready to burst with chromatic potential, which we may think of in relation to our infantile color perception. Then, as if to follow our imagined cognitive progression, he revealed upon opening the panels an explosion of tapestry-rich, full-intensity color in a panoramic world populated with teeming human presence. The vision of biblical history, moving from left to right, reaches from Edenic early morning brightness to a prophetic night of ice and fire. This mysteriously exuberant dance of light, color, movement, and promise (even with darkened stillness) fixes our attention on the interior of the *Garden of Earthly Delights*. But as beholders, we know that once opened this triptych must also close again, as if returning all creation to its origin. The *Garden of Earthly Delights* thus ends at the threshold of our first perception of warm and cool color neutrality.

Our awakened response to the pictorial order of the triptych includes the experience of a "closed" beginning, "open" fulfillment, and "closed" ending, followed by another "opening" and the beginning of a new cycle. Like the rising and setting of the sun, this temporal sequence mirrors the ratio of infinite and finite reality—permanence with change, eternity with transient existence, living with dying.

Bosch placed the figure of God holding a book (Logos-wholeness) on the left outer panel in an illuminated space surrounded by black clouds and visibly separated from the crystal orb of his creation. Two inscriptions (from Psalm 33:9) at the top of the facing panels proclaim the Lord's unchanging divine sovereignty:

> (left): *Ipse dixit et facta sunt* (For he spoke and it came to be)
> (right): *Ipse mandavit et creata sunt* (He commanded, and it stood firm)

The *Garden of Earthly Delights* is almost invariably taken to be a moralizing work of late medieval if not ecclesiastical art. Without denying the triptych's theological frame, is it possible to move beyond its time-bound reality to a timeless self-transcendent acknowledgement of our universally human condition of being?

In seeing past the cloud of complex iconographic decoding, an unsuspected clarion vision appears; one that anticipates what may be William Shakespeare's most enduring recognition: "Love is not love / which alters when it alteration finds / or bends with the remover to remove: O no! it is an ever fixed mark."[32] We return to the poetic clarity of this sonnet in chapter 8, for now we might listen to the reassuring and tender solace Shakespeare offers in another sonnet to the materialist obsessions and fears, not only of Bosch's contemporaneous patrons but also our own. If we were to behold slowly and contemplatively, the result might be the very presence of wholeness beyond the affliction of our mortal longing:

> Buy terms divine in selling hours of dross;
> Within be fed, without be rich no more:
> So shalt thou feed on Death, that feeds on men,
> And, Death once dead, there's no more dying then.[33]

Unfortunately, the most recent technical, highly refined, and tasteful installation of the Bosch gallery in the Prado is remarkable for an artistic estrangement that prevents our full engagement with the *Garden of Earthly Delights*. The triptych is supported on a platform next to the gallery wall with its two wings secured in place. Like uncertain cats, they are unwilling to come in or go out. Without the direct experience of seeing the triptych both closed and open, this fixed arrangement obscures the very vision this majestic work of art embodies.

(2.7) Bosch-Gallery, museum installation Prado, Madrid, Spain

Imagine with me, instead, a beholding alternative alert to the art of this work of art and the impact it would have on us as aware visitors from around the world. In place of its clinic-like presentation, primed for invasive observation and interrogation, the triptych might be supported in a separate room on an altar-like shelf and covered by a middle-value gray curtain. When invited into this dimly lit room we would wait for several calming and focusing moments of visual and psychological preparation . . . slowing down, being silent, listening . . . until the curtain gradually pulls back to reveal the closed exterior wings illuminated by soft, chromatically transparent light.

As willing beholders, we would have sufficient time to engage with the color neutrality of the paint and the ontological reality of the moment within the cosmic history of the image and our individual awakening. With care, we might imagine our physical presence swept up into the timeless reality of our being.

Then, slowly, reverently, the triptych would open, allowing its vivid color to realize the passionately fleeting dream of incarnation from beginning to ending. We might now almost hear the sound of acceptance and gratitude in the opening verses of Psalm 33 as a musical equivalent of Bosch's virtually synesthetic vision:

> Give thanks to the Lord [wholeness] with the lyre;
> Make melody to him with the harp of ten strings.
> Sing to him a new song;
> Play skillfully on the strings,
> With loud shouts of joy.
> (Psalm 33:1–3, New American Standard Bible)

After some fifteen to thirty minutes, however we use them and whatever thoughts and feelings open to us, the wings would close slowly, bringing this beholding occasion back to its beginning at the threshold—birth—of our conscious presence. With the protective curtain returned to the triptych, we beholders would be invited, when ready, to leave this now *sacral* place.

> *Pause with me in quiet contemplation, as we now behold with the* Garden of Earthly Delights *as though for the first time; perhaps even hearing the sound of a harp of ten strings.*

(2.8) *Garden of Earthly Delights*, exterior
(2.9) *Garden of Earthly Delights*, interior
(2.8) *Garden of Earthly Delights*, exterior

(Advance screen)

The Contradictory Space Between Infinite Light and Dark

Whether we encounter the continuum of finite perceptual value and color in "red-green" studio exercises (or in those using the remaining color pairs of blue and orange, purple and yellow)—or whether we engage with their application in complex works of architecture, sculpture, and painting, this consciously learned reality occurs in the contradictory space between infinite light and dark. In recognizing this, we may share Thoreau's knowledge that "thus the darkness bear its fruit, and prove itself to be good, no less than the light."[34] As though in a crib, we exist within an elusive cosmic interval that enfolds the physical and metaphorical incarnation of all conscious life.

As urgent and immediate as this living reality is, we must compete in our world with another equally compelling and (for many) dominant reality. Some will argue that modern technology has enabled us to escape our primordial crib and the reality of our mortal condition, freeing us to construct a post-corporeal, virtually eternal, if not immortal existence. What some may call an "invitation" and others, perhaps more aptly think of as a "temptation," takes its authority from an unarguably relentless campaign of efficiency, discovery, and acquisition propelled forward from the sixteenth century by the Renaissance Dream of Reason (see chapter 8), which promised to transform all darkness into light.

One vision of this reasoned disembodiment comes from Hans Moravec's *Mind Children,* published in 1990, in which the developmental curve of both computer power and nanotechnology offers evidence to hypothesize the complete "downloading" of the human brain into artificial materials.[35] Since then, current artificial intelligence and robotic engineering have almost brought us face to face with our own digitized versions—akin perhaps to the monster Dr. Frankenstein created—as if to affirm Václav Havel's essentially artistic observation that "man as an observer is becoming completely alienated from himself as a being."[36] This entirely plausible digital/mechanical empowerment may even have brought us full circle to that sense of despair and mortal shame, which, in the ancient world of Greece, gave meaning to the word *hubris*. Think here of the poet Hesiod donning the robe of the prophet, and the lament that concluded his sad account of the Iron Age in its last days:

> And then *Aidos* (Modesty) and *Nemesis* (Indignation) with their sweet forms wrapped in white robes, will go from the wide-pathed earth and forsake humankind to join the company of the deathless gods: and bitter sorrows will be left for mortals, and there will be no help against evil.[37]

Even if we don't despair at the disappearance of Modesty and Indignation, those divinities "with their sweet forms wrapped in white robes," we may well feel abandoned in our movement toward a "more human love" that would offer lasting solace to our longing.[38] At the very least, we may have the feeling of being lost and surrounded by apparent but unmanageable abundance of endlessly expanding information absent all meaning.

The View from Space

For many of us, succeeding cycles of day and night, friends, objects, work, and pleasure—that is to say, our lives—may have come to resemble little more than aimless movement in endlessly receding space, not unlike the "screen saver" on our computers. Fleeting intensities appear and disappear without trace or solace. An unnerving emptiness seems to await us in our every moment of quiet reflection. Indeed, if we are honest with ourselves, we would have to admit that feelings of separation, fragmentation, and unanswered longing constantly drive us to a deep loneliness: an unspoken fear we can't escape. The global pandemic that began in 2020 has of course intensified our isolation. Although reasons will vary, even the most fortunate among us may feel a gnawing hollowness.

Why? Why has the student's lingering purposeful and inspiring question—"so what?"—become a helpless, unanswerable ache? What, amid apparently incalculable wealth, is the impoverishment, at least for some, that whispers "counterfeit" in our ears even as we await the next mind-blowing technological wonder? And what of our numbness to distant natural disaster?

In other words, our human trajectory since the turn of the fifteenth century seems to have brought us to a point of shared desolation, which the superficial charisma of our dazzling accomplishments only partially obscures. Think of the gilded wonder of the renamed St. Petersburg in Russia, heroically restored after the demented destruction during World War II: rather than being seen as a meaningless remnant of a departed past, it might actually provide the very means of confronting the particular character of our current dilemma, releasing us from the nightmare of confusing our present circumstances with the human condition. The grandeur of the czar's Winter Palace and the sweeping dream of Peter the Great didn't fall to the fresh new vision of a revolution that sought economic redress. Rather they were overwhelmed—"killed"—by another form of hubris in the tyranny of self-centered fear demanding power to seize control and establish "our" order over everyone and everything else, while denying all other realities that might diminish this ultimate, commanding authority. Even the delicate healing potential of Russian spiritual aspiration, in the form of a Rasputin caring for the czarina's son who was dying of hemophilia, became grotesquely distorted in the culminating events of the half millennium that began with Columbus's voyage to the new world.

Constructed in the early eighteenth century on the inhospitable marshy delta of the Neva River, St. Petersburg took shape as though through sheer force of will, labor, and reason it might deny its subarctic reality by mimicking the imperial artifice of Rome, Florence, and Versailles.[39] Its improbable splendor may exemplify our headlong rush to give up the sensory perception—dismissed as the "flat earth" upon which we actually stand—in favor of an "enlightened" modern conceptual vision of a heliocentric universe as the exclusive foundation of a human rationalism that dominates all understanding.

Perhaps at stake here is what the paleontologist and evolutionary biologist Stephen J. Gould—not without controversy—identified at the turn of the twenty-first century as the essential truth that divides our existence. He called it NOMA, an acronym for "non-overlapping magisteria." By this, he meant two independent, but non-overlapping, areas of inquiry and experience, each of which constitutes "a legitimate magisterium of domain or teaching authority." One is a rationalized, objective, and presumably true science of "facts." And facts, as Gould would have it, are forever estranged from the other, namely religion, as being values-driven, idiosyncratic, and "subjective," though nonetheless equally coherent and organized, if not systematic.[40]

From the point of view we aspire to in this book, we might well think it is time to reimagine the swirling polar arguments *for* and *against*: to allow instead for the contradictory possibilities of clear distinctions as well as overlapping magisteria that, paradoxically, are without intersection. If we do so, multiple epistemologies (science, religion, art, and others still) will emerge from a singularly embodied human condition of separation and longing, refreshing what we mean by the word *cognition*, if not *wisdom*.

At the same time and in the same vein, in a collective act hardly less audacious than Peter the Great's improbable dream (or Steven J. Gould's cognitive clarity), we have now also seen Earth from space. We have seen it whole and gleaming within the surrounding darkness. By means of a contemporary high technology, equivalent to the splendid muscular unreality of St. Petersburg, we have seen it through new instruments that seem to free us from the ancient limitations of our bodies. We have seen our Earth weightless, disconnected, adrift, and alone. In fact, perhaps the singular icon of our time is the NASA photograph of Earth taken anonymously in 1968 by an astronaut who represented us all at the Archimedean point realized in the form of the Apollo 8 spacecraft.[41]

That is, from a certain point of view, our eyes have at long last observed our world, so that in the poet Archibald MacLeish's words, "man may discover what he really is." MacLeish continues: "To see the earth as we now see it, small and beautiful in that eternal silence where it floats, is to see ourselves as riders on the earth together, brothers on that bright loveliness in the unending night—brothers who see now they are truly brothers."[42]

(2.10) NASA, *Earth from Space*, 2002

MacLeish's ecstatic poetry on seeing the 1968 version of this photograph echoes our unanimous response to a sense of being liberated from primordial incapacity to see ourselves truly from the outside. In this compelling image, we are objectively displayed beyond all possible personal interaction, mechanically delivered up like an insect pinned on a laboratory wall: our world, our universe, our existence suspended for everyone to see. Even if we are not all literally brothers and sisters (but only symbolically so), this new perspective reveals our planet as though without interference, privilege, or bias. This remarkable and universally recognized image is an affective product of a precisely focused (and yet strikingly limited) way of knowing and relating to the world. As an image it realizes our contemporary conviction that truth resides in dispassionately observed phenomena, governed by immutable ("natural") laws. Being the result of a nearly incomparable act of remote observation (similar to microscopic and telescopic observation), this photograph distances us. It abstracts. It withdraws. Finally, to complete its task, it alienates its object. Taken from the hermetically enclosed space shuttle, this photograph records on chemically processed film an image of Earth in space independent of all embodied experience except optical sight. There is no "up" or "down," no "left" or "right." There is neither "near" nor "far"—no "here," no "there."

As though it were a purely abstract painting, seemingly disconnected, like a Jackson Pollock canvas from the artist's own hand, it exists as a perfected, immutable, unchanging reality seen by a neutral, disembodied observer. Like the medium of photography itself, this NASA photograph has become the virtual *vera icon*, the true image, of our secular "scientific" and objectifying faith.[43]

It aspires to pure "order" beyond change or human interference, recording the circle that remains a circle in infinite expansion comparable to the longed for *acheiropoeitos* or "divine image of God made without hands," like the miraculous medieval painted "Face of Christ" called the *Sudarium*.

Yet there is a second, related photograph that captures another, more immediate, and familiar reality that discloses the unspoken limitation, not to say bias, of the first one. During the same mission to the moon, on Christmas morning 1968, William Anders took the photograph that has come to be called *Earthrise*.

(2.11) William Anders, *Earthrise*, 1968

How different it is to see that perfect circle of the NASA icon fragmented. In the first image, we may choose to see an objective truth, seemingly beyond the reach of time and change, in which we are, indeed, somehow absent, everyone abstracted as "brothers." In the second photograph, change itself is manifest in the subjective presence of the moon's horizon. This photograph records our "experience" of movement; of rising and falling as Earth slips out of and returns into infinite darkness. Time and place now reverberate with the human construction of a timeless space. *Earthrise* has an embodied perspective. "Up" and "down," "near" and "far," "here" and "there" are once again alive in us.

Each of these photographs brings to the surface a different fraction of our human condition: objective absence and subjective presence. But seen together they begin, ironically, to precisely measure the enduring mortal limitation we still share. For somewhere between these commonly exclusive extremes of immutable order and phenomenal experience is the living actuality of such contradictory realities existing at the same time as the irrepressible source of an unavoidable need to seek their reconciliation. Could it be? Could it ever have been? Could we reimagine the human in this relentlessly "advancing" technological age? Could we ever reimagine the possibility of intimating such reconciliation in art, poetry, love?

(2.12) a. William Anders, *Earthrise*, 1968; b. NASA, *Earth from Space*, 2002

Come back to Earth with me. Let us return to the temporal and the art historical boundary of our modern world, specifically to the city of Bruges.

(2.13) Bruges, Belgium, early morning

Walking the unusually tidy and remarkably well-preserved streets of Bruges in modern day Belgium during the early morning hours, we have the distinct impression that Jan van Eyck (ca. 1390–1441), the best known of the Flemish painters of the fifteenth century, and any number of his contemporaries, are there with you. The half-light of the shadows, illuminated by the rays of the rising sun, creates a mysteriously rich space in which the buildings, the cobblestone streets, the vacant sidewalks—not to mention the countless silent figures of Mary holding the Christ Child, which are enshrined everywhere in stone niches above street level—collapse the vast distance of time and thinking that spans the half millennium separating us.

(2.14) Bruges, Belgium, *Madonna and Child* indicated

The uncommonly bright, dazzling, and fragmented light bouncing off the water of the canals animates the stillness as though those artists really were still there, constructing, as always, those visions that would annex time and transform the darkness of the night.

(2.15) Bruges, Belgium, *Madonna and Child* indicated
(2.16) Bruges, Belgium, Golden Hand Street, *Madonna and Child*

But, of course, those artists are not there. Their visions and their aspirations are long gone. Their world has been reconstructed by those new ideas that have brought us in our own time to the very eve of a virtual or, for some, even a post-bodily existence, made real and vivid by machines designed to extend our senses and mimic our minds. Having physically departed our planet, we have nearly stepped out of our bodies. We now stand in a new space: it seems to be as utterly foreign to the one that produced the wooden panels of Flanders, and those grand canvases of Haarlem, Delft, and Amsterdam, as that imperial Russian dream was to the mud flats of the Neva River in St. Petersburg. And yet, that first impression out of the corner of our eye, before the noise of the day breaks the spell, puts Jan and the others there with us, as real and vibrant as we feel ourselves to be. Can we wonder, then, what it might be like to see the world again in those images and through the eyes of the painters who made them? Is it possible to let the faint sound of the morning bell you hear in the distance fix this elusive moment as an occasion that we might call *re-membering*?

(2.17–2.27) Bruges, Belgium, *Madonna and Child*

Is it imaginable that we might almost brush against that permanence of time where even the irreconcilable discontinuities of our lives are whole again, if only for an instant?

Here I ask you to look again at the two photographs from space.

(2.12) a. William Anders, *Earthrise*, 1968; b. NASA, *Earth from Space*, 2002

Seen together, they are not only opposed as fleeting "experience" and immutable "order." They are also no less alike than they are different. The NASA icon reveals change in the random, organic shapes of the clouds and, conversely, an inexorable orbit haunts the rising and falling of the Christmas photograph.[44] This invisible but implicit complementarity may point us back to a mechanics of beholding in which absent others, our daughters and sons perhaps, and those who have preceded us or will follow us, are here also in this embodied threshold we all inhabit. Whether we are on this Earth or in space, we exist within our bodies, suspended in the impossible interval between these two photographs.

(Advance screen)

Beholding then—in space, in the crib, in the museum, or in life generally—will require a deliberate effort to embrace the eternally contradictory reality of our physiological and psychological being, including the left and right hemispheres of our brain and body, as well as the full range of conceptual order and phenomenal experience within a universal self-conscious condition of mortal separation and longing. The art of this beholding will invoke those intimations of re-membering, reunion, and wholeness that will redeem the spiritual aspiration of our living. Let this art be the foundation of our effort to reenter the threshold of love, which, by any other name, is that being our observing eyes had forgotten and that Milo's sleeping tears might refresh.

With this recognition, we may approach the elusive, but vital interval of discontinuity or void that will complement the habitual continuities of our lives—*gravity*—into which *silence* and Simone Weil's *grace* will enter and from which art, music, and science will emerge. Let us now think of eros and insight together as the reconciliatory longing of our mortal condition. And we may do so for no other purpose than to enact the eternal conversation between lover and beloved that would offer consolation to our "wandering mourning."

Where We Have Arrived . . . Where We Are Heading

Intimations of reconciliation are the art, beauty, and love manifest as the threshold of love we would approach. By their very nature, and because of our immanent reconciliatory longing, they engage with contradiction in an embrace of suspended disbelief; they exist as a "bridge state" that reunites even as they preserve contending realities. An art and practice of contemplative beholding, then, may allow us once again to encounter and to construct for ourselves those intimations of reconciliation among the countless contradictory realities of human being that will embody meaning in our lives and *bridge* the infinite chasm of solitude with compassion.

Now that we have arrived at the end of part I, "Preparation," let's look back at image 2.2, which represents the existential origin and goal of our journey. It reminds us of the perspective from which a dynamic coincidence of self *and* transcendence becomes the primal manifestation of the contradictoriness all conscious being entails. As a schematic rendering of the precondition for beholding, this image of separation and longing places before us the component realities of an art and practice of contemplative beholding.

(2.2) Conscious Awareness *in Relation with* Infinite Wholeness I

Each of the six images that follow elaborate on image 2.2 and anticipate the steps we will take in part II, "Setting Out." (Think of them as preliminary "maps" to guide our journey.) In succeeding chapters I reintroduce these schematic drawings and expand on concepts integral to them, so that step by step we may aspire to and realize an art and practice of contemplative beholding in our lives.

(2.28) Contradictory Epistemologies

The side-by-side lists in "Contradictory Epistemologies" echo the relationship between the two photographs *Earthrise* and *Earth in Space* as an extension of our infantile awareness of sensory "experience" and conceptual "order." The multiple ways of knowing and being I include in the lists illustrate the potential spectrum of adult cognition. (I invite you to add any contradictory epistemologies that come to mind.) The following schematic drawings further develop these two lists.

(2.29) Embracing Contradiction

"Embracing Contradiction" recalls the premodern definition of *ars* ("experience," in terms of sensory awareness, observation, practice, craft) and *scientia* ("order," in terms of reflection, theory, cerebral cognition) as mutually informing realities before their modern estrangement as Art and Science.

(2.30) Collaborating Epistemologies (*ars* and *scientia*)

"Collaborating Epistemologies" invites us to integrate *ars* and *scientia* so that neither is arbitrarily dominant; doing so allows us to construct those intimations of reconciliation—*cathedrals* of love—as an act of aspiration rather than mere acquisition. As we consider the reciprocity that exists between these two declarations—*ars sine scientia nihil est* (practice without theory is nothing) and *scientia sine ars nihil est* (theory without practice is nothing)—we may then recognize the active cognitive relation of "experience" and "order" that will bring us to *eruditio* (higher learning).[45]

(2.31) *Eruditio* (higher learning)

In this schematic we see *eruditio* (higher learning) emerge as the intimated reconciliation of contradiction. This higher learning, seen as the threshold of love, comprises (variously) art, eros and insight, and love the verb. By proceeding along this path of awakened self-transcendence and the embrace of all contradiction that conscious being entails, including contradictory and collaborating epistemologies, we will animate a Via Amoris leading toward *sapientia* (wisdom)—immortality insofar as mortals are able to know it.[46]

(2.32) *Sapientia* (wisdom)

As beholders we now see *sapientia* (wisdom) appear through artistic intimation as infinite wholeness, greater than which there is nothing: love the noun, the beloved, beauty, I–You. Again, you may add as you will to these verbal equivalents for infinite wholeness.

(2.33) Conscious Awareness *in Relation with* Infinite Wholeness II

Although this image looks the same as image 2.2 at the beginning of this chapter, I have made several specific additions. I invite you to add as you will to the verbal equivalents of both the "void" and the "infinite wholeness" we seek to embrace.

With our thoughts turned to wisdom, then, I offer these words from Thomas à Kempis. Toward the middle of the fifteenth century, on the first page of Book One of his devotional manual for the lay members of his monastic community, he wrote:

> This is the highest wisdom: to see the world as it truly is, fallen and fleeting; to love the world not for its own sake, but for God's [wholeness] and to direct all your effort toward achieving the kingdom of heaven [intimations of this wholeness].[47]

Although I have substituted my words for Thomas's theological language, his appeal to the "highest wisdom" corresponds precisely with our approach to the threshold of love. By replacing the more familiar monastic demand to "forsake," "renunciate," or "despise" the world with the admonition to "love the world," he conveys the universal humanity of his vision, even as he challenges us all to seek this "highest wisdom." In our next steps we will together follow the guidance of several exemplary persons whose goal was a comparable wisdom, including Rembrandt van Rijn, Johann Wolfgang von Goethe, and Piet Mondrian in part II; and in part III those creators of a Japanese spatial construction we may call *ai-no-ma*, as well as Albrecht Dürer, Leonardo da Vinci, and Michelangelo Buonarroti. Along this path, our approach to this "highest wisdom" will take shape in an art and practice of contemplative beholding.

(Advance screen)

II

SETTING OUT

CHAPTER 3

Focused Attention and Open Awareness: Rembrandt van Rijn

An activity which is meaningful in itself... cannot be accomplished except with an attitude of receptive openness and attentive silence.... There does exist something like "visual noise."

—Josef Pieper, *Only the Lover Sings*

Before we come face to face with Rembrandt van Rijn, let me guide your imagination once again, as we prepare to enter the interval of contemplative beholding.

BE STILL, silent. Breathe slowly. Pay no attention to the noises, loud and soft, around you. Let everything you hear fade into the periphery of your awareness. Remain silent. After a few moments, imagine ringing a brass bell softly. Listen now, as completely as you can, to the bell sound. Distinguish between that sound and random noise.

Ring the bell again: focus on it. Hear the movement of its sound from the sharp metallic clarity at the onset, to the slow diminishment of volume returning to silence.

Repeat the ringing several times; listen for the character of its sound from loudest to softest. Engage this sound in its particular transformation from distinct presence to absence. Let the bell's sound linger until it merges with the complementary sound of silence, which its passing will evoke with stunning, if unexpected, vividness.[1]

Pay attention to this silence. Be in this space. Remember the sound of the bell—its bright beginning, fading, and disappearance. Let the asymmetry of this aural movement begin to frame the space of silence you have entered. Remain silent.

Imagine ringing the bell again. Anticipate its sound. Ring the bell again to complete framing the space of silence. Repeat this sequence—bell sound . . . silence . . . bell sound—three times and then, slowly, allow yourself to become aware once more of the noises around you. Leave the space and sound of silence. Return to the day.[2]

> *Now experience the imagined bell meditation "for real," with no prompts whatsoever. Listen and reflect.*

(Advance screen)

***Bell meditation**

The Interval of Contemplative Beholding

Throughout this book I use the word *interval* to mean the infinite gap of discontinuity, where grace renders palpable all intimations (hints . . . inklings . . . suggestions) of infinite wholeness. Here's how we might imagine the aural experience of this interval of contemplative beholding in a visual schematic.

(3.1) The Interval of Contemplative Beholding I

(Advance screen)

Now let's relate this delicate interval to the act of awakening that Robert Frost implicitly invites us to engage with in "Mending Wall," his subtle and youthful homage to the art of poetry.

> Something there is that doesn't love a wall,
> That sends the frozen-ground-swell under it,
> And spills the upper boulders in the sun;
> And makes gaps even two can pass abreast.
> The work of hunters is another thing:
> I have come after them and made repair
> Where they have left not one stone on a stone,
> But they would have the rabbit out of hiding,
> To please the yelping dogs. The gaps I mean,
> No one has seen them made or heard them made,
> But at spring mending-time we find them there.
> I let my neighbor know beyond the hill;

And on a day we meet to walk the line
And set the wall between us once again.
We keep the wall between us as we go.

To each the boulders that have fallen to each.
And some are loaves and some so nearly balls
We have to use a spell to make them balance:
"Stay where you are until our backs are turned!"
We wear our fingers rough with handling them.
Oh, just another kind of outdoor game,
One on a side. It comes to little more:
There where it is we do not need the wall:
He is all pine and I am apple orchard.
My apple trees will never get across
And eat the cones under his pines, I tell him.
He only says, "Good fences make good neighbors."
Spring is the mischief in me, and I wonder
If I could put a notion in his head:
"*Why* do they make good neighbors? Isn't it
Where there are cows? But here there are no cows.
Before I built a wall I'd ask to know
What I was walling in or walling out,
And to whom I was like to give offense.
Something there is that doesn't love a wall,
That wants it down." I could say "Elves" to him,
But it's not elves exactly, and I'd rather
He said it for himself. I see him there
Bringing a stone grasped firmly by the top
In each hand, like an old-stone savage armed.
He moves in darkness as it seems to me,
Not of woods only and the shade of trees.
He will not go behind his father's saying,
And he likes having thought of it so well
He says again, "Good fences make good neighbors."[3]

Some of us might read "Mending Wall" as an unresolved narrative of division, separation, and contradiction because the poem begins and ends with declarative counter-statements—"Something there is that doesn't love a wall" and "Good fences make good neighbors"—that bracket several rational inconsistencies. For others of us, the poem might allude to moral choice. But as a work of contemplative art, "Mending Wall" offers us an occasion of artistic wisdom when we become open to and aware of Frost's attempt to reconcile the contradictions he embodies in the poetry, if not in the very structure of the poem.

Let's start by identifying infinite wholeness as it's implied in the first line, "Something there is that doesn't love a wall." (Later in the poem, Frost repeats this line and follows it with a terse affirmation: "... That wants it down.") Those lines merge across an asymmetrical *interval* with the irreconcilably contradictory finite idea of "good fences" that "make good neighbors" in the last line.

Frost's poetic challenge to us—to enter the "gaps" (intervals) between wholeness and fragmentation—occurs in the narrator's famous questioning of his neighbor. But before asking him bluntly, "*Why* do they make good neighbors," the narrator says to himself, "Spring is the mischief in me / And I wonder if I could put a notion in his head." This rhetorical interruption divides the poem asymmetrically between its "upper" and "lower" parts.

Now I suggest we step back for a moment to think about the poem's title and consider what a "mending wall" actually is. Perhaps we might ask why the title does not correspond to the poem's narrative activity, *mending the wall.* Might we wonder what Frost had in mind by omitting the simple article "the," which would have bridged the gap and removed any ambiguity? Could it be that this ambiguous phrase is a purposeful synonym for conflict resolution?

Metaphorically, a "mending wall" becomes the healing art of poetry that intimates reconciliation between the infinite "something" and the finite recognition that "good fences make good neighbors." A "mending wall" softens the harsh divisions, contradictions, and unalterable separations of conscious being. So too, it is the love to which we aspire.

In some sense we may ourselves be unable to articulate the experience of such elusive and even impossible reconciliation. And yet, with the narrator's question to his neighbor suspended before us, as well as the one implied by the repeated first line of the poem—"Something there is that doesn't love a wall"—Frost pushes us further toward a moment of potential self-discovery: we ourselves become the neighbor when the poem's narrator declares: "I could say 'Elves' to him / But it's not elves exactly, and I'd rather he said it for himself." We might now certainly imagine that Frost intended the title to be grammatically ambiguous, wanting his readers to see for themselves how art—his poetry—might reveal itself. Our habitual distance of disembodied analytical observation and interpretation will surely give way in meditation to an awakening of our own as beholders—unless we remain outside the thrall of this work of art as the neighbor does, "Bringing a stone grasped firmly by the top / Like an old-stone savage armed."

For those who have never seen a New England wall, and even for those of us whose paths through the woods have bordered along or traversed many a stone wall, I offer the next image—a brief interlude before we move on.

(3.2) New England wall

"Mending Wall" first appeared in Frost's collection of poems called *North of Boston*. Is it possible that he meant his title to echo Thoreau, whose determination to transcend the limits of habitual behavior led him to leave Concord for the "woods"?[4] Like *Walden*, "Mending Wall" is a quiet manifesto of new ways of feeling and thinking, carried along by the fresh spring air of epistemological "mischief." "Mending Wall" appears to amplify this new reconciliatory understanding in its determined structure of balanced asymmetry.

We can see just how "visible" this balanced asymmetry is when we turn the verbal poem on its side to create a long, horizontal rectangular form: notice the two unequally sized text blocks, and the interval text in blue—"Spring is the mischief in me / And I wonder if I could put a notion in his head."

(3.3) Robert Frost, "Mending Wall," horizontal schematic

In the next image we see that for Barnett Newman, Frost's "spring is the mischief in me" has become a "mending wall" in a sequence of ratios seeking intimated reconciliation between horizontal and vertical form, left and right, lower and upper, symmetry and asymmetry, wholeness and fragmentation—all this in a field of red calling out across an interval of silence to an absent green "something."

(3.4) Barnett Newman, *Vir Heroicus Sublimis*, 1950–51

(Advance screen)

A metaphoric interval of contemplative healing emerges especially gently for me in Max Bruch's second movement, the adagio, of his Violin Concerto no. 1 in G Minor, op. 26.

Pause to listen slowly for this composer's aural guidance into one particular occasion of intimated wholeness. Allow yourself to become present in this sublime "place" of experienced grace, as though you had just dreamed your way back into the moment before Milo's lament.

The introductory phrases lead to a series of quiet heartbeat-like sounds. Then notice how the middle section of the adagio "dawns" as though for a new day—homecoming—and ends with a heart-rending "evening" departure realized in the repetition of the opening notes. In the final section Bruch guides us back to the world of ordinary experience and *gravity*. We may encounter this adagio as a musical equivalent of the meditative sequence of "sound" ... "silence" ... "sound" that transforms random noise into music, words into poetry, and paint into art.

(Advance screen)

* **Max Bruch (1838–1920), Violin Concerto no. 1 in G Minor, op. 26: second movement, Adagio, performed by Joshua Bell**

(Advance screen)

Although bell exercises like the one we experienced earlier in the chapter are common in multiple forms to meditative practices around the world—and comfortably familiar to those of us who practice meditation at any level or attend the liturgy of the Mass—perhaps some of us have yet to experience how they can usefully serve as a preparation for approaching other forms of artistic realization. Such exercises are certainly foreign to contemporary museum expectations. If we were actually to use this approach in our attempts to open a path to the art of a painting, we would soon be sent packing.

The aural, spatial, and visual reality a bell exercise engenders, however, is a necessary step toward "beholding *with*" a work of art, rather than merely seeing or observing it. Blindness, to our probable surprise, is less of an obstacle to beholding than not being able to hear. Unlike optical observation, beholding draws on all the senses. I witnessed such an occasion when Elizabeth, an extraordinary student in my acquaintance who had been blind since birth, enrolled in an art history course on medieval architecture that I was teaching. Dumbfounded, I asked her how in the world she could possibly manage the visual presentation of projected images. Her answer was sobering. "Don't worry," she said, "I can hear space."

My own task from that "teaching moment" onward has been to connect sound and sight so that I might listen to the voice of paintings, just as she was able to see what she only heard. My responsibility to her was to describe, as clearly as possible, what a given image revealed of a constructed space, so that she could indeed hear it.[5] As a result not only I, but also the other students in the class, learned from Elizabeth how to move past the "visual noise" in our habit of distracted seeing and listening so that we might enter the deepest silent realities of the art of works of art—and, with care, even the sound of silence.

The occasion of a performance of Beethoven's *Leonore Overture II* brought this classroom lesson home to me. Unable to get a seat in the sold-out main section of the Concertgebouw in Amsterdam, I purchased a ticket for a proscenium seat in the elevated rows behind the orchestra, facing the audience. The conductor Leonard Slatkin entered the stage from behind me. He descended the stairs, took his place before the orchestra with his back to the audience, and set his baton gently on the podium. Everything was ready to begin. The hall was filled to capacity with expectation. The conductor stood silently, quietly, his arms at his side. Nothing moved. The musicians sat in rapt attention watching the conductor. Still nothing moved. The audience fell absolutely silent, waiting.

Unseen by the audience in front of the stage, the conductor looked at the musicians one by one. He engaged their eyes slowly, reciprocally. He stood silent. He closed his eyes for what seemed forever and then opened them. He raised his arms in a gesture of offering with his hands open, facing upward. Then he moved his arms forward and back, toward the musicians and toward himself as though he were drawing sound out of them—as though he were assisting in its birth. As intricately related notes slowly began to assume their form in the space of the concert hall, the conductor picked up his baton and music *filled the interval of sound and silence.*

Rembrandt van Rijn: Revisited

What kind of "noise" prevents us from hearing the whispered voice of Rembrandt van Rijn? Of any artist? Although the silent awareness of our being is manifest in our presence at the threshold before any work of art, this silence is only an opening gesture.

In our modern museums, that gesture is likely interrupted by the literal noise of disembodied "Acoustiguides" or in-the-flesh interpreters who with no small amount of sophisticated information drown out what Thoreau called "celestial music." But the most destructive "noise" may well be the art-historical wall between us and the object with which we would behold. Along with Václav Havel's stunning reflection that "as observers we have become completely alienated from ourselves as beings,"[6] recall the haunting words of Martin Luther, written in his defense against the charge of iconoclasm.

> I approached the task of destroying images by first tearing them out of the heart through God's Word and making them worthless and despised. . . . For when they are no longer in the heart, they can do no harm when seen with the eyes.[7]

The contemplative beholding that will animate the threshold of love requires something radically different from our habitual demand for ever-expanding information, explanation, and interpretation. For this, we must be willing to enter into the ineffable interval between discontinuous realities, reminiscent of John Keats's negative capability (the capacity of "being in uncertainties, mysteries, doubts, without any irritable reaching fact or reason").[8] Or we may recall Abbot Suger in the twelfth century describing his experience in the Basilica of St. Denis near Paris, where he meditated *anagogically*—that is, suspended within the luminous wisdom of intimated reconciliation. We too must be willing to visit what Suger called the "strange region of the universe which consists neither entirely of the slime of the earth nor entirely of the purity of heaven."[9]

As we approach the interval of silence between sounds, each of us might consider how long we remained quietly present in front of a given work of art—before moving on to the next—during our last museum visit: One hour, a half hour, ten minutes, five minutes, less than a minute, mere seconds? Whatever our current habits may be, imagine now slowing down by deliberately releasing ourselves into an unaccustomed and honestly unaccountable moment.

We may recall that to serve his unrelenting pursuit of transcendent knowledge, Goethe's Faust made a pact with Mephistopheles: if Faust were ever to "take ease upon a bed of leisure" or sink "into a smug complacency"—or utter the fateful words "Tarry a while! You are so fair!" upon encountering beauty that would bring his quest to a standstill—he would die and forfeit his soul to Lucifer.[10] For our purposes in contemplative beholding, we might repeat these words as a reminder to pause, reflect, and be open to vital realities beyond grasping, but present in our encounter with art, beauty, and a "more human love."

> *Each of us might now say to ourselves what Faust never dared: "Tarry a while! You are so fair!"*

A "Field Trip" to the Met

Now imagine we have come to New York City to behold *with* one painting by Rembrandt, to spend the entire day with the artist's vision and then return home drenched in the experience. The word in italics here—*with*—holds a significant purpose for an art and practice of contemplative beholding. It marks a fundamental conceptual shift not only in our relation with works of art and our relational awareness in general, but also, as we will increasingly discover, with love. Many of us may find this focused and sustained approach to a single work of art unfamiliar and perhaps unlikely, even those of us who would willingly engage during our visit to the Met with just one painting. But engaging this practice will certainly invite a simple question: "What now? We are here. We are willing, but what can we do to begin?"

(3.5) Gallery, Metropolitan Museum of Art, New York

First, we must suspend our habitual ordering capacities in favor of our neglected experiencing ones. Before interrogating the painting with the familiar rationally cognitive questions that we use to capture works of art and fix them verbally—to objectify and "order" them—let's try a new exercise. Quiet the noisy left-brain functions and open slowly the relational right brain. The nuanced relationship of so-called left- and right-brain and body functions need not obscure our multiple capacities for knowing and responding in the world. We need to forget everything we've ever known about the artist, the painting, and the history of art. When we enter the gallery and locate the painting *with* which we have come to behold, rather than remaining disembodied, though knowledgeable, observers, we will be present before it, become aware of our physical relationship with the room and the painting . . . and slowly . . . allow the painting to guide our beholding distance and position.

(3.6) Gallery, Metropolitan Museum of Art

Alone, in Front of the Painting

Pay no attention to the "noise" of labels, frames, distractions. Instead, focus your attention on the painting. Ignore, for the moment, detail, specific form, and even subject. Allow yourself to be in thrall to the whole painting. Let it draw you in. Be present with it with all of your senses: sight (shape, color and value); touch (tactile impressions); smell (olfactory impressions); taste (as a complement to smell); hearing.[11] Listen for the sound of silence. (Even in Paul Klee's famous *Twittering Machine*, with its open-mouthed birds on a wire, ready to sing at the turn of a crank connected to their perch, the implied "sound" is a product of artistic silence.)

As with sound, when you listen with full attention, let the work of art before you be the only definition of time. Become aware of your physical relationship with the painting. Enter into the experiential space—the interval—between you and the work of art. Be prepared to meditate *with, in the company of*, the art embodied by it. For that moment, in this contemplative interval, become the one in a hundred millions awake "to a poetic or divine life." Allow yourself to arrive alone, come face-to-face with the artist. Be present with Rembrandt van Rijn. He is here. Be vulnerable to him and his "mending wall."

> *Be attentive for several moments in silence . . . alone . . .*
> *then listen for the sound of the bell . . . enter the interval . . .*

(3.7) Gallery, painting, Metropolitan Museum of Art

After this initial encounter, close your eyes. Let the image appear in your memory. Then sketch what you are seeing. Don't reproduce the painting even summarily. Instead, on a small piece of paper make marks of any kind you wish that, without words, will remind you later of what you are encountering now: warm and cool color; light to dark value; horizontal, vertical, and diagonal placement; shapes, space, and size relationships; stillness and movement; symmetry and asymmetry; the rectangular format and scale of the painting as an object, its center and edge. After leaving the museum or just turning away from the image in your mind, characterize *verbally* as simply as possible your memory of this painting: your first impression or, if the painting is an old friend, your present, *refreshed* impression.

(Advance screen)

What Interferes with Our Beholding?

Having reflected on our individual experiences alone, in front of the painting, compare this encounter with our habitual museum routine, which to a large degree has been choreographed for us. Many modern museums are purposefully designed to attract visitors as consumers, rather than beholders. They often organize our relationship with works of art on display according to a particular "exhibition" rationale with a focus on ideas concerning the history of art that are frequently grounded in the time period, location, style, or "cause" for the works. The Barnes Foundation, formerly in Merion, Pennsylvania, which used to offer the collector's idiosyncratic preferences independent of art historical categories, has been moved to Philadelphia where even its original display format now conforms to the corporate museum model. On the other hand, the layout of The Robert Lehman Collection in the Metropolitan Museum of Art seeks to maintain some sense of its benefactor and collector. And The Philips Collection in Washington, DC, where gallery spaces expanded within the family home of its founder from 1921 to the present day, is for many an exemplary combination of personal, domestic experience and corporate order.

Museums, like all human technology, are not neutral repositories. They serve a cultural purpose that ironically and all too often obscures the art of the works of art they preserve. This hasn't always been the case: in chapter 9 we'll see that the Propylaea at the Acropolis in Athens served as the spiritual—hence, artistic—threshold to the sanctuary of Athena; objects placed in or near the Propylaea were meant to invoke reverent encounter with divinity, comparable to altarpieces erected in ecclesiastical settings. Modern museums, on the contrary, at least since Napoleon expanded the Louvre in Paris, have presented works of art as trophies or as objects of more or less obvious social and political propaganda. Contemplation in most museums requires a deliberate act of artistic awareness and the intentional focus to move beyond the "noise" of the setting.[12]

Unfortunately, within seconds of entering the Rembrandt gallery in the Metropolitan Museum of Art, we will be drawn not to a work of art, but to a nearby label. Its purpose is to instruct: we learn that the painting before us is called *Aristotle with a Bust of Homer*; that it is painted in oil on canvas; that it is 56 ½ inches tall and 53 ¾ inches wide; that it was painted by Rembrandt van Rijn (1606–1669) in 1653; and, importantly, that it is now owned by the Met.

(3.8) Gallery, painting with label, Metropolitan Museum of Art

The label currently displayed with this painting includes detailed iconographic and historical information, adhering to art historical protocol as if it were the passport required for our visit with the artist. Additional summary information might add brief stylistic and formal references: "high baroque," or "chiaroscuro" perhaps, referring to blended light-dark values. Again, all too often, the label becomes an experiential substitute for the work of art. It implicitly encourages us to privilege art historical information over direct encounter, to pigeonhole the painting, and move on.

(3.9) Museum label, information as the virtual equivalent of the painting it identifies

(Advance screen)

The sheer number of other works of art displayed in the same gallery, and throughout the other galleries of the museum purposefully connected to it, likewise compel us almost compulsively forward, on to the next labeled object. We rarely pause. We hardly dare tarry, even for a moment. By habit, we are determined to keep up; to move on. Satisfied with some minimal factual or interpretive information, we proceed dutifully. Or, out of vague curiosity, we seek out some momentary distraction. We stop briefly at another painting with its obligatory database compressed into its label, which is sometimes extended slightly into a gallery information sheet. Or, perhaps, we listen to a recorded description and analysis. None of this behavior on the part of the museum or its visitors is wrong. It is just limiting. Artistically, it is impoverished. It also restricts our experience of the work. Absorbing information, however extensive, is not beholding.

(3.7) Gallery, painting, Metropolitan Museum of Art

The diminishment of art in our Faustian rush through the museums of the world, large and small, mirrors the incomparably vast accumulation of art historical research in general. Rembrandt's painting, *Aristotle with a Bust of Homer*, is an exemplary case in point. The recent official Metropolitan Museum of Art catalogue of its Dutch painting collection, written by Walter Liedtke, is nothing short of a masterpiece of exceptionally detailed, thoughtful, thorough, logical thinking.[13] In the twenty-five-page section of this two-volume compendium of scholarly work, the account of this painting is exhaustive, worthy of a painting considered boldly by its owners to be the most important Dutch painting in America. Beginning with a careful technical record of the physical condition of the painting, the justly distinguished author of the catalogue summarizes the long trajectory of scholarly research and opinion, offers a very brief and general description of "form and content," and then concludes with a comprehensive annotated bibliography of virtually every publication concerned with the painting from 1814 to 2007.

We learn in precise and richly informed detail—including references to contemporaneous documentation for the initial commission of the painting by a Sicilian merchant named Don Antonio Ruffo—that Rembrandt made this painting for a man he did not know, and who did not know him. In effect, remarkably, the original patron's relationship with the painting is not unlike our own. Although Ruffo may have known of Rembrandt as a famous artist from the north, there is little evidence that he knew any more about the artist's intent than we do.

Nevertheless, despite ongoing learned debate, general agreement still currently identifies the figure in the painting as Aristotle, the sculpted bust as Homer, and the face on the suspended gold pendant as Alexander the Great. Hence, Aristotle (the philosopher who became the tutor for Alexander (the military genius and king of Macedonia) shares the pictorial presence of Homer (the poet they both admired, who lived in Greece roughly five centuries earlier). But the setting, contemporaneous to the artist and his patron, is generally understood to be that of a seventeenth-century scholar in his study surrounded by the materials of his trade, which often included books and a carved bust of a famous thinker. As beholders before this work of art, we occupy a timeless reality that reaches from ancient Greece to our present moment and from the Metropolitan Museum of Art to the world.

Given the apparent inattentiveness of the figure, the content of this painting has emerged as Aristotle *with* a bust of Homer rather than the more animated title of "Aristotle *Contemplating* a Bust of Homer," which was popular for many years.[14] One of the most enduring scholarly observations about the subject of the painting imagines that Aristotle's hand gestures—the one hand touching the gold chain, the other resting gently on the sculpted head of the poet—imply a moralizing distinction among wealth, power, and fame, contrasted with wisdom.[15] Similarly, scholarly research has proposed many echoes of humanistic themes grounded in traditions of art and immortality that would have presumably interested contemporary scholars no less than an ambitious painter. Some have pursued the potential association between this painting and Aristotle's own thought, most especially and appropriately his ideas concerning the senses of touch and sight.

After nearly two hundred years of written engagement with this extraordinary work of art, the scholarly envelope brims with glistening accounts of the painting's cultural, historical, and documentary significance, offering an unending source of art historical mystery and debate. But those of us willing to behold *with* Rembrandt and the oil painting he made and shipped to Sicily may be left asking: *What does all this add up to? Does all of the effort to give an objectively valid and logically supported account of this compelling work bring us any closer to its ineffable art and the artist's devoted effort to intimate wholeness?*

If we were to allow this painting to be more than a document in the history of art or a scholarly mystery to be solved, we might soon find ourselves in thrall once again to its art—its intimated reconciliation. From within this beholding reality, for a fleeting moment, the painting might become immeasurably more valuable: an incomparable occasion of deeply felt peace in which the artist shares his hard-won, palpable though momentary sense of well-being. In this sacral exchange, our beholding *with* this art will be like a deep in-breath after the exhausted out-breath of a surfeit of rational knowledge.

(Advance screen)

From Meditation to Contemplation

The abbreviated bell exercise we began with in this chapter imagined two distinct perceptual perspectives: focused attention and open awareness (as represented in image 3.1). Listening to the bell's sound separated from random surrounding noise creates an interval filled with silence, the memory of the departed sound, and anticipation of the one to follow. Multiple soundings of the bell seek to evoke the elusive relational reality of alternating sound and silence (always distinct from random noise). For this exercise to be effective, it is important to avoid using the bell sound as an invitation to free associate. Only our deliberately focused attention on the bell sound itself will serve the purpose of forming a space bracketed, and hence separated, on both sides from the ordinariness of noise.

Within this space, the new reality becomes the foundation of music, whether of simply two sounds flanking silence or of richly integrated multiple notes. In both instances, the fundamental components of relational sound and silence remain. Open awareness in this exercise allows the relational trajectory of this "music" to invoke cognitive insight beyond normal incremental understanding, echoing, perhaps, the composer Olivier Messiaen's word éblouissement (bedazzlement).[16] Such elevated cognitive knowing—in the form of bedazzlement or beholding—amounts to a directly experienced suggestion of wholeness, accompanied by our own sense of well-being.

> *Recall the soothing effect on the biblical King Saul's mental and emotional suffering, when the shepherd David (who would become Saul's successor), played the harp!*
>
> *Now listen again to Joshua Bell's performance of Max Bruch's adagio.*

(Advance screen)

* **Max Bruch, Violin Concerto no. 1 in G Minor, op. 26 (second movement, Adagio)**

(Advance screen)

How can we allow focused attention followed by open awareness to inform our encounter with Rembrandt's *Aristotle with a Bust of Homer*? To prepare the way back to this incomparably rich occasion of contemplative beholding, we must first meet the youthful Rembrandt van Rijn.

(3.10) Rembrandt van Rijn, a. *Blinding of Samson*, 1636, detail; b. *Portrait of a Young Lady*, 1626, detail

> *Independent of specific iconography or individual identification, imagine that these two images visualize opposing capacities of the artist's (as well as our own) complex human existence: unspeakable, noisy brutality; and quiet, thoughtful repose.*

Rembrandt was a young man when he painted these two polar images. Side by side, they frame the entire range of how, as human beings, we adapt to our "wandering mourning." Clearly and courageously, they span the range from "killing" to "love." On the left, clutching the severed hair that rendered the invincible Samson vulnerable to her betrayal of love, Delilah looks back in demonic satisfaction with what she has done, as one spectator recoils as if to challenge the casual viewer to comprehend or, perhaps, to behold.

(3.11) ***Blinding of Samson,*** **a. detail of Delilah; b. detail of witness**
(3.12) ***Blinding of Samson,*** **detail of blinding**

The clenched, angry fist at the very center of the illusory threshold of the painting, placed just above Rembrandt's signature, may be the artist's and our own confrontational reply: anger, even rage, before the calm that precedes new understanding.

(3.13) ***Blinding of Samson,*** **detail of fist and signature**
(3.14) a. ***Blinding of Samson*****; b.** ***Portrait of a Young Lady***

The figure in the *Portrait of a Young Lady*, on the other hand, is soft, gentle, and silent, enveloped by a dark shadow that mediates the space between us. Paradoxically, as we behold with these two paintings, the full drama of noise and torment in the awful blinding of Samson becomes eerily quiet, while sounds of domestic tranquility resonate in the young lady's portrait, as though Rembrandt had embraced, in his own beholding, all "war" and all "peace," all "noise" and all "silence," palpably drawing us in as experiential participants.

(3.15) ***Blinding of Samson,*** **in situ**

At the age of twenty-two, Rembrandt appears already to have directly challenged us to acknowledge and share our common condition of being. Although some doubt that Rembrandt himself painted *Scholar in a Lofty Room*, this work exists as a virtual extension of the young artist's own hand and method.

(3.16) Rembrandt van Rijn (?), ***Scholar in a Lofty Room,*** **ca. 1628–29**

At the very least Rembrandt's implicit "participation" is evident in the compelling, even urgent, presence of an inter-subjective confrontation that informs his vision from his earliest to his last years. In this painting, confrontation inexorably animates the contradiction between light and dark. This encounter is focused in the contour of the scholar's massive book and working table from which he stares outward to engage the viewer in the reciprocal interval of direct awareness: I ≈ You (I approaching You).[17]

Framed on all sides by deep shadow that envelopes our presence in this space, the scholar's world becomes our own. Dazzling light, warm color values, and velvet black assume a material presence to connect exterior and interior, public and private realities—the scholar's and ours. As we behold here *with* this painting, whoever actually made it, we may imagine ourselves face to face with a fragile monument to Rembrandt's living contemplation. *Scholar in a Lofty Room* is a remarkably small painting, measuring little more than 18 inches by 21 inches, and yet its monumental contemplative affect makes it a plausible threshold by which to approach once more the majestic moment embodied by *Aristotle with a Bust of Homer*, undoubtedly painted at the very height of Rembrandt's artistic career and redolent with a similar air of shared contemplative wisdom.

(Advance screen)

Focused Attention: *Aristotle with a Bust of Homer*

One of the most intriguing discussions in the scholarship on this painting is not whether Don Antonio Ruffo knew the artist of the work he commissioned but what, if anything, he knew about the *subject* of the painting. As a wealthy businessman in Messina, he may simply have ordered a painting from an exotic, rising celebrity artist from the far-off and prosperous Dutch Republic. Setting aside the sociology of art collecting in seventeenth-century Sicily and ignoring the interceding years of art historical interpretation, we might well imagine that Don Antonio was remarkably like us in our efforts to behold with this work of art. By acknowledging that the panoptic view of two hundred years of study may give way to an immediate, dizzying array—of alpine flowers, trees, and rocks—we can look past the "cairns" of scholarly construction to find another guide to our goal: the art of this work of art. Our challenge is to turn back to the painting itself to encounter it freshly, much as Don Antonio might have seen it glowing before him in 1653.

(3.7) Gallery, painting, Metropolitan Museum of Art

Let's return now to the Met, where *Aristotle with a Bust of Homer* is waiting for us to follow its contours home. Whether the figure is Aristotle or, as some have thought, the ancient artist Apelles, or a contemporary friend of Rembrandt in Amsterdam dressed up ambiguously in exotic clothing, reminiscent of a smoky Greek past no less than a luxurious present, the representational facts are few and vivid. The man standing obliquely before us, facing to our left and wearing a massive gold chain, is lost in thought. To his right, a carved marble bust of a man along with a small metal object rests on a waist-high table covered by a red cloth. A room-dividing heavy curtain suspended from an invisible ceiling has been drawn back behind the man to reveal several large leather folios stacked on a shelf in the adjoining room. To turn around then, we may start over by allowing the painting itself, like the contour of Cadillac Mountain, to be our guide and begin where the artist began: with paint.

Looking carefully and without interpreting, each of us may describe for ourselves precisely what we see.

(3.17) Rembrandt van Rijn, *Aristotle with a Bust of Homer*, 1653, detail of paint

This extreme detail from *Aristotle with a Bust of Homer* shows yellow, white, orange, and very dark neutral blue (virtually black) paint, heavily laid on the prepared canvas (technically, the word is "scumbled") in short, rhythmic strokes made with a brush and possibly a palette knife.

(3.18) Rembrandt van Rijn, *Aristotle with a Bust of Homer*

Raw brushstrokes of paint now appear clearly as links in a golden chain. Because the artist has applied these brushstrokes in particularly heavy impasto, they remain vividly present as material paint, especially the yellow and white. Although perfectly obvious to our attentive looking, the implications of these brushstrokes and the "gold" they suggest are essential for our beholding. Like the space between multiple soundings of a bell, these physical marks, and the image (the "gold") they produce, bracket a discontinuous interval. The yellow and white paint do not change alchemically into "gold" and then, when we turn away, revert to paint. They exist simultaneously as two incommensurate realities. Had Rembrandt diminished the physical presence of paint, the "gold" image would be predominant. We would see the image rather than the paint. Or, the reverse: had he not placed the impasto paint in a particular representational context, it would have remained visible only as paint. Given the high relief of his brushstroke, Rembrandt clearly meant to suspend the contradiction of material substance and illusory image before us as we view the painting.

Rembrandt's exaggerated use of impasto is well known and was recognized from the beginning. One early admirer suggested you could pick up a portrait Rembrandt painted by the subject's nose! Jan van Eyck, in contrast, in his justly famous *Portrait of Giovanni (?) Arnolfini and His Wife* in the National Gallery in London, systematically smooths out all painterly marks—except one!—to evoke a mirror-like image of reality.

(3.19) a. Jan van Eyck, *Portrait of Giovanni (?) Arnolfini and His Wife*, 1434; b. detail of mirror with random "brushstroke" indicated

The Arnolfini double portrait is often taken to be the epitome of "realism." But pictorially it is just another artist's alternative realization of the interval that exists along the same infinite continuum—of pure brushstroke to pure image—that Rembrandt occupies. As extremes along this artistic continuum, compare Franz Kline and Richard Estes.

(3.20) a. Franz Kline, *Chief*, 1950; b. Richard Estes, *Cafeteria*, 1970

We often invoke the predominance of medium (a "brushstroke," let's say) or illusion (an "image") to distinguish between so-called abstract and representational painting, as in the comparison of Kline and Estes above. But the pronounced mutual relationship of material substance and illusory image in *Aristotle with a Bust of Homer* reveals more than a simple stylistic choice made by a "baroque" artist. Rembrandt's pictorial discontinuity opens a "gap" that we experience between two utterly distinct and irreconcilable realities, as we will see in *Artist in His Studio*, one of his earliest paintings now in the Museum of Fine Arts in Boston.

Reflective Interval 1: Behold with Rembrandt's Two "Lights"

(3.21) Rembrandt van Rijn, *Artist in his Studio*, ca. 1628

The pictorial combination of brushstroke and illusory image in this painting is nothing short of a manifesto of artistic purpose.[18] This apparent contradictory pairing creates an incalculable void as if to reveal a silent presence that would "bridge" finite and infinite realities: another "mending wall."

One "light," perhaps from a nearby window, illuminates the table leg next to the standing artist, casting a faint, inconspicuous shadow. A second qualitatively different "light"—a "magical light"—remains suspended simultaneously at the center of the two-dimensional picture plane and the three-dimensional illusory space.

This second "light" opens an interval of "something," somewhere between the painter, standing in the background, and his work, even as it casts an impossible dark shadow that rakes across the wooden floor almost like a brushstroke—the painting itself is on wood!—to measure the contemplative reality of elusive artistic presence. Squint to allow this "spring mischief" to glow before you and, slowly, it will become a monumental epiphany of intimated wholeness—"light" beyond diminishment, suspended between the edges of the painting and the illusory shadow within the image—all this on a panel barely 12 inches wide. Like Robert Frost's "Mending Wall," Rembrandt's *Artist in his Studio* is a youthful embrace of art, poetry, and beholding.

Return to the art of *Aristotle with a Bust of Homer*, which also resides in a mysterious void or, more precisely, in the interval between "paint" and "gold." This "gap" is itself the invisible *sacral* space we would behold with, the space where the artist has hinted at the rationally impossible reconciliation of contradiction. The indescribable color, texture, weight and weightless, cloud-like sweep of the figure's sleeves only amplify the visual affect of paint that is "gold"—and I do mean "affect" here, in the sense of the paint as a psychological manifestation rather than a superficial result—no less than the illusory light is also eternal light radiant in darkness.

(3.18) *Aristotle with a Bust of Homer*

In these sleeves, paint has become material "white light" emerging, on our careful and attentive observation, from the full palette of the painting and the visible spectrum of color, including red, green, yellow, violet, blue, and orange.

(3.22) *Aristotle with a Bust of Homer*, detail of color

Rembrandt's experience realized in his craft reverses the conceptual engineering of Gothic stained glass, which converts ordinary exterior white light into an interiorized incarnation of mystical color. In *Aristotle with a Bust of Homer* applied color in the shadows of the philosopher's sleeves becomes transcendent white. Each constructed instance of this relational *ars* and *scientia*, resulting in a fleeting vision of *sapientia* through artistic *eruditio*, may echo across time with Claude Monet's spiritual collaboration with the Cathedral of Rouen. In this series of paintings, painted color suggests light beyond light in Monet's magical amalgamation of white pigment and color, in which "eye," "hand," "mind," and "brain" share in intimating self-transcendence.

(3.23) Claude Monet, *Rouen Cathedral, West Façade, Sunlight,* 1894

(Advance screen)

Reflective Interval 2: Behold with Rembrandt, Across Time and Space

Returning once more to *Aristotle with a Bust of Homer*, what must we do to move further toward an anagogical moment of beholding *with* the painting? Our path now leads us beyond the initial contradiction of material medium (brushstroke) and image ("gold") into a complex web of interlaced intervals, which—like silence, music, art, and love—can only be known contemplatively: that is, outside instrumental, even scholarly, time, space, and noise. Begin with the artist himself. Rembrandt van Rijn was forty-seven when he painted *Aristotle with a Bust of Homer*. For many reasons, he may have been especially alert to midlife reflection on the inevitable merging of youth and age.[19] Alternatively, the vast time span that pictorially joins the living philosopher (Aristotle), the long dead poet (Homer), and a contemporary model may well have caused him to consider a distinctly synchronic embrace of mortal longing across twenty-five centuries and beyond.

These intervals, of course, would not have been lost on Don Antonio Ruffo, nor do they diminish our own encounter with this painting today. The prominent gold chain anchors another subtle interval. In Rembrandt's era, similar chains were well-known tokens of public commendation and esteem. Two artists Rembrandt may have sought to emulate, Tiziano Vecelli (Titian) and Diego Velasquez, were honored in this way.

But with the chain in this painting, imagine that Rembrandt invites us to remember other, still-more elusive attainments no less familiar to him than to Henry David Thoreau: "to awaken to a higher life than we fell asleep from" and to aspire to be that "one in a hundred millions capable of poetic or divine life." For us to follow Rembrandt into the interval of his own poetic or divine aspiration means to step into a waking dream of no time, no space, no hearing, no being, and no contradiction—into the éblouissement (bedazzlement) of intimated wholeness. And, like the awakened infant given voice in a blessing by John O'Donohue, we step into the remembered "light of the world I am leaving" that would "shine through and carry me home"—at least until we blink or turn away from our beholding.

Now, move closer to the illusory world: into the interval of subjective experiential presence and objective order.

(3.18) ***Aristotle with a Bust of Homer***

As we adjust our eyes to the shiny brilliance of the gold chain, feel its considerable weight. Measure the contrasting textures of the soft, dark velvet tunic, often associated with depth in philosophic thought, against the glittering surface of the outer cloak with those luminous "white" sleeves. Smell the leather binding of the books. Let a sensual presence draw us further into this moment out of all time and space, suspended within an envelope of art and contemplation. Be with Abbot Suger in that "strange region of the universe" somewhere between "the slime of the earth" and "the purity of heaven." Tarry here a moment. Inhale the aroma of thought and learning and contemplation. For in the very process of scumbling paint, Rembrandt constructed a pictorial veil that joins not only the living and the dead, Aristotle and Homer, but also the material and immaterial realities of being and nonbeing each of us would know. If it were not for this artist's act of devoted beholding embodied here in paint, this work of art would have little or no value. Except for its art, *Aristotle with a Bust of Homer* is nothing but an oily rag, even as each of us is nothing but water, bone, blood, and flesh.[20]

Be patient. Suspend disbelief. What if you were to open your hands, turn them upward and extend them forward—a gesture by which you become present, waiting, vulnerable, trusting.

Let the questions you seek to live, now begin to take shape: Are you willing to encounter the art of art? To meet Rembrandt van Rijn? To see another human being like yourself who is fully awake? To imagine a new brightness, a new illumination that will bedazzle you like the sun? If you are . . . then approach Aristotle's hands.

(3.24) ***Aristotle with a Bust of Homer*****, a. detail of right hand; b. detail of left hand**

Here are Aristotle's painted hands. Here too is Rembrandt's own "hand," seen in the visible brushstrokes left behind by the artist, especially visible in the philosopher's left hand. Two discrete realities join as one in the moment of our contemplation when we realize a tangible proximity of someone and something no longer living, yet palpably present in our experience. The texture of paint and the artist's brush are the instruments of his knowing—his medium—no less than mathematics is the medium of the scientist. The interval here is between presence and absence, change and permanence.

Rembrandt may have revealed this essential contradiction of "experience" and "order" more openly than most, leaving both paint and image equally vivid, as if to enlarge the beholding threshold he would have us enter.

Here also, along with the imagined hands of Aristotle and the artist's hand as it actually moves before our eyes across the still-wet paint, we might approach yet another deeper, more immediate, threshold of awareness.

Compare these two gestures (image 3.24, a. and b.). The left hand appears actively to fondle the golden chain between the first two fingers. The right hand is still, resting lightly on the head of Homer. Measure their interval of movement and stillness. Both hands are richly sensual, even erotic. One moves in an absent-minded, not to say subconscious, private way. The other makes a declarative, public gesture of affirmation and reverence animated by deep affection, as though we were moved to caress the head of an elderly person or young child.

**(3.25) *Aristotle with a Bust of Homer*, a. detail of right arm;
b. detail of left arm**

Looking at image 3.25 we may now ask where, in the psychological interval defined by these hands, does the underlying impulse arise that would bring to life such contradictory gestures? Where pictorially, as well as emotionally, has Rembrandt suspended interior and exterior realities as one intersecting sensual and mental struggle?

As you behold with the next image, notice that Aristotle's attention is neither interior nor exterior, but suspended.

(3.26) *Aristotle with a Bust of Homer*, detail of face

Do sensual eros and reflective insight together carve out this image of Aristotle's face as they embrace the irreconcilable tensions of unalterable contradiction suspended here in paint and flesh? Were we to be engaged by this face—and by the affective hands of Aristotle and the artist's hand still moving before our eyes—we might enter yet another deeper threshold of awareness, the one where Simone Weil challenges us with the hardest reality:

> Contradiction experienced to the very depths of the being tears us heart and soul.[21]

Rilke, however, offers us affectionate promise:

> Love the *questions themselves* like locked rooms and like books that are written in a very foreign tongue.... And the point is to live everything [so that]...perhaps [we] will then gradually, without noticing it, live along some distant day into the answer.[22]

In *our* contemplation, eros and reflective insight come together as reassuring partners in a knowing embodiment: equal parts joy, sadness, and dignity that animate this face and presumably our own as we approach slowly, calmly, and mindfully. Beholding *with* this face—and, of course, *with* this painting—we may almost hear the apostle Paul again, speaking to the Corinthians. He invokes the theological virtues of faith, hope, and love as the necessary veil through which to see the elusive wholeness for which we long. But that wholeness remains well beyond the constraining limits of the cardinal virtues—prudence, courage, justice, and temperance—held before him by the ancients. If we do hear Paul's voice, hope will have become the animating "bridge" between faith and love.

(Advance screen)

Open Awareness

Now that we have meditated deliberately and slowly on several artistic intervals present in *Aristotle with a Bust of Homer*, we could reasonably stop here. Much of what we might have encountered during our first individual and silent response to this rich work of art may now resonate more vividly within each of us.

But if we proceed still further, from focused attention to open awareness, and then by moving on to a face-to-face encounter with the artist and his own "poetic or divine life," we may discover a more profound contemplative knowing, one that will reveal the art of this work of art. For this painting and this image made out of canvas and pigments is not primarily concerned with Aristotle's, Homer's, or Alexander's contemplative knowing. At its core, this work of art is not even *about* contemplative knowing at all. Nor is its purpose to challenge us through scholarly research to construct multiple accounts of its alleged narrative, discursive, or moralizing meaning, or thus to solve its riddle. Plausibly its meaning for us as contemplative beholders is not even exclusively within the limits of the material painting itself.

Perhaps most importantly for us, as it may have been for Don Antonio Ruffo and certainly for the person who made it, this work of art offers *an occasion for contemplation* for each of us who would be present to behold *with* it—even to the point where this mysterious work of art will, finally, disappear from view. We are now prepared to move deliberately well beyond familiar but disembodied observation, and even beyond careful meditation, to an embodied presence within the "poetic or divine" mystery of this work of art. In taking this next step, we may ask again: What would it be like to encounter ourselves, the world, and those around us from a threshold of contemplative artistic awareness? Can Rembrandt's *Aristotle with a Bust of Homer* guide us closer toward our goal?

(3.18) *Aristotle with a Bust of Homer*

For this discovery, you are alone again, in front of the painting.

Let the finite contradictory parts that make up *Aristotle with a Bust of Homer* come together before you with an initial recognition: this work of art does not exist as art until you engage with Rembrandt's own struggle within the continuum of "experience" and "order" (*ars* and *scientia*) aspiring through *eruditio* to wisdom (*sapientia*).

Place yourself, then, within one or another of the many intervals in this painting. Slowly, purposefully, embrace their contradictoriness so that you might share the artist's pictorial realization and feel his human longing as a synchronic extension of your own. Look beyond the painting as mere object, or as a visual narrative of Aristotle and Homer. Instead, allow yourself to be present within the intervals of contradiction constructed by Rembrandt. The intimated reconciliation that occurs within these intervals is the artistic aspiration toward wholeness that exceeds the sum of its parts by a factor of infinity.

Beholding with this painting will offer you, a willing pilgrim, a fleeting sensual moment of blissful wordless insight. Perhaps it will come to you like the late afternoon epiphany Thoreau revealed in the concluding section of "Walking," when "one day last November" the "rising ground gleamed like the boundary of Elysium, and the sun on our backs seemed like a gentle herdsman, driving us home at evening."

In this spirit, embrace Rembrandt's particularly robust artistic contradictions. Begin with those of the object itself (fabric and image: oil paint on canvas and "gold"); then light and dark; warm and cool; surface and illusory space (near, far, and middle ground); left and right; lower and upper; weight and weightless; consciousness and unconsciousness;

movement and stillness; flesh and being; mortality and immortality; past and future, poised in the present. Allow these contradictions and any others you perceive to manifest their full force of complementary denial and inexorable relation.

Simone Weil extended her observation that "contradiction experienced to the very depths of the being tears us heart and soul." Contradiction "is the cross," she wrote, adding:

> When the attention has revealed the contradiction in something on which it has been fixed, a kind of loosening takes place. By persevering in this course, we attain detachment.[23]

Allow this "loosening" and "detachment" to occur in you. Breathe slowly. Be grateful for Rembrandt's shared "loosening." In this fragile moment of your beholding with Rembrandt, Aristotle's oddly large black velvet hat, nearly lost in shadow, almost becomes a conferred crown rewarding the enduring presence of a silence and solitude that now exceed beyond measure the iconic golden chain and its limited honor. Remain aware of the easily forgotten asymmetry of this recognition, echoed throughout the form and content (brushstroke and image) of *Aristotle with a Bust of Homer*; it may return you to "ground zero" of conscious awareness and the unanswerable mystery of the begotten condition within which we all exist.

This shared interval between onrushing instances of noise is manifest in the relation of sound and silence—into which grace will enter. It now includes art along with music, not to mention science and any other deliberate act of contemplative imagination. These are the primal instruments of our universally human capacity for the contemplative knowing that informs our "poetic or divine life." The list of these "divine" and "poetic" accomplishments of our focused meditative attention and open contemplative awakening is, of course, limitless. But allow the shadowed light of Aristotle's hat to recall the night sky—with its stars, constellations, and celestial movement—as the universal point of departure.

(3.27) The Interval of Contemplative Beholding II

Entering the Interval of Our Being

To pursue our direct contemplative experience with *Aristotle with a Bust of Homer*, here are four meditations to guide us individually: pictorial movement, chromatic energy, contemplative arrival, face to face.

Pictorial Movement

Let's start with the format of the painting by comparing three empty rectangles—one horizontal, one vertical, and one square—with that of the actual painting.

(3.28) Three rectangles: horizontal, vertical, square

The rectangular format of the painting is just slightly taller than it is wide.

(3.29) Rectangular format of *Aristotle with a Bust of Homer* (53 ¾" x 56 ½") shown with vertical extension beyond the square

Experience how pictorial "movement" (*ars*) within the theoretical order (*scientia*) of the four sides, the diagonal corners, and the center activates the two-dimensional picture plane of this "elevated" rectangle.

(3.30) Schematic rendering of the theoretical two-dimensional picture plane

Compare the abstract schematic pictorial possibilities for any rectangular format with Rembrandt's actual painting.

(3.31) *Aristotle with a Bust of Homer*, schematic rendering of the theoretical two-dimensional picture plane with an image of the painting

Then look for his particular compositional choices within the image: left and right; edge, corners, and center; lower and upper symmetry and asymmetry. Do pictorial realities of practice and theory animate this image?

(3.32) *Aristotle with a Bust of Homer*, schematic rendering of planar rotation "up" and "down" from an imagined horizontal "base" with an image of the painting

Add now to this planar construction the illusory spatial organization of the painting.

(3.33) *Aristotle with a Bust of Homer*, schematic rendering of the theoretical picture plane and three-dimensional illusory space with an image of the painting

The immediate foreground occupied by the figure of Aristotle leads from the lower right to a transitional space occupied by the table and the bust of Homer. The foreshortened gestures of Aristotle's arms coincide visually with this spatial "movement" and the rising arc of the curtain that frames the books in the nearby distance on the left. A similar "movement" from the lower left, beginning with the shadow cast by the bust, reaches up past Aristotle to the darkened corner on the right.

Since the four sides of the image do not correspond with the four edges of the canvas, the illusory space of the painting remains open as though it were an extension of the actual place and time, within which both you, as the beholder, and the physical painting exist. Allow a gentle transitional integration of the space you occupy in front of this painting to merge with the intimate proximity of Rembrandt's dynamically compressed pictorial space and moment.

(3.34) *Aristotle with a Bust of Homer*, schematic rendering of an implied "bridge" to illusory pictorial space

The dashed blue line in image 3.34 may help to reveal and affirm a felt sense of shared presence between you and the painting, including palpable downward weight and upward release. Imagine a place or places in the two- and three-dimensional composition of the painting where these pictorial movements come to rest. Achieve a still-point...

Chromatic Energy

Beneath the surface of its compositional design, *Aristotle with a Bust of Homer* embodies a remarkably subtle but contemplatively compelling chromatic event. Rembrandt placed his signature in the lower left corner of the painting in a field of intense warm red color. The gentle diagonal movement following the shadow cast on the red cloth leads upward (in the picture plane) to the right, past the figure, and then to an area of distinct though quiet, darkened (but still relatively saturated) green just above Aristotle's elbow at the edge of the painting. A similar diagonal reverses direction from this green area and rises toward the left border to the neutral yellow spatial plane defined by the stacked books behind the curtain. This ascending movement, zigzagging within the picture plane, culminates in the undefined area of what appears to be dark neutral blue-violet behind the figure and across the upper border of the painting.

(3.35) *Aristotle with a Bust of Homer*, a. area of middle value, intense red; b. area darker, slightly neutralized green; c. area of neutral yellow (tan); d. area of dark neutral blue-violet (?) indicated

(3.36) *Aristotle with a Bust of Homer,* schematic rendering of chromatic movement from the lower left pictorial border to the center of the top border

As pure color, however, the relational energy of this event calls out across the interval between complementary red-green and then yellow and blue-violet, expanding upward within the vertical rectangular format of the painting.[24]

(3.37) *Aristotle with a Bust of Homer,* schematic rendering of chromatic complementaries

Measured within this organizing plane, these areas of color move as we encounter them. They partner in a cosmic dance, inviting us to engage, to let them resonate within us. Linger in awareness of the fixed symmetry of the vertical and horizontal axes and sides of this rectangle; allow it to animate the dynamic asymmetry of the moment. Feel this expanding pictorial movement, from paired white and black at the center of the picture plane to an aureole of animated color at its periphery.

(3.38) *Aristotle with a Bust of Homer,* schematic rendering of theoretical horizontal and vertical symmetry and pictorial asymmetry

Contemplative Arrival

The gilt frame that physically encloses *Aristotle with a Bust of Homer* may now also refocus Rembrandt's contemplative artistry, as though the painting had become something like a reliquary. It opens itself before us in the museum gallery, reminding us of time spent in contemplative meditation or beholding with images similarly framed by *rinceau* borders—their decorative motif of branching stems and leaves in vivid color or gold leaf—that we find in devotional Books of Hours.[25]

(3.39) *Aristotle with a Bust of Homer,* with gilt frame

Be still . . . silent . . . behold . . . seize, without touching, this moment of shimmering intimated wholeness.

Sound . . . silence . . . a deep resonance . . .

Share this silent interlude with another seventeenth-century master, the Japanese poet Matsuo Bashō. Allow it to resonate.

How quiet it is!
On the wall, where a painting
hangs—a cricket.
. . . .
A monk sips morning tea,
it's quiet,
the chrysanthemum's flowering.

Will our initial impression of *Aristotle with a Bust of Homer* be transformed as we continue to contemplate with this work of art? What may have first appeared to us as a direct confrontation of dramatically contrasting monochromatic light and dark (call it Rembrandt's artistic simplicity) might now slowly become (in all its genuine complexity) the presence of a luminous still-point shimmering in a constellation of richly incarnated color. Where the scientist Johannes Kepler knew "sacred ecstasy" in discovering the lawful planetary order behind the apparent randomness of the night sky, Rembrandt animates the infinite randomness of our earthly experience within a precisely calculated pictorial order. Scientific "order experienced" becomes artistic "experience ordered." *Ars sine scientia nihil est* (practice without theory is nothing) becomes before our eyes and body its ontological mate, *scientia sine ars nihil est* (theory without practice is nothing). On both occasions, the embrace of primal contradiction results in contemplative *eruditio* (higher learning) suspended in the *sapientia* (wisdom) of absolute silence, undisturbed by the noise of the day.

The illusory space of *Aristotle with a Bust of Homer* is shallow. The unexpectedly wide range of color values from warm to cool and light to dark realizes an image of expanding energy that is simultaneously centrifugal and centripetal (moving away from and toward the center axis, respectively), and at once monumental even though excruciatingly intimate.

Allow the heavy, gilded museum frame to disappear into memory, leaving behind only Rembrandt's threshold of inter-subjective encounter: his art and practice of contemplative beholding—his threshold of love.

(3.18) *Aristotle with a Bust of Homer*

Let's imagine that Rembrandt, as an artist, sought actively to embrace the contradictory realities our shared conscious being entails. With his deliberately constructed "order," he shaped a fragment of that living "experience." When the pictorial components of this painting are allowed to exist within their relational tension—each measuring the other—the work of art as a whole will begin to move before us. Each brushstroke informs others until they vibrate together in the pictorial equivalent of a human pulse. The art of this work of art emerges reverently from the shadowed interval of timeless silence and stillness bracketed by the noise of the busy world. Within this *sacral* space, Rembrandt whispers a virtual litany of intimated reconciliation: our direct and palpable invitation to behold, to enter into an act of contemplation itself, in which we live the very questions that he, Aristotle, and Homer once lived. If we were to behold with Rembrandt and his art, then we might well hear his voice, and perhaps see his face.[26]

In the painting itself we can find contemplative presence in the stone sculpture anchored to the table by its base, on which Rembrandt placed his name and the date 1653. The foreshortened horizontal plane of the tabletop presses against the lower edge of the image. That swath of warm vibrant red paint, the cast shadow, and the fleeting glint of the unidentifiable, metallic object behind the bust—all seemingly negligible, random details—combine with the horizontality of the heavy books as silent reminders of the very floor on which the figure and the beholder are standing.

The pictorial verticality of Homer, Aristotle, and the hanging pendant of Alexander all mirror our standing position. The rising accents of color, as well as the chain and the curtain, now actively resist the felt gravity of stone, paint, and flesh. The diagonal structure of the picture plane that defines the four corners of the canvas also carves out the illusory space you occupy. The lower right foreground gestures toward the opening beyond the curtain and the remembered scent of leather, books, and learning. The opposing diagonal from the luminous lower left corner leads past the figure of Aristotle to the darkened upper quadrant of the painting as though it were a shadowed echo of the philosopher's black tunic.

> *Now, engage again with the two- and three-dimensional rhythms of this painting. Allow them to bring you to an intimated resolution: in this "place" all contradiction gives way to a delicate, but always dynamic (asymmetrical) balance; there the lightest light "whiteness" of those sleeves embraces the darkest pictorial dark to allow finite pigment to cross an elusive, infinite gap to become "gold."*

Contemplate with this momentary permanence: all movement, all stillness . . . all silence . . . loosening and detachment . . . absolute simplicity on the farthest side of complexity . . . release . . . intimated wholeness . . . until you blink.

Close your eyes, pause, and allow the art of Aristotle with a Bust of Homer *to disappear into your memory. Come face to face with Rembrandt van Rijn.*

Now "look" again in silence as though experiencing a repeated musical theme (image 3.18). One pictorial diagonal draws the beholder's attention from Aristotle's left hand, across the chain of honor to the warm caress of the bust and on to the stacked heavy volumes. The opposing diagonal accent reaches from the illuminated table across the timeless introspection of the poet and the philosopher into the upper right corner of the painting. These intersecting diagonal paths meet near the center of the picture plane where the glowing sleeves, the black tunic, and the sweeping line of the "golden" chain have become unmeasurable lightness and darkness. The pictorial "light" on the poet and the philosopher brings them tangibly, almost theatrically, forward into your experience of the physical painting—even as it then disappears into that undefined and unrelieved shadowed darkness that permeates the whole image. For one brief moment Rembrandt's *Aristotle with a Bust of Homer* is a nearly perfect experiential exemplar of Henry David Thoreau's awakening to a "higher life" in which "the darkness bear its fruit, and proves itself to be good no less than the light." For an instant, you too exist within this illuminated darkness.

As a willing beholder, might you imagine the presence of grace that would enter this fleeting artistic void as it is made palpable in the lifting gesture of this painting? Like the slightly elevated rectangular format of the physical canvas amplified in the raised curtain, the expanding movement of created "colored light" relieves all gravity to become timelessly graceful, even as it merges perceptibly with the material presence of paint and the movement of the artist's brush, palette knife, and hands. Can you begin to resonate with, breathe with this presence? Does its grace diminish for just a second the weight, the gravity, the loneliness—the mortality—we all share? Does something begin to inform you? Reassure you? Gestate within you? Become embodied within you?

At this moment of beholding, however unfamiliar our journey together may seem, recall that we have left Concord for the "woods" of Walden. We have deliberately set aside the unconscious habit of looking at the world, of analyzing the world, of objectifying it, distancing it, observing it at the cost of becoming alienated from our being. We have come to Rembrandt's *Aristotle with a Bust of Homer* to contemplate with him. We are now beholding silently, patiently, and courageously with another human being, whose ontological dilemma of contradictoriness echoes within our own being and awakened presence. *Aristotle with a Bust of Homer* now mirrors us as we contemplate collaboratively with Rembrandt.

Even if we hesitate to articulate our inchoate sense of connection in this moment, we may, in our beholding with Rembrandt (again, until we blink), suspend the struggling, warring contradictions of all human being—not just the obvious ones like "experience" and "order" (*ars* and *scientia*)—but the truly difficult ones: life and art, the living and the dead, mortality and immortality, now and then, war and peace, you and I.

Slowly, almost imperceptibly—and quietly—alertness to time and space and your own separate existence (apart from this painting, standing staring at it), will have been changed. You now, along with Rembrandt, Aristotle, Homer, Alexander, and the anonymous model who posed for the artist have all entered an extraordinary interval of intimated wholeness. An incalculable silence will have become manifest in the deepest blackness at the very center of the painting, which will now measure the bedazzlement of the brilliant tangibility and presence of undiminished light. Artistically, the ordinary light of the day (*lumen*) has been joined like paint and "gold" with eternal light (*lux aeterna*). As you watched, grace entered the void made by grace. In the very blackness of this painting, you come home to an interior place—the vessel of your being—to that hidden reality you recognize in contrast to your experience of the world suspended before you. Synchronically, two solitudes have arrived face to face: you and the other artist, Rembrandt van Rijn.

> *Standing in front of a celebrated work of art—no longer unconsciously or unreflectively but now deliberately, as an embodied presence in this new place of intimated infinite silence, infinite stillness, and wholeness—release yourself into the deepest reality of your being. Be vulnerable. Open yourself to a moment of contemplative beholding in which all* ars *and all* scientia *will have become through* eruditio *purest, wordless sapientia—unbounded wisdom.*

Let's imagine tarrying a moment in this place in which the artist before us spent his entire life. By becoming silent now with his art, we might discover that there is no such thing as silence. For silence is not something. It is not the opposite of noise, or even greatly diminished noise. Being silent here will reveal that silence is no-thing. This intimated silence, which we can know only by its absence from the sound (not noise) that surrounds us, will open us to the most difficult contradiction of all: the nonbeing to our present being, which we are called on to embrace with all of the other contradictions of conscious awareness.

To approach the awakening of our own being as the measure of our nonbeing—remembered in the intimacy of Milo's lament—is only to recognize, again, that this "image" of Aristotle, Homer, and Alexander really is, in compelling material reality, only an oily rag.[27] And yet, its "image" embraces its nonbeing. Aristotle is not there, nor is Homer, nor, finally, is Rembrandt. Only their nonbeing is suspended in paint and canvas. Their memory, conjured up in the miraculous fiction of pigment, makes them present to us, reuniting then and now as one. They are there and here with us. Their voices speak with us across the no-thing of silence. They are present still, within infinite, inaccessible silence... and we can see them as vividly as we see anything and know ourselves to be present also in this moment and this place. Here the purest eros of bodily experience in the five senses (sight, sound, touch, smell, and even taste, a complement to smell) are manifest in Rembrandt's physical brushstrokes to realize for us an enduring grasp of our being and nonbeing. Rembrandt's contemplative beholding is his *eruditio*, in which he attempts to reconcile the warring and peaceful partners of all conscious existence. The result is a moment of "sacred ecstasy" he shares with us.

Consider here how Simone Weil described her sense of beatitude—a word we associate with a state of utmost bliss (or, in the Christian faith, blessedness; and in Buddhism, satori)—but which she considers to be a form of reconciliation:

> Contradiction is the criterion. We cannot by suggestion achieve things that are incompatible. Only grace can do that.... Man's great affliction, which begins with infancy and accompanies him till death, is that looking and eating are two different operations. Eternal beatitude is a state where to look is to eat.[28]

Like all true insight, the "poetic or divine life" to which we would awaken must exceed mere labor and intellectual exertion, as Thoreau reminds us. This vision must transcend sight as though we had to be blinded in order finally to see and, above all, silenced in order to hear. As each of us would struggle to contemplate with Rembrandt and to reorient ourselves in this unfamiliar transition to a sacral place, remember that Rembrandt knew only too well the reality of blindness, as he himself was threatened by the diminishment of his eyesight through inoperable cataracts. He also knew of course, as we do, that the visionary poet Homer was blind. In this knowledge, our habitual familiarity of third-person encounters with the world (he, she, it, they) will have become an unfamiliar but utterly reassuring "no-person" welcoming us into a threshold of love, experienced directly and sensually as an enduring, indestructible, and primal I and You as one.[29]

Perhaps for Rembrandt van Rijn as for Homer, blindness itself was the mortal occasion of awakening to Thoreau's "higher life than we fell asleep from" in which truly "the darkness bear its fruit, and prove itself to be good, no less than the light." Whatever Rembrandt knew or thought about Aristotle's writings will remain forever vague, subject to scholarly searching. But what resonates is his artistic vision, shared with Homer the blind poet and with us. So too, whatever the commissioned facts surrounding *Aristotle with a Bust of Homer* were in 1653, we might well imagine that its artistic life had begun to emerge in Rembrandt a year earlier, with his drawing of Homer reciting verses while surrounded by those who would behold with him.[30]

(3.40) Rembrandt van Rijn, *Homer Reciting Verses,* 1652

(Advance screen)

Face to Face

Be still. Be silent. Come face to face with Rembrandt.

(3.41) Rembrandt van Rijn, *Self-Portrait,* 1660

With this self-portrait, painted at the very height of his career in an act of intimated wholeness, the artist has brought the "image" of his painting to life, almost Pygmalion-like, as if to animate the very border of eternity between us: an eternity, suspended in the sliver of light floating weightlessly above the loaded palette he holds in his working hand.

The next time you find yourself struggling to be silent—with Rembrandt's *Aristotle with a Bust of Homer,* or in your own immediate experience with the noise of the world, or with nothing other than velvet blackness—ponder Aristotle's own enduring question: "Why is it that all those who have become eminent in philosophy or politics or poetry, or the arts"—namely Thoreau's one in a hundred millions capable of "poetic or divine life"—"are clearly melancholics?"[31] Is it their moodiness? Sadness? Or is it the unfathomable brooding experienced in the solitude of a sleeping interval of being/nonbeing that in truth we all share and know in one form or another of Milo's lament?

(3.42) a. Rembrandt van Rijn, *Self-Portrait*, 1660, oil on canvas, detail with crown-like studio headdress, b. *Bust of Homer*, Roman copy of Greek original, 2nd century CE, marble

Allow the man, the artist, the human being, like us, to be present.

(3.43) Rembrandt van Rijn, *Self-Portrait*, ca. 1628–29

This youthful self-portrait is an image of introspection. It shows the brooding young man as an interior presence, vividly subjective. The painting speaks and asks, "Who am I?"

(3.44) Rembrandt van Rijn, *Self-Portrait*, 1629

In this image, the same young man is startled by his own presence as his body casts a shadow on the wall. Interiority and subjectivity give way to exteriority and objectivity. This painting says, "Who is he?"

These two self-portraits, both possibly painted in the same year when the artist was barely twenty, are redolent with an awakening self-consciousness—I and the world. They reveal first- and third-person awareness—as though the presumed mirror in front of the young man was the very equivalent of the support upon which he would display the enduring contradictory interval of our human being. The art that would seek a possible reconciliation of this and every other contradiction an awakened life entails will include those "brushstrokes" made as the artist moved his hand while drawing with the reversed end of his brush through dark paint to reveal the lighter valued underpainting as the sparkling elusive "image" of "light."

(3.45) Rembrandt van Rijn, *Self-Portrait*, 1669

Might we recognize hard-won human and artistic attainment softly embodied in this last self-portrait Rembrandt painted? He is now sixty-three years old. His death is imminent. In this mirror of himself, the warring almost seems to have been stilled. Can we imagine with T. S. Eliot that "the fire and the rose" have at last become one? The pigment and the image plainly have. So too, subjective immediacy and objective distance merge in a singular, inseparable, though fragile, intimation of wholeness. Some of us, contemplating with this final account, might see a philosophic smile flash across those silent lips. Here is the fullest mortality of our "wandering mourning" without distraction or cosmetic retreat: a "more human love" that has conquered all need to "kill" in one of the bravest and most reassuring works of art I know. At this moment in his life, Rembrandt was financially ruined. Everyone he loved the most had died. He was alone in his infinite solitude, left with only the art and love that he gave freely. Here Rembrandt speaks to us, and what we "hear" echoes the words of the apostle Paul in his second letter to Timothy (2 Timothy 4:6–8):

> As for me . . . the time of my departure has come. I have fought a good fight, I have finished the race, I have kept the faith. From now on there is reserved for me a crown of righteousness, which the Lord, the righteous judge, shall give me at that day: and not to me, only, but unto all also that love his appearing.

(3.46) Rembrandt van Rijn, *Self-Portrait*, 165(7?)

Rembrandt's *Self-Portrait* in Edinburgh, Scotland, reveals him at the very height of his career as a painter. Lines like those in his forehead and under his eyes, here exposed in a bright raking light, emerged for many of us as we passed through our fiftieth year. So too, this painting, signed and dated in the 1650s, would make the artist himself roughly fifty. As with *Aristotle with a Bust of Homer*, approach this exceptionally vulnerable work of art slowly. Listen for it to speak directly with you. In absolute silence, it seems to say, kindly: *Go ahead and look. Look hard at me. Then go home and look at yourself just as hard and honestly. Then contemplate with me our shared existence. Enter the interval of our fullest human being with me; as it is.*

The velvet beret, separated from the dark ground of the painting by the faintest thread of glowing light, casts a surprisingly sharp shadow where the lightest light and the darkest dark values converge; it's as if an elevated light from above defined the cranial structure of the head, even as it reveals the honest signs of aging, including the first hint of graying hair. Like the large mysterious hat worn by Rembrandt's Aristotle, nearly invisible except for its shimmering gold and silver lining, this beret serves in a moment of unutterable recognition as a true martyr's crown worn by one who would faithfully and humbly carry the burden ("cross") of mortal contradiction. And now, perhaps, the white rag that covers the painter's head in the studio portrait of the artist in the Louvre where he is poised with working brush and palette in hand is no less a crown in which paint and light are mingled inseparably.

(3.41) Rembrandt van Rijn, *Self-Portrait*, 1660

Look again at Rembrandt's early self-portraits.

(3.47) a. Rembrandt van Rijn, *Self-Portrait*, ca. 1628–29;
b. Rembrandt van Rijn, *Self-Portrait*, 1629

The mysterious conflation of "brushstroke" and "image" that so profoundly informs and animates the artistic interval of *Aristotle with a Bust of Homer* is, in these two paintings, the haunting result of the artist's faithful effort to bring forth, by the movement of his hand, the presence of poetic light; that light, in the moment of our beholding, has become the enduring presence of divine illumination—grace.

(3.48) Rembrandt van Rijn, *Self-Portrait*, 1628–29, detail

To me the luminous calligraphy of these "lines" recalls the late lyrical paintings of Willem de Kooning (1904–1997) rendered all the more vital in the possibility that they were left behind by the hand of an artist released from the limitations of ordinary cognition by the lingering diagnosis of dementia, if not Alzheimer's disease.[32]

(3.49) Willem de Kooning, *Untitled XIII*, 1985

Now, having come face to face with Rembrandt, you might be ready to recognize how, in his *Aristotle with a Bust of Homer*, he has placed the contemplative "philosopher" together with you, the "beholder" in a threshold between "outer" and "inner" realities intersected by the picture plane and frame of the painting, even as a curtain divides illusory space.

(3.50) Plan of *Aristotle with a Bust of Homer* with beholder

Might you also imagine that a fleeting sensory experience has triggered this shared moment of deepest reflection? For the "philosopher" it is the passing touch of his hand on familiar objects as he stands at the entry to his study. For you, the one who would behold with Rembrandt van Rijn, it is the incandescent incarnation of "light," perceived for the moment as the relational unity of color and value. For both, reverie mimics Socrates pausing before entering Agathon's home, "lost" in contemplative suspension in the evening light before the famous symposium on love.[33] As Josef Pieper reminds us, "an activity which is meaningful in itself... cannot be accomplished except with an attitude of receptive openness and attentive silence."[34]

> *Pause here for one last meditation in thrall to* Aristotle with a Bust of Homer. *Soften your eyes . . . your body . . .*
>
> *Think again of Thoreau's aspiration to the wholeness of our human being: "To be awake is to be alive. I have never yet met a man who was quite awake. How could I have looked him in the face?"*

(3.18) *Aristotle with a Bust of Homer*

> *Let your sense of sight and our shared and habitual experience of objects give way to a feeling—a presence beyond observation and naming—an awareness . . . a wholeness . . .*
>
> *Allow the dark eyes of the "philosopher" to draw you close until they fade into the fabric of the painting to remain as a memory of intimated reconciliation brought forth for you in the imagination of Rembrandt van Rijn. Come face to face with solitude. Let your self-conscious involvement become implicated in the unmeasurable light of an inexhaustible You.*

(Advance screen)

CHAPTER 4

Embracing the Obverse: Johann Wolfgang von Goethe

Therefore, grasp without delay, the sacred open secret.
—Johann Wolfgang von Goethe, "Epirrhema"

WE'VE already seen how visual and scholarly "noise" can distract us and compromise our encounters with the art of works of art—how such noise impedes the development of contemplative beholding and thus obstructs our journey toward the threshold of love. But now a different kind of "noise" requires our awareness and attention. Having come face to face with Rembrandt and his artistry in chapter 3, we meet the multifaceted genius Johann Wolfgang von Goethe to see how this other "noise" challenged him during his short stay as a student in Strasbourg from 1770 to 1773.

In an experience easily imagined by any one of us who would travel to France to engage the Cathedral of Strasbourg directly, the young Goethe awoke—almost literally—to a "higher life" than he'd fallen asleep from the night before.[1] In a flash of the most intense combination of sensory apprehension and intellectual insight, he saw as if for the first time what had long been present, but was previously hidden beneath the blinding simplification of his perceptual and conceptual bias.[2] This life-changing vision came to him directly as he experienced the full artistic thrall of the cathedral. It opened the way toward a new kind of simplicity, a profound "living beauty" on the far side of complexity and contradiction—an experience that drew him well beyond what his prior knowledge of architecture, and his partiality for favored styles of the moment, could ever offer.

The Cathedral of Strasbourg, 1176–1439

Before turning to Goethe's own experience, let's begin, as we did with Rembrandt's *Aristotle with a Bust of Homer*, by approaching slowly. The experience for each of us will unfold gradually and at its own speed. Imagine, then, moving toward the cathedral from the northeast, alert to our own relational experience with form, presence, and the moment. Let it be early morning with the north tower of the cathedral as our guide.

Now, setting out alone, prepare yourself. Soon you and the structure will meet in a place illuminated by the soft reflected half-light as the sun rises in the east.

(4.1) Cathedral of Strasbourg, France, 1176–1439, from the northeast, early morning
(4.2) Cathedral of Strasbourg, France, from the northeast, morning

Moving physically closer let your eyes follow the forms that give rise to the south tower. Be open and vulnerable to them and their gesture toward you, just as the young Goethe might have been as he too stood wide-eyed and amazed in the cathedral square (parvis).

(4.3) Cathedral Square (parvis), Strasbourg, France, from the south, morning
(4.4) Cathedral of Strasbourg, from the south, foundation stones

Resist your inclination to step back to a more commanding view. Focus your attention on the foundation of the south tower. Note first the blocks of heavy horizontal stones at your feet; and then the slender attached colonettes, rising from their rounded bases to their pointed arches, delicate tracery, and triangular gables.

(4.5) Cathedral of Strasbourg, from the south, detail of stone tracery

Let the first two archways directly in front of you draw you in. Let them mirror and inform your standing position. Then, as your glance moves left to right from the first two archways to a third, respond to the very gentle rising.

(4.6) Cathedral of Strasbourg, from the south, detail of stone tracery

> *Allow yourself to be lifted slightly. Pause. Reflect. Be still. Enter the interval of transformation, as though between sounds. Listen for the silence of the moment. Hear the emerging space. Let it carry you up . . .*

Now everything is moving: fragile colonettes with their gables rise and multiply even as they expand beyond the first horizontal band (stringcourse) into a small niche (aedicula) occupied by a sculpted figure.

(4.7) Cathedral of Strasbourg, from the southwest, detail stone tracery and aediculae with sculptures

A stone pinnacle caps this aedicula and points still further upward to new levels that seem to rise like arrows...

(4.8) Cathedral of Strasbourg, from the south

To the right of your focus, there's an elevated railing (balustrade) with vertical balusters, or posts) above a double arched entryway. It introduces a sequence of rounded openings, culminating in a large pointed (cusped) window.

(4.9) Cathedral of Strasbourg, from the southwest

Move slightly back toward the southwest.

(4.10) Cathedral of Strasbourg, from the southwest

The next level of the south tower begins with another balustrade above a floral stringcourse that leads to a taller and narrower subdivided opening framed by bands of ornamental molding (archivolts). Further up, a projecting balustrade appears as the support for four aediculae occupied by horsemen that flank a series of still-taller gabled archways. Notice that these archways recapitulate their ground-level partners, which you saw when you started out. A fourth open and projecting balustrade seems literally to crown the south tower at its summit.

Now, as you take another step back, the south tower of the Cathedral of Strasbourg assumes its full form.

(4.11) Cathedral of Strasbourg, from the south

From this position, a fragile but real impression of an elusive wholeness may begin to stir within you. Your glance will have moved upward past four distinct stories framed by a paired sequence of foundation stones, rising colonettes, stringcourses, arches, gables, and aediculae. Meditate slowly on the form of this south tower and the multiple shapes that contribute to its soaring movement. The many separate parts of the overall structure now converge in your perception; as they ascend toward the high horizontal platform where the south tower ends, they become something akin to a musical crescendo. From here also, the north tower appears to begin reaching with its open staircases toward an infinitesimal climax suspended in light.

(4.12) Cathedral of Strasbourg, from the southeast with completed north tower

Recalling the "celestial music" that accompanies Thoreau's and now Goethe's awakening to a "higher life than we fell asleep from," we too might now resonate with the cathedral "music" of the early morning.

(4.13) Cathedral of Strasbourg, from the southeast with branching trees

Goethe described his own experience of actually standing on the platform of the "unfinished" south tower, and the transforming vision he had there, as though the poetic ascent of its form had been realized in his body. That rapturous feeling lingered as he looked from the tower, past the "noble city," to embrace the mountains, woods, and meadows surrounding his new "dwelling place" in Strasbourg: "It was exactly like being carried up into the air by a balloon."[3]

Now, return to the western parvis to confirm for yourself something of the climactic epiphany that resulted in Goethe's own youthful awakening.

(4.14) Cathedral of Strasbourg, from the southwest, midmorning

Seen from the ground below, where you began, nothing, it seems, could slow your own attentive ascent except, of course, the cold, heavy stone beneath your feet. From your vantage point of awakened awareness, the intervals realized as form and imagined sound will have delivered you into a transformative moment: the gravity of your presence, standing in the cathedral square, will be, if only fleetingly, "lifted" no less than the shadows around you are dispelled by the rising sun.

Do you recall in chapter 3 meeting my determined student Elizabeth, who was blind from birth yet able to hear space? I imagine how the structural "music" of the Cathedral of Strasbourg might embrace her—how through careful contemplative beholding, with my verbal descriptions above and the written ones Goethe left behind for us—she too might enter into the presence of its harmonic intimated resurrection.[4]

The precise frame of mind the young Goethe brought to his transforming encounter with the cathedral is unmistakable. His account, published in a 1772 pamphlet called *On German Architecture*, is worthy of its renowned place in the history of art:

> When I went to the minster [cathedral] the first time, my head was full of the general knowledge of good taste. By hearsay, I honored the harmony of mass, the purity of form, and was a sworn enemy of the confused capriciousness of Gothic decorations. Under the heading *Gothic*, as an article in the dictionary, I accumulated all the synonymous misunderstandings which had ever passed through my head of the undefined, the disorderly, the unnatural, the stuck-together, the plastered upon, and the overladen. No cleverer than a people which calls *barbaric* the entire unknown world, I called everything *Gothic* that did not fit into my system, from the turned, colorful dolls and paintings with which our bourgeois nobility dressed up their houses to the stern remains of the older German architecture, over which, because of certain bizarre scrolls, I agree with the common chant, "Completely smothered by ornament!" And therefore, as I went, I shuddered as before the sight of a misshapen monster.[5]

But like Thoreau, who left the dead hand of habit in Concord to find fresh meaning and purpose in the woods around Walden Pond, Goethe awoke to a new reality in his encounter with the Cathedral in Strasbourg. His words are exemplary for our journey:

> With what unexpected emotion did the sight surprise me as I stepped before it? A complete and total impression filled my soul, which, since it was composed of a thousand harmonizing details, I could easily relish and enjoy, but could by no means comprehend and explain. They say it is thus with the joys of heaven. And how often did I return to enjoy this heavenly-earthly joy, to embrace the gigantic spirit of our older brothers in their works! How often did I return from all sides, from all distances, in every light of day, to gaze at its dignity and splendor! It is hard for man's spirit when his brother's work is so exalted that he must only bow and worship.[6]

Goethe's joy and praise for the principal architect of the cathedral are direct and personal. Underneath the title of the pamphlet he included a dedication to "D. M. Ervini A Steinbach," which translates as "To the blessed spirit of Erwin from Steinbach."

> When I wandered around your grave, noble Erwin, seeking the stone which would point to me, . . . and I did not find it and none of your countrymen could show it to me so that I might pour out my veneration for you on the holy spot, I was deeply grieved in my soul. My heart, younger, warmer, more foolish, and better than now, promised you a memorial in marble or sandstone—as might be able—when I would come into the peaceful enjoyment of my [fortune].
>
> Of what use is a memorial to you! You have erected to yourself the most glorious one; and although the ants who crawl there worry little about your name, you have the same fate as the architect who piled up mountains into the clouds.
>
> To few was it given to conceive in their souls an idea of Babel so complete, so great, and necessarily beautiful to the smallest detail, like the trees of God. To fewer was it given to encounter a thousand willing hands, to dig the rocky ground, to conjure thereon steep heights, and then dying say to their sons: "I remain with you in the works of my spirit, complete the beginning in the clouds."[7]

This passionate and unusual, non-moralizing reference to the biblical tower of Babel may well point to the remarkable platform of the south tower that offered Goethe a view to his own expansive aspiration. His anger at those who would disparage the cathedral is no less immediate, vivid, and personal:

> "It is in trivial taste," says the Italian, and passes by. "Childishness," stammers the Frenchman and triumphantly snaps his snuff-box à la Grecque. What have you done that you dare to scorn? . . . Had you felt more than you measured, the spirit of the mighty pile at which you gazed would have come over you, then you would have not only imitated it because they did it and it is beautiful. You would have created your plans necessary and true, and living beauty would have surged from them.[8]

In effect, the young Goethe announced rather simply: *If this is ugly*—by which he meant, perhaps, barbaric, undefined, disorderly, unnatural, trivial, or childish—*then, based on my immediate experience, everything I know is wrong.*

But what did Goethe *know* as he stood spellbound before this Gothic building? His references to classicizing architecture in Italy and France clearly reveal the aesthetic attitude that informed his encounter in Strasbourg. He had been raised and educated in a world in which reason reigned supreme and classical form was the singular model. The name "Gothic" itself stemmed from Alaric the Goth, who had dared to invade eternal Rome, ransack the city's noble buildings, and desecrate its temples. Thus, "Gothic" had come to stand for a particularly egregious form of aesthetic sacrilege.

(Advance screen)

The Parthenon

What if we imagine that the intellectual and perceptual anchor that weighed on Goethe in Strasbourg could also be epitomized by one singular monument of classical vision, the sanctuary of the Acropolis, placed high above the city of ancient Athens?

(4.15) Acropolis, Athens, Greece, from the southwest

Ascend, then, to the Acropolis by following the Panathenaic Way from the sacred gate at the Dipylon cemetery. Pass through the agora (marketplace) and arrive at the entry to the sanctuary. Now, slowly, deliberately, and reverently, approach the inner space of this consummate monument to human reason and divine aspiration.

> *Stand face-to-face before the Parthenon, the temple dedicated to Athena Parthenos, the virgin goddess of all wisdom, military power, community, justice, and skill.*

(4.16) Parthenon, Acropolis, Athens, Greece, 448–32 BCE, from the west

As you engage with the western elevation of the Parthenon, change the focus I suggested for the Cathedral of Strasbourg; this time follow your inclination to step back for a more commanding view. Take in the whole form. The multiple layers of the ground-level foundation stones that form the base (plinth) and the elevated horizontal structure resting on columns (entablature), along with the relatively compressed triangular pediment, enclose the ribbon-like series of columns forming the Doric-order colonnade. The initial visual effect is a singularly horizontal rectangle, firmly anchored to the earth.

Now pay attention to the sculptural program, originally displayed in the pediment and in the band of rectangular panels with carved relief figures (metopes), which are flanked by rectangular blocks with vertical elements (triglyphs). Spread across the entablature these sculptural elements convey the heroic energy and grace of divinity literally sublimated in human form. The abacus, the flat slab at the top of each column, is a squared block of stone, echoing the horizontal heft of the foundation and at the same time forming a bridge between the lower and upper horizontal sections of the porch—and, no less, between mortal and divine existence.

A nineteenth-century painting by Thomas Horner affirms this perception of deliberate conceptual order based on layered horizontality in both the Parthenon and the Acropolis sanctuary.

(4.17) Thomas Horner, *View of the Acropolis*, 19th century

Numerous scholarly reconstructions of the site suggest a similar guiding horizontality.

(4.18) Acropolis, reconstruction, with Propylaea indicated by red arrow

Unlike the façade entryway to the Cathedral of Strasbourg that challenged the young student Goethe to climb from the cathedral square to the top of the unfinished south tower, the gateway to the Acropolis sanctuary, called the Propylaea, came at the end of the arduous journey from the city below. The next step was the Parthenon itself and direct encounter with embodied divinity.

(4.19) Parthenon, reconstruction, inner chamber

Imagine being the boy in the drawing (image 4.19) who kneels on the marble floor within the Parthenon's inner chamber. Now, at the feet of the colossal statue of Athena Parthenos, he (and you) have indeed reached the summit of human aspiration within the closed rectilinear vessel of her temple. Think now of how Goethe praised the architect of the Cathedral of Strasbourg: "It is hard for man's spirit when his brother's work is so exalted that he must only bow and worship." Those words and the kneeling posture differ only in the object of their adoration, whether human or divine.

Step "outside" the chamber for a moment to see an architectural rendering of the western elevation of the Parthenon made by Josef Bühlmann

(1844–1921), a professor of architecture and architectural perspective in drawing who also specialized in construction theory. His rendering underscores the apparent horizontality of this iconic structure that so informed the people of the Renaissance and the Enlightenment as they sought to emulate in thought and action the Greek ideal of rational stability and clarity.

(4.20) Parthenon, architectural rendering by Josef Bühlmann

Now imagine the youthful Goethe's shock when he arrived in Strasbourg entirely within the thrall of this ideal classical vision, only to find this:

(4.21) Cathedral of Strasbourg, west façade

Leaving aside for a moment Goethe's own response to the Cathedral of Strasbourg, engage with the incalculable amplification of the forms within this façade that make up the comparatively simple south tower. Among other elaborations, you might begin by attending to the separation of the slender colonettes and arches from the stone blocks of the façade wall and the shifting shadows they cast. In countless ways—think of Goethe's "thousand harmonizing details"—this structure confronts the timeless simplicity and stability of the Parthenon with the fleeting reality of a moment that disappears the very second it is noticed. Thus the cathedral façade *appears* to exchange all that is fixed, certain, and horizontal (that is to say, classical) for all that is shifting, uncertain, and vertical (that is to say—according to eighteenth-century convention—Gothic, even barbaric).

The "Living Beauty" of the Cathedral

What, then, did the young student standing in the parvis of the Cathedral of Strasbourg see that others no less grounded in the values of classical order had missed? We have already seen how passionately Goethe responded to the explosive verticality of the façade. He might also have seen a veiled presence in the dynamic structural illumination caused by the separation of the stone wall and its decorative fretwork (the interlaced, cutout patterning) of colonettes, gables, and straight and curved lines. But, perhaps most importantly, he engaged with what he called a "living beauty" that, almost plant-like, rose up and blossomed from the anchoring horizontality of the earth—the parvis—as though he were listening to the voice of genius that had inspired Erwin von Steinbach:

> Diversify the overwhelming wall which you are to build toward heaven so that it rises like a tall tree of God, which, with a thousand branches, millions of twigs and leaves as the sands of the sea, proclaims to the country roundabout the glory of the Lord, its Master.[9]

Once we notice it, this ascent emerges everywhere from its grounded—even seminal— horizontality. This groundedness is the source and measure of movement, not only upward, but laterally. It punctuates the perceived diagonal convergence of all verticals toward a single point far above even the finished north tower, let alone the originally conceived sequence of five towers. So too, this repeated horizontal anchoring forms the implied baselines of the myriad gables, large and small, that culminate the framing archivolts around the portals and windows of the façade. As a two-dimensional movement—an expansion and contraction—it complements the comparable three-dimensional spatial movement of the areas flanking doorways (portal jambs) that open outward, drawing us into the shifting luminous fabric of the façade and toward the doors to the interior.

As Goethe described his experience of this structural form, the physical objective presence of the façade became a sensual threshold that anticipates the interior of the cathedral. This time, as though Erwin von Steinbach had accompanied him into this transitional space and spoke to him directly, Goethe wrote:

> "What astonishes you?" he whispered to me. "All these masses were necessary, and don't you see them in all old churches of my city? Only their arbitrary size have I raised to a harmonizing proportion. How over the main entrance, which dominates two smaller ones on the sides, the wide circle of the window opens, echoing the nave of the church and was otherwise only a hole for daylight; how the belfry high above demands the smaller windows! All that was necessary and I formed it beautifully."[10]

(4.22) Cathedral of Strasbourg, west façade, center portal and rose window

Caught in the shifting light of day, "the wide circle of the window" miraculously occupies two places at once. It appears to be inside the wall and outside, recalling Goethe's life-altering insight in four lines from his poem "Epirrhema":

> Nothing is inner, nothing is outer,
> For what is inner, is outer.

Therefore, grasp without delay,
The sacred open secret.[11]

Structurally, this western rose window combines the horizontal, vertical, diagonal, straight, and curvilinear components of the façade, including the radiant leaf-like forms of the architect's "tall tree of God." Suspended near the center of the rectangular contour of the façade, the rose window becomes, within the direct experience of our perception, the interval poised somewhere between the ground and the elevated foundation of its transcendent north tower—echoing perhaps the invisible, but palpable, presence of the unfinished south tower. In the exact convergence of the circle with the horizontal and vertical sides of the square, this rose window embraces the contradictions of movement and absolute stillness, presence and absence, and maybe even sound and silence. From the smallest detail to the overall form of its structure, the façade of the Cathedral of Strasbourg thus realizes a poetic void manifestly surrounded by the noisy realities of the world.

(4.23) Cathedral of Strasbourg, from the west

The "living beauty" Goethe found in Strasbourg was not *Gothic.* His meditative embrace of the contradictions that are revealed in the façade of this cathedral opened him to a deeper beauty beyond the limitations of aesthetic, perceptual, and conceptual opposition. I ask you then, at this point in our journey together, to take a second look with me at the iconic ground zero of *classical* form: the Parthenon.

Approach the outer boundary that encloses the sacred interior. For this, you must stand next to one of the Doric columns that as a group define the horizontal rectangular form of the temple.

(4.24) Parthenon, base of Doric order

The perpendicular intersection of column and stone floor, emphasized by the sharp vertical lines of the first fluted drum, alter the anticipated horizontality of this Greek temple. From here, a perception of extreme verticality challenges our most cherished preconceived notions of classical groundedness, giving way to a soaring ascent, reminiscent of the thinnest sequence of Gothic colonettes.

(4.25) Parthenon, Doric order with capital and entablature

The repeated accents of the Doric order columns, the empty spaces between them, and the grooves in the triglyphs above them add an implied verticality to the dominant horizontality of the western elevation of the Parthenon. Even the precise spacing of the columns and their gentle swelling (*entasis*) hints at movement—think of how this swelling animates Goethe's "living beauty"—and suggests a very subtle bowing of the rectangular colonnade and the temple façade. This perceived vertical movement of the Parthenon may now complement the repeated horizontal accents of the Cathedral of Strasbourg. Seeing it from this perspective opens the way to Goethe's larger vision of the "higher life" that Thoreau challenged us to awaken to, and which Goethe himself so passionately experienced in Strasbourg.

(4.26) a. Parthenon, architectural rendering by Josef Bühlmann;
b. Cathedral of Strasbourg, engraving by Wenceslaus Hollar, 17th c.
(4.27) Parthenon, architectural rendering by Josef Bühlmann (vertical accents by author)
(4.28) Cathedral of Strasbourg, engraving by Wenceslaus Hollar (horizontal accents by author)

Here I invite you to meditate with the formal and structural realities—vertical and horizontal—as they are integrally embodied in the Cathedral of Strasbourg and the Parthenon in Athens.

While still holding these contradictory but mutually informing possibilities in your consciousness, imagine your own presence before these works of art. Allow yourself to behold with them and their art of intimated reconciliation.

Goethe's compelling eros (his fullest sensory alertness to the Cathedral of Strasbourg) generated for him (as it may for us) a new understanding or insight—the potential to replace the disembodied conceptual opposition of "classical beauty" and "Gothic beauty" by integrating and embracing their obverse realities. We too, with our fullest sensory awareness, can embrace the elevated horizontality of the cathedral and the grounded verticality of the temple. Both works of art become constituents—or counterparts—of a perceived wholeness far greater, by a factor of infinity, than the sum of their individual parts.

In a moment of contemplative beholding (knowing), Goethe was able to release a "living beauty" from the clutches of fragmenting bias. We too, on our journey to the threshold of love, might imagine our own direct entry into the thrall of such an awakening moment of intimated reconciliation.

(4.29) a. Parthenon, from the west; b. Cathedral of Strasbourg, from the west

(4.30) a. Parthenon, from the northwest, evening; b. Cathedral of Strasbourg, from the west, evening

(Advance screen)

Embracing the Obverse: Six Reflections

How might we further reflect on what it means to embrace the obverse, considering what we have experienced with Goethe in Strasbourg? Here are six brief thematic contemplations—think of them as comparable to the reflective interludes in chapter 3—in preparation for the next step of our journey, or perhaps to revisit at any time along the way.

Reflection 1: "Gentle intimations" that will "transmit the blissfulness of the gods to earth"

Goethe's embodied response to the Cathedral of Strasbourg took shape as he moved around it, near and far, during all hours of the day, especially early morning and late evening—matins and vespers. Here he reflects on how pleasure and understanding (let's say *eros* and *insight*) became one and the same.

> How often did the evening twilight refresh with friendly quiet my eyes made weary by their seeking, for the twilight made the innumerable parts melt into complete masses! These now standing simple and great before my soul, my strength unfolded itself rapturously to *enjoy* and *comprehend* simultaneously! There the genius of the great builder revealed itself to me in gentle *intimations* (*Andeutung*).[12]

(4.31) Cathedral of Strasbourg, from the west, morning

(Advance screen)

Let's shift our attention from Goethe's Strasbourg experience to our journey toward the threshold of love. Specifically, let's focus on the role eros and insight play on that path, as well as on the other contradictory realities of our conscious longing that result from our of mortal limitation and our aspiration for wholeness. Where, then, might Goethe's "gentle intimations" lead us in our deliberate shift to an open, contemplative awareness? To seek music in sound and meaningful silence, to seek art in the midst of "visual noise"? Do we sense Thoreau's "undulations of celestial music instead of factory bells, and a fragrance filling the air?" Can we too "awaken to a higher life than we fell asleep from [so that] the darkness bear its fruit, and prove itself to be good, no less than the light?"

In going to the woods around Walden Pond, Thoreau committed a deliberate act not to escape or oppose his city life in Concord. Instead, he meant to embrace its obverse in order to engage a larger reality that would point to the elusive wholeness of his being—"the essential facts of life." He did this so that "when [he] came to die, [he] would not discover that [he] had not lived." Similarly, Goethe's experience in Strasbourg may draw our attention outward, beyond architecture, to a larger reality, undiminished by bias, but born in irreconcilable opposition, in this instance, between so-called Gothic and classical values. Like Thoreau, Goethe challenged the limitation of mere opposition with the expanding possibility of integrating obverse realities. He saw the "living beauty" of an integral force of transcendent verticality emerging from the earthbound, horizontal foundation of the parvis. He was, at first, simply drawn to climb the south tower to its summit. In time, he came to know the simultaneity of weight and release that initially he had only sensed.

Conversely, we have also imagined a mirrored equality of beauty embodied in the Parthenon where subtle vertical elements animate its grounded horizontal form. Goethe's and our own contemplation of Strasbourg Cathedral, especially in the early morning and evening hours, allows otherwise opposed realities to evoke in our beholding a sense of how these contending (even warring) possibilities become instead obverse partners (or counterparts), present *together* in a whole that is immeasurably greater than any particular sum could name.

As we discovered earlier in the value and color-value exercises of chapter 2, such contemplative wholeness takes shape in the very interval that joins these partners, whether black and white or red and green. Since this interval includes an infinite number of possibilities (grays or neutral values), it is literally and manifestly an intimation of wholeness beyond calculation. From another angle, we might envision Simone Weil's void into which grace, replacing gravity, will flow, even as grace itself caused this void in which we, ourselves, were begotten. Goethe's closing words to his youthful declaration of joy challenge us as beholders directly:

> Hail to you, Youth, who is born with a sharp eye for proportions to practice [your talent] with facility on all [nature's] forms.... Accept... Heavenly Beauty, you mediatrix between gods and men... [who] may transmit the blissfulness of the gods to earth.[13]

Here we may ask: Was it merely exuberance that fueled the young man in Strasbourg? We might choose instead to see the reconciliatory longing we all share as the inspiration for those "gentle intimations" of art, beauty, and love as they each become the "mediatrix" that does the transmitting.

Reflection 2: The dynamic reconciliation of all things in relation

(4.32) a. Schematic rendering of the obverse realities of "experience"—"order";
b. Schematic rotation of obverse realities;
c. Schematic rotation of multiple obverse realities

In image 4.32 (a), **E** and **O** represent the relation of "experience" and "order." When rotated in any direction, the initial oppositional relation of "experience *over* order" becomes "order *over* experience" (b). As (c) reveals, their dynamic relations are integral parts of one continuous whole made up of animated obverse realities (counterparts), not biased oppositions.

Conversely, to maintain the duality of opposition in (a) or (b) is to obscure and deny this larger reality of a wholeness in which multiple, even contradictory, realities not only exist but inform each other. We don't have to stay with horizontal–vertical: imagine substituting for **E** and **O** other contradictory realities of concern (perhaps choose red–green, or round–straight).

But let's be cautious here, as we extend our choices. Despite our modern obsession with them, the terms "race" and "gender" cannot be individually reduced to the duality of opposition. Their many differences exist without being obverse. However stark the differences existing within them may appear, those differences are superficial to our common humanity. Some in the world are bound to see the refusal to accept anything as "absolute" or certain as a sure path to psychological, social, and intellectual anarchy. But from our open awareness, we will arrive at a sobering recognition and vulnerable acceptance that *all things* in creation, from their beginning, exist *in relation*.

Existential (and spiritual) questions about how we live now challenge us in many forms: What will this relation be? Where in the interval between sound and silence will we stand? What will our art be? How will we love? How will we seek to intimate reconciliation of irreconcilable contradiction in the full embrace of the obverse?

(Advance screen)

Reflection 3: "The sacred open secret"

From our earliest days, when we first perceive sensations of chromatic warm and cool, light and dark, or movement and stillness, obverse realities frame and animate an existential reality, one that is formed by, and which contains, the relational integrity of "experience" and "order" (*ars* and *scientia*), and thereby provides the cognitive foundation of true learning (*eruditio*) at the core of our universal longing and aspiration to wisdom (*sapientia*). When we come to recognize this, unalterably opposed and forever destructive acts—from fragmenting to alienating bias—will yield their position of primacy. In their place, acts of love committed as the deliberate embrace of the obverse will have become, silently, the alternative form of our "wandering mourning."

Though visible even in an unexceptional schematic drawing, this "more human love" is most intensely present and palpable in that "wide circle of the window," which Goethe saw at the center of the west façade of the cathedral "echoing [intimating] the nave of the church."

(4.33) Cathedral of Strasbourg, western rose window, exterior
(4.34) Cathedral of Strasbourg, western rose window, interior

Simultaneously exterior and interior, stone and glass, light and color, centripetal and centrifugal, complex and simple, the rose window now assumed its full presence for Goethe as if for the first time. From this new unbiased vantage point, he saw this rose window as nothing less than the membrane threshold (interval) to the sacral presence of Our Lady of Strasbourg. Precisely because of his passionate awareness of this elusive presence of wholeness, Goethe, the youthful pilgrim, knew that this glorious structure was "otherwise only a hole for daylight," a mere instrumental reality.

Let's extend Goethe's personal experience to our own beholding with the Cathedral of Strasbourg. As the result of the embodied physiological and cerebral longing at the very core of our conscious awareness, the work of art that is this cathedral arises from our immanent capacity for relating all experience and all order. Indeed, it opens the way to a contemplative integration of all eros and all insight. That integration will provide a moral vision of intimated reconciliation as the perceptual and ethical basis of understanding and action. In their obverse relation, "experience" and "order" take shape as the living components of that gravity, which for Simone Weil controls "all the *natural* movements of the soul." Her elusive "void," into which she imagined grace would flow, requires a deliberate transcending of this contentious condition, even as we acknowledge and suffer within it.[14] This affliction of gravity, whether in the form of literal weight causing fatigue, hunger, cold, fear, confusion, and loneliness—or, more abstractly, as hierarchy, bias, and opposition—will be *healed* only by those acts of love to which we aspire and that are to be realized only within the threshold of a contemplative beholding (knowing) that reaches for wholeness.

(4.35) Schematic rotation of obverse realities: gravity—grace

The vision of this wholeness beyond limitation—love the noun, or "blissfulness," alive in the very embrace of the obverse—can begin to reveal Goethe's "sacred open secret" as the animating center of our being with its ever-expanding, window-like ripples of grace that would redeem a world of gravity. Again, reflect on Goethe's insight.

> Nothing is outer, nothing is inner.
> For what is inner, is outer.
> Therefore, grasp without delay,
> The sacred open secret.

Reflection 4: The sound of silence (wholeness) in the interval of the morning and the evening

If we were to reimagine Thoreau's awakening "accompanied by the undulations of celestial music . . . to a higher life than we fell asleep from," we too might discover that the "darkness bear its fruit, and prove itself to be good, no less than the light." Accepting this revelation, we would no longer be inclined to define evil, knowing that to do so is to assure the commission of evil. We would recognize that in the embrace of the obverse, the hint of a "more human love" will have appeared on the horizon. We will have learned to stand in the discontinuous interval of the morning between night and day, as though prayerfully at matins and vespers, and hear the sound of silence beyond reckoning.

(4.36) Takaragaike, Kyoto, Japan, early morning

(Advance screen)

Reflection 5: "At the serene core all that befalls us is pure"

Goethe clearly put down the burden of bias with which he arrived in Strasbourg. His awakening to a higher life in his embrace of the obverse returns us to the beginning of our path toward the threshold of love, where we first encountered Rainer Maria Rilke's extraordinary observation about killing. Rilke's words seem to leave us with no escape. According to Rilke's own commentary, hunters hung curtains in caves near Karst on the Dalmatian coast so that, when the curtains were shaken, their shimmering light would entice confused and frightened birds to fly out of the darkness to their death.[15] Although they lowered these curtains as false banners of peace, the hunters don't deserve to be judged. They did what hunters do, because, in the lingering truth of the final verse of Rilke's sonnet:

Killing is a form of our wandering mourning... [16]

This killing is but *one* form of our "wandering mourning." The poet's unfinished sentence calls out, even to the "hunters" among us, to aspire beyond killing, presumably, toward the "more human love" that would "protect and border and salute" the solitude of another's "wandering mourning."

Perhaps we, too, then, like those vulnerable birds, seek light as we reach out for wholeness from our darkened condition of mortal limitation. In Strasbourg, standing before the massive west façade of the cathedral, Goethe may have experienced what Rilke suggested to a young poet a century later: "*Live* the questions now. Perhaps you will then gradually, without noticing it, live along some distant day into the answer."[17] Goethe himself lived into the *purest* answer to the poetic question raised by the curtains of Karst. For here, the hunters' killing—or for that matter, bias in any form—will have given way not to just another act of killing, but to a "more human love." Rather than remain merely an instrumental "hole for light," the western rose window became to Goethe's awakened eyes a luminous membrane that would join the exterior and interior of the cathedral vessel. And, in the active, loving embrace of the obverse realities of brightness and shadow, the window would faithfully translate white light into the living, yet divine, incarnation of color.

We find little explicit reference to color in Goethe's Strasbourg text. But he did develop a scientific theory of color that drew on his experience of how light, when it passes through a prism, results in the presence of color in the interval between light and dark. The theory may recall not only the western rose window of the Cathedral of Strasbourg but also everything else he learned there and shared with us.[18]

(4.37) Cathedral of Strasbourg: a. western rose window, exterior; b. western rose window, interior

So too, Rilke's concluding words to this particular sonnet to Orpheus are nothing if not radiant with the transcendent simplicity reminiscent of Gothic stained glass:

> At the serene core
> All that befalls us is pure.[19]

Look again, in image 4.36, at the ripples in the early morning light as they animate the still water of the pond at Takaragaike . . .

(4.36) Takaragaike, Kyoto, Japan, early morning

Meditate with them. Let them move, expand, give way—like the sound of the bell—to stillness and silence. Be in this interval . . .

Now, allow the transparent movement of the western rose window at Strasbourg to merge with our memory of Rembrandt's moving hand. Think of how he transformed the material color of pigments in an intimation of eternal whiteness suspended in the sleeves of the philosopher. Join with Claude Monet again at the Cathedral of Rouen to contemplate with the interweaving mystery of white and colored light, from early morning to oncoming darkness as the evening anticipates the dawn. From this universally begotten center, chromatic ripples will open endlessly toward that white light we first saw and felt as infants in the inchoate form of warm and cool sensations. Only later did those sensations become the contending categories of red and green, orange and blue, yellow and purple arrayed across the full value range of the lightest light and the darkest dark.

(Advance screen)

Return to Strasbourg now. Relish the following glimpse into Goethe's personal life, and a passage he wrote to conclude his memories of his sojourn in Strasbourg, where he arrived as a "youthful pilgrim" of twenty-one.

Goethe's desire to engage with the harmonies embodied in dance prompted him to sign up for lessons with an instructor who would introduce him to the "act of whirling around in the waltz."[20] Before long, he was caught up in a drama with the instructor's two young daughters, entangled in their tribulations of jealousy and unrequited love. One daughter, Emilia, was "fresh and good-natured," but seemingly superficial. The other, Lucinda, was "reserved and quiet...concealing wonderful depths within." According to Lucinda's self-assessment, she had a "warm, true spirit," but her sister had a "cold and selfish heart." Caught in the middle, Goethe fled the scene, "with the firm determination never to enter [their] house again." He left Strasbourg with Lucinda's words ringing in his ears:

> "I know that I have lost you; I make no further claims on you. But you shall not have him either, sister!" With these words she took my head between her hands, thrusting her fingers in my hair, and, pressing my face to hers, kissed me over and over again on the lips. "Now," she cried, "fear my curse! Woe upon woe, for ever and ever, to her who kisses these lips for the first time after me! Dare to have anything more to do with him! I know heaven hears me this time. And now, Sir, be gone, be gone as quickly as you can!"[21]

If we interpret even *slightly* metaphorically the irreducible contradiction in the attentions paid to Goethe by Emilia and Lucinda—their contradictory impulses, let's say—we can place the awakened young Goethe in his fateful threshold of love, departing on a path toward his poetic accomplishments in art and science.

Reflection 6: From seed to flower: the metamorphosis of change, growth, and transformation

> *Jeder neue Gegenstand, wohl beschiet, schliest ein neues Organ in uns auf.*
>
> Every object well contemplated opens up a new organ [of change, growth, and transformation] in us. (Goethe)

Here Arthur Zajonc's sharp focus on the cognitive and spiritual empowerment of Goethe's famous observation will guide us further into an art and practice of contemplative beholding.

> You have to attend carefully. "Every object well contemplated"—not just casually contemplated but well contemplated, attended to

> over time, repeatedly—changes who you are, changes who you are to the point where you begin to see things that you didn't see originally, and perhaps which no one before you has seen.[22]

Over many years, in my personal endeavors and repeatedly in my profession as a teacher, I have returned to Goethe's writings and especially my own experience with the Cathedral of Strasbourg, as a source of aspiration. As a result of that careful attention, I have arrived with a clear sense of awakening to a higher reality beyond the limitations of bias and fragmentation.

Goethe published his *Metamorphosis of Plants* in 1790, roughly twenty years after leaving Strasbourg. If we trace the process of "flowering" and fruition he describes in that work and apply it to his vast poetic and scientific accomplishments, we can imagine that his sojourn in Strasbourg was the "seed." If so, his life-altering experience there will encourage us all to embrace the awakened potential of such "flowering" in our own lives. We might now even say that every individual advance in an art and practice of contemplative beholding will enhance all human aspiration to wholeness.

The language of Goethe's first scientific study offers a comforting echo of compassionate—virtually ecological—reconciliation as he characterizes a relationship of organism to organism "in which one species is created, or at least sustained, by and through another."[23] By this means, we may hope that anyone's interior metamorphosis of change, growth, and transformation will ripple outward from seed to flower to fruit, and to the formation of a new seed, to all people, animals, nature, the world, and wholeness beyond reckoning.

Moving Ahead on Our Path of Contemplation

In chapter 5 we will find that for Piet Mondrian the combined color, value, and movement in his own lifelong embrace of the obverse is akin to the devoted search for Goethe's "Heavenly Beauty" as the "mediatrix between gods and men." Although the justly famous dance of color realized in Mondrian's *Broadway Boogie-Woogie* clearly animates one of his best-known works of art, our path of contemplation will move from his singular vision, called simply *Painting No.1*, to the enduring transformation embodied by his last known painting, *Victory Boogie-Woogie*, left unfinished at his death in 1944. In both of these paintings purest white pigment becomes another "serene core" where "all that befalls us is pure." This delicate perception recalls once more John O'Donohue's blessing, in which the voice of the child entering the world speaks to the aspiration of us all:

> In everything I do, think,
> Feel, and say,
> May I allow the light
> Of the world I am leaving
> To shine through and carry me home.

(Advance screen)

CHAPTER 5

Measuring Contradiction: Piet Mondrian

> *When the attention has revealed the contradiction in something on which it has been fixed, a kind of loosening takes place. By persevering in this course, we attain detachment.*
>
> —Simone Weil, "Contradiction," *Gravity and Grace*

TO PREPARE for the next stage of our journey toward the threshold of love, listen once more to the apostle Paul as he invites the citizens of Corinth to imagine an awakening beyond their current limitations. Think of Thoreau's awakening to a "higher life than we fell asleep from."

> *Set aside the ecclesiastical implications that Paul's words will have for many. Welcome and allow them to open within all of us an experience of new awareness.*
>
> *Absorb Paul's words in silence and stillness. They contain a key to our work—not information but precisely the intimation of a new life.*

> For we know only in part, and we prophesy only in part; but when the complete comes, the partial will come to an end. When I was a child, I spoke like a child, I thought like a child, I reasoned like a child; when I became an adult, I put an end to childish ways. For now we see in a mirror, dimly, but then we will see face to face. Now I know only in part; then I will know fully, even as I have been fully known. And now faith, hope, and love abide, these three; and the greatest of these is love. (1 Corinthians 13:9–13)

Moving from the Habitual

Returning to our path of contemplation now, focus intently on the following circle of color for several minutes without thought or anticipation.

Simply embrace the immediate experience of color as fully as possible. Then close your eyes gently and wait to see what happens...

(5.1) Colored circle

Did you free associate with the color red? Did you remember occasions in the past summoned forth by that color? Did you have thoughts about its meaning, its potential symbolism, its effect on you? Or did you wait quietly, patiently, openly for something to occur? If you did—which would likely signal a conceptual change from habitual objectification to direct engagement—what happened? What did you "see"?

Did a blue-greenish glowing (almost shimmering) form take shape? Did a shifting and soft edge, rather than a hard one, begin to appear? Did this colored form move and even pulsate as you observed? Did it withdraw slowly and disappear, leaving you aware of something vividly real, but just beyond your grasp?

Contemplating this circle without fanfare or the slightest thunderclap of recognition—like the inconspicuous frog in the Bashō poem, breaking the silence of an ancient pond—you might have experienced something akin to what Thoreau achieved in his experimental trip from Concord to the unfamiliar woods at Walden. That is: you may have experienced moving from the habitual to a fresh, new awareness.

If a faint blue-green color without specific shape appeared before your closed eyes, you "saw" the chromatic and formal complement of the "red" circle. What happened? As a material event, explained by the physiology of your eyes and animated by the vascular movement of blood, you will have experienced a natural, physical relation. Reflecting on the experience, you might have found yourself stepping beyond the boundaries of your familiar, even exclusive, reliance on merely finite, material, logical, critical, and essentially causal thinking. In that case, in that calm, seemingly negligible, and virtually inchoate moment of the "greenish" epiphany, you were in fact poised within the threshold of an awakening to a "higher life," one born in your own immanent capacity for complementary existence in the world. Your own faithful, uninterrupted, unbiased experience offered you presence and absence: closed "red," open "green;" fixed "red," moving "green;" opaque "red," transparent "green."

By all outward appearances nothing remarkable happened, either in you or in the world—except, perhaps, that you had a direct experience of a cognitive reality, once present in your infancy, but forgotten and buried since then in the habitual rationalized behavior of your adult life. To "put an end to childish ways" involves nothing more than recovering as an accessible state this newly begotten childlike potential to bring back together again our fullest powers of *ars* and *scientia*: experience and order. In fact, in their natural, given, integral wholeness, such a conjunction of "experience" and "order" can become the foundation of our human capacity for that "higher life" of contemplative beholding (*eruditio*), concretely embodied in the delicate intersection of sensual yearning (eros) and cerebral insight: not one or the other, or even one and then the other, but both together, yoked by (and to) the urgency of immediate "presence."

Indeed, in this undramatic but exemplary instance, it is possible that in embracing and being embraced by obverse realities you experienced not only the thrall of "red . . . green," but also an unsuspected "deep resonance" of an elusive wholeness that we can identify as wisdom (*sapientia*).

Let's pause in this place of contemplative beholding, accompanied (metaphorically at least) by "celestial music and a fragrance filling the air." Such necessary and contradictory realities of our conscious being are continuously informed by (and become vehicles for) intimations of wholeness beyond all limitation and contradiction. Such intimations are nothing other than the purest water for our endless thirst, nourishment for our hunger, rest for our tired bodies, clarity in the face of confusion, courage where we were afraid, companionship for our enduring loneliness, and solace when suffering grief. They are, by any other account, the love that softens our longing. And grounded in physical being, they will be the grace to enter the void we experience between the discontinuous manifestations of finite and infinite realities.

Such intimations, present in direct experience but not limited to the immediate perception of "red . . . green," can begin to build a bridge between the conscious mortality of our being (thirst, hunger, loneliness, for instance) and Thoreau's "higher life," where "darkness [will] bear its fruit and prove itself to be good, no less than the light."[1]

Might we now recognize the possibility that grace penetrating ordinary palpable experience will redeem the *gravity* (or burdensome weight) of our lives if we allow it to do so? Perhaps now the familiar phrases with which our journey started will also begin to take on a deeper meaning, similar to the way in which the complementary presence of "green" pulsates with the fixed order of "red," or the reverse.

(Advance screen)

The Sacred Open Secret of Seeing "Green"

In the classroom with my students, I intended this "red . . . green" exercise as a very small extension of the color-value charts we worked with earlier (see chapter 2). It proved to be much more difficult than I expected. One devoted student named Jenny, who was particularly alert to the problem of avoiding "free association," experienced repeated failures in which nothing appeared to her other than the usual darkness of her closed eyes. Then one day without warning, after the class had moved on to new challenges, she came to my office to announce with unrelieved enthusiasm, "I saw green!"

Was Jenny's excitement simply the result of a dutiful completion of a past assignment? It was not. For in her written reflections about the exercise, this capable student understood that something more than a mere physiological response had occurred. The hard, tangible, and fixed world of the red circle painted into her color-value chart had merged with the elusive, intangible, and pulsating open presence of the complementary absent color *with no apparent or measurable link or bridge from one to the other*. She now knew two utterly separate realities: one lay on the desk and the other lived within her. They were joined in her singular experience. What she knew to be separate now flowed together mysteriously, transcending ordinary material explanation. Having set aside the "childish ways" of exclusive rational continuity, she discovered a new, perceptually discontinuous, but nonetheless "whole" reality.

In calm reflection, Jenny "saw" green with her eyes closed. She set aside the "noise" of "red," with all of its remembered connotations. By simply being silent, open, and waiting, she entered an interval of color simply as color, generated in the physical construction of her body. As though "seeing" beneath the ripples of sound, she found the deepest resonance of absolute silence beyond all noise. In seeing "green" she experienced that "loosening" that precedes detachment:

> I SAW GREEN!
> [On another occasion] I was looking at the familiar *ars, scientia* and *eruditio* chart that Professor Upton often puts on the screen. I was staring at the solid red circle representing "order" and I glimpsed at my white notebook and SAW GREEN! I had been so frustrated

> when I did not see green on October 6. I had tried so intently to find green that day, but I could not. Today, without trying, without even thinking about it, I saw green! This has been one of the most exciting mini-awakenings for me in my time as a student in "Eros and Insight" and also as an Amherst College freshman. This flash of green was incredibly encouraging after my disappointment and frustration on October 6. I believe the way in which it happened is indicative of awakenings in general. You cannot wake up one morning and decide "I am going to have an awakening moment today." Just as you cannot stare at red and tell yourself over and over again "I will see green, I will see green, I will see green . . . " This happened spur of the moment because I was open to seeing green, but I was not forcing myself to see something that was not there.
>
> Today, I was looking at the single green word, "solitude" [in class] on the screen. I didn't think anything of it. The green word started glowing, and I saw a faint redness glowing around the word. When I looked away, I saw the flash of red. It was like my revelation was supplemented! I was so excited when I first saw green, and seeing red just reinforced my awakening moment! Seeing green earlier was definitely a turning point for me in this course. I was afraid that this was beyond my grasp, but I realize that contemplative knowing is attainable! I am of course not fully awake, but I see intervals in my everyday life, I even see contradictions! I really have seen a progression in the way that I think.[2]

Although ordinary by the measure of broadest human experience, Jenny's classroom discovery may be compared to that of the young Goethe in Strasbourg. Just as she came to see green in obverse relation to red, as two parts of a larger unbreakable whole, so too Goethe found the biased opposition of *Gothic* and *classical* form resolved in the inextricably complementary pairing of vertical and horizontal, interior and exterior. Goethe's ecstatic recognition of beauty beyond the invidious categories that he had learned would emerge as a poetic declaration of the ubiquitous and universal "sacred open secret" that is key to any contemplative beholding. Being embraced by the light of the stained-glass western rose window of the Strasbourg Cathedral confirmed that revelation for him.[3]

Jenny's hard-won experience of Goethe's "sacred open secret" thus moves us another step toward the "higher life" embodied in the youthful encounters of both. Each emerged from direct experience of utterly unbiased presence, followed by thoughtful reflection.

One question underlying our journey toward beholding—*What would it be like to engage with (encounter) oneself, others, and the world through contemplative knowing?*—comes into slightly different focus if we ask another question: *What would it be like to find oneself endlessly falling in love?* We can look for an answer in the impossible and contradictory circumstances of the celibate monk Thomas Merton, who wrote in "A Mid-Summer Diary for M" about his relationship with his hospital nurse, a woman half his age. The following reflection from this journal evokes the memory of the delicate moment when he and "M" knew they were falling in love:

> I find myself back at the beginning.... I will never forget that Wednesday in Holy week, that rainy night when you came in before going to Chicago, and when we were too tongue tied to say what we almost knew. And the night after that when I lay awake and realized that I loved you. And that Good Friday when I decided to leave you a note for you to write to me. (How glad I am that I did that.) And your first letter, with its "opening." And my letter, impulsive and "intense" that began everything.[4]

In his diary for M, Merton reveals love for his God incarnate in his love for her. This most faithful Trappist monk, filled with absolutely irreconcilable and vulnerable longings, expresses the dilemma like this: "When we began, we knew it could not be understood... and it never was. There is nothing *understandable* in love."[5] He allows himself to voice his hope for a transcendent, eternal reunion with his beloved only at the very moment he accepts the inevitable fact of their physical separation, his return to the hermitage, and life in solitude.

> Between now and then I will obey my nurse as best I can. I have got some barrels of fresh water (there has been no rain, and this water is actually *clean*). The hermitage is relatively sanitary. I killed a wasp in the bedroom and sprayed it with a bug bomb.[6]

As these words reveal, Thomas Merton, the ordinary man with extraordinary vision, remained grounded in the present moment of embodied conscious human being. He ended his diary for M with this Zen-like statement: "And I washed my feet good, and cut my toenails straight." Such seemingly dismissive words don't even approach the range of thought and emotion either he or M had experienced, but they do acknowledge the circumstance in which contradiction embraced them both.

In his *Letters to a Young Poet* Rilke underscores this intimate yet paradoxical interweaving of solitude, love, and human being that we will return to explore in chapter 7:

> For one human being to love another: that is perhaps the most difficult of all our tasks, the ultimate, the last test and proof, the work for which all other work is but preparation. For this reason young people, who are beginners in everything, cannot yet know love: they have to learn it.... But learning-time is always long, secluded time, and so loving, for a long while ahead and far on into life, is—solitude, intensified and deepened loneness for him who loves.[7]

The apostle Paul's words remind us that leaving behind our childish ways precedes the potential for our awakening recognition: mortal contradiction is the veil we are invited to look through. In doing so we may discover for ourselves the "sacred open secret" that gives meaning to the words "faith, hope, and love," with love being the greatest among them.[8]

Absence Within Presence

On our path toward the threshold of love, that veil may now take further shape in the paintings of Piet Mondrian. The artist's own intense lifelong attention to contradiction offers another encounter with Simone Weil's *grace* and the "loosening" we might all wish to share.[9]

See, look at, take in . . .

(5.2) Piet Mondrian, *Geinrust Farm in a Watery Landscape,* ca. 1905–06

Notice first: the rectangular format; the warm and cool tones in watercolor applied with pastel and crayon to white paper. See forms physically present as marks comparable to Rembrandt's yellow and white painted brushstrokes.

Second: trees . . . a field . . . water . . . two buildings . . . all pictorially present as an "image" of a farm in a watery landscape.

Soften your gaze. Enter the interval between these two contradictory realities ("brushstroke" and "image") by allowing the event of your experience of them to be present in your awareness.

Hold the contradictory warm/cool colors and values from high to low together in your perception. Let these physical forms and their discontinuous "image" exist together. Allow them to emerge, like Jenny's "green" in relation to "red," as "space" in relation to the flat surface of the paper, as a "place," a "moment"—as "light." Note how the implied complementary diagonals—one rising gradually from the lower left of the rectangle to the upper right and another rising chiasmally from the right to the left—expand the "image" beyond its edges: beyond the physical frame of the painted object.

Be there in this interval in which the white "light" of the distant sun, beyond the invisible horizon, spills forward through the silhouetted trees and into the watery landscape to become the fabric of the paper on which the artist left his name.

(5.3) *Geinrust Farm in a Watery Landscape,* ca. 1905–06, detail of signature
(5.2) *Geinrust Farm in a Watery Landscape,* ca. 1905–06

Do you feel the gentle, but palpable movement in (and of) the moment? Can you feel it suspended in the balanced horizontal and vertical components of the "image" . . . and focused very near, but not at, the crossing of the vertical center of the white paper and the horizon of the landscape? Let the leafing tree (or is it a plume of smoke?) to the left of the farm buildings, animate this very delicate asymmetrical balance.

Focus your attention on an emerging catalogue of contradictory realities: mark/image, geometric/organic, object/space, near/far; symmetry/asymmetry.

Allow an intimated reconciliation of these pictorial contradictions to appear so that the art of this work of art—watercolor, pastel, and crayon on paper—might begin to inform your direct experience . . .

Has ordinary white paper become the elusive presence of an infinite "whiteness," beyond all measurable color, brought home in the fading light of the day? Does evening now invite a new reverence for time and eternity, presence and absence? Do you see "green"?

Now, prepare to behold with another painting by Mondrian.

(5.4) Piet Mondrian, *Composition with Red, Yellow, Blue,* 1930

First: physical presence; red, yellow, blue, white, and black oil paint applied to canvas; horizontal and vertical lines.

Second: Is there an "image" here? Is there "space," a "place," a "moment," "light," as in *Geinrust Farm in a Watery Landscape*? Is there "movement"—a rising diagonal from lower left to upper right? Allow this "movement." Experience it. Are there also complementary "movements"? A smaller blue square expanding into a much larger red square? A "distant" yellow almost disappearing at the lower right? Balance, symmetry, asymmetry, contradictions? Measure them. Respond to them. Be present with them as you might have been present with the moment of the setting sun at the Geinrust Farm. Is this "image" any less real?

Our habitual contemporary bias tells us instantly that these two paintings are incommensurable. One is figurative: it is *realistic*. The other is nonfigurative: it is *abstract*. According to the logic of "modernist" thinking, one is more "advanced." Goethe was confronted with an established opposition—*classical*, although chronologically earlier, was considered superior to degenerate *Gothic*—and now we too are confronted by an opposition that obscures the art of both works of art.

> *Look again at both paintings. Allow and embrace the contradiction.*

(5.2) *Geinrust Farm in a Watery Landscape*
(5.4) *Composition with Red, Yellow, Blue*, 1930

Both works of art contain pigment and color values on a shaped support, nothing more—except for the interval we might enter between their material composition ("brushstrokes") and their "image." If we were to behold with these works of art rather than observe them from an objectifying distance, we might find ourselves approaching an affectingly consistent threshold. Imagine it like a riverbank rising between immutable "whiteness" and the self-aware, grounded presence of color, movement, change, and transformation: this threshold exists in the paintings and in ourselves.

Here our beholding with the art of each painting might draw us beyond our familiar response to fixed opposition—and, continuing the riverbank simile, imagine riparian zones that serve as interfaces between land and river—into a palpable realization of an experience approaching a "relativity of simultaneity." I understand "relativity of simultaneity" (a term from physics that I use here and elsewhere in the context of artistic beholding) to mean an overarching "presence" in which multiple frames of perceptual reference, and manifestly different and contradictory events within a cosmic reality can be realized—borrowing from Einstein—in the nearest approximation of infinity in the speed of light.

Yet, as different as these two paintings obviously are, they both approach a singular reality. The square format of *Composition with Red, Yellow, Blue* serves the same purpose as the evening twilight of *Geinrust Farm in a Watery Landscape*. They intimate the elusive "bridge" between the worldly and pictorial asymmetry of randomness and immutable perfection that allows the "whiteness" of infinity, beyond all change, to show through the subtle veil-like palimpsest of experience.

At this point, as we meditate on and contemplatively behold with these two paintings, we may ask ourselves whether a "loosening" has occurred in their apparent opposition as "figurative" and "nonfigurative" works of art. Can a larger awareness move from the familiar objectifying categories of so-called realism and abstraction toward a shared artistic and cognitive aspiration for intimated reconciliation?

Assuming such "loosening" has occurred, let's practice leading our vision through the physical presence of material realities to an unbounded wholeness.

> *Let go . . . let infinite variability become this singularity:* Composition with Red, Yellow, Blue. *Let time, change, and transformation give way to an openness, to completion beyond reach.*

Be present to the possibility that such beholding allows our "seeing" to be more richly embodied, so that a work of art as a discrete entity emerges instead as a phenomenal process. Its art and its being move ever toward but not closer to completion. In the language of beholding, this *intimation* as love the verb is an act approaching infinite love the noun: the beloved.

(Advance screen)

Detachment

The familiar frame of reference in the world, in which exclusive objectivity characterizes the things in it (and the ways it operates), would have us focus on the differences between these two paintings. This conventional view implies that the chronologically later one—*Composition with Red, Yellow, Blue*—is the more evolved accomplishment in the life of the artist. Such a view is consistent with the general conviction that the history of art itself evolves from figurative or representational form to nonfigurative or nonrepresentational form. These classifications overwhelm our direct experience of (and with) the artistic event: they give primacy to the "naming" and the "positioning" of the object of observation rather than to engaging directly with its particular relational sensation of color, line, and shape. In short, our habit privileges the ordering of all experience into fragmented parts that necessarily obscure their intimated reconciliation: their wholeness and their art.

But if we eschew objectification and allow multiple possibilities to exist simultaneously, our "vision" will become less clouded—our mirrors less dim, to invoke Paul once again—even as we open our presence to the practice of an art of illumined reconciliation. In this sense, to see and move beyond the superficial differences in these two works of art is to proceed toward that threshold of love where we seek to experience an active process, a living embodiment of intimated reconciliation arising in our detachment from self-centered separation.

Return for a moment to Geinrust Farm in a Watery Landscape . . .

(5.2) *Geinrust Farm in a Watery Landscape,* ca. 1905–06

As your gaze moves from left to right, right to left, top to bottom, and bottom to top, the "farm image" remains contained within a horizontal/vertical grid, while simultaneously expanding diagonally to the four corners of the paper support and beyond. But then . . . if you make a deliberate transition—if you focus your attention on distinction and difference to allow open awareness—a larger wholeness of integrated contradiction appears. Within this wholeness, movement and stillness are one, and centripetal closing and centrifugal opening are poised, held suspended in trembling balance. Near and far merge into a timeless place where horizontal grounding, vertical ascent and descent, along with diagonal possibility, all flow together in a singular stream of illuminated awareness that transcends the discrete content of the "image."

Hold this apparition of undying "light."

Now, shift your gaze back to Composition with Red, Yellow, Blue . . .

(5.4) *Composition with Red, Yellow, Blue,* 1930

Here, in this painting's extreme and apparent reduction of form to constituent parts, another instance of an intimated reconciliation emerges, this time in your perception of how the black horizontal and vertical lines of varying width—and red, yellow, blue, and white paint—form differently sized rectangles all precisely "positioned" within the field of the canvas. The dynamic relation of large and small rectangles, the presence of full intensity primary colors—both warm and cool, resonating with their absent but complementary secondary colors (full intensity and neutral)—and, above all, the very delicate asymmetrical tension between the physical center of the canvas and the implied "center" of the obliquely ascending red square, result in a vivid pairing of irreconcilable stability and change.

This formal choreography of *Composition with Red, Yellow, Blue*, we now see, is comparable to that of *Geinrust Farm in a Watery Landscape*. As we approach both paintings with Paul's "face to face" vision—in the self-aware process of our contemplative open awareness—each painting becomes a "whole" that is always greater by a factor of infinity than the sum of its parts.

Each work of art is now "alive" within our own presence, independent of its objectifying identification as "representational" or "nonrepresentational."

Attentively now, look . . .

(5.5) Piet Mondrian, *Blue Tree*, ca. 1908–09

The "image" here appears to be a tree—an object—set in illusory space. Starkly silhouetted against a background of blue sky, it rises from a field with a distant horizon that anchors a vivid landscape.

Look again, be open to new contradictions.

Can you now begin to see this painting differently? Allow it to become an event born in the inherent contradiction between identifiable physical objects in space—the image—and a complex gathering of sensations generated by watercolor paint on paper with particularly distinct brushstrokes, including drips of paint. Can you see both at once? Hold the contradiction. Let each exist so that you might enter into the measuring event between them. Let Mondrian guide you. Let him teach you and share with you his living embrace of contradiction.

(5.6) Piet Mondrian, *Gray Tree*, 1911

In this painting, by contrast, the so-called figure/ground opposition—the tree as an object distinct from its surrounding space—collapses visually. Compared to our first image of an isolated, distinctly silhouetted tree (image 5.5), what we see now moves toward pictorial abstraction—more brushstoke than image. As though to soften pictorial contradiction, Mondrian painted this work of art nearly monochromatically; he applied light to dark through middle values without preference to construct an image of value variation for its own sake. The tree, sky, and space—what some might choose to see only as components of the image—share equally in an event (the interaction of sensations) reminiscent of Goethe's "law of required change," or even of the physicist's "relativity of simultaneity." In either case, it is primarily the stark contradiction of variable light and dark values that Mondrian has suspended before you.[10]

This painting, called *Gray Tree*, pictorially represents the painter's experience of a moment of seeing in which values between the lightest light and darkest dark merge dynamically as contending primal realities made vivid in the noonday sun. Here, what is sometimes named "negative" space—everything that is "figuratively" non-tree—is perfectly positive from our vantage of contemplative perception. It is no less actual or palpable than the "tree" itself. In engaging with the pictorial event as a process of value interaction including intersection, overlapping, and juxtaposition, *Gray Tree* emerges in our direct experience more like a dance or a musical adagio. Reimagining this pictorial world as the embodiment of Mondrian's animated experience of contradictoriness—his embracing of living, form-giving contradiction—multiple frames of reference come to exist in relation simultaneously.

If we let this work of art reveal itself—this painting that is simultaneously a physical object (made of canvas and paint, ranging monochromatically from light to dark) and an "image" of a tree in space—then we will have entered the artistic "event" or interval. Within this interval irreconcilably contradictory realities exist separately, even as they are joined together in an elusive whole: canvas, paint, painting, image. From our position within the experience of this particular "relativity of simultaneity"—which is the art of this work of art—our ordinary objective "seeing" can once more become an act of *beholding with* a discontinuously immutable reality. Think of that reality as metaphorically analogous to the speed of light: always present, always the same, always approaching infinite wholeness.

Could it be the painter's contemporary equivalent of the physicist's famous thought experiments in relativity? If Einstein offered the world a conceptual mathematical path to this wholeness, Mondrian provides us with a vivid intimation of that wholeness, not at the speed of light, but in the slow, steady interrelationship of brushstroke and image. This interrelationship formulates a pictorial reality inviting us to behold with a vision that is equal parts presence and absence.

> *Look again at Mondrian's painting traditionally identified as* Blue Tree . . .

(5.5) *Blue Tree*, 1908–09

We might now notice that the "tree" is not simply blue. True, there is much blue pigment in this painting, but the "tree" is actually composed from several sweeping brushstrokes that appear to the eye as dark neutral blue-purple. A very rich pattern of other blues, applied in varying values from light to dark and opaque to transparent paint, covers the sheet of paper.

The paper on which these swirling brushstrokes have been placed is a slightly neutralized and relatively light-value orange color. Orange is, of course, the color complement of blue. Recalling Jenny's color-value experience with red and green, we may look at the "blue" to see "orange" and the "orange" to see "blue," both simultaneously present and absent, yet joined in our perception. If we allow a "loosening" to occur in our fixed attention on chromatic contradiction, a remarkable new detachment from the ostensible subject of the painting will occur as its complementary colors, multiple values, and transparencies all begin to move with the animated rhythm of a lyrical dance.

> *As you might have "seen" green, now ease into this pictorial "event." Be liberated by it.*

What happened? All that is "not-tree" has almost ecstatically, if not miraculously, become warm and cool, orange and blue, shimmering, sparkling "light," its brightness measured by the brooding darkness of the blue-purple tree paired in our immanent memory with an absent, but undying yellow. From the perspective of contemplative knowing then, this painting is nothing if not a moment of extraordinarily intense and vibrant emerging sunlight that must be both seen and felt.

We must be there, present with Piet Mondrian as he saw and felt it—not in the Dutch landscape in time and place, but in the artistic imagination and action that was capable of realizing a fleeting and now absent moment in such a way that it was nevertheless still present to immediate experience. This painting is not—at least its art is not—an objective re-creation of a past event or distant reality. It is, insofar as we engage with it, an ongoing, shared experience of expanding light beyond diminishment: infinite light . . . *lux aeterna* . . . the promise of unfading eternal light that illuminates the morning.

Again, be still . . . look . . .

(5.7) Piet Mondrian, *Red Tree*, 1908

Engaging with Piet Mondrian's contemplative "measuring," by experiencing contradiction with him and by sharing his being in the world, you will have become implicated in a universal "relativity of simultaneity."

The painting now before you will no longer be just another silhouetted tree, another "figurative" image. Seen through the hard-won veil of art and contemplative knowing, this painting as an object becomes an endless event occurring in the very experience of your being. For a beholder it is another animated embodiment of a moment lifted out of self-limiting time and space to become its own event. In this painting the event occurs in the form of still another dance between blue and a slightly asymmetrical complement of red/orange, in which fragile "light" again becomes palpable in the pulsating "image" of a lonely tree. Objectively, this tree is identical to the trees in Mondrian's *Blue Tree* and *Gray Tree* paintings. The difference is the time of day. Morning and noon have passed into evening.

What you might have previously thought was a solid tree set against a blue background is actually diffuse, broken up, fragmented into countless shards of paint. Conversely, what you took naturally to be diffuse—the light and air—are as solid and real as the very paint seen face to face, no longer through clouded vision, but with your awakened eyes. The "event" (the interval) into whose thrall you have wandered is the transitional twilight between the day and the night. You, like the tree, are enveloped by this twilight, suffused with it. Like the tree, you are informed and perhaps transformed by it.

Interlude 1

If you doubt your potential to identify with the tree, you might for a moment step back in time. In the so-called middle ages of our past history, when contemplative knowing was as natural as sunlight, and before exclusive rationality took away our childlike wonderment and mystery, evening was called vespers (from the Latin: *vesper*, the evening star). The canonical Hour of Vespers, unlike the factory bell sounding out the mechanical clock-time that rules our lives, was a focused moment of attentive prayer, called Vesper Prayer, tied to the setting of the sun. It preceded the Hour of Compline—completion—the time of night and sleep. This moment, realized here in the very paint of *Red Tree*, embraced the passing of the day, the turn to darkness, and the eternal promise of a new day—and by any other name, rebirth in the morning at the first Hour of Matins.

This painting named *Red Tree*, when seen through artistic and contemplative eyes, is less a tree than a vesper prayer enacted with and within you. You only have to "put childish ways" behind you—like the exclusive objectification of all things accompanied by the resulting disembodiment of art—and allow a magical "relativity of simultaneity" to exist before you and in you. From the perspective of contemplative knowing, all you need to do is embrace the contradiction of painted "brushstrokes" and their discontinuous "image." Let them be. Join with them. Be in their thrall. Fall in love.

Try to imagine yourself alone with these paintings, one by one, in their home where they are preserved. Be still. Be silent. Let them open to you. Allow yourself to be open to them. Wait. Be in the embrace of their most fragile art. Remember, when you blink, all will be gone. The material world will be as it was, except that you will be changed ever so slightly in the direction of the immutable white light whence you came.

(5.8) *Red Tree*, 1908, in situ

(Advance screen)

And so, our journey now proceeds along the path Piet Mondrian blazed. We have seen how varied, but equally powerful moments—human relational events—constructed by the now-absent artist for himself and for us, take shape in our own experience, doing so by and with their art.

> *Learn to share Mondrian's living contradiction. Measure the inexplicable realities that lie beneath and beyond the "childish" objectification of all things. Let presence and absence coexist so that Piet Mondrian might be present here, now.*

We may also think of the following works of art by Mondrian as prayers, just as Albert Einstein's roughly contemporaneous $E = mc^2$ may be as much cosmic prayer as it is primal physics.

(5.9) Piet Mondrian, *Flowering Trees,* 1912

In this painting, organic transformation, bound up in an implied horizontal and vertical grid, fragments into the shards of a stained-glass window animated by a whitening crescendo of brightness emerging from luminous shadow. Like new blossoms in the spring air, pictorial expansion and value lightening become the rising "light" that would animate promise, birth, and growth.

> *Ask yourself: Is this painting another prayer? Does a spiritual "relativity of simultaneity" exist here as the subtlest transforming variation of complementary yellow and violet-purple paint?*

It really is as simple as this. Can you imagine approaching "the speed of light" again? The name of this painting is *Flowering Trees*, but its art is the undying reality of absolute renewal.

(5.10) Piet Mondrian, *Flowering Apple Tree,* 1912

Now engage with this painting, titled *Flowering Apple Tree*, where vivid white with a shimmering leaf-like overlay of yellow and violet-purple, reminiscent of medieval incarnations of divinity, are interlaced with the bluish green of cool, fresh celestial air. Feel the "presence" of contradictory human mortality and divinity embodied in the paradisal fruit of conscious awareness, which is germinating and expanding before you.

(5.11) Piet Mondrian, *Composition No. 2,* 1913

Release yourself once again from the habitual constraints of noisy explanation, discursive interpretation, and rational analysis. As you respond to image 5.11, can you allow yourself to be intently, deliberately attentive, and completely open, even vulnerable, to the relational simultaneity this painting offers? Piet Mondrian named this work of art simply *Composition No. 2*. Will you allow yourself to be drawn into its longing as it reaches from relations of sharp focus at the center toward limitless "presence" at the periphery? Will you share in its awe, its mystery, its silence, while the "image"—except for the artist's name, written in the lower right corner—disappears from view at the four edges of the canvas so that continuous finiteness and infinity might at last be joined in artistic aspiration, Mondrian's and our own?

Enter the contemplative interval that would intimate reconciliation within irreconcilable contradiction. If this seems too difficult, David Bohm, a physicist renowned for his unorthodox contributions to quantum theory, offers these words: "The analysis of the world into its constituent objects has been replaced by its analysis in terms of events, processes."[11] Ernst Mach, the physicist whose name was given to the speed of sound, came to a similar conclusion a half century earlier: "No things [exist] in themselves, rather only complexes of sensations."[12] Might then even such scientific "analysis" now give way to alert, truly human, contemplative being in the world—to being in relation together?

(5.12) Piet Mondrian, *Composition with Red, Yellow, Blue*, 1937–42

Listen to the sound of your voice as you speak or silently say the name of this painting: *Composition with Red, Yellow, Blue*. In the act of beholding, the words, the image, and the work itself are all manifestly the same thing. Engage objectively with the constituent parts of this particular complex of sensations: red . . . yellow . . . blue . . . black . . . white . . . horizontal . . . vertical . . . varied rectangular shapes within a nearly square format. All are "joined" in relation simultaneously with binary "meaning" (by which I mean *this, that*) and trinary "measuring" (*this, that*, and *everything else*, including implicit diagonal form and movement, and absent "secondary" colors of green, purple, orange).

> *Allow an artistic interval to open before you. Let each discrete color become the triangulated interval for the other two "primary" and "secondary" colors.*
>
> *Think of the color-value chart from chapter 2 (image 2.5), where red joins triangularly with yellow and blue; yellow with red and blue; blue with red and yellow; so too with green, purple, and orange, even as horizontal, vertical, diagonal, black, and white pulsate together like a beating heart, just as you are breathing in . . . out . . . in . . .*

In the art of these works of art, it's as though Mondrian had seized hold of space/time and sought to engage them, measure them, live them, breathe with them, contemplate with their infinite mutual sensation and unalterable reality, consistent with the laws of physics. Although vividly and precisely ordered, as though fixed forever, this "image" is also simultaneously random, idiosyncratic: alive—like you!

It is a remarkable fact that Mondrian's paintings, despite their apparent simplicity, are, I understand, immune to faking. Not because they are hard physically to paint, but because they are impossible to duplicate as, notwithstanding cloning, you are. Piet Mondrian's paintings—as "complexes of sensations" (events) that he lived—are manifestations of his own unalterably unique being, his *genius*, and are simultaneously related to everyone and everything else that makes up wholeness, of which we are all a part.

From the vantage point of our humble, respectful beholding with the artist, Mondrian's paintings emerge as particular realizations of his devoted search for variation within the immutable condition—"the speed of light"—of our enduring existence. His "sensations," incarnated in his art, embody the very intersection of finite and infinite reality resonating in the presence and absence of our mortal and immortal experience of human being. *Composition with Red, Yellow, Blue* (1937–42), in London's Tate Museum, is but one of an infinite number of potential arrangements of red, yellow, blue—implicitly paired with the equally elusive shimmering presence of the absent green, purple, orange—as well as horizontal and vertical, also paired with their innumerable diagonals, not to mention black and white, with endless discrete values in between.

Interlude 2

Although this particular formulation apparently came later as rationalist critique, the scholastic goal of the question, "How many angels can dance on the head of a pin" was to touch the intersection between finite and infinite realities. How many angels, indeed. The post-medieval world of Renaissance and Enlightenment rationalism rejected this quest as irrational and hence ridiculous. Gustave Courbet, in the positivist France of the nineteenth century, articulated a "Realist" manifesto in these challenging words: "Show me an angel and I'll paint one." No wonder he never did.[13]

But what if we suspend Courbet's disbelief? If we were willing to look again contemplatively and behold with Mondrian's art, we might rediscover with him that elusive, even angelic, interval that pilgrims of an earlier time honored within their contemplative imaginations. From this point of view,

Mondrian's artistic life might be seen as a similar attempt to "count angels" dancing on the head of a pin.

(5.13) Piet Mondrian, *Composition No. 11, 1940–42—London with Blue, Red, and Yellow*, 1940–42

Like the Tate *Composition with Red, Yellow, Blue* (1937–42), Mondrian painted *Composition No. 11, 1940–42—London with Blue, Red, and Yellow* during World War II. With the brutal chaos of that time, the world witnessed the disintegration of what some had understood to be the cosmic order of society. Can we imagine contemplatively that for this expat Dutch artist living far from Europe, the war was a most compelling occasion to "count angels"—to rediscover infinite wholeness in the face of disintegration and virtual despair?

Consider "red," not as a conceptual category, but as a primal experience. Similarly, "blue" and "yellow." With awakened eyes, see through the veil of the object: its canvas, its paint. Be open to receive the embrace of the relational mystery they embody. Ask yourself: Where does this exceptionally calibrated ("ordered") moment merge silently with eternity? Repeat, as if they were a prayer, the words *red, yellow, blue, horizontal, vertical, black, white*. Do so, however, not as if they were a constituent reality, but rather another incarnated dance of finite and infinite wholeness.

Together, these paintings (images 5.12 and 5.13) are like two human figures; remarkably similar and distinct, as you and I are humanly similar, and also absolutely unique: two solitudes within the infinity of our being. Think of Ernst Mach again: "No things in themselves, rather only complexes of sensations"—like each of us at some level, perhaps.

For the determined materialists among us—those of us who are convinced that the whole really is a sum of its parts and still cling to calculable constituent reality—here are those parts:

(5.14) Graphic: red, yellow, blue, black, white, horizontal, vertical

And now . . .

(5.4) *Composition with Red, Yellow, Blue*, 1930

Here they are again, uniquely interrelated as *Composition with Red, Yellow, Blue*, informed by Thoreau's "poetic or divine life" as art: dancing before us as though on the head of a pin, angels affirming a "higher life than we fell asleep from." Within their now-visible celestial realm, the diagonally rising "red" measures the "blue" anchored at the lower left, while "yellow" almost disappears from sight.

Attend quietly to this next painting.

(5.15) Piet Mondrian, *Composition No. II with Red and Blue*, 1925 (original date 1929): a. without frame; b. with frame

Soften your eyes. Be present. Wait. Engage. Respond. "Measure."
In a word, "live" this "complex of sensations," this particular "relativity of simultaneity." Do you see visible and invisible angels?

Repeat to yourself or aloud the prayer or mantra:
horizontal . . . vertical . . . black . . . white . . . red . . . blue . . .

Enter the sacral intervals of this stationary image, which is both absolutely stable and at the same time moving at the speed of light: ride the beam of artistic light.

Now rest in the silence, in open awareness, waiting.
Slowly and gently close your eyes.

Say "yellow." Do you see the invisible yet implicated "yellow" of the primary chromatic triangle? Isn't this absent "yellow" now as vividly present as the next note on the other side of silence in a phrase of music? As "green" echoes "red" in your meditative eye, pulsating before you? As real as dancing angels are real?

(5.16) Piet Mondrian, *Composition 12 with Blue*, 1936–42, with red initials and date indicated

*Again, with image 5.16, repeat as a prayer or mantra this pictorial realization of a "poetic or divine life": black . . . white . . . horizontal . . . vertical . . . blue . . . red . . . **yellow** . . .*

Let the absent "presence" of *yellow* join the accumulating angels as you count slowly, openly. Allow the angelic dance to be visible to you . . .

This painting is nearly a square; itself a geometric reconciliation of the infinitely variable dimensions of rectangles. Do you behold with *yellow* in

Composition 12 with Blue? Do you behold with wholeness beyond the veil of incarnated color, with infinite implied diagonals?

(5.17) Piet Mondrian, *Composition No. 9*, 1939–42

Vary the absent presence: this time allow blue to appear before you. Repeat

horizontal . . . vertical . . . black . . . white . . . red . . . yellow . . . ***blue*** *. . .*

Now allow . . . absolute presence within absence . . .

(Advance screen)

"Tarry a While! You Are So Fair!"

Approach the next work of art as if it truly were absolute simplicity on the farthest side of complexity—almost a painted equivalent of $E = mc^2$. . .

(5.18) Piet Mondrian, *Composition with Blue (Schilderij No. 1)*, 1926, precisely 84.9 cm. square

Now count these angels:
horizontal . . . vertical . . . black . . . white . . .

What has happened? What is the "sensation"? Two black lines, set asymmetrically on a field of white paint and suspended within a square format raised forty-five degrees above grounded horizontality, remain poised as the interval between movement and stillness.

Continue counting angels.

(5.19) *Composition with Blue (Schilderij No. 1)*, 1926, detail with initials "PM" and date "26"

Open yourself to colors—blue in the precise triangle at the intersecting lines, and red in the signature letters "PM" and the date "26" nearby on the horizontal line—and let these colors animate this silent prayer and open its threshold epiphany: blue . . . PM 26 in red . . . ***yellow*** *. . .*

(5.18) *Composition with Blue (Schilderij No. 1)*, 1926

In *Composition with Blue* (image 5.18), a broad ground of white pigment becomes, in our perception (our beholding), the absent yellow that completes the primary triad of red-yellow-blue as the chromatic, pictorial bridge to infinite wholeness. Goethe called this "Heavenly Beauty" the "mediatrix between gods and men." At the time of its first exhibition, Mondrian named this assembly of "angels" *Schilderij No.1* (Painting No. 1) as though it were the origin of his beholding.[14]

> *As you engage with this transforming moment, allow an invisible presence to appear, expand outward to the periphery of the object and then disappear in the surrounding darkness.*

In our contemplative beholding with the art of this work of art, our relation with ourselves, each other, and the world may now include a fleeting vision of infinite reality beyond all variation: reality beyond all contradiction where white, black, red, yellow, blue are one. Here all color, all value—lightest to darkest—become indistinguishable and interchangeable at the speed of light. Here in this place, in this moment, earthbound *lumen* gives way to the whiteness of *lux aeterna*: gravity gives way to grace.

> *Do you doubt your unbiased, open response to this painting? Has something happened? Did change occur in the blink of an innocent eye? Do you doubt you have reached the speed of light?*

Ask yourself: Is space embodied in this square, apparently flat, painting—space rotated, raised up, elevated, even sublimated? How far do those black painted lines extend past the frame, this particular "frame of reference"? Imagine a grid pattern enlarged beyond all grasping. Pick one right-angled intersection. Hold this immediately finite, tangible, and almost measurable reality in your eye, mind, and body, even as you also reach out for its colossal outer limit.

Now notice, with very gentle, steady, virtually prayerful attentiveness, that the horizontal black line is slightly broader than the vertical black line. Consequently, we might perceive this horizontal line as perceptually closer than the vertical line. In fact, it lies physically behind the vertical line, which is painted directly over it (image 5.19). Mondrian painted the red initials "PM" and the date "26" on this, the larger and more "distant" line, perhaps to place himself (in space and time) within infinite wholeness.

(Advance screen)

How deep is the "space"? Can you measure it? Enter it? Remember your own common experience of the night sky, which has no perceivable depth. The "stars" all appear, as they have since the beginning of human experience, as though they exist in a single domed plane, arching over us to form what used to be called the "dome of heaven." Each "star" does seem to be equidistant. Some are larger; some brighter, but all are perceptually equidistant. As we all now know conceptually, of course, some of these "stars" are not "stars" at all. Some are planets; some are moons; some are suns. They are also separated in space by many multiples of the distance light travels, at the speed of 186,000 miles every second, to a number beyond our counting. Being clearly well beyond our human sight, this "space," like every other perceptual discontinuity we experience, remains unreal except for our capacity to engage trans-perceptual vision beyond the limits of finite measurement, which by any other name is beholding, whether mathematical or pictorial.[15]

Reflection 1

Now let's return to Mondrian's irreducible prayer in paint, a surpassing work of pictorial art, at once so simple, so complex, and so mysterious: *Composition with Blue.*

(5.18) *Composition with Blue (Schilderij No. 1)*, 1926

By animating the elusive connection that unites "red" and "blue" (present in material paint) with visibly absent "yellow," the interval between material and trans-material realities emerges slowly within the threshold of patient contemplation:

First: notice how the fixed, rational positioning of horizontal and vertical resonates with endlessly variable nonrational diagonality in the rotated canvas.

Second: notice how proximity and immeasurable distance appear in the delicate physical change in the width of the two black painted lines—"brushstrokes"—as they echo the silence of the discontinuous image within the planar singularity of vastly separated "stars."

Third: notice how the veil of paint and canvas opens toward an undiminished whiteness of light comparable to what we "saw" of the setting sun in *Geinrust Farm in a Watery Landscape* (image 5.2), measured by the imminent darkness of the night and the coming of the dawn.

Fourth: enter into the thrall of a life-affirming art; embrace it as an utterly nonecclesiastical and nonreligious, purely human and spiritual instance of "that poetic or divine life" to which we have been challenged to awaken and which here almost echoes the words:

> I am the resurrection, and the life. Those who believe in me, even though they die, will live, and everyone who lives and believes in me will never die. Do you believe this?" (John 11:25–26)

Thus, in fullest contemplative awareness, the tangible presence of this work of art merges perceptibly into infinite wholeness, even as the painted lines converge and expand asymmetrically. As if speaking directly with you, the beholder, Mondrian signed this product of his art at this intersection of two discontinuous solitudes. And in naming it *Painting No. 1* he may have invoked Martin Buber's concept of primal relation regarding I and You: the conscious awakening to the indissoluble "oneness" of all being. Imagine this painting as if it were the "first one" reaching back to the very core and moment of our conscious human awareness and being—and recalling for us all, if you will, Milo's lament and these words of Albert Einstein.

> The most beautiful experience we can have is the mysterious. It is the fundamental emotion that stands at the *cradle* of true art and true science. Whoever does not know it and can no longer wonder, no longer marvel, is as good as dead, and his eyes are dimmed.[16]

(Advance screen)

Reflection 2

What would it be like to experience yourself, those around you, and the world through deliberate and disciplined contemplation?

(5.20) Piet Mondrian, *Farm near Duivendrecht*, ca. 1916

Mondrian painted *Farm near Duivendrecht* at the threshold of the twentieth century. Encountering it now, at the beginning of the twenty-first, we may wish to tarry a while, to behold with its fair beauty: to behold with it as an intimation of an evening before the dawn of an era that would witness a near transformation of all preceding history, including Albert Einstein's cosmic awakening vision of time, space, mass, and energy.

The unusually bright lingering light of this sunset suspends the farmhouse here as it did in *Geinrust Farm in a Watery Landscape* (image 5.2) as if it were another solitude surrounded by the endless contradiction of its self-aware presence. Like so many of Mondrian's images of solitary objects—single flowers, windmills, piers reaching into the ocean—this painting prepares the way for a path into an art of contemplative beholding and the radical questions it entails: What is real? What is reflection? What is paint? Image? Light? What are horizontal, vertical, diagonal? Standing? Sleeping? Here? There? Then? Now?

As you imagine living these questions of our shared existence, allow your own sensations of being and self-awareness to intersect with those of Mondrian and the world around you. Is it possible that this painting is offered to you, the beholder, as an explicit act of ancient faith, hope, and love, an act that would leap the infinite gap of discontinuity at the center of all our questions, born within the realm of our conscious separation and longing? Does this luminous painting embody Piet Mondrian's most devoted search for intimated reconciliation within our acknowledged mortal human condition? Is *Farm near Duivendrecht* another vesper prayer? As you *behold* in stillness and silence, can you hear Milo's lament?

Journey Toward Wholeness

(5.21) Piet Mondrian, a. *Self Portrait,* 1900;
b. *Self Portrait,* 1918

Of the two side-by-side self-portraits, Mondrian painted the first (on the left) when he was twenty-eight and the second (on the right) at forty-six. The portrait of the young artist embodies heated presence in the moment. The huge, wide dark eyes are open, alert, receiving, and vulnerable. Pictorial color combines warm neutralized red, intensified and focused in the lips, with areas of equally warm green, as though this youthful image were an anticipatory event of potentially full chroma red and—if you are willing and able—green (!) and blue, orange, violet, yellow, as well as the infinite range of other manifestations of warm and cool perception that animate our living from infancy to death.

By contrast in the second self-portrait, the artist turns to observe himself, his work, the world, and, presumably, also us—all in the focused attention of purposeful reflection. Where the first portrait seems to embody the chromatic equivalent of eros, the second renders visible in its color neutrality our complementary capacity for thoughtful insight. It is as if these two portraits, like Rembrandt's own youthful confrontation of subject and object (images 3.43 and 3.44), seek to bring "warm" and "cool" together in our human journey toward wholeness.

Two late magisterial works of art bring our meditation with Piet Mondrian to a close: *Broadway Boogie-Woogie* (1942–43) and *Victory Boogie-Woogie* (1942–44).

(5.22) Piet Mondrian, a. *Broadway Boogie-Woogie*, 1942–43;
b. *Victory Boogie-Woogie,* 1942–44

From one perspective, these paintings reiterate the integral mutuality of the two self-portraits (*Broadway Boogie-Woogie* corresponds to the later portrait and *Victory Boogie-Woogie* to the earlier). They also echo remarkably the contradictory realities—subjective presence and objective absence—we found in the photographs of *Earthrise* and *Earth from Space* (images 2.11 and 2.10). Seen together they return us to Paul's admonition to leave behind "childish ways" so that we might come "face to face" with our being.

In beholding with these two paintings from the end of Mondrian's life's work, we encounter the full spectrum of separation and longing—fullest eros and fullest insight—merging into a single elusive realization, not only of faith and hope, but of a muscular love that offers the only alternative to the sobering recognition that "killing is a form of our wandering mourning?"

(5.23) Piet Mondrian, *Broadway Boogie-Woogie*

The first obstacle ("killing") to our beholding with *Broadway Boogie-Woogie* is its well-known celebrity within our culture of objectification. This painting is one of the "stars" on display in the renovated Museum of Modern Art. Without a deliberate effort to resist, a casual visitor will be led into an amazingly forceful response of hurried recognition and observation bordering on artistic entertainment, if not voyeurism. The pervasive mall-like atmosphere of this usually crowded and frenetic museum diminishes the necessary environment of quiet, slow, and reflective—even reverent—presence that beholding requires. The second obstacle, ironically related to the first, is the title itself and the ostensible content of the painting that easily divert our attention from its art and toward all manner of free association, such as the well-known grid pattern of city streets, the ubiquitous presence of imagined "yellow cabs" darting from here to there, all of it informing an image of urban bustle, analogous to the syncopated rhythms of jazz and the boogie-woogie dance so popular when Mondrian lived in New York.

To begin beholding with *Broadway Boogie-Woogie*, we might imagine the painting in a different setting, one in which its particular formal presence would be less harshly isolated in the unrelieved stark white wall space of the contemporary museum. Mondrian himself, we are told, actually "softened" the otherwise nearly immaculate world he worked in by allowing an occasional flower, or colored panels suspended from the walls, to decorate his studio. This is how Charmion von Wiegand, an artist/journalist friend of Mondrian, who also helped him translate his essays into English, described his studio in New York studio:

> Everything was spotless white, like a laboratory. In a light smock, with his clean-shaven face, taciturn, wearing his heavy glasses, Mondrian seemed more a scientist or priest than an artist. The only relief to all the white were large mat-boards, rectangles in yellow, red, and blue, hung in asymmetric arrangements on all the walls. Peering at me through his glasses, he noticed my glance and said: "I've arranged these to make it more cheerful."[17]

In his Paris studio, Mondrian had used flowers to make it more cheerful: one tulip in a vase, an artificial one, its leaves painted white.

> *So, try re-situating Broadway Boogie-Woogie in your mind into a "more cheerful" environment that will allow its art to inform your contemplative encounter.*
>
> *Be still. Be silent. Look without thinking. Be present. Allow contradictoriness. Slowly, allow the fragile potential of intimated reconciliation to reveal itself.*
>
> *Wait for "green" to appear . . .*
>
> *With Goethe, allow for the obverse . . .*

Look again at (5.20). Mondrian's focus on the triad red-yellow-blue need not discount green-violet-orange, notwithstanding his own seeming disaffection for green.

(5.20) *Farm near Duivendrecht*, ca. 1916

Even so, the art critic David Sylvester speculated:

> As Mondrian was probably incapable of irony, the tulip was unlikely to be a wry joke about his having had to produce flower pieces between 1922 and 1925 when he no longer wanted to

> because there were no buyers for his abstracts. It could, of course, have been a revenge for the agony a compromise of that sort must have cost him. More likely, it was simply a part of the general revulsion against green and growth, which made him, when seated at a table beside a window through which trees were visible to him, persuade someone to change places.[18]

(5.23) Piet Mondrian, *Broadway Boogie-Woogie*

Now, as you behold with *Broadway Boogie-Woogie*, a deeper reality may emerge in the spiritual intensity of Mondrian's art. The story about his turning away from green recalls Thomas à Kempis's sobering insight that the closer the devoted pilgrim approaches the goal (whether God or infinite wholeness) the greater the pain of separation. Rather than an arbitrary rejection of green, violet, and orange, Mondrian's nearly absolute focus on red, yellow, and blue virtually confirms their complementary absent presence as we recall yet again Milo's lament of separation and endless longing.

Thinking back to chapter 3 and our first encounter with Rembrandt's *Aristotle with a Bust of Homer*, we may begin by focusing our attention on paint. Let's look at a precisely defined square and two horizontal rectangles composed of carefully blended brushstrokes of yellow and gray paint in an area near the center of *Broadway Boogie-Woogie*.[19]

(5.24) *Broadway Boogie-Woogie*, detail, yellow and gray paint

As color (hue), these two applications of paint form vividly distinct shapes: one gray (or you could describe it as very light neutral violet) and the other yellow (the color complement of violet). As value, however, this chromatic distinction fades into a single relatively light monochromatic vertical rectangle. To see this color-value distinction, squint your eyes gently until hue difference slowly fades into common value.

From one vantage point—hue—multiple rectangles are distinct. From another—value—they lose their separation, even as this distinct "rectangle," just left of center in the painting (image 5.23), opens upward to form yet another yellow and gray pictorial "alliance" with the horizontal axis.

(5.23) *Broadway Boogie-Woogie*

Here it becomes the obverse partner of hue distinction, veil-like, across the entire image. Hence, in our direct experience of a single focused pictorial event—yellow and gray (or neutral violet) together—the two contradicting but overlapping realities (hue and value) exist simultaneously within a larger perceptual whole. Taken together, they combine to create an image of active geometric and chromatic vibration, including the "absent" partner of less than full hue intensity.

From this attentiveness to one detail of the material fabric of *Broadway Boogie-Woogie* and its generative pictorial presence, we may proceed further into Mondrian's artistic event. Without the distraction of the title or imagined narrative content, enter into the elusive interval between material "brushstrokes" and their discontinuous "image," in which the art of this work of art emerges.

In this painting, Mondrian's familiar black horizontal and vertical lines enclosing variable rectangles of white, and various combinations of red, yellow, and blue have evolved into an overall shifting pattern that is simultaneously present and "absent" depending on our momentary focus. Rectangular shapes coalesce perceptually into lines, yet they remain separate. As color and value, they appear relatively light and dark, distinct and blended, pulsating and stable, random and ordered, symmetrical and asymmetrical. Our embrace of these animated pictorial contradictions within the pattern of shimmering "lines," "colors," and "values" must approach the direct experience of éros pur—that is, our innate reconciliatory longing—tentatively and momentarily suspended within the ordered square format and frame of the painting. The contemplative art of this exceptionally rich work of art is perceptually incarnated as a primal energy of coexistent multiplicity and unity—and that energy is palpable, perhaps, as a universal dance of life, recalling the transcendent reality present in Bosch's *Garden of Earthly Delights*.

Piet Mondrian named *Broadway Boogie-Woogie* so suggestively, presumably drawing on the syncopated order and randomness of urban life manifest in the music and movement he found in his adopted home of New York. The "local" title does not diminish the universal transcendence of this painting. It is artistically plausible that Mondrian's purpose in the very act of painting, and perhaps in his written theory, was to underscore the necessary gap between "brushstroke" (paint) and "image" that would preserve the infinite silence of a hard-won art. Surrounded by the noise of the rationalized debate over so-called figurative and nonfigurative works of art that dominated the first half of the twentieth century, Mondrian's own artistic manifesto appears to reach beyond the false choice imposed on the essential abstraction of all art.

In his embrace of a trans-rational vision of discontinuous reality, Mondrian's passion was to approach in material paint the "face to face" presence of an "absent" infinite wholeness. In this daring, his art may well be the mirror of Jan Vermeer's earlier anti-iconoclastic wager with God. That is, his conviction that faithful artistic intimation of wholeness would redeem his creation of "graven images," proscribed in the second of the Ten Commandments that appear twice in the Old Testament (Exodus 20:4 KJV, Deuteronomy 5:8 KJV).[20] A fuller contemplative encounter with *Broadway Boogie-Woogie*, however, requires another step of measuring its art with that of *Victory Boogie-Woogie*.

(5.25) Piet Mondrian, *Victory Boogie-Woogie*

Victory Boogie-Woogie occupied Piet Mondrian during the time he completed *Broadway Boogie-Woogie*, but it remained unfinished at the time of his death in 1944. Its art embodies the identical longing that imbues his life's work and his devoted acts of contemplative knowing—a virtually prayerful progress toward an unattainable but visible goal. As a painting realized in the ecstatic ascent of human aspiration, *Victory Boogie-Woogie* closes our meditation with Piet Mondrian as the necessary partner of *Broadway Boogie-Woogie*. Even though its name cannot be attributed directly to the artist himself, the face of "victory" is everywhere present in this most unusual work of art.

The physical components of *Victory Boogie-Woogie* are oil paint, pieces of cut paper, plastic tape, and black charcoal on canvas. The support is square (127 x 127 cm), identical to *Broadway Boogie-Woogie* (127 x 127 cm). Unlike *Broadway Boogie-Woogie*, however, the "square" canvas of *Victory Boogie-Woogie* has been rotated forty-five degrees with a vertical axis of 179 centimeters. Although Mondrian once again transformed the black lines common to most of his geometric paintings into sequences of colored rectangles, in this instance the fragmenting rectangles are not all painted. Many are simply pieces of colored tape the artist has loosely applied here and there as though testing their visual and psychological effect within the composition before fixing their form in paint.

(5.26) *Victory Boogie-Woogie,* detail with pieces of added tape visible

Because Mondrian died suddenly before finishing *Victory Boogie-Woogie*, we can only speculate about what the completed work would have been. But he did leave behind the actual process of his method of deciding on the precise relationships of form, color, and value as though he had just a moment ago lifted his hand from his work to reflect.

Victory Boogie-Woogie is literally an ongoing emergent event of artistic intimation. It may remind us of the impression left by so many Dutch still-life paintings that someone in the room has just departed, leaving behind an immaculate array of presence in absence—moving beyond gravity and noise into sound and silence. Without anticipating what he might have decided next, we can look over the artist's shoulder (as in Vermeer's *Art of Painting* in Vienna) to become implicated in the unfolding of a dynamic asymmetrical movement radiating from the pair of white and yellow, nearly square, shapes at the intersecting horizontal and vertical axes of the raised diagonal image. Other than the clear suggestion of upward transformation, consistent with the tilting of the canvas, there is no discernable resolution within the image. It remains remarkably fluid, entirely in flux—still seeking.

We can now engage directly with both works of art (seen together in image 5.22), imagine them as a pair, and move still further into their artistic reality very much as Mondrian presumably did during the years when he divided his attention between them.

(5.22) a. *Broadway Boogie-Woogie*, 1942–43;
b. *Victory Boogie-Woogie*, 1942–44

Focus your attention on these two consummate works of art. Hold them side by side. Allow them to resonate together as partners engaged in a universal and timeless pas de deux. For all of their movement and, we may reasonably imagine, sound, there is a place of stillness and silence at the geometric center of each painting.

Be present here without thought . . . be open to this moment . . . be present in the irreducible primal reality they seem to embody. Breathe with them . . .

The precise geometric center of *Broadway Boogie-Woogie* is a white vertical rectangle, paired on the left with yellow and gray and on the right with areas of red, yellow and blue, separated by the narrow white rectangle.

(5.27) *Broadway Boogie-Woogie*, with one dotted circle at the geometric center (indicated by diagonal red lines and horizonal/vertical white lines) and a second dotted circle at the periphery of the canvas; both surround left and right color areas that flank the central white rectangle

Chromatically, the central white rectangle is unchanging. The others to the left and right are different. One, as we have seen, changes according to our perception: now yellow and gray; now all gray—all color, all value. The right-side area of paint, rather than merging color and value, opposes them. As though we had returned to the very origins of our evolving infantile perception, the physical and pictorial core of *Broadway Boogie-Woogie* embodies irreducible shifting "experience" and stabilized "order."

> *Be present with this familiar opposition. Embrace it across the interval of immutable whiteness, even as it radiates outward in every direction to the edge and frame of the painting. Allow contradictory dynamic movement to fill the interval between a stilled center and periphery.*

By comparison, the geometric center of *Victory Boogie-Woogie* occurs at the intersection of the vertical and horizontal axes of the painting in the asymmetrical pairing of two slightly different rectangles—one yellow and one white—that together form a horizontal rectangle in which color and value remain as the unchanging, unrelieved opposition of implacably obverse realities: *this* versus *that*. No squinting will relieve this color-value distinction or diminish their asymmetry.

(5.28) *Victory Boogie-Woogie*, detail of yellow and white painted rectangles

Two additional rectangles below the optical tension of this pair combine to form an implied square shape asymmetrically aligned with the vertical axis of the painting.

(5.29) *Victory Boogie-Woogie*, with horizontal and vertical axes and off-center square

In image 5.29 the focal area along the horizontal axis of the rotated square canvas overlaps another rectangle and animates an expanding asymmetrical energy that rises from the lower half of the painting toward an irregularly shaped culmination at its apex. The perceptual result resembles a compass-like magnetic north in relation to east, west, and south.

(5.30) *Victory Boogie-Woogie*, with horizontal and vertical axes and extended asymmetrical rectangle

Unlike *Broadway Boogie-Woogie,* where asymmetrically random movement is suspended between perfect symmetry at its center and periphery, *Victory Boogie-Woogie* realizes an obverse intimation of wholeness, reaching upward and outward through unrelieved asymmetry.

If we were to contemplate with these two works of art (seen together in image 5.22)—dancing as two discrete solitudes, joined by a singular impulse to wholeness—we might proceed still further into their art.

(5.22) a. *Broadway Boogie-Woogie,* 1942–43;
b. *Victory Boogie-Woogie,* 1942–44

Broadway Boogie-Woogie possesses a pulsating aura, generated at the heart of our human capacity for reflection. This animation is based in a perceived distinction between color (hue) and value. In this literally vital "image," the asymmetry of our conscious awareness finds tentative resolution in the grounded symmetry of the painting's square format and the unchanging luminosity of pure white paint at its irreducible center... until, of course, this momentary peace moves again, as it does in *Victory Boogie-Woogie,* to a dynamic asymmetry in which symmetrical bliss is caught up once more in a renewed ecstasy, and rises upward and outward in the centrifugal process of endless generation.

Undistracted by the noise that surrounds us, we may sense that the human aspiration of Mondrian's artistic beholding inherent to both paintings is nothing if not primal existential reality. Each painting in its own way resonates with our being by drawing us into our conscious presence as intensely and completely as any in the long history of art. Side by side, these intimately related paintings embody the living contradiction of "order" and "experience" at the core of our being.

Think once again of Rembrandt's *Aristotle with a Bust of Homer*, where the reconciliatory interval that merged the material brushstroke of scumbled yellow and white paint with the elusive image of "gold" in the philosopher's chain of honor may have seemed too much to grasp, too wide to cross, too tall to climb. In these two paintings, however, Mondrian has narrowed both the formal and ontological interval. His art has brought the irreconcilable obverse pictorial realities of brushstroke and image to a point of virtual unity, as though he had returned to the poised moment just prior to Milo's sobbing lament of separation and longing. In our effort to behold with Mondrian, we may have returned also.

And we are not alone. T. S. Eliot, at almost the same time and place as Mondrian, is there with us:

> At the still point of the turning world. Neither flesh nor fleshless; Neither from nor towards; at the still point, there the dance is, But neither arrest nor movement. And do not call it fixity, Where past

> and future are gathered. Neither movement from nor towards, Neither ascent nor decline. Except for the point, the still point, There would be no dance, and there is only the dance.[21]

On our path toward the threshold of love and the elusive interval between discontinuous realities, one nearly immovable obstacle still stands in our way. To proceed, we must be willing to confront, and then break, the law of the excluded middle. Again, on this path we are not alone. Nor are we limited only to voices of Western imagination. Our next meditation will occur in Kyoto, Japan, where we began our journey. By entering into a most unfamiliar realm of Japanese *ai-no-ma* we will discover yet another form of intimated reconciliation in a spatially spiritualized *pas de deux.*

Before moving on, pause once more to behold with Piet Mondrian in stillness and quiet . . .

(5.31) *Broadway Boogie-Woogie,* in situ
(5.32) *Victory Boogie-Woogie,* in situ

These two masterly works of art literally culminate Mondrian's career. Together, they embody the enduring dynamic contradictions that inform our conscious awareness of living and dying. Where *Broadway Boogie-Woogie* is eros contained by insight, *Victory Boogie-Woogie* is the insightful release of erotic impulse. In the interval of their art, the white paint of these two inextricably joined images becomes the undiminished "light" of intimated reconciliation, pressing through a veil of endlessly variable color to "carry us home."[22] From this contemplative vantage point, *Broadway Boogie-Woogie* and *Victory Boogie-Woogie* merge as Mondrian's faithful summation of our mortal separation and longing. So too, the "vesper light" in his early *Geinrust Farm in a Watery Landscape* (image 5.2) may now have the unexpected new vitality of a reconciliatory expectation of the dawn that anticipates eternal resurrection.

(5.2) *Geinrust Farm in a Watery Landscape,* ca. 1905–06

In this work of art, the artist's prominent signature remains as a nearby cenotaph of his enduring presence: Piet Mondrian, 1872–1944.

(Advance screen)

CHAPTER 6

Breaking the Law of the Excluded Middle: *Ai-no-ma*

> *In fact, our conception of physics itself, and even the principles of chemistry, would probably differ from that of Westerners; and the facts we are now taught concerning the nature and function of light, electricity, and atoms might well have presented themselves in different form.*
>
> —Jun'ichirō Tanizaki, *In Praise of Shadows*

EACH time we return for inspiration and guidance to Thoreau's sojourn at Walden Pond we remind ourselves of his purpose for going there: to break with his habitual behavior in Concord, even from his dependence on his teacher and friend Ralph Waldo Emerson. Leaving the familiar behind at a similar juncture of our journey, we now prepare to enter a foreign place of unanticipated discovery—in the full knowledge that, on our return, even the most familiar will have been changed.

> *Imagine, then, walking in Thoreau's "woods." After several hours of strenuous hiking, you grow tired. Your body weighs heavily on you. You are hungry and thirsty. There is no relief in sight. Your burdens seem unrelenting. Then you come to an opening in the trees.*

(6.1) View of Walden Pond with the location of Thoreau's cabin to the left of the rock cairn

The pile of stones on the left of this photograph identifies the site of Thoreau's cabin: his sanctuary. The pond ahead is immaculate, filled with clear, pure, cool water: something you had not expected, perhaps something the likes of which you have never seen before. What do you do? Stand back?

Become disoriented? Be fearful? Run home to Concord, where familiar food and rest await you? Will you cling to comfortable and reassuring habit or will you move slowly, gently, deliberately forward into the water, first only dipping your toes, and then carefully immersing yourself in the refreshing but still incomprehensible pond?

(6.2) Thoreau's Cove, Walden Pond, ca. 1900–10

What would it be like to enter, figuratively, the pure water of the pond? How might you share this experience with a friend who stayed at home? How would you describe it? Would you begin to sense a gradual recognition of profound change, growth, and transformation? Would your pond experience generate still others?

(Advance screen)

Aristotle's Law of the Excluded Middle

What is the law of the excluded middle? Why might we want or need to break it? At this point in our journey, we *must* break it because we have now entered the pure water of contradiction—where the possibility of infinite intervals between discontinuous realities opens a place of rejuvenation capable of refreshing even the most tired of worn-down wanderers.

Actually, our journey has already brought us face to face with these questions, even if we haven't identified "the law" in specific terms. We've confronted it, for instance, in the discontinuous interval of silence following sound, in the interval between pigment (yellow and white paint) and image, and between the finite part and finite whole of our color-value charts, whose beholding would point us toward infinite "wholeness." Our experience has thus already moved from the familiar world of incremental, causal, and narrative continuity to the possibility of mysterious, infinitely open intervals in which art appears. We might then say that in our previous experience, without knowing it, we have already broken the law of the excluded middle. This imagined pond we entered by way of the familiar Walden Pond may be called *ai-no-ma*.

But step back a moment to recall the cognitive reality that has governed Western thinking, behavior, and ethical vision since ancient times.

According to Aristotle and countless subsequent variations, the law of the excluded middle requires that something is what it is, until it is not, and then it is something else; the finer the distinction the better.[1] Ever sharper and clearer differences only confirm the division of all reality into component parts: either *this* or *that*. In the language of philosophical and mathematical logic, the law of the excluded middle is stated simply as P or Non-P. In our familiar language of possession, currently crumbling under the weight of digital reproduction, we own, borrow, or steal—with no "middle" alternative. Something is yours or it is not yours. Sharing is divided ownership. But the law of the excluded middle precludes the possibility of something being in two places at once or simultaneously in the possession of multiple owners.

Simply saying the phrase "law of the excluded middle" can have the effect of throwing a pebble into a pond. Circles will begin to radiate outward from the point of impact, even as the idea behind the phrase will sink ever deeper into complexity until it disappears from view without a trace. If for a moment we were to exchange the laws of thought for the immediacy of experience, we might hold the pebble in our hand. By attending to the pebble, we might move closer to a complementary way of knowing and being in the world. Rather than our habitual either/or exclusivity, we might discover multiple mutual realities in the form of both/and. That is to say, breaking the law of the excluded middle results in PnP.

As we engage with the pebble in our hand, we might even recall Jenny's moment of "seeing green" after her intense focus on "red." Her subtle awakening to the essential asymmetry of our conscious being mirrored in our physiology—brain, as well as our left- and right-handed bodies—may focus the question of "possession" and "ownership." Her awareness of an unbiased, innately existing complementarity—previously obscured by her habit of thinking exclusively of objective, rational opposition (this is red not green)—opened new possibilities reaching toward the otherwise hidden origins of art, and even, perhaps, love itself. Recovering this intimation of Edenic wholeness required Jenny's deliberate openness to a natural integration of obverse realities that even her most simplified contemplative practice had offered. She quieted the *noise* in her head, body, and surroundings. She slowed down and allowed her own being to assume its natural function. She entered the cooling water of the pond.

Imagine that each of us is that pebble held in our hand. Is it possible that the seemingly unalterable circumstances of owning or not owning (remembering that even sharing is divided ownership) might begin to soften? Even change? Habitually, one cares for one's own and what one owns, not for what one does not own—or, at least, one cares less so. If we were capable of owning and not owning simultaneously, the possibility of reciprocal mutuality might slowly appear before us. Rather than choosing this *or* that, we might "see green" and thereby discover the endless potential for this *and* that in dynamic conjunction, together and at times compassionately related.

Our willingness to enter into Thoreau's pond might now move us in the direction of a fateful implication with ourselves, others, and the world around us. By attending all the more carefully to red in order to see green, we could begin to imagine multiple ways of knowing and being in the world, merging even as they remained gloriously distinct. The dry hollowness of Stephen J. Gould's NOMA—the acronym for his concept of "non-overlapping magisteria," explored in chapter 2—might now begin to fill up again with multiple interrelated ways of knowing that rise upward toward a common human goal. And our profoundest human capacities for "experience" and "order"—*ars* and *scientia*—might be reunited as *eruditio* without bias to release our longing for wisdom—*sapientia* (as I illustrated in image 2.32). Our knowledge would now embrace more than isolated bits of meaningless information and our knowing would once again be embodied.

> *As we think of our longing for* sapientia*, we might also recall the words of Niels Bohr: "The opposite of a fact is falsehood, but the opposite of one profound truth may very well be another profound truth."*

To hold and to engage intently with the pebble, then to watch its immersion into the water result in the outward concentric flow of ripples, is to return to our ontological perspective, which began with Milo's lament. We may now understand it to be the foundation of all contemplation, all art, and—as we increasingly will come to see—love.

Many of us recognize these words from Hamlet's soliloquy, "To be or not to be: that is the question," as one of Western literature's most anguished contemplations on the nature of life and the uncertainty of what lies beyond. We might now think of the implications if we amend Hamlet's words: *To be and not to be: that is the fateful condition of our being*. From the perspective of contemplative knowing—understood as the willing embrace of contradiction and the seeking of intimated reconciliation of separation and longing—we might rediscover an innate source of compassion. As such, Parker Palmer's urgent sense that epistemology is ethics—enlarging the way we know by acknowledging the paradoxical nature of our being—will foster not an abstract idea of compassion, but its animated embodiment in each one of us, as well as in the world we would embrace, and by which in turn we would be embraced.[2]

A Meditation with *Ai-no-ma*

Imagine again stumbling toward an unfamiliar pond along your path, one you have never seen before, and entering its incomprehensible and yet potentially refreshing water.

(6.3) Kyoto, Japan, looking west

The following meditation with *ai-no-ma* offers a contemplative occasion for us to approach our relationship with ourselves, one another, the world, and the mystery of our shared human being in a way that differs radically from what many in the West have assumed and accepted without doubt or even questioning. In my experience in Japan, where *ai-no-ma* is the assumed natural relational reality, *ai-no-ma* is a given. After I gave a presentation of a variety of instances of *ai-no-ma* to Japanese colleagues in Kyoto, the response was simply: Of course. How else could it be?

> *Our goal now is to make visible and animate what we habitually assume is utterly invisible and immaterial—namely space—in order to approach another possibility of knowing and being.*

To begin, I introduce Jun'ichirō Tanizaki, one of Japan's most revered writers.[3] His widely regarded serialized novel (and later popular movie), *The Makioka Sisters*, explores the personal and social interactions of family in the precarious years, from 1936 to 1941, leading up to the Allied occupation. We'll focus though on his short essay about space and light, *In Praise of Shadows* (*In'ei Raisan*), which will bring us into the unfamiliar place of *ai-no-ma*.

In Praise of Shadows endures as far more than a sidebar to Tanizaki's literary fiction, conveying as it does his thoughts about traditional Japanese culture in the midst of encroaching Western influence: not only the spreading implications of the Enlightenment, but also the industrial development transforming his homeland and the world; these conditions would lead to a devastating world war in which Japan, of course, was instrumental. When completed in 1933, *In Praise of Shadows* was prophetic: as an evocation of yearning for the shadowed softening of the harsh realities of life, which was disappearing in the glare of electric lights; and as a commentary on the dangers of material progress at the expense of appreciation for the organic. Like all good prophecies, Tanizaki's is still true. The electronic transformation of our lives multiplied exponentially by digital developments is, if anything, more robust and culturally voracious than ever.

Yet in its characterization of the Japanese house, Tanizaki's essay points to his transcendent awareness—his art—with an approach that is intimate, sensual, and physical. Despite its expanding global relevance, the art that Tanizaki writes of and embodies originates at the core of a domestic and Japanese sense of space, time, and light.

To make our way toward this place of *ai-no-ma* and prepare to enter Tanizaki's house in image 6.4, let me propose what will likely be an unfamiliar idea: space does not exist solely as an a priori, absolute, and universal reality, identical everywhere and independent of experience and willed action. From this perspective, our conscious existence within space-time takes shape as we construct it, leaving us free to imagine space-time according to our deepest human needs. When those needs are not being met, we are free to reimagine even the reality we had come to take for granted as being fixed and unalterable.

(6.4) Alcove (*tokonoma*) in Jun'ichirō Tanizaki's home in Kyoto, called Sekison-tei (House of the Stone Village)

Tanizaki's home, which he occupied in Kyoto on and off until his death in 1965, reveals his own artistic sensibility and spatial construction. I photographed the meditation alcove (*tokonoma*) in the reception room (*shoin*) of his home to present a slightly angled view into the space. Having removed and left my shoes in the entryway to the house (*genkan*), I knelt on a floor of woven straw tatami mats. My viewpoint reveals the fixed form and scale of this particular space. The electric lights were turned off to allow natural shadows and darkness to measure and animate the shifting light and space consistent with the explicitly interactive function of the *tokonoma*.

If we were to linger here patiently with the meditative welcome of this alcove, the vivid, almost palpable, presence of the small white jar on the side shelf to the left and the subtle aroma of the tatami mats would be among the many vibrant but hidden discoveries we would experience. For the moment, however, let us simply accept and enjoy the artistic presence of the fresh flower arrangement (ikebana) as our host's personal invitation to enter this place—this deliberate animation of space. As we do so, without any previous cognitive understanding of *ai-no-ma*, its reconciliatory mutuality already becomes part of our experience.

Ironically, Tanizaki said he could never actually live in the house he described in his famous essay. He, too, as we all must, had to find the seam between the ideal and the real. He imagined the shadowed world he described, embodying in it the aspiration to wholeness from his immediate, acknowledged condition of physical limitation. While this noble aspiration may strike us as perfectly familiar, similar to our own longings and those of the other exemplars we have met, the space in which Tanizaki's life takes shape will challenge our understanding of this reality at its core. Tanizaki—the artist—knew this. In what must be one of the most radical claims he made in his essay praising shadows, Tanizaki wrote:

> There are those who hold that to quibble over matters of taste in the basic necessities of life is an extravagance, that as long as a house keeps out the cold and as long as food keeps off starvation, it matters little what they look like. And indeed for even the sternest ascetic the fact remains that a snowy day is cold, and there is no denying the impulse to accept the services of a heater if it happens to be there in front of one, no matter how cruelly its indulgence may shatter the spell of the day. But it is on occasions like this that I always think how different everything would be if we in the Orient had developed our own science. Suppose for instance that we had developed our own physics and chemistry: would not the techniques and industries based on them have taken a different form, would not our myriads of everyday gadgets, our medicines, the products of our industrial art—would they not have suited our national tempers better than they do? In fact, our conception of physics itself, and even the principles of chemistry, would probably differ from that of Westerners; and the facts we are now taught concerning the nature and function of light, electricity and atoms might well have presented themselves in different form.[4]

Are we ready to move away from our automatic, habitual, unreflectively familiar assumptions about ourselves and our world and into the unfamiliar terrain of Tanizaki's world? If so, we may take a step toward that particular construction of space—*ai-no-ma*—as the virtual spatial equivalent of the kind of physics, chemistry, light, electricity, and even atoms that Tanizaki imagined. In my understanding, this form of space has been constructed in Japan as far back in time as the Japanese creation myth in which the sun goddess Amaterasu is the "bridge" between heaven and earth.[5] *Ai-no-ma* is clearly manifest in contemporary Japan: in baseball, film, politics, literature, garden design, architecture, and in other realizations of Japanese culture and life.[6] Insofar as it has not yet become a casualty of our high-tech disintegration of all shadows and all mystery, *ai-no-ma* exists and is pervasive. As a deliberately constructed space, *ai-no-ma* is an interval in which two solitudes are simultaneously whole, while remaining entirely distinct within the infinite condition of our existence. It offers a profound alternative to our habitual assumptions about an unalterable reality of space-time. For this, we must dare to enter the water of this unfamiliar pond.

(6.5) *Ai-no-ma* (pictogram)

So, what is *ai-no-ma*? Reading the individual pictograms (*kanji*) from the right: *ma* is "space"; *no* is the possessive "of"; *ai* is variously, "merging" or "connecting." Hence *ai-no-ma* is literally "merging or connecting space." But this transcription of the composite pictogram for *ai-no-ma* and its transliteration into English barely approaches this new world: say, a first toe in the pond. The pictogram is itself spatially suggestive.

(6.6) *Ai-no-ma* (pictogram), "merging space"

Here the pictogram directly embodies the connective character of *ai-no-ma* in the symmetrical bracketing of the possessive "*no*"—like the space between two structural pillars or two posts of a threshold gate. This is perhaps the primal meaning. Technically, as an architectural term, *ai-no-ma* identifies the merging or connecting space between the two distinct buildings comprising a Shinto sanctuary known as a Hachiman shrine.[7]

(6.7) Hachiman shrine, Usa, Ōita Prefecture, Japan, 8th century, with *ai-no-ma* indicated

Ai-no-ma in this sense joins a designated place of worship with a separate place of divine presence. That is, the intermediary space of *ai-no-ma* functions as a conceptual bridge between human beings and Shinto divinities, called *kami*, who descend into such a deliberately constructed space. For our purposes of contemplative beholding and its intimation of infinite wholeness, we may note as well that these *kami* are the divinities of that *wholeness* manifest throughout nature in mountains, rocks, trees, waters, and so on.

In addition to understanding its architectural and devotional formation, turning to the literary realization of *ai-no-ma* will take us more fully into this water.

(Advance screen)

Interlude with Murasaki Shikibu

As my Japanese colleagues have explained, altering the *kanji* for *ai* changes and expands the definition of "merging" or "connecting."[8] Although to my knowledge the altered *kanji* does not appear in written form, its implied presence is vivid in the amorous protocols of the Heian court of the eleventh century, including allusive letters and poems, as well as in the very process of their delicate exchange.[9] Today, a simple "Google translate" investigation confirms that in modern Japanese "ai" means "love." *Ai-no-ma* becomes literally "a space/place of love." It resonates precisely with the elusive relation between finite substance and infinite presence embodied by that "more human love" we are seeking. We may thus experience *ai-no-ma* as a threshold place of mysterious meeting—inaccessible to rational calculation—as in the fateful encounter of lovers.

One iconic literary source for this implicit presence of *ai-no-ma* must certainly be Murasaki Shikibu's *The Tale of Genji*.[10] In the first chapter we learn that the Shining Prince Genji is the love child of the emperor and one of his concubines. Shortly after Genji's birth his mother dies, leaving the emperor utterly bereft, isolated, and infinitely separated from the beloved he'd imagined being with forever. As the certainty of death approaches, the couple recognize the necessary contradiction inherent in conscious separation and longing. Here we may be reminded of Milo's lament as their passionate presence with each other, each being aware of their mortal fate, opens and sustains this tale of complicated suffered love:

> The emperor returned to [the apartments of his beloved] and still could not bring himself to the final parting.
>
> "We vowed that we would go together down the road we all must go. You must not leave me behind!"
>
> She looked sadly up at him. "If I had suspected that it would be so"—she was gasping for breath.
>
> "I leave you, to go the road we all must go. The road I would choose, if only I could, is the other."[11]

The tenderness in this fleeting, delicate exchange may easily pass unnoticed. For a beholder, it animates the remaining fifty-three chapters of *The Tale of Genji* as they flow toward the reality that lies in an unending search for lost love beyond the events of the last chapter, "The Floating Bridge of Dreams."[12] As another threshold to the infinite interval between solitudes, the events of this chapter are the void into which grace would enter. Although they take place long after Genji's death, they involve two young men, one being Genji's grandson, who pursue the same woman. As a result of their advances, she feels trapped and considers a death by drowning. Like the full range of amorous aspiration that fills the pages of Genji's story, this famous last chapter reveals the joy and lingering sadness of the eternal mystery of love and human being. Anticipating by a thousand years David Foster Wallace, Murasaki Shikibu *knew* that even if we are oblivious to it, tears and weeping are the water in which we all swim, most especially those who love.[13]

Tradition in eleventh-century Japan embraced polygamous marriage as well as multifarious amorous adventures. But Genji's relentless pursuit of love originated, not only under the influence of his culture, but equally from the loss of his mother: separation drove his conscious struggle in search of *wholeness* through love. To limit or judge Genji's behavior as mere licentious privilege is to lose sight of a poetic path of "romantic affinity" as a living though complicated, always contradictory, epistemology of love.[14]

In keeping with Heian court culture, Genji's first wife is presented to him (in chapter 1, "The Paulownia Court") as a gift at his coming-of-age ceremony (he'd turned twelve!), where the Minister of the Left deemed Genji suitable to marry his only daughter. A poetic exchange between the emperor (Genji's father) and the minister conveys the hopes of each for the marriage. The emperor speaks first:

> "The boyish looks are now bound up, a man's.
> And do we tie a lasting bond for his future?"

The girl's father replies:

> "Fast the knot which the honest heart has tied.
> May lavender, the hue of troth, be as fast."

In Edward Seidensticker's translation, *murasaki* (lavender, and also purple) suggests "romantic affinity."[15] The color in various shades pervades the text in floral images, in allusions to scents (wisteria and lavender, used both in incense and dye), and with the mention of violet root, a symbol in Japanese poetry of love and constancy. In chapter 5 ("Lavender"), the now-married Genji's attentions turn to a ten-year-old girl, then in the care of her grandmother. She would later become the great love of his life in spite of other wives and infidelities.

> "I long to have it, to bring it in from the moor.
> The lavender that shares its roots with another."[16]

Like Genji's mother, she would die at a young age. This character, called Lady of the West-Wing in the original text, came to be called Murasaki, as eventually was the author herself.[17] Murasaki as a name thus identifies the living embodiment of longing for wholeness from an unalterable condition of immanent limitation, the force behind Genji's endless search for intimations of reconciliation: for love.

Like Tristan and Iseult's impossible contradictory love—dying whether they were together or apart—Genji's intimate affairs may be understood as urgent attempts at "romantic affinity," the narrative equivalent of *ai-no-ma*.[18] As such, they also resonate with the elusive "love from afar" (*amour de loin*) that animated the troubadour path of "purified love" (*fin'amor*) as it flourished in Europe around the same time (see chapter 7).

We may even find in Murasaki Shikibu's tale a counterpart to the "magic potion" in the myth of Tristan and Iseult. That Celtic potion transformed an ordinary wooden boat, as it carried Tristan and Iseult on an instrumental voyage across storm-tossed waves from Ireland to Cornwall, into a place of mysterious encounter that would alter their fate.[19] In *The Tale of Genji*, the color purple serves in the same way, and perhaps to the same end.

Some years ago, during a visit to Tanizaki's home near the Shimogamo shrine in Kyoto, I met a neighbor who had known him. She spoke about "Kyoto purple," regretting that those days of a "*murasaki* presence" were sadly long gone. The next morning, while walking a path at Takaragaike near the quintessentially modernist Kyoto International Conference Center (Kokusaikaikan), I witnessed an undeniable presence of Heian court "romantic affinity" in the form of "*murasaki* purple," the noblest color in Japan.[20] Notwithstanding the melancholy I'd felt the day before in Tanizaki's home, it appeared that such intimations of reconciliation—love—are always present, waiting only for us to allow them to appear.

(6.8) Takaragaike, Iwakura, Japan, early morning, *murasaki* purple

Simultaneous Distinction and Reunion

A further step into the mystery of *ai-no-ma* extends its implications for our journey, becoming a sensually vivid moment within, but also separated from, ordinary time and space. As an intense phenomenal instant, such contemplative *ai-no-ma* offers us an explicit sensation of absolute peace and wholeness. It vanishes the second we perceive it but is no less real or extraordinary because of its fleeting suddenness and paradoxical ordinariness. As such, it is a potent complement to the enclosing certainties that pervade our habitual Western way of exclusive rationalistic knowing and being.

Direct encounter with *ai-no-ma* as a form of contemplative knowing may well be a Japanese spatial equivalent to the "kind of loosening" that takes place, as Simone Weil describes it, "when the attention has revealed the contradiction in something on which it has been fixed."[21] Or, think of Olivier Messiaen's "bedazzlement" (the internal perception of colors in music), or the act of beholding as we seek it. It also resonates with Kenneth Rexroth's identification of a "poetry of sensibility" in Japan.[22]

The schematic drawings in image 6.9 will bring us closer to an understanding of *ai-no-ma*, in which a new awareness might loosen our habitual obedience to the law of the excluded middle and encourage us to imagine purposefully breaking it.

(6.9) a. Either P (this) or Non-P (that); b. multiple ways of knowing

The solid wall in the top drawing (a) literally and figuratively blocks any intersection of P or Non-P, represented here by the two standing figures. This separation results in the familiar reality of our universal human being, in what we may perceive as isolation or enclosure: something is what it is until it is not however minute the difference may be; notice P or Non-P in the lower drawing (b) on the left. The reality is the same for color values or individual people. I see red, not green. I am me, not you: the world seems to surround me objectively and distinctly as Buber's "he, she, it, they" rather than "I and You." We may visualize "I and You," with the lower drawing (b) on the right, as PnP.

So too, as suggested in chapter 2 (image 2.32), this opening applies to multiple and collaborating ways of knowing. Shakespeare's *Hamlet* comes to mind again: "There are more things in heaven and earth, Horatio, than are dreamed of in your philosophy" (act 1, scene 5). Recall as well: the infinite range of neutral color values.[23]

How does our understanding of *ai-no-ma* change our most familiar experience and understanding of space? The structural components of *ai-no-ma* transform the exclusivity of our Western model of spatial and psychological enclosure into a flowing intimation in which the very concept of "interior" and "exterior" disappears.

Pause here to recall the photo of the Hachiman shrine from image 6.7. The annotated drawings in the next two images, showing two different views of the shrine, will help us visualize the change in our perception of space.

(6.10) Hachiman-style sanctuary and worship hall, plan
(6.11) Hachiman-style sanctuary and worship hall, elevation

Notice how the extended eaves of the sloping roof over the *engawa* in image 6.11 create a shadowed area between inside and outside, replacing the fixed defining "wall" with a fragile integrative openness. (The Japanese word *engawa* literally translates in English as "side-river." It is easily mistaken as a mere veranda, and thus is often referred to that way.) The familiar distinction between object and void collapses within a continuous sequence of overlapping realities. Air, wind, light, and shifting scents are integral to the space and our experience within it. When it rains, a veil of water activates the outermost plane of this delicate interval, which we can see depicted in the elevation of the space.

This construction of space according to the principles of *ai-no-ma* results in the simultaneous distinction and union of separate entities. The worship hall and the sanctuary of the *kami* unite the worshipper and the deity. The interior and the exterior of the buildings merge in the "side-river" (*engawa*), and the sloping roof brings sky and ground into a diverse wholeness. As in Martin Heidegger's well-known concept of "fourfold," where "earth and sky, mortals, and divinities" come together in a built form by the nature of the "dwelling" taking place within it, otherwise separate realities are joined here in a gentle place of mysterious meeting, as in the fateful encounter of lovers.[24]

To move from description to actual practice, compare two distinct constructions of space, the first seen in a series of defining walls and the second in a bridge that appears to soften its points of contact.

(6.12) a. Roman Empire (ca. 117); b. walled Rome (ca. 330); c. Aurelian wall, Rome (ca. 270); d. Hadrian's wall, Northumbria, United Kingdom (ca. 122); e. Christo and Jeanne-Claude, *Running Fence,* Sonoma and Marin Counties, California, 1972

From its political center in Rome, reaching out to the limits of its authority and presence, the Roman Empire was defined by the signifying structure of a wall that indicated not only inside and outside, but divided the known world into the "civilized" and "uncivilized"—Roman and non-Roman peoples. Not even the poetic and temporal fragility of Christo's *Running Fence* disguises the underlying and enduring clarity of a habitual sense of space—if not thinking, knowing, and being—grounded in the law of the excluded middle: this, not that; either inside or outside.

(6.13) Utagawa Hiroshige (1797–1858), *Sudden Shower at the Shin-Ōhashi Bridge*, 1857

Utagawa Hiroshige's *Sudden Shower at the Shin-Ōhashi Bridge* embodies pictorially the radically different spatial conception and construction of *ai-no-ma*. Although the bridge connects two banks of a river, the points of contact with the bridge remain undefined, elusive, open, so that the river itself (like the *engawa* of the shrine) and the bridge together become the place of mysterious meeting. Even the rain in this woodblock print serves to "connect" the space outside the image with the illusory space within it by conflating the two- and three-dimensional realities of the object. The Japanese inscriptions in the upper right and left lower corner, which identify the image and name the artist, likewise bring the print (as object) and its image into a discontinuous but singular reality.[25]

If we are willing to break the law of the excluded middle, we may now try to enter this place of mysterious meeting, with all of its potential for complementing, augmenting, and even transforming our relational presence in the world.

Entering the Pond

(6.14) Kyoto, Japan, looking toward the northeast and Mt. Hiei

From this view of Kyoto, Japan, we look toward Mt. Hiei (Hiei-zan). For the Japanese, Hiei-zan is a spiritual entity said to protect the city against evil from the northeast. Divinities (*kami*) that inhabit the mountain are celebrated in the Shimogamo shrine next to Tanizaki's home.[26] Traveling north from Kyoto, we will come to the secluded monastery of Sanzen-in in the village of Ōhara.[27]

(6.15) Road to Ōhara, Japan, mountain rice field
(6.16) Steps to Sanzen-in, Ōhara, Japan

After a lengthy but gentle climb past a stream, and along a path lined with shops selling ordinary souvenirs and snacks, we arrive at the steps leading to the main gate of the monastery of Sanzen-in, and then into the central compound. The monastery has been associated since the tenth century with the Tendai sect of Buddhism. Our passage from the city to this mountain retreat leads us to a place of felt solitude, stillness, quiet, and anticipation.

(6.17) Sanzen-in, South Gate

The large and imposing south gate to the monastery of Sanzen-in does what gateways do anywhere: it manifestly distinguishes areas in space, suggesting familiar interior and exterior realities. But from the perspective of *ai-no-ma*, this gate suggests connection as much as separation and enclosure. The rhythmic sound of chanting monks provides an unexpected aural dimension to the early morning experience of departure and arrival.

Pause here now . . . each of us will enter individually.

Allow this moment of felt imminence to envelope you.

Moving past the heavy wooden door of the south gate to approach the nearby gatehouse, where you will exchange your shoes for slippers, brings you to the *engawa* of the guesthouse.

(6.18) Sanzen-in, guesthouse (*kyakuden*) veranda (*engawa*), with *shin*-shaped pond and Temple of Rebirth in Paradise (Ōjō Gokuraku-in) in the distance

Kneeling in the space of this *engawa* under the extended eave, attend first to the garden that has been precisely constructed to appear utterly natural, untouched by human hands. Then look past the trees, moss, and water toward the fragmented outline of a building bracketed by trees and the sky. Assess for yourself how the familiar experience of "inside" and "outside" changes. Notice how space around you has been transformed into a series of deliberately articulated intervals that join you, the *engawa*, the pond, and the garden together. The seemingly unexceptional pond even resembles the pictogram (*kanji*) for *shin*, meaning heart *and* mind together.

(6.19) Sanzen-in, main garden, looking from west to east toward the Temple of Rebirth in Paradise

Attend now to the main garden space of Sanzen-in. This space has been carefully, thoughtfully, and purposefully organized to focus your attention. Think of it as a cathedral of trees. Walking on the moss floor among the maples, cypresses, and pines (all of which respond dramatically to the passing seasons and changing weather, to the slightest shift of wind or light), you might feel as if you've just entered Paradise—or, more precisely, the constructed equivalent of Paradise. This monastic setting anticipates the sense of wholeness in the "Pure Land," a place of eternal bliss, experienced in the present moment. At Sanzen-in, the garden itself embodies *ai-no-ma*, realized as the interval between here and there; now and then. Having entered this space, you might find it very difficult to leave. Allow this particular place of mysterious meeting to embrace your presence.

(6.20) Temple of Rebirth in Paradise, view from the southeast

The building you see now, the main hall (Hondō) of the monastery, was first built by the monk Eshin in 985 and rebuilt of wood in 1493. This Hondō is known as the Temple of Rebirth in Paradise (Ōjō Gokuraku-in). As you look, allow the structure to blend with its surroundings. The massive overhanging eaves, the stone base, the wooden stilts, the cypress bark shingles will then slowly merge to form a singular reality of integrated parts. The rising outline of the roof, meanwhile, echoes the natural flow of the tree branches to animate, rather than occupy, space. In approaching the Temple of Rebirth in Paradise, you will be drawn ever deeper into its presence, and into the presence of Amida Buddha, Lord of the Western Paradise, who is enthroned here.

From this vantage point, the *engawa* that surrounds the Temple of Rebirth in Paradise is the shadowed gateway to the Buddha's eternal presence. The stark difference between this opening and the familiar massive stone façades of Western cathedrals or the articulated gates of the Roman Empire underscores the movement from familiar walled enclosures into a new place and occasion of seamless reunion.

(6.21) Temple of Rebirth in Paradise, view from the southeast with single illuminated candle

Engage with the Temple of Rebirth in Paradise across an interval of space defined in the intersection of ground and sky, mediated through the soft luminous surface of the moss and the harder calligraphy of tree branches.

Having done so, you may feel as if you've already entered the sacral throne room of the Buddha. Such a prefiguration of being "inside" while remaining "outside" draws on the subtle, barely visible, spatial effect of a single candle radiating its light outward from the darkest velvet black of the surrounding shadows.

(6.22) Temple of Rebirth in Paradise, view from the east with two illuminated candles
(6.23) Approaching the Temple of Rebirth in Paradise

The tree branches here are no accident. They are trimmed and shaped, "encouraged" to form the connecting screen between you and the Buddha, whom you now approach. In the fall, these delicate maple leaves provide brilliant red contours that accentuate a deliberate, contemplative movement through space.

(6.24) Arrival at the Temple of Rebirth in Paradise

From here, the spatial and temporal interval joining all of us with the goal of our pilgrimage, Amida Buddha, has become an irresistible invitation in shadowed space.

(6.25) Entry into the Temple of Rebirth in Paradise

At the bottom of these steps you remove the slippers used to walk in the garden and enter the *engawa* of the Temple of Rebirth in Paradise to be in the immediate presence of Amida Buddha. This sculpted figure is an integral part of the space you entered through the monastic gate. Its aura extends to the outer reaches of the monastery and beyond, echoed in the sounds that attended your arrival and your passage through the garden toward the candlelight. This anticipation intensifies as you kneel in the *engawa*, directly before the enthroned figure of the Buddha, and recognize that the space you've entered is the connecting interval between the garden and the Buddha's presence in his intimate sanctuary.

You have arrived at the point of mysterious meeting between yourself and the embodiment of wholeness. You are within the thrall of intimated reunion.

(6.26) Temple of Rebirth in Paradise, with gilded figure of Amida Buddha

Looking up from your kneeling position, you will see enthroned before you an idealized portrait of an Indian prince who became in his enlightenment the Buddha. Surrounded by a luminous halo, decorated with a rippling series of smaller images of the Buddha, this aristocratic icon reveals a slight but real animation, as though the compassionate Buddha might turn his gaze toward you to acknowledge and confirm your place in his presence. In this moment, a new light translates the faint and flickering glow of candles into gold.[28]

(6.27) Temple of Rebirth in Paradise, face of Amida Buddha

The experience of immediate spiritual presence in the *engawa* of the Temple of Rebirth in Paradise is remarkably similar in personal tone and psychological effect to the familiar Judeo-Christian verbal benediction:

> The Lord bless you and keep you; the Lord make his face to shine upon you, and be gracious unto you; the Lord lift up his countenance upon you, and give you peace. (Numbers 6:24–26)

A Spiritual Invitation, Arrival, and Welcome

As a matter of spatial fact, the impression of universal arrival and transformation is not entirely farfetched. Nor is it merely our subjective response in the moment. According to the traditions of Amida Buddhism, we would be welcomed into the Western Paradise simply by faithfully reciting this phrase: *Namu Amida Butsu*, Buddha I beseech thee. As we kneel in the intermediary space between the monastic garden and the innermost core of the Temple of Rebirth in Paradise and imagine this simplest of prayers, the two attendants on either side of Amida Buddha become spatially significant as the agents of spiritual invitation, arrival, and welcome.

(6.28) Temple of Rebirth in Paradise, Amida Buddha with Seishi and Kannon

These two figures of Seishi and Kannon normally *stand* flanking the Buddha. But here, at Sanzen-in, they kneel as we do, at this precise moment of spatial, temporal, and spiritual transition. Seishi (on the left, representing wisdom), prays for us. Kannon (on the right, representing mercy), holds out a lotus blossom to receive our soul. Beyond this iconographic welcome, however, it is the spatial animation that reinforces the actual intention of this constructed setting. Seishi and Kannon are not only kneeling, but they also clearly lean forward, bowing toward us in a traditional gesture of welcome into a Japanese home.

(6.29) The Goshima in the entryway (*genkan*) to their home, Kyoto

By leaning forward to enter physically the space where we are, Seishi and Kannon physically animate the interval between them and us.

(6.30) Temple of Rebirth in Paradise, Seishi and Kannon bowing

As a sculptural metaphor of spiritual fulfillment, expressed primarily spatially and socially, these two figures bring us closer to our waiting lotus blossom, upon which our eternal soul will reside.

Reflection at Sanzen-in

(6.31) Temple of Rebirth in Paradise, Seishi
(6.32) Temple of Rebirth in Paradise, Kannon
(6.33) Temple of Rebirth in Paradise, detail of lotus blossom
(6.34) Temple of Rebirth in Paradise, altar with Amida Buddha, flanked by Seishi and Kannon

Feel how this deliberately constructed space fosters the personal and ritual equivalent of well-being we experienced earlier, walking in the garden that surrounds this Temple of Rebirth in Paradise. The contemplative sensation here is one of universal belonging with the goal of our profoundest desire manifest in the luminous figure of Amida Buddha.

Whatever private spiritual thoughts you may hold, imagine kneeling quietly in front of this altar as you recite the prayer: Namu Amida Butsu.

At Sanzen-in it is hard to resist direct, palpable connection between ourselves and everything else, a connection that exists in the moment and across time. In this intermediary area between the monastic garden and the intimate sanctuary of Amida Buddha, we might recall Martin Buber's primal word "I-You" and feel the subject "I" merging with the transformed object "You," now the Amida Buddha and Pure Land Buddhism.[29]

For all of us who would come without bias or prior expectation into this construction of *ai-no-ma*, the wordless, even post-verbal, post-cognitive feeling of wholeness and peace is irresistible: we come here, and we do not want to leave. To be present at Sanzen-in at any time in our lives—and during any time of the year, most especially at the peak of seasonal transition, or during a gentle rain that swells the moss at our feet and drips from the branches overhead—is to confirm Simone Weil's conviction that "grace fills empty spaces but can only enter where there is a void to receive it." And further, "it is grace itself which makes the void."

Autumn Meditation at Sanzen-in

(6.35) Welcomed guest in thrall to the Temple of Rebirth in Paradise
(6.36) Temple of Rebirth in Paradise, grounds
(6.37) Temple of Rebirth in Paradise, grounds
(6.38) Temple of Rebirth in Paradise, viewed from the imperial meditation room through entryway and *engawa* with rolled bamboo curtains as connecting veil
(6.39) Temple of Rebirth in Paradise, viewed from the imperial meditation room
(6.40) "Will you turn toward me? I am lonely too, this autumn nightfall" (Matsuo Bashō)
(6.41) Amida Buddha with Seishi and Kannon

Spend a quiet moment of reflection with Rainer Maria Rilke's poem "Buddha in Glory."

Center of all centers, core of cores,
almond self-enclosed and growing sweet—
all this universe, to the farthest stars
and beyond them, is your flesh, your fruit.
Now you feel how nothing clings to you;
your vast shell reaches into endless space,
and there the rich, thick fluids rise and flow.
Illuminated in your infinite peace,
a billion stars go spinning through the night,
blazing high above your head.

But *in* you is the presence that
will be, when all the stars are dead.[30]

Pause for a moment of private contemplation before departing Sanzen-in.

(6.42) At the departure gate; holding fast to the fleeting joy of the moment

(Advance screen)

Our experience of spiritual connection and belonging within a discontinuous, trans-rational wholeness, has been realized by means of the logically open "interval" that would embrace all contradiction—an interval we are calling *ai-no-ma*. Such experiences of wholeness assume particularly vivid presence in what may be the best known of all the Buddhist temples in Kyoto, those associated with Zen Buddhism.[31] To pursue our meditation with this unfamiliar but complementary way of knowing and being—to do so as a way of softening the hardest contours of our habitual reliance on oppositional duality—consider three consummate Zen temples: Shinju-an, Ryoan-ji, and Daisen-in. From our contemplative perspective of *ai-no-ma*, embrace and be embraced by the combined power and subtlety of these constructed spaces. Without this acceptance, and especially for those who remain outside the path of our particular journey, they might appear as little more than elegant, exotic destinations.

Shinju-an, Kyoto, Japan

(6.43) Shinju-an, Outer Gate from the west

The sub-temple of Shinju-an is one part of the larger temple complex in Kyoto called Daitoku-ji.[32] Without comparing in detail the corresponding Zen philosophy that this temple serves, it is fair to suggest that the space beyond this gate is not unlike the sacral sanctuary of Sanzen-in. Here, however, befitting the Zen focus on meditation rather than Pure Land devotional practice, a Zen garden replaces the golden icon of Amida Buddha. Here the changing seasons, the light of the day, the breezes, the moss, the rocks, and trees are the primary focus in which nature herself has become the occasion for Buddhist enlightenment.

Before we arrive at the outer gate as pilgrims to Shinju-an, we encounter a series of preparatory gates: the "outer" East Gate that admits our entry into

Daitoku-ji, the Imperial Messenger Gate, and the Triple Gate of the temple complex.

(6.44) Daitoku-ji, East Gate
(6.45) Entry into Daitoku-ji
(6.46) Imperial Messenger Gate
(6.47) Triple Gate leading to the Dharma Hall (Hattō) and Main Hall (Kondō)

Now that we've passed through this sequence of spatial transitions, we are prepared for our meditative arrival at the outer gate of Shinju-an.

(6.48) Shinju-an, arrival from the west

Our next step crosses a gap of discontinuity—*ai-no-ma*—leading into the temple interior.

(6.49) Shinju-an, discontinuous transition

The gracefully bowed arch of the Inner Gate before us is a traditional decorative form with aristocratic and even imperial connotations, presumably signifying the elevated importance of our next step through this gate.

(6.50) Inner Gate and *genkan*, from the west

This gate is actually a separate small building placed at a right angle to the Abbot's quarters (Hōjō) within. Characterized by its extreme simplicity, clarity, and stark emptiness, the space is immeasurably more than a mere physical entryway; its quiet beauty, which draws on its spatial function as a place of waiting and preparation, offers devoted pilgrims an occasion for psychological and spiritual prefiguration, anticipation, and beginning. Roughly translated, this *genkan* is an "entryway to a mystery." As in Japanese domestic settings, here we remove and leave our shoes.

(6.51) Inner Gate and *genkan*, facing southwest
(6.52) Southern veranda (*engawa*), facing west

The measured proportions, the polished but muted tones, and the deep russet colors of cedar and cypress wood combine with white plaster in this *engawa* to transform what in Western experience might appear to be just another porch into a genuinely sacral and hallowed space, giving the English word "veranda" an entirely new significance.[33] Paper- and wood-framed sliding panels (*shōji*) simultaneously enclose and open the main room of the Hōjō connecting this "interior" space with the *engawa* and the garden.

(6.53) Southern veranda (*engawa*), facing east

(6.54) Southern veranda (*engawa*), with visitors kneeling at the entrance to the altar room of the Main Hall (Hōjō)

We see in image 6.54 that visitors have come here to pay their respects at the main altar of the temple. The altar enshrines a sculpted figure of Ikkyū, who was both the founder of the Pearl Temple and teacher of Buddhist aspiration. As at other Zen temples, teaching itself at Shinju-an becomes a form of *ai-no-ma*.

Following this southern *engawa* around the Hōjō to the eastern *engawa* will bring us to this entryway to the teahouse of Shinju-an.

(6.55) Eastern veranda (*engawa*), with entryway to the anteroom room and tea house

The diminutive structure on the right of this image is the teahouse of Shinju-an. The highly stylized tea ceremony performed in this space is one of the ultimate refinements of Zen Buddhist thought and practice. Several delicately overlapping planes with stencil-like interlacing of wood and shadow combine to form this threshold, which leads into the anteroom of the teahouse. From the *engawa*, this anteroom appears impenetrably dark.

(6.56) Anteroom to the tea house

It is impossible to exaggerate the effect of entering this space. The scale is intimate. The rectangular tatami mats measure three-by-six feet, and the wooden slatted ceiling is barely six feet above them. In every sense, this space is an antechamber to the room and ritual of the teahouse. There is no furniture in this room: only shadowed but nonetheless luminous light fills the space. Tinted paper walls (*fusuma*) decorated with monochromatic mountainous landscapes evoke the vast exterior world as light filters through translucent white-papered "panes" in the wood-framed sliding panels (*shōji*).

As your eyes adjust, be still and silent. Slowly, allow the room to awaken and heighten all your senses. Imagine kneeling on the soft tatami mats made of surprisingly aromatic rice straw. Although it's barely audible, listen for the sound of water dripping slowly in the nearby tea garden.

To the Western visitor whose idea of interior space assumes bright light, openness, and, above all, expansiveness, this room will at first appear sinister, dark, and even claustrophobic. But those who constructed this space envisioned it as consummate and reassuring poetry. In the warmth of this diminished light, we can discover something extraordinary if we are willing. The objective infinite realities of our existence, embodied at Sanzen-in by the image of Amida Buddha, merge silently in this room with an intimate and subjective interiority illuminated by a pervasive golden glow.

(6.57) Anteroom to the tea house, with visitor

Still meditation in this place opens the way to an unavoidable sensation that our private awareness has become the *ai-no-ma* or interval of intimated reconciliation. Here subject and object are mysteriously joined. So too, as individuals, we no longer look outward to see the Buddha reality but discover it within, thereby animating the scale and intersecting meaning of this otherwise "empty" space.

(6.58) Abbot's *genkan* to the Hōjō, with sandals

The private entryway (*genkan*) of the Abbot of Shinju-an is a place of spare, humble, and self-evident affirmation of this awakening moment, this *enlightenment.*

(Advance screen)

Ryoan-ji, Kyoto, Japan

The tangible realization of an internalized infinite awareness is nowhere more compellingly experienced than at Ryoan-ji, the Zen Buddhist temple on the western border of Kyoto—the temple where we began our journey toward the threshold of love.[34] Ryoan-ji is justifiably one of the best known of all of Kyoto's roughly 2,500 temples and shrines. Here I offer a suggestion from the seventeenth-century poet Matsuo Bashō: "Go to the pine if you want to learn about the pine, or to the bamboo [*bashō*] if you want to learn about the bamboo. And in so doing you must leave your subjective preoccupation with yourself."[35] His words assume so tangible a form that we can actually feel our ego-selves being absorbed and transformed by this place and its particular construction of space: its *ai-no-ma*.

Recall our approach to Ryoan-ji in chapter 1, as we walked along the winding stone path that leads to the main gate of the temple.

(1.1) Outer gate I
(1.2) Outer gate II
(1.3) Curving path
(1.4) East Gate

Passing through the East Gate now, we return to the pond, those two otherwise ordinary rocks, the soft spring light and, of course, Bashō's own poetic inspiration.

(1.5) Pond with moored boat
(1.6) Pond with two rocks
(1.7) Pond with two rocks and still water
(1.8) Pond with ripples
(1.9) Matsuo Bashō, text, "Breaking the silence..."

Two water lily blossoms, suspended silently in this venerable old pond, assume new meaning in this world of *ai-no-ma*.

(0.1) Two water lily blossoms, Ryoan-ji, Kyoto, Japan

Their presence resounds within us: just as they are implicated, one with the other, so too are we.[36]

(6.59) Ryoan-ji, lingering light

> *Now, with awakened presence in the late afternoon light, follow the gravel path that leads to the dry rock garden* (karesansui)*, the source of Ryoan-ji's renown and the center of its contemplative purpose.*

(6.60) Gravel path
(6.61) Fountain I

The inconspicuous purification fountain along the path reminds us that everything at Ryoan-ji serves to focus our concentration on the immediate experience of the present moment. The plop of a frog into a pond of unknowable depth and age transforms an ordinary incremental moment into a connecting space located in time somewhere between infinite silence and the slightest movement or sound.

The "deep resonance" experienced in such a moment will be different for each of us. Countless unique and unrelated memories will ripple outward from this fleeting event, which is already in the past. Yet our shared experience in the world will be changed from this moment on. Perhaps our thoughts will turn back in time to recover earlier realities, or forward to those moments that lie beyond immediate awareness, perhaps to that time when our very existence, like the fading light and the delicate cherry blossoms it illuminates, will also be gone. Can the moment we might have experienced even as it lingers in the disappearing disturbance of the "ancient pond," or in the dripping sound of this fountain, carry us further into the mysterious promise of Ryoan-ji?

(6.62) Fountain II

Something we took for granted only a moment ago—fixed and unalterable, given our idea of space and time—might now seem somehow fresh and open to unimagined possibilities. In this moment, we might see how the very unfamiliarity of *ai-no-ma* resembles that wooden boat on the far side of the pond, waiting, secured to its protected mooring. This boat is there to carry our thoughts to a place beyond habitual thinking. Once there we might rediscover and reclaim something that had become so familiar it had disappeared from sight and lost its power to inform and shape our lives: like an inconsequential frog . . . until it jumped: like a familiar pebble we once held in our hand until the moment we threw it into the pond . . . only to discover that we are that pebble. Think of the rain shower at Hiroshige's Shin-Ōhashi Bridge . . . and imagine that the awakening reality of this moment, like expanding ripples of water and even the scratching sound of the gravel beneath our feet as we walk, will guide us toward the threshold of timeless authenticity realized in the dry rock garden at Ryoan-ji.

(6.63) Steps to the *genkan*
(6.64) Approaching the *genkan*
(6.65) *Genkan* gate
(6.66) *Genkan* interior

Here we have entered into another *genkan*, a place of waiting, preparation, prefiguration. But everything has changed. The shadowed light, the stillness and the quiet are familiar, but this is a new moment, a new point of entry into a gateway of endless mystery.

(6.67) *Genkan* window with sliding paper and wood panels (*shōji*)

This window, with its *shōji* open, offers new meaning for our understanding of illumination and enlightenment. After all, this space, despite its humble simplicity, poised between "outside" and "inside," is as refined in its spiritual reach as any of the monumental stained-glass windows of Gothic France. Where rich color is the agent of incarnation there, here in this *genkan* made of stone, plaster, wood, and paper, the soft indefinable merging of light and shadow together animate this space. If we were inclined to linger, we might pause and, sitting on the empty bench, reflect on our progress... and then follow the corridor around this Hōjō from east, to north, to west, culminating in the southern *engawa*, a place of meditation with the dry rock garden. Might this "walk" be a limited, but focused pilgrimage toward increased understanding?

(6.68) View from the *genkan* toward the eastern veranda (*engawa*)
(6.69) Eastern veranda (*engawa*)
(6.70) View of the study alcove (*shoin*) with *tokonoma* and *shōji* window, from the east veranda (*engawa*)
(6.71) Northern veranda (*engawa*)
(6.72) Western veranda (*engawa*) I
(6.73) Western veranda (*engawa*) II
(6.74) Main devotional hall (Hōjō), from the western veranda (*engawa*)
(6.75) Main devotional hall (Hōjō) with the founder's altar, from the western veranda (*engawa*)

The central altar of Ryoan-ji, containing sculpted figures of its imperial patrons and two former abbot-teachers, is situated at the north wall of the Hōjō opposite the south-facing meditation *engawa*. The white plaster strip between the ceiling and the upper horizontal beam is an aesthetic *ai-no-ma* that transforms the massive literal weight of the structure into a so-called floating roof.

(6.76) Main devotional hall (Hōjō), with view to the east and south toward the meditation veranda (*engawa*)
(6.77) Meditation veranda (*engawa*), facing west

This structure is not merely a separate porch, tacked onto the main hall but closed to its space. Nor is it what the casual visitor might assume is a convenient viewing platform for the rock garden. Like the "side river" (*engawa*) of the Hachiman Shinto shrine and the *engawa* at Shinju-an, this structure is a precisely constructed space meant to facilitate silent meditation and connection. It is a place . . . an opportunity . . . an occasion to enter the *ai-no-ma* between all that is interior, private, and subjective and all that is exterior, public, and objective: not one reality or the other, eternally estranged, but both, dynamically integrated in our very experience.

(6.78) Meditation veranda (*engawa*) and dry rock garden (*karesansui*), facing west

This *engawa* is nothing if not a place of convergence and ultimate contemplation with that elusive wholeness we are all a part of, and from which our conscious awareness appears to separate us.

(6.79) Meditation veranda (*engawa*) and dry rock garden (*karesansui*), with visitors I

A skeptic might well respond, "Fine, but so what? Objectively, physically, this garden contains nothing other than five groups of fairly ordinary rocks, laid out in a bed of raked gravel—not much different from any common stone driveway on which we park our cars." To which we might respond: "Like Rembrandt's yellow and white paint, these rocks have been deliberately ordered—that is, constructed, in a subtle arrangement of discrete parts—to open an interval between finite material components and an elusive, but no less real, "image."

And like Rembrandt's painting *Aristotle with a Bust of Homer*, this garden is a masterpiece of artistic attainment and devotional engineering. Slowing down to contemplate here without bias or purpose, we might find ourselves entering into a Japanese equivalent of the same essential *ai-no-ma* that suspended paint, brushstroke, and "gold" in our act of beholding with the painting in the Metropolitan Museum of Art—and thus discover for ourselves a tentative answer to the lingering question that concerns the deeper value of our seeking.[37]

(6.80) Meditation veranda (*engawa*) and dry rock garden (*karesansui*), with visitors II

(6.81) Meditation veranda (*engawa*) and dry rock garden (*karesansui*), with my student Josh

(6.82) Meditation veranda (*engawa*) and dry rock garden (*karesansui*), with an anonymous visitor

Without trying to articulate how—whether technically, formally, and even institutionally—this *karesansui* serves its intended spiritual purpose, or why by any standard it is unquestionably a surpassing work of art, let me propose one way we might experience its contemplative effect.

> *Imagine that you are sitting quietly in the center of the engawa. Slowly, gently, soften your resistance. Engage with the garden, with the moment. With focused attention, follow individual rock groups. Unhurriedly, release your habitual skepticism, your guarded, distanced relationship with the world. Choose your group. Choose a rock. Attend to it. Savor it. Embrace it. Be embraced by it.*

(6.83) Rock grouping # 1

(6.84) Rock grouping # 2

(6.85) Rock grouping # 3

(6.86) Rock grouping # 4

(6.87) Rock grouping # 5

> *Hold "your" rock group in your focused concentration . . .*

(6.88) Rock grouping # 5 in shadowed light

The ripples of raked gravel simultaneously frame and identify individually each rock group, even as they tie them into the garden's shadowed light. The devotional act of raking itself, like Rembrandt's brushstroke, has become a purposeful gesture of interconnecting *ai-no-ma.*

(6.89) Rock grouping # 5, with "ripples"

Now reverse your focus. Allow your attention to open up; to drift outward with these ripples that echo the ancient pond "outside" this garden and the concentric circles a frog makes when it jumps; or that ducks make when they swim.

(6.90) Pond with two rocks and widening ripples

(6.91) Pond with Mandarin ducks

Recall the sky; the trees; the gravel path that led to this garden; the fading light, the cherry blossoms...

(6.92) Dry rock garden (*karesansui*), facing southwest

Finally, release "your" chosen rock group. Allow it to become absorbed back into the garden... and the fullest reality of this moment. Take the time for this movement to occur in your experience. Wait until you "see green."

> *As you attend to the entire garden, imagine "your" rock (yourself) absorbed into the larger order of things with which we are implicated—distinct, unique, individual to be sure, but inexorably and immaculately joined with everything else.*

In this garden there is nothing to "see." There are no precious religious objects, no figure of the Buddha, no icon. In a sense, there are only ordinary rocks, moss, and gravel—nothing but "paint" perhaps—but there are also extraordinary ratios that would embody the interval between "brushstroke" and "image." As with Rembrandt's art, we will find ourselves once again in a contemplative place of mysterious meeting, as in a fateful encounter of lovers.

From the middle of the meditation *engawa*, looking out at the axial center of the garden, we discover that there really is nothing exceptional at its core, only ordinary gravel. This "emptiness" is the *ai-no-ma* of Ryoan-ji, now incarnated by contemplative awareness and understanding beyond words, things, and the limitations of conscious distinction. As a place of mysterious meeting, this "void" (within our experience of this constructed moment) is the grace of all fullness, all abundance. This intimation of wholeness that reconciles intense yet fleeting self-awareness with simultaneous universal and eternal absorption is the ontological purpose of the space and this elusive contemplative awakening—no more or less fragile or real than an overlay of rock and shadow. Momentary bliss...

(6.93) Dry rock garden (*karesansui*), detail of the gravel center

This "enlightenment," in which infinite truth merges with the finite experience of endless contradiction, is the goal of our visit to Ryoan-ji. For the Buddhist pilgrim, it is *satori*. For us it may simply be wisdom, felt everywhere and once felt, felt always—until, of course, as with all art, we blink and need to begin the steps toward contemplative awareness all over again—especially after the winter cold, encouraged by the renewal of spring blossoming and endless stained-glass-like affirmation in the transformation of light into pure color.

(6.94) Dry rock garden (*karesansui*), with snow and leafless cherry tree
(6.95) Dry rock garden (*karesansui*), with blossoming cherry tree

(Advance screen)

Daisen-in, Kyoto, Japan

(6.96) Daisen-in, approaching from the west in early morning, entry indicated; Shinju-an in the distance
(6.97) Outer Gate and *genkan*, from the southwest in early morning
(6.98) Dry rock garden (*karesansui*), view toward the southwest

Contemplative wisdom is the irreducible goal of the rock garden at the sub-temple of Daisen-in at Daitoku-ji, located next to Shinju-an.[38] Unimpressive ordinary mounds raised up in a field of straight and curved rows of raked gravel invoke, in purely abstract language, a grounded cosmic wholeness, comparable to that of the iconic image of Amida Buddha at Sanzen-in or, as we have seen, two inconspicuous rocks in a stilled pond at Ryoan-ji.

(6.99) Dry rock garden (*karesansui*), detail with two mounds of raked gravel
(6.100) Meditation veranda (*engawa*) of the main devotional hall (Hōjō), facing west

Experience in this *engawa* will respond to those questions that our shared human longing raises, including those that defy categorical answers. Its purposeful merging of "exterior" and "interior" realities informs an *ai-no-ma* based in Japanese cultural values that may now extend outward to include the profoundest realization of all our human aspirations to wholeness, those aspirations originating from our acknowledged universal condition of limitation and fragmentation. This particular *engawa* is the site of daily Zen meditation and ritual performed by the abbot of Daisen-in.

(6.101) Abbot Soen Ozeki standing in the *genkan* wearing formal dress

It is also the site of frequent lectures by this especially loquacious abbot, offered to anyone who would come here to learn. One day in my own experience, the abbot of Daisen-in, Soen Ozeki, was talking to a group of people who were severely afflicted with Minamata disease, barely able to walk, let alone sit still, listen, and focus—or comprehend the abbot's words.[39]

(6.102) Abbot Soen Ozeki, wearing working clothes and lecturing from the garden

A young man in a blue shirt to the right of the nearest post was the most uncomfortable. As the abbot started to speak, this man began to move uncontrollably, extending his twitching feet over the step of the *engawa*.

(6.103) Abbot Soen Ozeki lecturing; showing the agitated man's white-socked feet extended

Just when it seemed to me that there was no hope of communicating anything to these suffering people, just when their pain became unbearable to *me*, something wonderful happened. The abbot, dressed not in his finest formal monastic regalia but in the work clothes he wears when he rakes the rock garden, leaned forward, as Seishi and Kannon do at Sanzen-in. As he knelt on the front step of the *engawa*, he touched the feet of the agitated young man to the delight of everyone except the woman facing me.

(6.104) Abbot Soen Ozeki kneeling into the veranda (*engawa*), touching the feet of the agitated man

With this gesture the interval between each of us—the infinite gap of our solitudes—swelled with the profoundest human expression of all: the compassion by which the *ai-no-ma* of intermediary space between all that is separate can be mysteriously bridged. In this remarkable act, committed in this setting and moment, the deepest lingering questions of life gave way to simple, wordless comprehension; and even, perhaps, the ecstasy of an unutterable but felt sense of calm and well-being.

(6.105) Abbot Soen Ozeki sitting with the group of visitors in the veranda (*engawa*)

From this quiet moment of recognition, we may begin to sense the radical reorientation Jun'ichirō Tanizaki offers in his poetic praise of soft shadows—as they diminish the harsh glare of unmediated electric lights, the hard edges of separation and distinction, and, perhaps, something of the potential alienation of modern instrumental reason.

The next steps along this path of love—the third part of our journey in this book—will begin to lead us home to the lived reality of our embodied human being.

(Advance screen)

III

HEADING HOME

CHAPTER 7

Lust to Solitude: From Grasping to Acceptance

What is necessary, after all, is only this: solitude, vast inner solitude.
—Rainer Maria Rilke, *Letters to a Young Poet*

OUR EXPERIENCE with *ai-no-ma*, that place of mysterious meeting, has allowed us to see the potential open to us in all our relationships with the world—if only we dare to break the law of the excluded middle, where something is either *this* or *that*, with no possibility of anything in-between. This recognition brings us to a critical point on our journey toward the threshold of love, where the noisy logic of our exclusively rational and materialistic thinking still lingers. With its devotion to power, control, possession, and authority, such thinking threatens the promise Rainer Maria Rilke's fervent advice held for a youthful poet and holds for us all: a more human love born in the infinite silence of solitude may lead us home to the quietly humble threshold toward wholeness. We may well be thinking: *What homeward-bound steps might we follow now?*

Now indeed is the time to appreciate how far we've come and to reorient ourselves to the perspective that an art and practice of contemplative beholding depends on. Perhaps we can start with T. S. Eliot's wise counsel from "Little Gidding" (see chapter 1) as we imagine arriving home to where we started and knowing it for the first time.

Next, we might recall Milo's lament (see chapter 2) and the existence of reconciliatory longing born in the moment of our conscious awakening. Remember that "separation" and "longing" require us to embrace contradiction and to seek *intimations of reconciliation*—as inklings or hints, or as productive ambiguities rather than impacted certainties—in this and every other contradiction our conscious being entails. In its most ordinary presence, this existential condition will be momentarily relieved by water to our thirst, nourishment for hunger, rest for fatigue, courage in the face of fear, clarity where there is confusion, and, of course, some form of companionship to diminish loneliness and solace to soften the grief.

Recall, too, that intimations of reconciliation mend (rather than remove) the gaps between the irreconcilable distance that separates finite and infinite realities. These include our deepest longing for some sense of regained wholeness, peace, and well-being—call it "happiness"—reminiscent of Milo before he wept. Imagine this coming home in the biblical sense as a return to Paradise through the East Gate, where Adam and Eve were once expelled. Or think of it simply as the bliss Thomas Merton remembered so vividly when writing about the moment that he and "M," against all rational objections, were falling in love. So too, we respond to the joy of meeting a friend, of seeing something "beautiful," or just feeling well. Our conscious capacity for "homecoming," then, requires our sensual alertness to sound, sight, smell, taste, and the texture of the world around us. Let this sensory awareness be "experience."

We are also endowed with the capacity to organize and fix otherwise fleeting "experience." Let this be "order." As we have seen, "experience" and "order" are dynamically related. Neither exists entirely without the other. The color red remains inchoate, ocular warmth absent conceptual red, and this red is a meaningless abstraction, absent raw experience of ocular warmth. In the tradition of *ars* (sensory experience, observation, craft, practice) and *scientia* (reflection, theory, cerebral order) the dynamic convergence of "experience" and "order" is *eruditio*. This understanding of "higher learning," which leads to *sapientia* (wisdom), helps to shape the perspective I describe as an art and practice of contemplative beholding.

In an earlier era, it was precisely because of this experiential and theoretical overlap that the "cathedrals" of our highest spiritual aspiration—despite all the difficulties and turmoil that attended their construction—stood firm, tall, and resplendent, inviting each one of us sooner or later into their luminous intimation of absolute wholeness.[1]

Beholding with Rembrandt van Rijn (in chapter 3) brought us face to face with the artist's own pictorial intimations of reconciliation, where his art led us to the threshold of universal being-nonbeing, and where we stand with him in contemplation of timeless presence. Johann Wolfgang von Goethe (in chapter 4) reminds us of the "sacred open secret" of interior and exterior wholeness in his passionate, unbiased encounter with the Cathedral of Strasbourg. Piet Mondrian (in chapter 5) draws us into his reciprocal "dance" with light beyond light.

Coming back once more to *ai-no-ma* (chapter 6), we recall the place of mysterious meeting where the fateful encounter of all lovers evokes a homecoming to the immanent wholeness of our living. Think further back in time, as though for a moment we are reunited with our infantile, preconscious condition at the very origin of our being.

This reflection brings us to a clearing along our path, and a return to the words *eros* and *insight*, which have been reverberating implicitly beneath all I have said and all we have seen so far.

Eros and Insight

Together, eros and insight animate the elusive but vital intimations of reconciliation that make possible the love of Love we depend on to bring us to a Via Amoris and our homecoming. I introduced these two terms briefly in the introduction. But I've postponed until now our explicit encounter with them because an unfortunate confusion occurs when eros is misinterpreted as "lust," and when "reason" is understood to be the same as insight. Eros and insight are fundamentally different from their antithetical pair, as we will see. Plus, there's a further distinction in the dynamic relation between eros *and* insight contrasted with the opposition in the standoff between lust *or* reason.

Eros, of course, identifies the Greek god of love. Eros in our time, being the root of the word "erotic," denotes sexual desire, and for some the very "life force" that sustains us. But sexual passion was only one of the many realizations of love in ancient Greece as we see it expressed by the following words: *storge* (parental and filial affection), *philia* (friendship), *ludus* (playful love), *agape* (divine, universal love), *pragma* (enduring love), and *philautia* (love of self). As eros applies to the nature of being, and specifically to our journey here, it reaches beyond sexual desire to embody our fullest sensual awareness, including sexual desire. Insight, on the other hand, complements the physical urgency of eros with our capacity to transcend reason by way of heightened intuitive perception and understanding.

Let's return for a moment to the idea of eros and insight as the animating partners of our human capacity for reconciliatory longing. Such longing softens and redeems the "affliction" in our conscious separation from wholeness. Together eros and insight form a constellation of active energy in which love the verb seeks love the noun—the beloved—a wholeness beyond all rational calculation. This is the constellation of our inherent aspiration to wisdom.

To progress on our journey means to move from the alienating effects of lust–reason (as it is grounded in the law of the excluded middle) to the dynamic energy of eros and insight that is alive in the infinite and ever-expanding space of existential solitude. We move by way of change, growth, and transformation from "noise" to the sound of silence—and, with Simone Weil, from the laws of gravity to those "empty spaces" (the void) filled by grace. If we were to agree that we have encountered such grace in the exemplary art of Rembrandt van Rijn, Piet Mondrian, the all-encompassing vision of Goethe, and the reconciliatory experience of *ai-no-ma*, we may now reimagine an epistemology of love—hence a new ethics of love—where the radical change from grasping amid the alienation of lust–reason moves toward the infinite embrace and acceptance of solitude.

> *The threshold of love I propose here is grounded in solitude, in being intimately awake to oneself, to others, to the world, and to the fateful condition of our mortal-immortal human being, even as we remain infinitely separate, each of us a unique solitude.*
>
> *Think here of the words I formulated for Milo's lament: to be is to be separate . . . and being separate, we long to be whole.*

In this affirmation of solitude we may face an apparent danger, where selfish misunderstanding and behavior lead to isolation, alienation, and despair. But solitude is distinct from the selfish individualism (self against *other* of all kinds) that results in Rilke's "killing is a form of our wandering mourning." If we embrace the unavoidable paradox of solitude (separation *and* wholeness), solitude itself will become the very means of igniting eros and insight as the source of love the verb. That embrace will empower us all to transcend "killing" in even its most innocuous forms, in order to love Love. Perhaps, like Heidegger in quoting the poet Friedrich Hölderlin (1770–1843), we too will come home to the hard truth: "But where the danger is, grows the saving power also."[2]

The personal, social, political, and even spiritual urgency we felt as we set out on this path might help us to recall our embrace of Rilke's irreducible definition of a "more human love . . . which consists in this, that two solitudes protect and border and salute each other." This understanding may lead us to consider the singular achievement of *fin'amor* (refined or purified love). What if it allows us to rediscover the lost, but not forgotten, aspirational importance of eros *and* insight as the animating realities of embodied solitude, freed of the fragmenting limitations of either lust *or* reason? Our rediscovered presence within the solitude of our being is precisely the precondition of a "more human love," which in the end may be identified with an art and practice of contemplative beholding.

The Inspiration of *Fin'amor*

The path and practice of a purified love known as *fin'amor* emerged as courtly love in Aquitaine, France, during the twelfth century and shone brightly until it was obscured by the dazzling Renaissance "Dream of Reason." It was a revolutionary, historical, and essentially feminine inspiration that sought to reclaim eros from the jaws of lust and release insight from the bonds of transactional reason.[3] This impulse washed over the spiritual and secular culture like a dissolving agent. It liberated sensuality from the chains of egotism, and placed it in the service of love, at a time when brutal knights of the medieval court dominated the pervasive masculine privilege—never mind power, control, and authority. Refined, pure *fin'amor* restored the true meaning and transformative experience of eros and raised insight beyond the grip of reason that would dominate all behavior. As a result, a new, influential, and creative feminine culture of love was created. In addition to the well-known poets and *jongleurs* who gave it lyrical voice, many extraordinarily capable religious lay and cloistered women realized the spiritual significance of what was at stake. Their lives offered, and offer still, reassuring hope to all who would listen.[4]

One of these women, Marguerite Porete (1248/50–1310), likely belonged to the Béguines, a then-widespread spiritual order of lay Christian women. She may also have been affiliated with the heretical Brethren of the Free Spirit. She is a particularly moving and instructive exemplar on our path.[5]

(7.1) *Béguinage*, Bruges, Belgium

We know almost nothing about Marguerite Porete's life before its tragic end on June 1, 1310. On that day she was burned at the stake in Paris at the Place de la Grève. Her offence? She wrote a book replete with alleged "errors" and heresies, including the anarchy of antinomianism (spiritual resistance to official order) and self-deification. Even more egregiously in the eyes of the Church, she refused to stop promoting and circulating her controversial book, called *The Mirror of Simple Souls*.

Porete's birthplace is unknown, but she appears to have lived most of her life in the area of Hainaut, adjoining what is now the Belgian border with France. Although we know little about her social standing and the circumstances of her work, she must have had considerable resources to pay for writing materials and for scribes to make copies of her book. She found at least three "qualified" supporters, including a Franciscan, a Cistercian, and, most importantly, Godfrey of Fontaines, a celebrated Regent Master at the University of Paris and a prominent secular Master of Theology. Evidence exists that Meister Eckhart (ca. 1260–ca. 1328), a prominent and popular German theologian and mystic, whose teachings received renewed interest in the nineteenth century as source of inspiration for diverse spiritual practices and traditions, read her book and was influenced by it. She wrote in vernacular French, was well read in the vernacular literature of *fin'amor*, and was herself familiar with contemporary philosophical and theological concepts. As others have pointed out, echoes of Augustine, Bonaventure, Richard of St. Victor, and Dionysus the Areopagite can be heard throughout her book. But her own words are the ones that will lead us directly to the radical proposal central to our path; words that so angered the ecclesiastical authorities that they silenced her by condemning her to death. Should it be necessary, the account of the extraordinarily calm and dignified demeanor she displayed at her execution provides compelling evidence of her deep sense of solitude and the inner peace that informed her embodied vision of Love.[6]

The Mirror of Simple Souls takes the form of an allegorical conversation in which Love (also named Lady Love), Soul, and Reason seek to give an account of the free, simple, and "annihilated" (liberated) condition of becoming Love. In what amounts to a most intimate interior dialogue, Lady Love is the primary authority aided by the longing of a determined Soul (Marguerite Porete personified). Throughout the conversation Reason struggles to understand, asking repeatedly, "What is the meaning of what you have said?" As the exchange progresses, it becomes clear that for Soul to become Love—"annihilated"—Reason must be transcended to allow for another kind of understanding to arise, one sustained by an ability to embrace the ever-recurring presence of opposites, contraries, and contradictory truths:

> Ah Love, says Reason, . . . I pray you to make clear and explain to ordinary people these double words that are hard for their understandings to grasp. . . . Reason, says Love, I will answer for the benefit of those on whose behalf you make this compassionate request.

> Reason, says Love, where are these double words that you beg me to explain for this book's listeners, who dwell in will and desire—this book which we call *The Mirror of Simple Souls*?
>
> My reply to this, Lady Love, says Reason, is that this book says amazing things about the Soul. It says that she does not care for me or for honour, for poverty or for riches, for comfort or for discomfort, for love or for hate, for hell or for paradise. It says too that the Soul has everything and has nothing, she knows everything and knows nothing, she wills everything and wills nothing.... It is certain, Love, says Reason, that no one can understand this according to my way of understanding unless they learn it from being taught by you.... And so I say that no one will understand this book by way of understanding, unless they understand it by virtue of Faith and the power of Love.... And yet, says Reason, I say this much that he who has these two strings in his heart, the light of Faith and the power of Love, has permission to do what pleases him, by witness of God himself [wholeness], who says to the Soul, love Love, and do as you will."[7]

Anticipating by more than three centuries these words from the great French mathematician, physicist, and religious philosopher Blaise Pascal—"the heart has its reasons which reason does not know"—as well as our own era's encounter with the rational mysteries of quantum physics, Marguerite Porete's vision opens the way to a Via Amoris that is forever poised on paradoxical intimations of reconciliation. It is grounded in our awakened acknowledgement of the infinite reach of our existential solitude.

Let's move now from the self-contained limitations of lust–reason to the elevated energy of dynamically integrated eros and insight as we consider the most immediately and dramatically radical proposal of *The Mirror of Simple Souls*.

In the third chapter, Porete recalls for her readers her own transforming action, challenging them to do likewise:

> Therefore, I say: Virtues, I take leave of you for evermore. Now my heart will be free and more at peace than it has been. Indeed, I know well that your service is too burdensome. Once I pledged my heart to you without separation: you know this well. I was obedient to you in all things. Oh, I was then your servant, but now I am liberated from servitude to you. I know well, I set my heart on you

completely, and so I put up with great servitude for a long time, suffering many grievous torments and enduring many pains. It is a wonder that I have escaped with my life. But now I do not care, because it has come about that I have left your dominion, in which I have been many nights and days, so that I was never free. But now I have departed from you, and so I dwell in peace.[8]

Porete essentially says here that once the Soul is no longer subservient to the Virtues, they serve her freely. She has now left the dominion of Reason, the Virtues, and the Law to enter the free domain of Love. Today, her radical challenge may fall on deaf ears—and the reaction from those who actually hear or read such words can be all too easily dismissive, articulated with a reflexive "So what?" But to take leave of the medieval cardinal virtues of temperance, fortitude, prudence, and justice—and the theological virtues of faith, hope, and love—shocked the ruling authority of the Church, all the more so when she called it the "Church of the Little." For us, these are still just words, abstractions from a bygone era that has since been written off as irrational, driven by arbitrary edict and superstition. We might think of Porete's transforming action as a revolutionary act but hardly worthy of a tortured death.

Still, presumably, those who condemned her knew her perfectly well and feared the reach of her vision and its liberating role in our human wellbeing. Perhaps they were right. In truth, were we to pause to reflect, might we not say: "Wait a minute, doesn't Marguerite Porete's blunt announcement speak to the very nature of our being? Might her words "Therefore, I say: Virtues, I take leave of you evermore" not bring us abruptly back to the burning center of the ontological dilemma each of us must confront sooner or later?

Rilke's own account of our misunderstanding of love, with which we began, echoes the circumstances and longing that fostered *fin'amor* in the first place. It is worth reading again and paying attention to his definition of "more human love."

> Someday there will be girls and women whose name will no longer signify merely an opposite of the masculine, but something in itself, something that makes one think, not of any complement and limit, but only of life and existence: the feminine human being. This advance will (at first much against the will of the outstripped men) change the love experience, which is now full of error, will

alter it from the ground up, reshape it into a relation that is meant to be of one human being to another, no longer of man to woman. *And this more human love (that will fulfill itself, infinitely considerate and gentle, and kind and clear in binding and releasing) will resemble that which we are preparing with struggle and toil, the love that consists in this, that two solitudes protect and border and salute each other.*[9]

(Advance screen)

Taking Leave of Our "Virtues"

Although rediscovered only as recently as the 1930s, Marguerite Porete's impassioned declaration speaks to us in our time as though it were offered directly to us, much the way Rilke's was to the young poet he addressed as "My dear Mr. Kappus." To test its primal authenticity, try a simple, if momentarily disorienting, thought meditation. In place of the medieval virtues, list for yourself as many of the values—the principles and noble constraints, as well as the inherited preconceptions—that guide your life and offer you comfort and stability. That is, list what you have learned. Choose from those taught by your grandparents, parents, elders in your community, friends, teachers, mentors, religious leaders, political leaders, thinkers, critics and commentators, artists, writers, and coaches. Add to the list personal and social moral values, ethical norms, and legal boundaries you have learned to respect on your own.

Then, with your list prepared as fully and frankly as possible, find a secure and quiet place to be alone. Sit comfortably in silence. Relax. Then do what Marguerite Porete did:

> *Take leave of your "virtues." Let go of the things you think you have learned, one by one. Set them aside; empty yourself of them. Separate yourself from everyone and everything that now guides you through each day and night.*

Remember that this thought meditation is meant to mirror the reality Marguerite Porete lived, and within which her vision of love emerged.

> *Allow that potent experience of emptiness to fill your being as true silence does. Sit with it. Then, when it seems right, blink . . . and once again, the world will be as it was.*

Now, repeat the experience. Imagine yourself again without the familiar support structure that defines your life. Be still once more, and silent. Embrace and be embraced by an unfamiliar presence at the origin of your being: existence within the infinite reality of absolute solitude. Remain in the experience of this meditative moment as long as you can. Repeat this exercise as you will without naming, defining, interpreting it. Simply take leave of *your* "virtues" in silence and stillness.

Now, reflect on this meditation. Was it difficult to accomplish? Were you able to take leave of the "virtues" that guide and support you? If not, what prevented you from succeeding? What did you feel or sense as you proceeded: Gratitude to those you love and respect and who taught you? Disorientation? Fear, anger, isolation, despair? Did you feel lonely? Or...

> *Did you sense an opening . . . a possibility . . . a change? Did you, like Marguerite Porete, come to "dwell in peace?" The full account of how you experienced your meditative moment will be valuable to you as we proceed.*

There can be no question that this meditation is fraught with difficulty and danger. I once asked a group of Elder Hostel visitors taking my class to prepare a self-portrait, by any means available to them, as preparation for encountering Rembrandt's painted self-portraits. One of them asked in an agitated voice, "Do you think I have spent my whole life avoiding who I am, only to begin looking at myself now?"[10]

It may be easier to begin by taking leave of those "virtues" that we already sense dominate and enslave us, and then slowly, bit by bit, allow the cherished ones to recede. From the beginning of this journey, we have experienced the value of resisting virtuous interference. The apostle Paul in his letter to the Corinthians acknowledged that he himself had left behind "childish ways." In front of Rembrandt's *Aristotle with a Bust of Homer* we tried to encounter Rembrandt's art without the burden of art historical intermediaries. Goethe's discovery of a complex contradictory beauty similarly required his recognition and rejection of the bias imposed by his former education when he said in effect, "If this is ugly, then everything I know is wrong!" Piet Mondrian resisted the false choice of "figurative" or "nonfigurative" painting to realize instead an art of related sensations in the form of line, color, space, and time. Engaging with *ai-no-ma* explicitly allowed us to deny the arbitrary despotism of the "law of the excluded middle."

For those of us who might be more confident with visible guides to Marguerite Porete's courageous act, Vincent's *Wheatfield with Crows*, which is so often described as the last apocalyptic vision of a dying and desperate man, will actually offer new hope.

(2.1) Vincent van Gogh, *Wheatfield with Crows*, 1890

Is it possible that the artist himself will bring us to a more optimistic understanding—not only of this exceptionally powerful image but also of our own experience of solitude? In a letter Vincent sent to his brother Theo on returning from Paris to Auvers, he wrote: "Once back here I set to work again—the brush however almost falling from my hands and—knowing clearly what I wanted I've painted another three large canvases, . . . immense stretches of wheat fields under turbulent skies, and I made a point of trying to express sadness, extreme loneliness."[11]

Let's look at the original French of that sentence, actually just the final clause, which reads "*et je ne me suis pas gêné pour chercher á exprimer de la tristesse de la solitude extrême.*"[12] Note that the word *solitude* in French can mean either "loneliness" or "solitude," so we may never know which meaning Vincent intended. Now, compare the frequently cited translation quoted above (from the compendium of Vincent's annotated letters) to my more literal translation, which follows, and see that mine reads rather differently: "I did not hesitate to try to express the sadness of extreme solitude."

The next sentence in Vincent's letter to Theo holds the key to help open our optimistic understanding of the artist: "You'll see this soon, I hope—for I hope to bring them to you in Paris as soon as possible, since I'd almost believe that these canvases will tell you what I can't say in words, what I consider healthy and fortifying about the countryside."[13] Several days later, in a letter to his mother and sister, he wrote: "For the present I feel calmer than last year, and the turmoil in my head has really abated so much. . . . I often think of you both, and would very much like to see you again."[14]

By avoiding the unresolvable debate about Vincent's tragic end that seeps into written analyses of his life and work, into biographical films, and even into retrospective exhibitions of his work, we may well turn again to the best known of the three canvases he mentions to reflect on the possibility that in solitude he found his capacity to express in his art what he could not say in words.

Although there is danger in distinguishing "solitude" from "loneliness," there is reason to try. Vincent clearly suffered from unrelenting loneliness, even isolation from those around him. A brother who died at birth a year before Vincent was born, whose name was also Vincent, intensified the loss of attachment he felt to his mother, as she surely grieved and suffered her own loss. Nevertheless, his prolific number of vivid self-portraits, no less than his haunting image of sunflowers contained in a vase with his signature across the bottom, create a virtual metaphor in which the painting itself becomes the vessel of his solitude.[15] His *Wheatfield with Crows*, seen from the vantage point of his most vital sense of the sadness of solitude he knew, offers us an occasion of beholding as it lifts the heavy veil of loneliness to reveal what Vincent considered "healthy and fortifying about the countryside."

In form and iconography, the art of *Wheatfield with Crows* provides a beginning as clearly as an ending. The reversed perspective of the roads converging near the center of the lower border marks the origin of a rising serpentine line along the central vertical axis of this exceptionally wide horizontal rectangle, leading toward a still invisible horizon. Meyer Schapiro's suggestion that the formal move from complexity to simplicity in this painting—as though one were counting again from zero—one, two, three—echoes Vincent's own words of optimism. Rather than conveying a state of mind in despair, *Wheatfield with Crows* stands as a resolute statement from an artist reclaiming his freedom.[16]

(Advance screen)

Something of this courage is also implicit in Marguerite Porete's challenge to let go of the virtues, for the Love she becomes is synonymous with freedom. For some of us more at home with modern psychological accounts, Porete's taking leave of the virtues resembles Robert Kegan's developmental movement from normal infantile behavior to pre-adolescent and adolescent dependence on others, and then to full realization of adult independence and mature responsibility.[17] Unfortunately, this psychological approach risks losing sight of the vital selflessness of Porete's spiritual attainment.

In whatever way we are willing and able to engage with it, this meditative exercise clearly requires great trust and no small amount of courage as we venture out of the familiar into the unfamiliar (and presumably forgotten) terrain of our primal being—the name of which for Marguerite Porete is Love. In other words, the purpose of the meditation is a renewed encounter with the very origins of our conscious awakening. The most intense and immediate parallel to this awakening moment may still be Milo's lament, which we experience, you might say, going in the opposite direction: we are returning to start over with "a second birth," and Milo is setting out for the first time. But the recognition is the same: to be is to be separate . . . and being separate, we long to be whole. It is the path to wholeness. It acknowledges that letting go of the isolation of separateness allows the contradiction of separateness and wholeness to be one reality—just as it happened for Marguerite Porete in letting go of the virtues.

In either direction, whether we take inspiration from Milo or Marguerite, we will have arrived at the irreconcilable contradiction of our infinite solitude commonly felt in the thirsts, hungers, fears, confusions, and loneliness that accompany all conscious being. To take leave of the virtues is to accept this reality and to act accordingly. What will follow for us, then, is the beginning of a free relationship with Virtue itself—and thus also with ourselves, others, and the world around us—and especially with the source of all being. For Porete this meant leaving behind the official "Church of the Little" (*l'église la petite*) for the "Great Church" of God's infinite love (*l'église la grande*).

Perhaps less ambitiously we may prefer simply setting out with a renewed aspiration to wholeness within our unalterable condition of humble longing. In either case, on this path, quiet change from the unrelenting opposition and the ironic, grasping similarity of lust–reason to the reality of solitude will bring us to the threshold of love in the embrace of eros and insight.[18]

This interlude with a fragment of Marguerite Porete's teaching assumes still greater meaning as we now actually begin to take leave of our blind, addictive obedience to the seemingly unalterable opposition of lust–reason in all aspects of our living. If we acknowledge the vital distinction between observation and possession, as contrasted with beholding in an act of reaching without touching, we enter the place of our solitude where lust–reason will be transformed into love the verb, forever seeking intimations of reconciliation that mirror the beloved. With this distinction established, let's approach a second component of *fin'amor* known as *amour de loin*—love from afar, at a distance. Porete's revolutionary vision of love as set forth in *The Mirror of Simple Souls* begins with an illustrative tale.

> Now listen humbly at the beginning to a brief exemplum of worldly love and understand its application to divine love. Long ago there was a lady, a king's daughter, who was of great distinction and of

> noble nature, and who lived in a foreign land. It so happened that word came to this lady of the great courtesy and great generosity of King Alexander, and she fell in love with him for his noble graciousness and his great renown. But this lady was so far from the great lord on whom she had set her love that she could neither possess him nor see him; and so she was very often miserable, because no love but this could satisfy her. And when she saw that this distant love, so near to her, was so far from her, she thought to comfort herself by imagining some figure that would bear the likeness of the one she loved and for whom she felt her heart so often wounded. And then she had an image painted, that represented as closely as possible the appearance of the king whom she loved so much. And by looking at this image, *along with other observances*, she was relieved; and thus she comforted herself with the representation of her love, so that she was raised from misery.[19]

Another brief story brings us face to face with this counterintuitive awakening. Jaufré Rudel (1113–1147), Prince of Blaye, was a troubadour in the last quarter of the twelfth century, a time when the Holy Land drew the mind and heart of Europe as the earth draws the plumb bob. Jaufré's court welcomed the streams of pilgrims as they paused to saunter through the various holy sites along their way. (Recall here, from my introduction, Thoreau's purposeful use of the word *saunter* to mean walking reflectively in search of simultaneous physical and transcendent reality.)

From one such noble traveler, a pilgrim returning from Antioch in Syria, Jaufré first heard of the Countess of Tripoli's great beauty. Her soul was said to radiate angelic purity and virtue. It shone through her body so intently that she seemed to hold within her slender frame the beauty of the world itself. Though he had never seen her, Jaufré fell in love, cultivating in his heart a deep fidelity to her image. For years thereafter, dwelling continuously in her image, Jaufré composed verses in her honor. All that time he yearned to see her. Finally, he could stand it no longer, and, in the words of his Provençal biographer, "took the cross and put out to sea."

Just then, when his dream was about to be fulfilled, Jaufré fell deathly ill. The ship was hardly out of port, but there was no turning back. Reaching Tripoli, he was carried on a stretcher to an inn. He lay there dying. When news of his arrival reached the countess, she rushed to meet him, came to his bed, and took him in her arms. Hearing her voice and sensing her presence, as if in a fragrant profusion of wildflowers and blossoms, Jaufré knew that this woman was the countess. Birds sang around them. It was spring. Rejoicing, he praised God that life had finally brought him this joy. Then, turning toward her, face to face with her, he died. The countess, too, felt something stupendous, like an opening or awakening. She had Jaufré buried with full honors in the house of the Templars and, that very day, true to her grief, she took the habit of a nun.[20]

This distant or "faraway" love (*amour de loin*) may remain remote to our modern experience, even with its potential to redeem our condition of mortal longing (our aspiring to wholeness) and to be realized in the most intense and immediate experience of sensual delight. Present everywhere in the poetry and music of the *jongleurs*, the exquisite longing of *fin'amor* amounted to a virtual religion of love. It required absolute obedience to one's *Lady*—the invariable embodiment of infinite wholeness. And, to avoid all of the limitations of legally imposed power and possession, the lover and the beloved who engage in *fin'amor* do so in adultery rather than within bonds of marriage. Though fleeting in its historical life, this seemingly fragile and ineffectual *fin'amor* became a muscular moral force that claimed love as the primary agent of ethical behavior.

In Marguerite Porete's vision, love is similarly an active verb eternally seeking the immutable perfection of Love the noun. In this conviction she echoes directly St. Augustine's admonition to love Love, and do as you will.[21]

The Noisy Presence of Crows

"Now what?" we may ask, having taken leave of our virtues only to discover ourselves alone and naked and on our own in infinite solitude. The very starkness of the moment, as with extreme thirst, hunger, fear, and loneliness—or, perhaps, simply being lost in a forest—may be the very impetus to encourage us on the path toward that "more human love." Accepting the embrace of our newly awakened solitude, we are challenged as never before to replace external authorities that had been for us, as they were for Marguerite Porete, the painful source of our servitude. If prepared to end our "childish ways," we too might see "face to face." That is, with nothing intervening, emptied of all that we think we know, all contents of a consciousness formed of memory and fragmenting desire, we will come close to the threshold of change, growth, and transformation. We might also come to the recognition that to "protect and border and salute" the solitude of another, we will have to give up protecting, bordering, and saluting our own solitude. Here, unselfish humility will be the essential cairn to guide us on our way and bring us home.

Let's listen to Simone Weil once more: "All the natural movements of the soul are controlled by laws analogous to those of physical gravity. Grace is the only exception. Grace fills empty spaces but it can only enter where there is a void to receive it, and it is grace itself, which makes this void."

> *Allow yourself to be this void: this "empty" vessel. Allow yourself to be even slightly detached from all the governing forces in your life. Be inattentive to those "virtues" you named. Take leave of them deliberately. Don't worry. Remember, when you blink, they will all be back controlling your every move, almost like gravity; except that they, and perhaps even the Church of the Little, will now be informed by grace.*
>
> *Let this opening remain. Let it widen. Be with Marguerite Porete and Simone Weil. Share their solitude.*
>
> *Let the noise of your "virtues" give way to the clear sound of a brass bell and the silence that follows its fading. Be in this silence. If you feel panic, let it subside. Even if you feel all alone, resist the urge to reach out to your familiar authorities. Imagine your own interior dialogue in which Lady Love speaks with you as she spoke with Marguerite Porete, guiding you also to move beyond the uncomfortable feeling of being adrift to a new place where you will love Love and, in turn, be loved by Love.*

From deep within our solitude and well along the path to the threshold of love, here is the challenge to our well-being: to know and be Love rather than retreat into the grip of those "virtues" that constrain us and weigh us down. To animate love the verb that would move ever closer to Love the noun, we must confront this inevitable temptation to momentary comfort, whether physical or cerebral. Why? Because love the verb that would guide us toward Love the noun is an embodied reality, as lust and reason are. But love the verb is neither lust nor reason. We will seek the threshold of a "more human love" elsewhere.

Look again at the black crows over Vincent's wheatfield, so easily and frequently "read" as symbols of death.

(2.1) Vincent van Gogh, *Wheatfield with Crows*, 1890

They may not be symbols at all. Imagine instead that the crows are, in paint, the existential presence of gravity: the antithesis of Simone Weil's grace that fills the void.

Pictorially, these ominous crows are the visual equivalent of raucous "noise" that would distract us from the poetic or artistic gesture of silence that opens the curving path in the field with its unknown, but certain, end. So too, the exclusionary opposition of lust *or* reason is also the "noise" that obscures the immanent presence of the void. Where lust or reason offer the unrelieved separateness of alienation, the silence of solitude brings us an intimation of wholeness embodied in the integration of eros and insight. If we were to find ourselves in the primal solitude of our conscious existence, the question would no longer be, "So what?" It will have become, "What will I do?" Rather than argue endlessly and exclusively about the meaning *of* everything, we might begin to rediscover occasionally the beauty of meaning *in* everything, including Vincent's compassionate revelation of endless new beginning.

Marguerite Porete's response to the existential question ("What will I do?") emerges in her passionate interior dialogue recorded in *The Mirror of Simple Souls*. The allegorical figures of Reason and Love *live* this question in the presence of her Soul. On our path to contemplative beholding, our own interior dialogue may begin to take shape as the effort to distinguish genuine eros from lust and transformational insight from mere reason: the effort to know true, rather than counterfeit, abundance. Counterfeit abundance, no matter how immense it appears to be, is never wholeness, just as lust is never eros, regardless of its intensity or allure. Like the "noisy" presence of the crows, countless variations of lust press in on us with tremendous force. So too, reason drowns out the silence of that solitude where love resides. Turning our attention, then, to the opposition between lust *or* reason will refocus the urgency for reconciliation at the core of both the art of works of art and an active love the verb.

(Advance screen)

The False Choice Between Lust *or* Reason

Conventionally—habitually, or wherever the lust-driven rationalistic logic of the excluded middle prevails—we accept the false choice between lust *or* reason, although they are, in their grasping, essentially the same. During the era of courtly love, even the philosopher Peter Abelard may have stumbled over this hurdle, calling his heated affair with his student, Heloise, nothing but lust. To which Heloise disagreed vehemently and beautifully, insisting by her words that the very courtly religion of love was her guide:

> God knows I never sought anything in you except yourself; I wanted simply you, nothing of yours. I looked for no marriage-bond, no marriage portion, and it was not my own pleasures and wishes I sought to gratify, as you well know, but yours. The name of wife may seem more sacred or more binding, but sweeter for me will always be the word friend [*amica*], or, if you will permit me, that of concubine or whore. I believed that the more I humbled myself on your account, the more gratitude I should win from you, and also the less damage I should do to the brightness of your reputation.
>
> Tell me, I say, if you can—or I will tell you what I think and indeed the world suspects. It was desire not affection, which bound you to me, the flame of lust rather than love....
>
> I wish I could think of some explanation, which would excuse you and somehow cover up the way you hold me cheap.
>
> I beg you, think what you owe me, give ear to my pleas, and I will finish a long letter with a brief ending: farewell, my only love.[22]

Given the choice of lust *or* reason, why not side with reason? Is not the cerebral, thoughtful, considered, restrained, "virtuous" behavior of noble human beings easily superior to the presumably unrestrained, so-called instinctual behavior associated with lust? This behavior is not only sexual, of course. It appears as avarice, anger, gluttony, pride, envy, and sloth, which, along with lust itself, are the "seven deadly sins" of medieval morality. These sins were experienced as being endlessly in conflict with the virtues of temperance, fortitude, prudence, justice, faith, hope, and love. So naturally, like any good medieval Béguine, we would choose reason rather than lust.

This obvious choice entails a sharply, even tragically, disembodied reality. It denies our normal physical desires for water, food, warmth, and other "creature comforts," as well as sexual pleasure. It also loses sight of the integral contradictory wholeness of sensual and cerebral experience. When we unreflectively, or even purposefully, accept this moralizing choice—lust *or* reason—we encounter an unfortunate fragmentation of our natural human being and usually end up "sinning" anyway.[23] To put it less theologically, we live an odd schizophrenic life, exhibiting so-called lower or animal behaviors, even as we praise the superiority of rational rectitude in our obedience to our preferred "virtues."

The rationalistic choice of lust *or* reason is limiting, even humanly disabling. But if we have left behind our "virtues" and "vices," at least temporarily and meditatively, and especially when it comes to exclusive, virtually lustful reason, we might now deliberately imagine replacing this choice by accepting the obverse realities of sensual and cerebral knowing. By doing so we can embrace the possibility of reconciling contradictory eros and insight. At this point, contemplating the simple verbal difference between saying lust *or* reason compared to eros *and* insight will help to clarify our challenge.

Let's look at another empty choice we habitually make between togetherness *or* loneliness, which itself generates a more destructive choice. Assuming that we choose to love in an effort to avoid loneliness, rather than consider love an existential necessity like oxygen, we believe our next step is to choose between proximate love and distant love. Without a second's reflection, our individual responses will sound something this this: "Are you crazy? I'll take proximate love, thank you. I want my love near to me always." The medieval vision of *amour de loin* is good for poets, many of us would agree, but not for ordinary life, and not for *our* lives. "Love from afar" seems to offer little comfort, certainly not sensual or sexual satisfaction.

On reflection, though, we might avoid choosing between togetherness *or* loneliness by recognizing the profound existence of solitude at the core of our human being. As Rilke reminds us, solitude "is at bottom not something that one can take or leave. We *are* solitary."[24] Solitude is the condition of our conscious being. Milo knew this. When we slow down, remain calm and are present, we know it too. We exist within the solitude of our longing. Each of us embodies our own solitude separate from every other embodiment of solitude. Regardless of proximity or distance, infinite solitude remains. If this is so, only one conclusion is possible. There is no other love than distant love. To be in love is to be in the thrall of *amour de loin*! Distant love *is* true love. Even so, when lived, it is infinitely intimate: no more remote than the re-oxygenated blood in our veins by which we are endlessly reborn. Or, let's say, no more remote than the renewed oxygen that enters our lungs because of the vacuum—the void—caused by the autonomic movement of our diaphragm. This is both fact and poetry. The real choice is how, when, and where we will begin to seek those intimations of reconciliation that are themselves the art of art and authentic love.

From the place of this awakening, we can set aside the false choices of lust *or* reason and proximate *or* distant love. We can move a step closer to a purposeful embrace of eros *and* insight together as the very engines of an active vibrant love that would seek Love the noun, or what we may otherwise name as wholeness, the beloved, and, for Marguerite Porete, God. What then is eros? What is the fateful partner of insight? How are eros and insight related? Unlike the estrangement of either/or, eros and insight cannot exist without the other. As we will soon see, each is informed by the other.

One more behavioral choice grounded in rationalistic exclusivity deserves our consideration: the choice between lust *or* avoidance. In this either/or case, lust emerges in the separation of eros from love (that is, when *eros* is limited to sex), no less than love from the world. Such separation reverses the deepest inspiration of *fin'amor*, which sought to embody love in sensual delight. Peter Abelard even praised the brutal loss he suffered (castration) as a result of his desire for Heloise because it ensured him an unencumbered means to love God.

Choosing between lust *or* avoidance not only loses love's animating joys, but its eroticization of eros also diminishes our fullest capacities for insight leading to wisdom. By breaking the relation of embodied knowing and sensual delight, it leaves behind nothing but estranged, disembodied, disengaged, and "childish" grasping after fleeting pleasures, moribund knowledge and fictitious power, control, and authority. Absent from this impoverished experience is that enduring sense of integrated wellbeing we might have experienced as bliss. Body and mind are alienated in life as well as in the education that would prepare us for life. In our schools, so-called academic pursuits—including meaningless information beyond what we may begin to absorb as well as unexamined "critical reasoning"—contend with unrestrained license and entertainment. Even eroticized sexual pleasure is reduced to exclusive genital arousal. The stakes are high.

There is an alternative path. By acknowledging the divisive energy embedded in the familiar behavior of lust–reason, we might reanimate our innate capacity for a love that integrates true eros and true insight. That integration extends, perhaps, even to *ars* and *scientia* as we aspire toward *eruditio*, which brings us closer to *sapientia* (wisdom) as it is revealed in the face of the beloved.

To avoid the debilitating limitations and invidious superiorities inherent in either/or dualities—lust or reason, togetherness or loneliness, proximate or distant love, lust or avoidance—we are challenged to reimagine the habitual dualities we normally accept as given: mind or body, cerebral thought or sensual behavior and, most notably, "science" or everything else (including art, religion, eros and insight, and also, presumably, love). What would happen if we were to reject the moralizing pieties of false choice in a deliberate effort to rediscover that "more human love" at the center of our lives—and, just possibly, at the heart of a redeemed academic enterprise generally, not to mention our own individual journeys of continuing change, growth, and transformation? Might we not move toward an ever more subtle and noble way of being human?

On the horizon before us, as we take leave of the virtues that diminish our freedom to be, is the higher, "poetic or divine life" Thoreau pursued so diligently during his solitary sojourn in the woods around Walden Pond. This effort to redeem the false choice summed up as lust *or* reason—even when the choice is disguised within supposedly separate areas of inquiry and experience—reanimates eros *and* insight as our irreducible birthright. The alternative, if we don't make such an effort, condemns us to a condition of painful, confusing, and finally hollow estrangement. Could it be that our singular shared purpose of being is to reclaim love from the clutches of false choice and the hopeless division of all things and all people into ever smaller circles of anger, fear, distrust, and disappointed craving?

What if we seek Love the noun, *amour de loin*, intimately, erotically alive within us, lifting us up through sensual, intellectual, poetic, and musical delectation? How might we avoid precisely the lust that has stolen away eros and insight as enduring partners who together are the parents of an embodied love forever *sauntering* toward the beloved? Is it still possible to envision such longing, such beauty, such grace? What, indeed, might eros and insight look like to the eyes and body of one guided by an art and practice of contemplative beholding?

The Face of Eros

(7.2) Cover illustrations: a. *Cosmopolitan*, April 2000; b. *GQ*, summer 1976

Long before words and images exploded in online magazines, *Cosmopolitan* and *GQ* (*Gentlemen's Quarterly*) enjoyed long reigns as print-media arbiters of fashion, style, and culture. Today they are but two of countless sources where we encounter the eroticized alienation of sensual and intellectual life. Comparing the visual and verbal language of these magazines with Jaufré Rudel's poetry of *fin'amor* starkly reveals what something is by what it is not—a ground zero, perhaps, for any effort to distinguish eros from lust:

> Whoever brings me to this *love*
> *from far away*, I will consider my lord—
> yet, though I've received one good thing,
> I get two bad; this love is far away;
> ah God! I want to be a pilgrim, walking,
> then would I see my stick and my cloak
> a second time in her gorgeous eyes![25]

The eros of contemplative sensuality is redolent in both the poetry and music of *fin'amor* and resides at the heart of art across time and cultures. Since the word *eros* comes to us from ancient Greece, we can declare, in the manner of Goethe and based on our culture's interpretation of the erotic: *if* Cosmopolitan *magazine is eros then everything I know is wrong*. Pause to look again at exemplary sculptural embodiments of eros as the living partner of insight. When they become one again, they will raise human aspiration above the grasping of lust–reason to the acceptance of love beyond longing.

(7.3) a. Eros as infant, 2nd–3rd century BCE; b. Milo

In image 7.3 we see the Greek deity Eros as an infant paired with Milo's innocent wonderment. Although we will return to the subject of eros as the living impulse to love when we attend Plato's symposium in chapter 9, the image of Aphrodite, goddess of love, will help us to remember what love itself once looked like in the Greek imagination.

(7.4) *Crouching Aphrodite*, 1st–2nd century,
copy after 3rd-century BCE original

Marble seems palpable as flesh in this image of Aphrodite. She is alone, kneeling at her purifying bath within the absolute solitude of her being. She is present and yet unaware of anyone or anything, except perhaps the scent and the feel of the refreshing water. All interior and all exterior exist in perfect unity: eros in stillness and silence; the goddess of love and the world as one.

(7.5) Edgar Degas, *Bather*, 1886

Positioned so similarly, yet so utterly different: Edgar Degas's *Bather* is not alone. Someone is present with her in her bathing room. The artist's skillful marks cast window light on her body as if to bathe her in our gaze. The image evokes an artistic ambiguity that resonates presence, separation, and potential possession—observation contrasted with beholding that would seize without touching. Degas's art conjures exquisite self-conscious tension. *Crouching Aphrodite*, on the other hand—however intently we engage with the sculpture—remains alone, pure, unambiguously primal, untouched.

Recalling Rembrandt's palpable artistic interval between material paint that is simultaneously "gold," attend as you will with the interval of marble and "flesh" realized in the following images of Aphrodite . . .

(7.6) Torso of *Aphrodite*, 2nd century BCE
(7.7) Torso of the *Knidian Aphrodite*, 2nd century CE
(7.8) Torso of the *Esquiline Aphrodite*, 2nd century BCE, Musée du Louvre, Paris

The slightly smaller than life-sized scale of these figures allows us to relate to them more intimately than to some monumental sculptures. Aphrodite is self-absorbed, self-aware, and alone, but neither isolated nor observed. Absolute psychological symmetry between the goddess and the world ensures an enduring mutual reverence, even as an extremely subtle formal asymmetry animates a living, moving, breathing presence with us. These sculpted images are the consummate realization of courtly love. Precisely created to inspire the troubadour's "love from faraway" (*amour de loin*), they invite us to behold with an art that evokes an intense sensual response in the presence of the goddess's undisturbed solitude, confirming perhaps our own solitude before her. So powerful is the contemplative allure of these sculptures, we might not even notice their lost heads or arms. Despite this incremental fragmentation, their suggestion of wholeness beyond limitation is intact.

(7.9) *Esquiline Aphrodite*, 2nd century CE, Palazzo dei Conservatori, Rome

With the finely chiseled marble of her head and delicately curled hair still in place, the *Esquiline Aphrodite* in Rome glances down without focus, looking neither inward nor outward. Her bathing vase and cloth are at her side. Her body moves ever so slightly in a quiet gesture of physical ease and psychological contentment. Beyond any possible disturbance, she stands gently and directly before us. She is intimately nearby and infinitely far away, created not as an abstract conceptual reality, but as a vividly alive incarnation of wholeness, at once completely physical and ephemeral. She is the goddess of all love.

(7.10) *Aphrodite with Flowing Gown*, Roman copy of Greek original, 2nd century BCE

Known as *Aphrodite with Flowing Gown*, this goddess of love seems unbothered by or oblivious to the possibility of intimacy with us. She hears the sound of silence, as we remain speechless, in awe and reverence in her presence. Almost two thousand years later (image 7.11), Rembrandt found this goddess in a cool stream, perhaps captivated by her very faint smile of self-recognition in the watery reflection of her body. Like the marble of these sculptures, his tangible paint leaps the incalculable remoteness of such distant love to remind us of our mortal longing.

(7.11) Rembrandt van Rijn, *Woman Bathing in a Stream*, ca. 1655
(7.12) *Aphrodite Bathing*, 3rd–2nd century BCE

Contemplatively self-aware, *Aphrodite Bathing* raises her arms as though she were about to put on a necklace. We might also imagine her about to dry her body with a fine perfumed cloth, and even imagine such a cloth rendered translucent in the morning light. Eros as the immaculate and timeless sensual presence of solitude transforms the hard metal of bronze gone green with age into a vessel of purest, erotic gracefulness. The diminutive scale of this statuette (approximately 18 inches high) only amplifies its near magical reach from finite materiality to infinite wholeness brought close in virtually hand-held intimacy.

(7.13) Praxiteles, *Knidian Aphrodite*, 2nd-century Roman copy of 4th-century BCE original

Still apparent even in this Roman copy of Praxiteles's original sculpture, the infinite gap between us, everything, and everyone around us informs Aphrodite's attention and ours as we behold with the goddess of love the paradoxical condition of our being. Her movement implies the subtlest possible change from singular contentment to deliberate alertness. Her left hand grasps a bathing robe in a new gesture, simultaneously purposeful and unconsciously modest, while her right hand unselfconsciously covers her nakedness. Aphrodite now looks up and turns her gaze outward.

Come slowly to this primal moment, guided by this gentle vision. Tarry a moment. Be with this figure of Aphrodite from the ancient city of Knidos . . . accept her invitation to behold.

From the hands, mind, and heart of Praxiteles, among the greatest of the nearly incomparable sculptors of ancient Greece, the *Knidian Aphrodite* returns us to the fragile threshold between sensual self-awareness and awakening consciousness of *other*. Like Thoreau's awakening to a higher life at Walden, with "fragrance filling the air," the suspended art of marble now becomes cloth, hair, and flesh, and fills the infinite interval between substance and immaterial reality. A fleeting instant of living transformation occurs while we stand before her; feeling and seeing her before our very eyes. The perfect geometric symmetry along the grounded vertical axis of the water vase, asymmetrically placed next to Aphrodite's casually bent leg, provides an immutable measure of our identification with this sculptural merging of palpable eros with equally potent psychological insight.

(7.14) *Eros Asleep*, 3rd–2nd century BCE
(7.15) *Crouching Aphrodite*, 3rd century BCE

All too quickly, of course, this exquisite balance between before and after passes into the full consciousness of separation and its endless longing. Where the baby Eros had been asleep, now he is awake and active.

With his almost playful touch and pointed arrow (image 7.15), the little love-god awakens Aphrodite, who turns in his direction.[26] In her explicit response to Eros, Aphrodite and Greek art have brought us back to the barely perceptible moment of Milo's lament: developmental separation and the beginning of our conscious human need for reunion with that now distant wholeness. This sculptural awakening also stirs eros into being as an immanent impulse, not only to psychological presence, but to our continuing sensual and intellectual reconciliation of all the contradictions that conscious living demands. It is water to our every thirst. Eros here is the animating agent of our paradoxical separation, of self-awareness, and longing of every kind. It is the very engine of love endlessly seeking the beloved.

(7.16) *Capitoline Aphrodite*, Roman copy of 3rd-century BCE original

Aphrodite at her bath now clearly and unambiguously covers herself before our aroused, but still reverent, presence. The art of this sculpture, which mediates between our erotic proximity to its marble-ness (or physicality) and its imagining of a distant love, seizes our attention, as her awareness of another must include us. The contradiction of our self-conscious involvement (separation and longing) now mirrors that of Aphrodite herself.

After the Fall

The tension of our implication within the psychological reality of the Capitoline Aphrodite must also inform its Renaissance transformation by Masaccio (1401–1428) into a new image of shame at the moment of expulsion from the garden of Paradise and our biblical Fall from Grace.

(7.17) Masaccio, *Expulsion*, 1427

In this famous early Renaissance fresco in the Brancacci Chapel of the Church of Santa Maria del Carmine in Florence, Eve covers herself with an urgent gesture like that of the *Capitoline Aphrodite*, while Adam hides his disgrace with his hands. What ancient Greek art had apparently defined as the natural evolution of conscious awakening has here become an emblem of moralizing recrimination at the failure of reason to constrain the temptation of our desires. Moral directive has replaced the delicate embodiment of Aphrodite's love. The fact that Adam in this image does not cover himself as Eve does may even inform our sense of gender politics in fifteenth-century Italy: here we might trace the conversion of an art in which eros and insight were integrated as the constituent components of this love rather than separated in their opposition as lust and reason.

In the latter years of the fifteenth century, a Flemish artist, Hugo van der Goes, portrayed the Fall of Adam and Eve as the loss of timeless, summer-like perfection, resulting in self-conscious anxiety, embarrassment, and even neurosis (image 7.18). In remarkable anticipation of the modern era, the Fall here is virtually a psychological pathology seeking remedy.

(7.18) Hugo van der Goes, *Adam and Eve*, ca. 1470

Albrecht Dürer represented Adam and Eve as emblems of his own fascination with rational perfection and proportional moderation in contrast to the idiosyncrasies he rendered in the forest that surrounds the figures, including the goat precariously perched at the edge of a distant cliff. Titian's *Adam and Eve* offers another objectified image of the idyllic Greek human form as the "beautiful" embodiment of rational control before its imminent loss to the ravages of lustful desire.

(7.19) Albrecht Dürer, *Adam and Eve*, 1504
(7.20) Titian, *Adam and Eve*, ca. 1550

By comparison, it appears that Rembrandt van Rijn subjectified the moment of the Fall. He brings us close to the ongoing struggle with the paradox of life's corporeal burden of conscious human being.

(7.21) Rembrandt van Rijn, *Adam and Eve*, 1638

The tree and the lurking reptile that frame and open the brightly illuminated illusory space cast "us" in shadow, even as a distant elephant reveals the heavily grounded vantage point of our presence as beholders in the darkened foreground. Adam's virtual blessing, his gesture protecting the apple, and Eve's humble acceptance, would seem to confirm the sacral fragility and enduring reality of the very moment of our self-awakening. Each of these masterful works of art, independent of their other accomplishments, reveals the fraught tension between lust–reason and the elusive healing of eros and insight, reaffirming our challenge to confront this affliction face to face.

Diane Arbus, in the art of her photography, may unwittingly or not offer us a warning about fatigue in our natural struggle with the paradox of this awakening. Her haunting incarnation of Adam and Eve as two utterly vacant naked people standing aimlessly in the woods surrounding their nudist camp might encourage us to reaffirm love as we reach to reconcile the necessary contradictions of our self-aware being.

(7.22) Diane Arbus, *A husband and wife in the woods at a nudist camp, N.J.*, 1963

Integrating Extraordinary Delight and Understanding

The bronze statuette *Aphrodite Bathing* (image 7.12) is identified iconographically as *Venus naturalis*—a figure of innocence (as in *eros pur*)—unaware of anything other than herself in seamless, unconscious relation with her surroundings. Like the *Capitoline Aphrodite* in Rome, the *Medici Venus* in Florence's Uffizi (image 7.23) is traditionally known as *Venus pudica*, sensually present to herself, but also erotically aware of others, as we are of her. Her gesture is one of modesty, not shame.[27] See the Venuses side by side in image 7.24.

(7.23) *Medici Venus*, 1st-century BCE Roman copy of 4th-century BCE original

(7.24) a. *Aphrodite Bathing* (Natural Venus);
b. *Medici Venus* (Modest Venus)

Both "natural" and "modest" sculptures were placed in temples of Aphrodite with the intention of ritually evoking the strongest possible (erotic) desire in the presence of the goddess of love. In thrall to such desire, how might we discover Love the noun as an embodied, living divinity on both sides of human conscious awareness? These two sculptural realizations of natural and modest eros invite our thoughtful contemplation and consideration along a developmental and conceptual continuum, one before and the other after awakening.

As we have seen, other figures of Aphrodite remain magnificently ambiguous. Like the *Knidian Aphrodite* in Munich (7.13), whose attention moves outward, the sculpture known as the *Kallipygos Aphrodite* (or colloquially as "Aphrodite of the beautiful behind"), turns her head as if to acknowledge another presence.[28] Her backward glance, perhaps toward her reflection in the still water of her bath, suggests that the goddess admires herself as much as we may.

(7.25) *Kallipygos Aphrodite*, 1st century BCE, front and back

In either instance, front or back, this sculpture is clearly present to us as the sensuous embodiment of divinity. Any pilgrim to the Temple of Aphrodite who sought to experience the integration of extraordinary delight and understanding would find it within the artistic interval between polished marble and the image of a woman's body. The intense erotic experience it evokes distinguishes such occasions of our contemplative involvement from even the most alluring of our familiar and essentially voyeuristic constructions—photographic or otherwise—whose exclusive purpose is material and commercial arousal. (Let me pause here to stress and contrast the negative result of fragmenting and alienating desire with the embracing affirmation of aspirational delectation.) The arousal elicited in us by commercial popular imagery has nothing to do with either eros or insight, certainly not their vital integration.

In the Greek spiritualization of our common humanity, masculine images of transformation from unconscious movement to willful action complement the femininity, innocence, and modesty palpable in countless sculptures of Aphrodite. The standing figure of a young man known as a *kouros*, which once marked a burial site, will extend this circle of artistic aspiration.

(7.26) *Kouros* (male youth), ca. 6th century BCE

The asymmetrical placement of the feet of this *Kouros* figure in New York's Metropolitan Museum of Art loosens the otherwise rigid symmetry of the body and imbues the stone with an inherent physical vitality appropriate to the contemplative insight attending human burial of the dead. The well-known formal development in Greece of muscular specificity conveyed with precise proportions follows an evolutionary arc toward the sculptural incarnation of divine willfulness in our earthbound existence.

(7.27) *Kritios Boy*, 5th century BCE
(7.28) *Young Athlete*, 4th century BCE
(7.29) *Hermes with the Infant Dionysus*, 4th century BCE, copy after Praxiteles
(7.30) *Charioteer of Delphi*, 470 BCE
(7.31) *Apollo* (*Apollo Belvedere*), 2nd century, Roman marble copy of 4th-century BCE Greek bronze

(Advance screen)

The Face of Eros and Insight

The fullest realization of infinite divinity in the integration of both eros and insight in female and male form exists in two of the best-known masterpieces of all Greek sculptural inspiration.

> *Pause to allow the elusive interval of intimated wholeness embodied by two magisterial works of art to open up before you and in you . . .*

(7.32) *Aphrodite of Milos*, ca. 150–125 BCE

The armless sculpture known as *Aphrodite of Milos* in the Louvre may allow us to recover something of the quiet, contemplative ambiguity she once possessed for herself and offered to those who came in reverence to her. The contradictory presence of natural and modest eros we have seen elsewhere stands forth here as the immutable perfection of purest sensual and cerebral presence. All noise ceases as she turns in response to an inner voice from the realm of absolute silence. Poised stillness now accompanies her graceful, curved movement while all space and all time give way to an undeniable sense of well-being, joy, and peace we feel in the deepest reaches of our being. Wisdom has become Love.

(7.33) *Zeus of Artemision*, 5th century BCE

Zeus, the divine progenitor, lover, and warrior, is poised to throw a missing spear—or a thunderbolt, given his mythical powers. The finality of this muscular, horizontal action, frozen in time, complements the formally ascending s-curve of the *Aphrodite of Milos*.

In these two figures, divinity approaches human awareness while remaining infinitely distant, untouched and untouchable, undiminished and undiminishable. The contradictoriness of mind and body, separation and wholeness, finite and infinite reality fades away in our contemplative experience. What emerges for us is the seamless intersection of immortal and mortal presence: theirs and ours. In thrall to this Greek artistic longing and sculptural aspiration, we come face to face with *amour de loin*.

(7.34) a. *Aphrodite of Milos,* torso; b. *Zeus of Artemision*, torso

To behold with the complementary female and male figures of Aphrodite and Zeus is to replace the moralizing opposition of lust *or* reason with an elevated vision of eros informed by insight, no less than the reverse of insight informed by eros. This Greek vision of divinity illuminates these two sculpted bodies with almost precisely the brilliance that Thoreau anticipated in meeting someone who was "quite awake." The rippling waves of carefully dressed hair and beard radiate outward to affirm the sun-like bedazzlement of our beholding.

> *Recall here also, from John O'Donohue's blessing, the light shining forth to carry an infant home, as well as Mondrian's immutable white light.*

(7.35) a. *Aphrodite of Milos,* face; b. *Zeus of Artemision*, face

In these two faces, so redolent with intelligence, we have at last found the embodied primal intersection of eros and insight. Let it animate those acts of love that would aspire to wholeness from within the solitude of our mortal condition and our feelings of limitation, fragmentation, and longing.

> *Allow the scent clinging to the freshly washed body of Aphrodite, who has just stepped from her aromatic bath, to fill the air. . . . Imagine Zeus's eyes filled, as they once were, with sparkling, radiant gemstones . . .*

Come home to this profoundest of all our awakenings—to these lost, forgotten realities—to St. Augustine's prophetic conviction that there will be "such poise, such grace, such beauty as become a place where nothing unbecoming can be found." In whatever form it will appear, we will discover ourselves, as Jaufré Rudel once did, reflected in the beauty that our beholding in solitude summons forth—face to face.

(Advance screen)

Entering the Interval of Silence

What if we have taken for granted that as human beings our natural tendency toward greed rather than love—and our resignation that killing is unavoidable if we are to survive—has been all along the worst of our "childish ways"? Is this really so?

The moralizing opposition of lust *or* reason itself may well be the distraction that most deafens us to the sounds all around us that, if we will but listen, would guide us gently into the interval of silence in which music, art, science, and love the verb will emerge. The very distinction between the dehumanizing estrangement inherent in the opposition of lust–reason, as contrasted with the dynamic alignment of eros *and* insight, will reveal a clearing in front of us. And beyond that, our path is open and waiting for us to proceed.

If eros turns out to be an irreducibly sensuous, physical, longing for momentary encounters with (or even hints of) wholeness, stillness, and peace beyond all limitation—greater than which there is nothing—then this eros reaches outward from all our senses and all our inborn human capacities to feel, to think, to respond, to resonate, and to embrace all life. If eros leads to true abundance, then counterfeit abundance is the grasping goal and limit of lust.

Like all counterfeit abundance, lust is fundamentally empty, having little or nothing to do with our fullest being. Here I mean us to reach beyond the concept of lust as one of the seven deadly sins of medieval behavior and acknowledge that it need not be dismissed merely as bad, evil, or hateful. In the reality of our experience, it is simply closed. Lust can never *reach beyond itself* or be fulfilled by anything that is not itself. Lust is the ultimate psychological and physical realization, not of self-awareness, but of selfishness. Lust is separation and division without hope of reunion. It is first isolation, then alienation, and then loneliness beyond hope. Lust is incapable of loving

Love. In its focused limitation of eros to genital arousal, lust generalized as eroticism remains exclusive unto itself and satisfied for itself only. The experience is compelling and, of course, it sells.

What then is love that would take leave of all habitual "virtues" to allow for our acceptance of an unmediated animation of eros and insight together?

Reflection

> *Soften your eyes . . . your face, your body . . . your thoughts . . . be present . . . breathe . . . in . . . out . . . be still . . . silent . . . listen again to Marguerite Porete . . .*

> This Soul, says Love, swims in the sea of joy, that is, in the sea of delights that stream from divine influences. She feels no joy, for she herself is joy. She swims and drowns in joy, for she dwells in joy without feeling any joy. Joy is in her in such a way that she herself is joy, by the power of joy that has changed her into itself. Now the will of the beloved and the will of the Soul are turned into one, like the fire and flame, for Love has changed the Soul entirely into himself.
>
> Ah, sweetest pure divine Love, says the Soul, what a sweet union this is, that has changed me into the thing I love more than myself! I who can love so little have lost my own name for the sake of Love. Thus I am changed into the thing that I love more than myself, that is, into Love, for Love is all I love.[29]

The face of the beloved never shone more brightly. In these extraordinary words of passion, the Soul is both female and male as though this flowing together of genders might be a Love beyond all distinction. Here, action and contemplation also merge as one—"fire and flame"—to become that "sweet union" in which all longing is "changed into the thing that I love more than myself, that is, into Love, for Love is all I love." Marguerite Porete in *The Mirror of Simple Souls* found her way back from the essential alienation of lust–reason to that place of infinite harmony, forever secure in the interior dialogue of her solitude. For this reason, and no other, the grace with which she faced her immolation left no one present unmoved.

What could have happened to diminish Marguerite's sublime embodiment of Love, so vivid in the imagination realized by those glorious, sculpted figures—male and female—from ancient Greece?

(7.36) "The champagne panty. At the soda-pop price." n.d.

We might find a partial answer in the provocative imagery of the countless popular magazines that surround us. Let image 7.36, an admittedly charming newspaper advertisement, focus our attention on the seductive allure of our contemporary instrumental "virtues." Note its message: "The champagne panty. At the soda-pop price." The fleeting but intimated wholeness of courtly love has given way to a virtually ubiquitous presence of estranged incremental lust in dedicated service to the power of commerce.

(Advance screen)

Approaching the Threshold

As a space with all manner and occasions of inexorable contradiction—call it the "mending wall" of poetry—the threshold of love holds the silence of solitude that signals the presence of infinite wholeness in the embodied experience of our mortal being. Entering this elusive space is the active precondition that enables an art and practice of contemplative beholding.

Solitude animated by eros *and* insight, rather than lust–reason, is where this threshold of love resides. To enter this threshold is to know that to love is to suffer love, and to love actively is to become Love. Milo entered his threshold at the age of five months and ten days. In his poetry, Jaufré Rudel wrote of reaching the threshold when we see ourselves reflected in the eyes of the beloved. This is the epiphany, the Holy Grail, we would approach, knowing full well perhaps, as Thomas à Kempis reminds us, that the closer we come to wholeness, the greater the suffering—as in the pain of conscious separation. From this vantage point, an art and practice of contemplative beholding is the deliberate lifelong action of replacing lust–reason (alienation without hope of reunion) with those precious intimations of reconciliation we can know as the art of works of art. They will evoke infinite beauty and co-passion (compassion) and redeem the necessary limitations of all consciousness.

In 1890, at the dawn of our own modern era, Vincent van Gogh's heroic struggle may have been to hold fast to solitude. His art emerged from an increasingly personal, interior place where loneliness threatened him. Scientific objectivity surrounded and further isolated him. If we've been encouraged by the words in Vincent's letters, we may now be willing to imagine that he painted *Wheatfield with Crows* (and all the rest)—not as an act of desperation but of love sent forth confidently to Theo, his wife Jo, and to all who would seek to behold with him. Although the circumstances of his death remain an obsession for many, Vincent's art is not a puzzle to be solved nor, finally, is his death. He was *and is* an artist whose loving gifts remain vivid.

> *To know this love that will emerge in our experience of "extreme solitude," imagine yourself at the convergence of those roads at the foreground border of* Wheatfield with Crows. *Listen for the raucous cawing that disturbs the peace . . . then hear, at last, as you behold with the art of this painting, the infinite sound of silence . . . and feel the liberation Vincent knew of intimated reconciliation—the love—that would bring him home.*

(2.1) Vincent van Gogh, *Wheatfield with Crows*, 1890

(Advance screen)

Accepting Solitude

Continuing our own journey home along a Via Amoris, we now turn to a new chapter, "Dream of Reason." Yes, we will witness breathtaking accomplishments of the Renaissance in Europe. But at the same time, despite the promise and the glory we attribute to this era, we will come to understand how this dream sacrificed the suffering that love requires, and instead gave in to the seductive certainties of power, control, and authority. By acknowledging the limitations hidden within the initial enthusiasms of the Dream of Reason, we may reawaken to an enduring, humble reality, where our immanent solitude is the source that will affirm and engender the love we seek.

The events that began in the sixteenth century in Europe transformed Marguerite Porete's anagogical wisdom of aspiration into a relentless campaign of efficiency, discovery, and acquisition. With her inspiration, we have already engaged with the challenge to take leave of the virtues that imprison us. Now we might expand the challenge with a choice: Do we cling to the false promise of counterfeit abundance? Or do we turn our attention to the promise of abundance that aspires to wholeness, even under the condition of limitation—whether thirst, hunger, fear, confusion, uncertainty, or loneliness—that loving entails?

We may find encouragement to seek the promise of love's abundance in the words of Joseph Bédier. As a scholar of medieval France, he was known for his studies of the poetry and music of the *jongleurs*, the French epic poems called *chanson de geste*, and especially for his lifelong devotion to reviving interest in the stories of Tristan and Iseult:

> The good singers of old time, Béroul and Thomas of Built, Gilbert and Gottfried told this tale for lovers and none other, and, by my pen, they beg you for your prayers. They greet those who are cast down, and those [sick] in heart, those troubled and those filled with desire, those who are overjoyed and those disconsolate, all lovers. May all herein find strength against inconstancy, against unfairness and despite and loss and pain and all the bitterness of loving.[30]

During the Renaissance "Dream of Reason," the very voice that had been allegorically incapable of understanding Love in the inner dialogue of the medieval Béguine now became dominant. At the turn of the sixteenth century, this voice nearly eclipsed all that had come before, including the fragile promise of *fin'amor*. Even so, the lingering and hopeful longing that guides our journey will appear again in the unsuspected consequences of this dream, realized in the art of Albrecht Dürer, Leonardo da Vinci, and Michelangelo Buonarroti. These artists will challenge us again and again to reach beyond the mechanics of limitation and instrumentality in order to approach "a higher life than we fell asleep from." And by accepting that challenge we might find our way back from the dead end of lust–reason to our begotten solitude, where a self-transcendent eros and insight together will illuminate the threshold of love.

(Advance screen)

CHAPTER 8

Dream of Reason: Redeemed by Humility

We have long projected into our forgotten myths... perhaps what has always lain dormant within us as archetypes. That is, the awareness of our being anchored in the earth and the universe, the awareness that we are not here alone nor for ourselves alone, but that we are an integral part of higher, mysterious entities against whom it is not advisable to blaspheme.

—Václav Havel, "The Need for Transcendence in the Postmodern World," 1994

(8.1) Sunset at Chartres, France

AT THIS point in our journey, we may ask: What could possibly have caused artists, poets, philosophers—at so critical a moment as the Renaissance—to turn from their pilgrimage along a Via Amoris? What made them abandon the path of love from afar (*amour de loin*) and the chance to realize an embodied love that aspired to wholeness beyond change? Why stray from that constant love evoked by William Shakespeare in "Sonnet 116," written in 1609, even as radical change was occurring?

Let me not to the marriage of true minds
Admit impediments. Love is not love
Which alters when it alteration finds,
Or bends with the remover to remove:
O no! it is an ever-fixed mark
That looks on tempests and is never shaken;
It is the star to every wandering bark,
Whose worth's unknown, although his height be taken.
Love's not Time's fool, though rosy lips and cheeks
Within his bending sickle's compass come:

Love alters not with his brief hours and weeks,
But bears it out even to the edge of doom.
If this be error and upon me proved,
I never writ, nor no man ever loved.[1]

Why leave behind the most intense and palpable longing of the troubadours, *jongleurs*, and the Béguine Marguerite Porete, with their beckoning vision of a Love that would be, in the great bard's words, "the star to every wandering bark"? Why forsake even the face of Dante's beloved?

The woman I adore carries ecstatic love in her eyes.
Whatever she looks at grows less worldly.
When she walks past, each man turns to look at her;
And if she notices him, his chest trembles.

And then, his eyes on the ground, he turns pale;
He can feel his inadequacies inside his heart.
Self-absorption and self-mothering leave ahead of her;
All you women, help me to say this rightly.

When a man hears her voice, sweetness and thoughts
Of ways to serve others come into his body.
I say then, much praise to the first man who glimpsed her.

And when she smiles, for even a short time, there is a feeling
Of someone I cannot speak of, nor keep in remembrance.
This is all some sort of miracle, fresh, amazing.[2]

As time passed, this shimmering promise became little more than a faint candle in a forgotten chapel, outshone by a new dream that saw the path we have been following as dark, brooding, superstitious, and irrational—in sum, barbaric, or "Gothic," a word derived from the assault on eternal Rome by Alaric the Goth. The Renaissance Dream of Reason repudiated all that had guided our pilgrims.[3] Centuries of increasingly biased divisiveness would eventually greet the young Goethe in Strasbourg, where the cathedral there, denounced as "Gothic," sparked his awakening to—and embrace of—its transcendent, universal beauty.

(Advance screen)

Cathedral Light Eclipsed by Daylight

From the moment the Dream of Reason emerged, there could be no doubt that the frail, elusive longing of love from afar (*amour de loin*) would be overwhelmed, perhaps even by the very same forces it had sought to soften.[4] Purified love (*fin'amor*) was simply no match for the new muscular dream that promised to transform all darkness into light. All too soon, it eclipsed the incarnate color of stained glass, exchanging the glow of a rising and setting sun for the brightest possible—that is to say, enlightened—illumination of high noon.

Nicholas of Cusa (1401–1464), a mathematician, ecclesiastical reformer, and cardinal of the Church who drew from the philosophies of his predecessors to shape his own thought, constructed an enduring insight that itself informed the Renaissance Dream. He concluded that an infinite God—a "coincidence of opposites," as he phrased it—exceeds our conceptual reach *and* the grasp of our language, and as such is approachable only in the finite results of His earthly creation. But even as Nicholas asserted that this infinite God was beyond our understanding, he believed our efforts to comprehend the depth and implications of this assertion would result in "learned ignorance."[5]

Contrast this view with Jan van Eyck in fifteenth-century Flanders. The mysterious presence of Mary had been comprehensible for him as the pictorial embodiment of rationally incompatible humanity and divinity. His was an entirely different kind of knowing, experienced in the ineffable yet visible combination of both natural light (*lumen*) and an incorruptible eternal light (*lux aeterna*).

(8.2) Jan van Eyck, *Madonna in the Church*, ca. 1440

The obvious scale discrepancy in this painting, so jarring to our post-Renaissance eyes, would have appeared in its day to be as natural as the rising sun in the morning, evoking nothing so much as the sound of a prayer at Matins and the presence of eternal wisdom (*sapientia*). In fact, Jan van Eyck inscribed an excerpt of the opening words from one such prayer in Latin, including the words for "sun" and "light," on the hem of Mary's blue gown.

Now read aloud the words of this prayer personifying Mary as the brightness of eternal light.

For she is more beautiful than the sun
and above all the order of stars:
being compared with [natural] light,
she is found before it.
For she is the brightness of eternal light,
the unspotted mirror of God's majesty.[6]

The poetic words of the Matins prayer continue:

After this cometh the night, but against
Wisdom evil doth not prevail;
She reacheth mightily from one
end [of the world] to the other.[7]

Erwin Panofsky, renowned for his study of early Flemish painting, observed that pictorial light enters from the left, casting two bright, warm pools on the stone floor. Given the common west to east orientation of most Flemish churches at this time, Panofsky suggested that this light very probably invokes the presence of "northern" light rather than geographically accurate light that would flow from the right, or the south side of the church.[8]

Compare this pictorially constructed "light" illuminating the church interior to the light that hits the trompe l'oeil frame.[9] Poetically, prayerfully, even artistically, then, this "light" exceeds the ordinary light reflected from the frame that encloses it. Accordingly, this pictorial light "reacheth mightily from one end [of the world] to the other" as though this image were contemplatively a reliquary of divine reality. Suspended before our beholding eyes, its reach transcends the limits of passing night and day, life and death—with literally dozens of particular kinds of observable light that could never be visible simultaneously in direct experience, but which the artist gathered from his devoted, lifelong, and prayerful observation. Millard Meiss, the great scholar of medieval and Renaissance art, reportedly said *Madonna in the Church* was the most important work of art he had ever encountered.

Let's pause here to reflect that Jan van Eyck realized in paint the contemplative epiphany Abbot Suger had experienced in the Basilica of St. Denis some three hundred years earlier. Recall our earlier encounter with the abbot, who had just completed the restoration of the mortuary site of French royalty:

> Thus, when—out of my delight in the beauty of the house of God—the loveliness of the many-colored gems has called me away

> from external cares, and worthy meditation has induced me to reflect, transferring that which is material to that which is immaterial... then it seems to me that I see myself dwelling, as it were, in some strange region of the universe which neither exists entirely in the slime of the earth nor entirely in the purity of Heaven; and that, by the grace of God, I can be transported from this inferior to that higher world in an anagogical manner.[10]

Abbot Suger experienced a vividly subjective reconciling of both finite and infinite realities—the "slime of the earth" and the "purity of heaven." Like Jan van Eyck's art, his contemplative beholding embraces the contradiction of our human condition—fleeting mortality and endless being—no less than earthly *lumen* and celestial *lux aeterna.*

At its core, the huge step into the Dream of Reason replaced this sense of discontinuity suspended across a gap of infinity—Suger's "anagogical" bridge—with the analogical reality of incremental continuity, grounded in material analysis, rational thought, and finite calculation. Although the brilliance of unencumbered rationality emerged everywhere in Europe, it unfolded most dramatically in the artistic attainment of three men: Albrecht Dürer, Leonardo da Vinci, and Michelangelo Buonarroti. Putting aside whatever accounts for its cause, the full effect of the Renaissance Dream of Reason, so powerfully revealed in their art, puts us in position to measure its promise. After all, we are the children of this dream, free as Goethe was to engage it as we will, informed by a lingering memory of that wholeness Nicholas himself called "learned ignorance."[11]

As history unfolded, this new vision quickly became a remarkably practical attempt to live a good life on this earth, to utilize our human capacities to their fullest. Briefly stated, this new era, moved with unbridled confidence beyond the supposed shortcomings of the so-called medieval world. In the Enlightenment it emerged again most powerfully as moral optimism. Later that optimism would find eloquent, if ironic, restatement during the brief period between, and then following, the two industrialized World Wars of the twentieth century.[12]

In one stroke, it seems, Albrecht Dürer in the north transformed the spiritual dimension of Abbot Suger's vision into an objective account of earthbound acquisition through power, control, authority, and the imagined possession of God-like capacities. At stake was the aspirational humility of Marguerite Porete's *fin'amor* and the elusive mystery of *amour de loin.* An emerging Reason, which had been unable to comprehend Love, now challenged that poetic threshold of love in which intimations of reconciliation, animated by love the verb, sought always to reveal Love the noun, the beloved: wholeness beyond calculation.

As we approach the magisterial accomplishments of the three greatest masters of the Renaissance Dream of Reason, pause briefly to remember Marguerite's words of patient restraint from the opening of *The Mirror of Simple Souls*, and within those words her urgent acknowledgment of humility:

> You who would read this book,
> If you indeed wish to grasp it,
> Think about what you say,
> For it is very difficult to comprehend;
> Humility, who is keeper of the treasury of
> Knowledge
> And the mother of the other Virtues,
> Must overtake you.
> Theologians and other clerks,
> You will not have the intellect for it,
> No matter how brilliant your abilities,
> If you do not proceed humbly.
>
> And may Love and Faith, together,
> Cause you to rise above Reason,
>
> [Since] they are the ladies of the house.
> Even Reason witnesses
> In the Thirteenth Chapter of this book,
> And with no shame about it,
> That Love and Faith make her live
> And she does not free herself from them,
> For they have lordship over her,
> Which is why she must humble herself.
> Humble, then, your *wisdom*
> Which is based on Reason,
> And place all your fidelity
> In those things which are given
> By Love, illuminated through Faith.
> And thus you will understand this book
> Which makes the Soul live by love.[13]

(Advance screen)

Albrecht Dürer (1471–1528)

In a large painting, presumably made for use in the Holy Mass, Albrecht Dürer saw Mary as a distinctly earthbound reality. She is an ordinary local woman (save for her fiery-colored gown and crimson cape), with flowing blond hair who holds her fleshy baby in her lap. She is comfortably seated in a garden filled with an array of flowers and recognizable fauna.[14]

(8.3) Albrecht Dürer (?), *Madonna and Child* ("The Madonna of the Iris"), ca. 1500–10

Symbolic references to divinity still exist here, but they recede before a wave of botanical description. The poetic *lux aeterna* that merges imperceptibly with Jan van Eyck's careful observation and choreography of natural light has become the tangible geography of a sun-filled earthly landscape. With Columbus's discovery only a few years earlier that the earth was a globe to be circumnavigated, mapped, named, colonized, and controlled, the distant watery horizon in the background of this new landscape was no longer a threatening place of moral and physical oblivion. It had become God's newest challenge to humanity. Almost overnight, it seems, the seas were the birthright of human beings to navigate and explore. The world was calculable; it was manageable. Mary was no longer shown to us as the symbolically iconic Throne of Wisdom (Latin, *sedes sapientiae*) nor as the Madonna of Humility seated on the ground. She now sat on a raised bank of earth and stone wall under a trellis made of wood. In the earliest moments of the new world, it is almost as though the spiritually elusive presence of divinity had become palpable in its absence, like the silence that follows the whispering sound of boiling water extinguished at the end of the Japanese tea ceremony. With the presence of God in the celestial distance, plants just outside the artist's studio door became occasions for natural portraiture.

(8.4) Albrecht Dürer, a. *Iris,* 1503; b. *Tuft of Cowslips*, 1526

The transformation around the turn of the fifteenth-to-sixteenth century was truly exciting. Its value was seemingly beyond all doubt or argument, as though someone had returned from deep space to report on another world "out there," where there is no pain, no starvation, no sickness, no killing. In this new world, there would be no limitation of any kind that would prevent human progress from being completely within our rational grasp, both temporally and spatially continuous with our immediate experience and understanding. The transcendent City of God envisioned by St. Augustine was now within reach. No longer related to this world only metaphorically, it now became, in the Dream of Reason, the result of a human-made perfection—a literal utopia. T. S. Eliot's "Quick, now, here, now, always" (from "Little Gidding") assumes entirely new meaning measured against the exuberance of this kind of a miraculous Dream. This radical transformation was anything but remote. It existed vividly and immediately with people, including Dürer's own parents—not suspended as it was for Abbot Suger "in some strange region of the universe which neither exists entirely in the slime of the earth nor entirely in the purity of Heaven," but at home.

(8.5) Albrecht Dürer, a. *Portrait of His Father* (attributed), 1497; b. *Portrait of His Mother*, 1514

Even the commission of a large liturgical altarpiece with portraits of the emperor Maximillian and the Pontifex Maximus of the Holy Roman Church offered the opportunity to study human presence in the face of Pope Julius II.

(8.6) Albrecht Dürer, *Pope Julius II* (?), 1506, study for *Feast of the Rose Garlands*

Unarguable evidence of this Dream of Reason at our human fingertips similarly informs an astounding self-portrait made by Dürer at the tender age of thirteen. In one small drawing done in the most demanding technique of silverpoint, he demonstrated near total control of description and self-determination.

(8.7) Albrecht Dürer, *Self-Portrait*, 1484

Those eyes and that hand, which come together in an unequivocal gesture of radically self-conscious purpose and direction, would soon become no less intently engaged with the most delicate creatures of God's creation. Where Mary had become for Dürer a young German mother, the beating hearts and warmth of innocent animals soon came to replace theological symbolism with a similar tangible, physical presence.

(8.8) Albrecht Dürer, *Hare*, 1502

The contour shape, focused eyes, and grasping talons of Dürer's *The Little Owl* transformed iconic "wisdom" into immediate and personal face-to-face encounter.

(8.9) Albrecht Dürer, *The Little Owl*, 1508

No less convincingly, in portraying his hometown of Nuremberg and, later, Antwerp, Dürer exchanged the biblical allegory of the Heavenly Jerusalem with the immediacy of his own daily, diary-like, record of his travels.[15]

(8.10) Albrecht Dürer, *View of Nuremberg*, 1496–97
(8.11) Albrecht Dürer, *View of Antwerp*, 1520

Before long, Dürer even realized the earthbound focus and precision of Nicholas of Cusa in two explicitly instrumental prints. Compared to Jan van Eyck's *Madonna in the Church* (8.2) in which a church structure and the painting itself capture and hold eternal light, Dürer's mechanical demonstration of pictorial foreshortening literally describes a tool for recording finite, physical perceptual reality.

(8.12) Albrecht Dürer, *Draftsman Drawing a Lute*, 1525

In place of Jan van Eyck's elusive mystery of eternal light, enclosed within a trompe l'oeil marble frame with funereal connotations, a quadratic wooden frame now serves as a device for calculating truth incrementally, square by square, anticipating nothing so much as our own idea of unquestioned photographic and digital verisimilitude embodied in the Benday dot printing process of the nineteenth century, as it is employed in Roy Lichtenstein's comic book–inspired pop art, or what we refer to today as "pixelated" images.

(8.13) Chuck Close, Working photograph for *Phil*, 1969

The American artist Chuck Close (1940–2021) clearly challenged this imagined continuity in numerous revealing portraits of himself, his friends, and other artists (see the composer Philip Glass in image 8.13). Close used his gridded photographs as models to capture versions of the "same face," whether in paint, aquatint, linoleum cuts, or other printing techniques, by adopting more and more elaborate processing methods. Neither Close nor Dürer employed this system to compensate for a lack of skill but each instead reached further toward an artistic vision. For Close his art evolved in the infinite variety of swirling brushstroke shapes, each one a solitude, that join individual people with universal humanity. In image 8.14, with Dürer's great skilled hands even Love herself could be "captured" in a startling allusion to the Goddess of Love, in which Aphrodite appears as the model before the working artist, her consort Hephaestus, the master craftsman and smith.

(8.14) Albrecht Dürer, *Draftsman Drawing a Recumbent Figure of a Woman* (Aphrodite and Hephaestus?), 1525

In all of these images and others, Albrecht Dürer, the man, has become the creator—not just the measure—but the measurer of all things.

(8.15) Albrecht Dürer, *Self-Portrait in a Fur Cloak*, 1500

Dürer's *Self-Portrait in a Fur Cloak* appears to show the artist as God's earthly regent, challenged with the task of revealing truth as though he were endowed with divine power. We will find no more inviting "cairn" along the way of the Dream of Reason than this justly famous portrait of art and the artist.

Thus Jan van Eyck, who would mirror God's creation according to his self-deprecating artistic motto "*Als Ich Can*" ("as I am able"), made way for an artist who is now a sovereign in his own right. A comparison with Jan van Eyck's magisterial image of divine sovereignty in the *Altarpiece of the Mystic Lamb*, which Dürer saw in the cathedral church of Ghent during his trip to the Netherlands, should diminish all doubt about this artistic trajectory and its self-conscious presence within the Dream of Reason, redolent in the art of *Self-Portrait in a Fur Cloak*.

(8.16) Albrecht Dürer, a. *Self-Portrait in a Fur Cloak*; b. Jan van Eyck, *God the Father* from the *Altarpiece of the Mystic Lamb*, 1432

Even so, we cannot neglect the subtle gesture of Dürer's powerful right hand fondling the fur collar of his cloak at the center of the lower border of the painting nearest to the beholder, intimating perhaps some measure of doubt.[16]

(Advance screen)

Leonardo da Vinci (1452–1519)

(8.17) a. Villard de Honnecourt, *Geometric Man* (ca. 1230); b. Leonardo da Vinci, *Study of a Male Nude* (ca. 1503–09)

Heading deeper into the Dream of Reason we encounter another compelling "cairn" to guide us: Leonardo da Vinci's drawing of a male nude figure. First compare how the ideal geometry used by Villard de Honnecourt in his stylized, thus indirectly experienced forms, now gives way to Leonardo's direct encounter with human flesh.

(8.18) Leonardo da Vinci, *The Proportions of the Human Figure* (after Vitruvius), ca. 1490

Then, in his iconic image of the Vitruvian Man (8.18), Leonardo brings the engineering and aesthetic wisdom of the ancient past into the present moment of his immediate experience, and into the very presence of his self-portrait.

Courageous Explorations in Leonardo's Sketchbook

The text and imagery of Leonardo's richly detailed sketchbook, preserved at Windsor Castle, records his extensive and courageous exploration into the corporeal temple of God's divine creation.[17] Almost echoing Dürer's daring portrait of human dominion in his *Self-Portrait in a Fur Cloak*, Leonardo traces the tendons and peripheral nerves of the hand, whose opposed thumb and forefinger evoke man's primal creative capacity.

(8.19) Leonardo da Vinci, *Studies of the Human Hand*, ca. 1490

Related to this, in one of the most startling of all the images in the sketchbook, the so-called genito-urinary system, Leonardo may have been seeking physiological evidence of ancient theories about the soul's entrance into the embryonic human being at conception.

(8.20) Leonardo da Vinci, *The Sexual Act in Vertical Section* ("genito-urinary system"), ca. 1490

Although it's doubtful that Leonardo observed this particular cross-section in real life, its precision is testimony to the scientific tension between observation and theoretical knowledge. In this instance, the idea clearly influenced the observation.[18] Similarly, his stunning image of the fetus in utero is a virtual portrait of human existence as if it were still in the biblical garden of Paradise.

(8.21) Leonardo da Vinci, *Embryo in the Womb*, ca. 1510

To measure the presence of this artistic intimation of existence before the Fall, compare this image to related illustrations in modern biology textbooks and to an analogous artistic counterpart in the Book of Hours, known as the *Trés Riches Heures du Duc de Berry*, from the first years of the fifteenth century.

(8.22) a. Textbook image of an embryo in utero, 2010;
b. Limbourg Brothers, *Paradise,* from the *Trés Riches Heures du Duc de Berry*, 1416

Leonardo's translation of divine creation into corporeality extends into several views of the brain on a single sketchbook page, specifically in how the drawings as a composite appear to distinguish and embrace the right and left hemispheres.[19]

(8.23) Leonardo da Vinci, *The Brain* (of an ox?),
injected to demonstrate the shape of the cerebral ventricles, ca. 1490

A descriptive drawing of the human skull serves as an artistic memento mori of our mortality.

(8.24) Leonardo da Vinci, *Study of the Human Skull in Sagittal Section,* from front, 1489

Leonardo's well-known fascination with technological engineering complements his focused attention on the mechanics of the human body. Ever the practical man—and not inconsequentially, the youth who had envisioned the kitchen as both a studio and a laboratory when he worked as a line cook in the court of Ludovico Sforza, the future Duke of Milan—he designed a giant whisk with a human operator placed within it.[20] Whether or not his desire had been to foster both efficiency and power by bringing technology and the body together, he precociously anticipated the consideration of human factors in modern industrial design.

(8.25) Leonardo da Vinci, *Giant Whisk,* ca. 1490

On the other hand, the backwards "mirror" script Leonardo used in the sketchbook for his verbal descriptions and reflections may suggest he valued the distinction between rational human "mystery," with its intent to conceal, as contrasted with the transcendent reality of the liturgical "mystery" of divine revelation manifest in the Holy Mass.

Timeless Voice and Timely Presence in the Last Supper

Leonardo's *Last Supper*, his second most famous painting—and here some would arguably place his *Mona Lisa* first in the world by any artist—was completed for the Church and Dominican Convent of Santa Maria delle Grazie in 1498. It may well be his most important given its subtle moral reverberations into the present moment no less than the early years of the Dream of Reason. For a beholder, his *Last Supper* reveals a particularly timely though subtle presence of humility in the face of unbridled power, control, authority, and the onrush of material success.

(8.26) Leonardo da Vinci, *Last Supper*, 1495–98,
Convent of Santa Maria delle Grazie, Milan, Italy

In his unique iconography for this biblical event, Leonardo brings us close to the critical divide between tangible and intangible realities at the heart of the Dream of Reason. Here we may pause to approach the art of this work of art deliberately. As always, we benefit by looking beyond our habitual reliance on photographs of this work of art or the experience of hurried visits to Milan.

> *Given the overwhelmingly noisy tourist invasion of the once quiet refectory where you will find this painting, imagine instead that you had entered into a place of undisturbed silence.*
>
> *Seek to engage slowly and directly with the art of the* Last Supper. *Be open to it; vulnerable to its inherent—embodied—artistic intimation of reconciliation that will, occasionally, when you are ready, offer you some degree of the joy and peace and wisdom we seek.*

Begin with the painting itself. The *Last Supper* is a large horizontal rectangle. Its dimensions—15 feet and 1 inch by 29 feet—are architectural as much as pictorial. This is important. At first glance, it is clear that Leonardo intended the illusory space of the image to appear as an extension of the actual space of the refectory.

(8.27) Refectory wall, 15th century, Santa Maria delle Grazie

We may imagine that Leonardo's purpose was not only to offer the *Last Supper* pictorially for those who would enter this space, but to involve them experientially in the charged reality of the moment. Although the painting is raised some fifteen feet above the floor, just below the coats of arms of wealthy patrons who commissioned it (the Sforza family among them), the perspective construction of its illusory space imagines it to be at eye level, hence face to face. This apparent contradiction is important.

The well-known narrative of the painting is particularly direct, even abrupt. It animates the precise moment when Jesus spoke to his disciples, saying, "One of you will betray me." Not surprisingly, his startled disciples respond vigorously. Being justly famous for the skillful visual portrayal of their emotional reactions, Leonardo captures how they question, complain, accuse, and in some instances retreat in fear. In the midst of this turmoil only John, tired and barely awake, and Jesus remain still and calm.

(8.28) *Last Supper*, a. detail of disciples to Jesus's right;
b. detail of disciples to Jesus's left)

Allow yourself to hear those stark, blunt words of rebuke. Admire Leonardo's capacity to engage you in the emotional verisimilitude of the moment.

For monks in the refectory who experienced this nearly life-size *tableau vivant* of Jesus and his disciples from only a few feet away, the drama is difficult to overstate.

Now return to the overall image in 8.29. The linear perspective that "joins" actual and illusory space places Jesus just slightly to the right of the so-called vanishing point, which coincides with the horizon of the distant landscape and is to the left of the central axis of the figures.

(8.29) *Last Supper*, linear perspective; central axis of figures indicated in red

Leonardo began work on the *Last Supper* by putting a hole in the plaster wall to precisely fix its linear perspective, so his deliberate positioning of Jesus is not trivial. While he sits in the middle between the disciples to his left and right, he is asymmetrically located in relation to the space of the room and the world outside. His body, silhouetted against the bright light of the triple arcade behind him, is visibly and unmistakably to the spatial right of the illusory center but directly opposite the monks who viewed it in the refectory space.

This nearly imperceptible, but no less real, pictorial tension underscores the intersecting realities of implacable calm and emotional drama. The geometric order of the single-point linear perspective not only defines the illusory space, but it also establishes a very subtle contrast between symmetry and asymmetry that measures, even as it amplifies, the disturbance among the figures. The slight collapsing of the space of the foreshortened room emphasizes the apparently deliberate contrast by bringing the luminous arcade forward and drawing our attention to Jesus's outstretched arms, which mirror the slant of the receding walls.

(8.30) *Last Supper*, detail of the figure of Jesus

His left hand, reaching for a small loaf of bread, faces upward. His right hand, visible through the transparent glass of wine, is face down. These gestures must certainly refer symbolically to the bread and wine of the Eucharist, but their artistic significance ripples outward beyond the walls of this refectory.

(8.26) *Last Supper*, 1495–98, Convent of Santa Maria delle Grazie, Milan, Italy

Other hands on the right side of the image face up, even including an upward pointing finger that anticipates Raphael's famous figure of Plato in his *School of Athens* in the Vatican. On the left side, they face downward, most especially the left hand of Judas hovering above a loaf of bread, the clear antithesis of the pointing finger. Beyond their apparent dramatic effect, however, these hand gestures, like the symbolic presence of bread and wine, mirror the familiar medieval tradition of representing the Last Judgment that we will look at in more detail later in the chapter.

At the Church of St. Lazarus in Autun, for example (image 8.114), the weighing of souls is accompanied by the weightless ascent of the "saved" and the heavy burden of the "condemned." The narthex tympanum of La Madeleine in nearby Vézelay repeats Leonardo's implication of the Last Judgment by placing closed books in the hands of disciples on Christ's left and open books on his right. Although reversed left to right, Jesus's hand gestures resemble those of the risen Christ in Michelangelo's *Last Judgment* in the Sistine Chapel (image 8.48). Reaching still further, Leonardo's *Last Supper* fairly recalls the monumental image of ultimate Christian triumph at the center of the royal portal of the Cathedral of Chartres. In the central tympanum, Christ, enthroned within an aureole of light, is surrounded by the four beasts of the apocalypse with his disciples arranged below him in four groups of three (looking ahead to chapter 10 and image 10.15), precisely comparable to their assembly in the *Last Supper*.[21]

Clearly, Leonardo's image invokes more than the startled dispute among his disciples. The pictorial presence of contradiction guides us toward what may be the timeless artistic vision literally "embodied" by this work of art. The apparent, if gentle, visual tension between the symmetry of the room and the asymmetrical placement of the figures in this constructed space, conjures our awareness of both actual and illusory space. Although this visual conflation would have been a considerably more powerful sensation in the year 1498 than in our own era of digitized reality, it remains present for an alert pilgrim to Milan.

Easily overlooked, but no less important as a fundamental irreconcilable contradiction, especially for Leonardo the painter, is his determination to combine the architectural capacities of fresco's water-based tempera with the transparent layered luminosity of the "hi-tech" invention of oil painting imported into Italy from Flanders.[22] The fact that the incompatibility of these two media soon deteriorated his work hardly diminishes his lifelong determination to reach beyond known habitual conventions. Indeed, this particular effort may even point us in the direction of his fondest desire. In his mixing of water and oil, he not only sought to expand the visual effect of transparent light beyond the scope of what painting on wood panel could bring to the north wall of the refectory, but he must have also been alert to the Christological implications of bringing together the water of baptism and the sacrificial oil of mercy, embodied by the central figure of the *Last Supper*.

> *Might we now approach a fresh encounter with what has become one of the most disembodied—clichéd—works of art in our culture of abstracted material commodification?*

The monetized tourist invasion of the Convent of Santa Maria delle Grazie is well known to anyone who has tried to see Leonardo's *Last Supper*. But when we acknowledge and embrace all manner of contradiction—beginning with the very nature of our human being as the precondition of contemplative beholding—we will find noise giving way to silence, movement to stillness, and fleeting time to timeless presence. If we are lucky enough to reserve our tickets and reenter the refectory of Santa Maria delle Grazie—not as observers, interpreters, or tourists, but as contemplative beholders—we will be prepared to receive the incalculable mystery of the art of Leonardo's gift to us all, but to do so with a gesture of open reaching, not grasping. Setting aside our habit of distanced photographic interrogation and audio-guide interpretation-seeking, we might now stand, or were it possible, kneel before the *Last Supper*. We may now see it as a heroically endowed prefiguration of Ernst Mach's nineteenth-century observation that "no things [exist] in themselves, rather only [as] complexes of sensations."[23]

Allow its monumental intimation of reconciliation to reveal itself, to speak with us. Be still. Silent. Wait . . .

(8.31) Refectory, Convent of Santa Maria delle Grazie

The recently and lovingly restored *Last Supper* invites us to listen again to Jesus's blunt words. For despite its material frailty, its voice remains strong. Jesus spoke about spiritual endurance directly to his disciples gathered to celebrate the Passover meal with him. As we will see, this work of art may have been particularly reassuring for Leonardo. His unfinished *Adoration of the Magi* from a decade earlier (image 8.78), to which we turn later, reveals an almost unanswerable doubt in need of such encouragement. To the monks who ate and prayed in the refectory at the turn of the sixteenth century, those same words would have re-ignited their faith in the liturgy of transubstantiation—for them an act of aspiration to infinite wholeness from their acknowledged condition of mortal limitation. The painting, raised up before them like the host in the Mass, was the visible embodiment of the sacred mystery (the intimation) of human and divine presence.[24] For those who would now come to Milan, open to the promise of contemplative beholding, Leonardo's *Last Supper* implores the world not to betray our universal human capacity for seeking ways to reconcile the contradictory realities of all conscious existence, independent of individual and collective difference. Its timeless voice summons all who would behold with him to commit acts of art, love, and beauty that would diminish the pain of loving.[25]

**(8.32) Refectory with visitors, 20th century,
Convent of Santa Maria delle Grazie**

In the context of the Dream of Reason, Leonardo's powerful hymn of praise to psychological, liturgical, philosophical, and mathematical, not to say pictorial, discourse would seem to deny the absolute stillness and silence, as one might imagine it in the refectory of the monastic site built on the rock of Scissy and called Mont Saint Michel.

(8.33) Refectory, Mont Saint Michel, 13th century, Normandy, France

And yet, the presence of pictorial drama enveloped by actual devotional silence in front of the *Last Supper* recalls Bernard of Clairvaux's visionary poetry so palpable in the refectory at Mont Saint Michel. "The coming of the Word was not perceptible to the eyes; for he has no color, nor to my ears, for there was no sound."[26]

> *Imagine beholding in the Convent of Santa Maria delle Grazie . . . allow Leonardo's art to offer hope in the prophetic quiet before the storm.*

(Advance screen)

Michelangelo di Buonarroti (1475–1564)

The contribution of Michelangelo di Lodovico Buonarroti Simoni to the Renaissance Dream of Reason remains richly present because of his participation in the transformation of St. Peter's Basilica in Rome. From the late fifteenth century onward the basilica, begun in Constantine's capital city, experienced radical change. The so-called old basilica of St. Peter gave way to its more familiar modern version, plainly visible in this sixteenth-century engraving of the seven pilgrimage churches of Rome.

(8.34) Antoine Lafrery, *Seven Pilgrimage Churches of Rome*, 1575, with the old basilica of St. Peter indicated

The complexities entailed in the historical and architectural transformation of the basilica are obviously beyond exaggeration. Religious, political, social, and, of course, spiritual implications inform nearly every aspect of this singular monument as it evolved from ancient times to premodern and modern European times. The conceptual significance of this history for the purposes of our Via Amoris, however, is remarkably simple. In effect, this vast architectural transformation tracks the transition—from the idea of a biblical "sacred" history, culminating in the appearance of the prophetic "Heavenly Jerusalem" toward our present, modern "scientific" history of earthbound continuity and power, grounded less in the metaphorical "City of God" than the papal Vatican City State.

Although Michelangelo was engaged with the design and structural work of the new basilica, he is best known for his fresco decoration of the ceiling of the Sistine Chapel. Less well known perhaps is his radical change to the original iconographic program of the first basilica. As the new building replaced the old one, the program of images that once informed spatial movement east to west was destroyed. The original program began with the apocalyptic imagery of the outer gate, followed by the large "Edenic" atrium and the royal portal, the Old and New Testament narratives on the north and south walls of the double aisles and nave, then to the triumphal arch at the entry to the transept decorated with prophetic imagery from the Book of Revelation, to the apse wall, and, finally, to the apse itself, where the risen Christ, flanked by Saints Peter and Paul, is enthroned in a celestial paradise.[27]

(8.35) Old basilica of St. Peter, Rome, conjectural reconstruction, ca. 1450

(8.36) Old basilica of St. Peter, 4th century, a. conjectural reconstruction of the interior program; b. apse mosaic (after Maffeo Vegio)

Most importantly, the point of explicit physical and temporal discontinuity between earthly history and prophetic celestial history, marked by the orthogonally placed transept, also disappeared, to be replaced by a new centralized structure over the burial site of St. Peter in the form of a Greek cross surmounted by a massive dome, designed by Michelangelo himself. Beyond the dome and altar, St. Peter's throne (made by Gian Lorenzo Bernini) replaced the apse mosaic image of the resurrected Christ in the old basilica.

(8.37) a. Old basilica of St. Peter, 4th century, plan showing longitudinal movement east to west; b. Michelangelo, plan for the crossing of the new basilica of St. Peter, 1546–64

(8.38) a. Old basilica of St. Peter, a. conjectural reconstruction of the nave, transept, and apse; b. New basilica of St. Peter, view of the chancel beyond the dome from the nave, centered on the *baldichino* of Gian Lorenzo Bernini, 1624–32

One part of the original, extremely detailed trajectory of Christian redemption was preserved in Michelangelo's "modernized" version painted in fresco on the ceiling of the Sistine Chapel.

(8.39) Sistine Chapel, Vatican, Rome, a. before 1508; b. after 1512

The extensive Old and New Testament narratives of the program in the old basilica had led through space and biblical "time" from the Creation to the figure of Christ placed beyond the transept and enthroned in eternal Paradise. For his ceiling, Michelangelo selected scenes from the Creation, concluding with the Drunkenness of Noah, thus preserving only the initial moments of the old program.[28] Michelangelo apparently also chose—certainly not without papal concurrence—to focus on the contrast of divine power and human frailty rather than on the discontinuity of apocalyptic fulfillment. Celestial order animated by the Dream of Reason and embodied by the pope was threatened prophetically by its inebriated loss, visible in the scene portraying Noah. Michelangelo placed it directly overhead at the entrance to the Sistine Chapel, where movement toward the altar begins.

(8.40) Michelangelo, *Drunkenness of Noah*, ceiling of the Sistine Chapel, 1508–12

(8.41) Ceiling of the Sistine Chapel, viewed from east to west with *Drunkeness of Noah* indicated

No less importantly, Michelangelo reversed the direction of the narrative events. Rather than approaching the altar in a temporal narrative sequence as in the "old" program, the biblical history of the Sistine Chapel ceiling now begins directly over the altar and proceeds toward the entrance to the chapel, confirming perhaps the papal message of authority and power. This fundamental reorientation of the narrative flow essentially repositions its generative force from the space and time trajectory of the original program to the person of the pope himself. The altar where the pope would celebrate the Mass appears below the sequence of images moving from the *Separation of Light from Darkness* followed by the *Creation of the Sun, Moon and the Planets* and the *Gathering of the Waters*, all the while expanding with an inexorable outward force from its liturgical center.

(8.42) Ceiling of the Sistine Chapel, viewed from west to east (lower to upper), *Separation of Light from Darkness* indicated

(8.43) *Separation of Light from Darkness*, ceiling of the Sistine Chapel

(8.44) *Creation of the Sun, Moon and Planets*, ceiling of the Sistine Chapel

(8.45) *Gathering of the Waters*, ceiling of the Sistine Chapel

Thus, in the papal chapel of the Vatican City, at the center of the Holy Roman Catholic Church itself, the origins of God's Creation are displayed monumentally as a drama of titans who would inhabit the earth, give it shape, dominate, and control it. Unarguably, the most famous and most pointedly identified new hero appears directly after the scene depicting God's gathering of the waters, in the *Creation of Adam*.

(8.46) *Creation of Adam*, ceiling of the Sistine Chapel

The vital spark of life that God sends to animate Adam also closes the infinite (discontinuous) gap between God and humanity. It thus shifts the prophetic vision of the Heavenly Jerusalem not only to earthbound human power but also, with the anxious face of Eve in his glance, toward sensual as well as intellectual desire. By comparison, that heavenly world—now left behind by this new heroic Dream of Reason—remains in an image of the same primal moment with God cradling Adam's head as a sculptor might, or as a parent might caress a child. Exemplifying what has changed (or been lost) in the Cathedral of Chartres in France, innocent animals share the moment of creation and affection now left amazingly empty, even desolate, in the landscape of the Sistine Chapel.

(8.47) a. Cathedral of Chartres, France, 12th–16th century, north porch, location of sculpture indicated; b. detail, *Creation of Adam*

As the site of the pope's divine election, the Sistine Chapel is the ultimate seat of Holy Roman apostolic authority, reaching directly from God through Christ to Peter and then, individually—that is, incrementally—to each succeeding pope.[29] Unlike the public institutional role of the basilica, the Sistine Chapel is the personal location of papal ecclesiastical, political, social, and private spiritual power. It's not insignificant, then, that in Michelangelo's massive image of the Last Judgment, placed on the wall directly behind the altar, a now Herculean Christ dominates, performing the eternal separation of the blessed from the damned with one muscular gesture, as though the pope below were now understood to be the human agent of this divine authority.

(8.48) Michelangelo, *Last Judgment*, 1534–41, altar wall of the Sistine Chapel

The conceptual departure of Michelangelo's art becomes clear by comparing Mary, cowering beneath the arm of her son in the Sistine Chapel *Last Judgment*, with her *Coronation* at the Cathedral of Reims in France. There she and her son are together, poised weightlessly in the design of the façade—as Abbot Suger would suggest, somewhere between the "slime of the earth and the purity of heaven."

(8.49) a. Cathedral of Reims, France, 13th century, west façade, *Coronation*; b. Michelangelo, *Last Judgment*, figures of Christ and Mary

(8.50) Cathedral of Reims, center portal of west façade
(8.51) a. Cathedral of Reims; b. Sistine Chapel

(Advance screen)

From Feminine Spirituality to Masculine Humanism

We've seen how, in the fifteenth century, Mary had become the consummate artistic image of wholeness with her corporeal embrace of humanity and divinity (image 8.2). But now, at the turn of the sixteenth century, the young shepherd who gained biblical fame for astonishing musical talent, for slaying the giant Goliath with his sling, and later, as King David, is the clearest single embodiment of the humanist Dream of Reason, both its promise and its danger. Michelangelo's *David*, originally placed at the entrance to the Palazzo della Signoria (Palazzo Vecchio) in Florence, welcomed its beholders to a new world that privileged a fusion of muscular strength and rational knowledge over anagogical wisdom and maternal mercy.

(8.52) Galleria dell'Accademia, Florence, Italy, with Michelangelo's *David* and visitors

This colossal marble figure—17 feet tall—now resides in Florence's Galleria dell'Accademia. In contrast to the recumbent form of Adam in the Sistine Chapel, David rises up as an awakened and alert man, animated by explicit self-conscious intellect. Michelangelo's immediate predecessor in Florence, Donatello, provides an especially apt introduction to this particular incarnation of the Dream of Reason. Donatello's marble and bronze sculptures of David from the beginning of the fifteenth century can help us bring into focus the particular artistic realities of Michelangelo's iconic work of art from the turn of the sixteenth.

> *Pause here to meditate with these two masterpieces from the early moments of the Renaissance. Be present with them. Try to avoid your almost automatic invidious assumptions of development and progress from the fifteenth to the sixteenth century, from "Gothic" to "Renaissance" form, from feminine spirituality to masculine humanism.*

(8.53) a. Donatello, *David*, 1408–09, marble (6' 2");
b. Michelangelo, *David*, 1501–04, marble (17')

Recalling Goethe's embrace in Strasbourg, allow these two sculptures simply to emerge in your immediate response as two particular artistic realizations of contradiction. Let them reveal their art, their beauty, and perhaps even their human spirituality to you. Imagine each to be a sculptural equivalent of love the verb seeking the face of the beloved from different paths.

(8.54) Donatello, *David*, 1408–09

Donatello's marble figure of David is, if at all, only slightly larger than life size. Compared with Michelangelo's titanic scale, it is intentionally intimately human. Dressed in a stitched leather tunic with a leather cape around his shoulders and a crown of laurel on his head, the elegant young man stands passively without the slightest expression on his face. Resting his left hand on his hip, he extends two long fingers to reach above his waist. His right arm and hand point "unconsciously" toward the severed head of Goliath at his feet. The slight tilt of his head and the passive placement of his hands form a poised gesture of delicate physical gentleness that evokes an unexpected serenity, given the stunning brutality of the occasion so dramatically underscored by the stone embedded in Goliath's forehead.

Note how two intersecting "S" curves animate the form of this gesture—anchoring it to the sculptural base and lifting it upward toward the right—thus affirming its counterintuitive lyrically graceful tone. The perfectly balanced vertical and, importantly, horizontal asymmetry that joins the two faces reveals the possibility of embracing human dignity in the impossible presence of justifiable killing. With its formal and thematic center of gravity suspended within its overall closed shape and focused by the young man's two arms, the sculpture becomes an emblem of moral clarity concerning the eternal struggle of human virtue and vice. The figure's apparent beauty balances the paradoxical weight of his fateful choice.

Our second guide to Michelangelo's *David* is the bronze sculpture that Donatello made of David roughly twenty years after he carved him in marble.

(8.55) Donatello, *David*, ca. 1430s, bronze (5' 2¼")

This figure is probably the first freestanding nude in European art since antiquity, reminiscent of Polyclitus' *Doryphorus* and countless other male divinities and athletes.

(8.56) Polyclitus, *Doryphorus* (spear-bearer), ca. 450–440 BCE, marble Roman copy after bronze original (6' 6")

In this case, the bronze figure of David, unlike the generalized youthfulness of the marble David or the muscular idealism of the *Doryphorus,* is plainly an adolescent boy wearing greave-like boots and a leather hat with a laurel crown. The victorious boy again stands over the head of Goliath, which he has just severed with the sword he holds in his right hand. This time, however, the connection between the boy and the dead giant has changed dramatically. A feather from Goliath's helmet caresses David's naked leg as he fondles the hair of Goliath's beard between his toes.

(8.57) Donatello, *David,* ca. 1430s, a. detail of feather against David's leg; b. detail of Goliath's beard between David's toes

(8.58) *David,* ca. 1430s, viewed from front, side, and back

Skin in the form of highly polished bronze replaces the leather tunic of the marble *David* and gilt highlights sparkle in his hair. The graceful dignity of the earlier work has become explicit sensuality—even as a similar asymmetrical structure within a closed shape of the sculpture provides another gesture of counterintuitive poise and reflection. If anything, the intentional *beauty* of this bronze David, revealed at the moment of his murderous victory, is even more prominent. We might think that Donatello seized on the allegorical struggle between virtue and vice to portray a pointedly sensuous adolescent boy. The apparent contradiction of justifiable killing, redeemed in the art of the marble *David,* has seemingly given way in this bronze *David* to delectation for its own sake. Unless, of course, we might imagine that Donatello, with no less skill and determination, has here embodied the triumph of eros and insight, artistically sublimated beyond the contending forces of lust and instrumental reason, resulting in another emblematic jewel of art and beauty that aspires poetically to wholeness at the very dawn of the humanist Dream of Reason.[30]

Entering the Galleria dell'Accademia

Modern visitors to the Galleria dell'Accademia in Florence will discover Michelangelo's *David* as the culmination of a corridor lined with his "unfinished" marble "slaves," many burdened not only by the weight of their sculpted forms but also by the stone block that prevents them from standing free.

(8.59) Galleria dell'Accademia, with Michelangelo's *David* and *"Slaves,"* ca. 1530–34

Placed just above eye level, the massive naked body of the biblical hero stands as the singular emblem of the Renaissance promise of rational triumph over presumed ignorance, and presumably limitation of all kinds.

(8.60) Michelangelo, *David*, viewed from below

Clearly associated with the virile, masculine power of the emerging city-state of Florence, and symbolic of its will to freedom, this magisterial work of art also reveals the problematic reality of all human aspiration—especially, perhaps, when grounded in the exclusive application of reason. Taken together with the adjacent presence of the *Boboli Slaves*, the arrangement of these sculptures resembles the primal relation of "experience" and "order" in the two NASA photographs from space (image 2.12)—that is to say, the subjective tension of the slaves and the pure objective order of David.

(2.12) a. William Anders, *Earthrise*, 1968; b. NASA, *Earth from Space*, 2002

For all of his power, control, and, presumed authority, the *Captive Atlas* remains forever unable to throw off or deny the experienced limits of his mortal condition. Nor, as we will see, can *David*.

(8.61) Michelangelo, *Captive Atlas*, 1530–34

Viewed from the front at even a slightly elevated level, with David's head in profile and his body turning, the dramatically objectified gesture of this iconic sculpture (image 8.62) opens toward the right.

(8.62) Michelangelo, *David*, raised view

Unlike the centered, formally, and narratively "closed" focus of Donatello's two figures of David (images 8.54 and 8.55), Michelangelo's *David*, for all of its compelling presence, invokes in both form and narrative an unmistakably absent reality essential to its art. Gone is the severed head of Goliath, so crucial to Donatello's art and the conventional allegorical iconography of virtue over vice. As a result, we encounter a deliberately "opened" narrative. David now looks toward the world he will conquer or, as I can imagine, back at the scene of his frightening battle. Donatello's quiet graceful delectation has become in Michelangelo's hands anxious self-reflection.

The artistic reality of this moment carries a conscious existential implication: if to be is to act, then to act is to become. Michelangelo has placed David, and those of us who would contemplate with his art, into the very moment of this moral awakening. Michelangelo's *David* as a work of art emerges in our encounter with its profound ambiguity as an occasion to see beyond the ostensible triumph of reason over ignorance and limitation, to peer into the problematic reality of the Dream of Reason itself. Our beholding with the art of the young Michelangelo draws us into those shared questions at the heart of our own "wandering mourning," questions that assumed their full force when we became conscious in "Paradise" and experienced separation coupled with its inevitable longing. Along with all of the thirsts and enduring hungers that animate us endlessly, we will ask: *What am I? Why am I here? What will become of me?* And, inevitably: *What have I done? What, indeed, have I become?*

Certainly, the physical absence of Goliath's head in Michelangelo's sculpture of David is not itself enough to suggest intimated reconciliation of the contradictory realities of "before" and "after" that these questions imply. But if you were to walk around the sculpture to the right, you would discover a completely different artistic gesture—a stunningly different *David.*

(8.63) Michelangelo, *David*, viewed from the right

The familiar and powerful objective potential of the iconic elevated frontal view of the figure with its head in profile—the angle commonly shown in textbooks—is, from this new oblique vantage point, an equally compelling but contradictory image of subjective reaction. A vulnerable body now folds in on itself protectively, while the eyes, brow, and face seen directly reveal intense responsive reflection.

(8.64) Michelangelo, *David*, detail of face viewed from the right

In "opening" both the form and the narrative of the sculpture, Michelangelo created a dynamic artistic threshold of moral awakening that seems to question rationally justifiable killing at its core. The noble serenity of Donatello's marble *David* is past. In our beholding with the art of Michelangelo's *David,* we become no less implicated than the youthful David and, perhaps, the young artist himself. For what his contemporaries saw as this artist's terribilità suggests more than the "frightening power" of his artistic skill. Born of the infinite separation and endless longing that is our "wandering mourning," the terribilità of this art was, and is, the enduring faithful struggle that our conscious condition of being entails for us all, as it still lingers with us from our own existential experience of Milo's lament.

(8.65) a. Donatello, *David*, head and face in shadow;
b. Michelangelo, *David*, head and face

The fateful implications of Donatello's gracefulness and Michelangelo's emergent humility rest gently before us in Emily Dickinson's poetic divinity:

Tell all the truth but tell it slant—
Success in Circuit lies
Too bright for our infirm Delight
The Truth's superb surprise
As Lightning to the Children eased
With explanation kind
The Truth must dazzle gradually
Or every man be blind—[31]

(Advance screen)

Remembrance and Reflection

Where did the promise of the Dream of Reason lead? It led, of course, to our contemporary world: to modern medicine, to industrial technology, to space exploration, the life-transforming internet, smart-phones and tablets with "apps" beyond counting, and more ultra-high-tech devices at every turn. Much of the world has now experienced the fulfilment of its promise, which has produced unarguable benefits and allowed—for some—previously unimaginable physical well-being, so that no reasonable person could deny its apparent and presumably abundant gifts. The contradictory reality of the Dream has been no less compelling in its concomitant consequences. These are grounded, for example, in increasingly expanded justifications for killing by ever more refined means. No wonder, then, that David's sling and rock reappear as rifles in Francisco Goya's *The Third of May 1808*. The still, black silence and abject pleading humility of this painting belie the faceless brutality of the slaughter it portrays.

(8.66) Francisco Goya, *The Third of May 1808*, 1814

Goya's rifles soon became bombs that destroyed whole cities in air-born devastation. Pablo Picasso's great scream of agony, painted on the occasion of the annihilation of a small Spanish town, resounds louder still in a photograph of Picasso's *Guernica* by Elliott Erwitt. The child stands opposite a flower (at the center of the lower border) emerging from a hand that holds a broken sword.

(8.67) Elliott Erwitt, *Boy Viewing* Guernica, 1995

(Advance screen)

By now, even these lethal slings have become new weapons in which atomic fusion turns promise into mass destruction on an unimaginable scale. Here we may recall that at the first successful test of an atomic device, J. Robert Oppenheimer spoke these chilling words from the Bhagavad Gita: "Now I am become Death, the destroyer of worlds." They confirm the enduring reality, as the threshold of moral awakening conveyed by Michelangelo's *David* might remind us, that all killing occurs with a single person's willingness and decision to kill.[32] Shortly after Oppenheimer's poetic reference to divine powers of destruction, one person gave the command to use the first two atomic weapons to incinerate two Japanese cities and their noncombatant citizens, including men, women, and children on their morning walk to work and school. Of course, the debate over the efficacy or the tactical and strategic need to detonate these weapons goes on.[33]

But no matter what each one of us concludes, the effort to establish rational justification for killing remains unchanged. The choice is never simple. Mindless passion notwithstanding, the choice ranges from divine obedience to self-protection or to membership in an organization, which itself implies a prior decision based on considered thought, such as a lethal gang, vigilante group, militia, police force, military unit, or civilized state. In every case, individual willingness to kill is the rational precondition. The astronaut Rusty Schweickart has made a moving acknowledgment of his own conscious preparation in 1959 as a bomber pilot on duty at an airbase in Taiwan—waiting for pending orders to deliver nuclear weapons on designated targets—that echoes the honesty and irony of Michelangelo's young David. Years later, says Schweickart, he reversed his certain decision that had the orders come (they never did), he would have obeyed them and dropped the bomb:

> I began to understand how much human frailty and subjectivity were woven into the most critical decision making.... As a young man I was unwilling to trust my own sense of rightness when facing a momentous moral dilemma. I now understand that we can't pass along such decisions to higher authority, for there is no higher authority than that which exists in each of us, individually, as we face our complicated and ambiguous world.... These personal moral choices, when repeated and aggregated in the behavior of families, of communities, of nations,... are the very essence of our survival.[34]

The fateful double-edged promise of the Dream appears nowhere more vividly than in the engraving by Francisco Goya, made during the years immediately following the apotheosis of the Enlightenment in the French Revolution, which sought with such passion, purpose, and certainty to replace all that appeared evil with self-evident rationally assured good.

(8.68) Francisco Goya, *The Sleep of Reason Produces Monsters*, from *Los Caprichos*, ca. 1798

The French Revolution's ostensible goal had been to replace "medieval superstition" and monarchical abuse with modern reason and democratic liberties. In this context, the inscription on this print—*El sueño de la razón produce monstrous*—may presumably be read as "the sleep of reason produces monsters" and, equally, "the dream of reason produces monsters." That is, when reason does not prevail (when reason "sleeps") monsters (chaos) will result; if reason does prevail (even as a hope or prayer), monsters (chaos) will result. In Goya's haunting vision, the "silence" of this print becomes all the more powerful in remembering that the artist was himself deaf. Thus on May 3, 1808, he couldn't hear the roar of those rifles, only inches away, any more than we can now, as we behold with him—despair beyond hope or pleading.

Reason and liberties aside, there is no doubt that careful rational thought led to creation of the device and the decision to bomb Hiroshima on August 6, 1945, and then Nagasaki two days later. The killing and destruction caused by these two bombs was accomplished with extreme control and precision. Evidence of military presence in and near both cities anchored the rational judgment, articulated like this: the use of atomic weapons—despite or sadly even because of, their devastation to the civilian population—was justified by the confident identification of evil as the legitimate basis of action in the service of virtue. The irony remains. By defining evil, one is led to commit the evil of killing. The enduring question of whether the bombings were even necessary avoids the much harder question of justifiable killing. David's fateful existential question still reverberates loudly in the haunting moral silence that followed the two atomic detonations. *What have I become?*

A full list of questions remains: *What will I . . . now . . . after this horror, freely choose to be? Am I only the material causal result of forces beyond my control, burdened by the unredeemable legacy of the past and of institutions to which I would belong or crusades I would serve? Or, will I be free to be free in my reaching out for the beloved along an evolving Via Amoris?*

In a third variation of the story of David, Gian Lorenzo Bernini suspended, as if forever, the very act of killing in the interval between anticipation and reflection. His incomparable artistic merging of marble as flesh ("brushstroke" and "image") in the moment of action opens an occasion for further reflection on both the combined strength and vulnerability of the Dream of Reason and the potential even now for change, growth, and transformation.

(8.69) Gian Lorenzo Bernini, *David*, marble, 1623–24

Contemplative Beholding with Four *Davids*

(8.70) a. Donatello, *David*, 1408–09; b. Donatello, *David*, 1425–30; c. Michelangelo, *David*, 1501–04; d. Bernini, *David*, 1623–24

Donatello's two figures of *David*—whether as the noble warrior triumphant over evil or as the sensually beautiful adolescent promise—realize an illusory idealism that softens, if not redeems, the essential brutality of killing. Michelangelo's *David* reopens the question in the figure of a colossal adversary brought down by killing. Finally, Bernini's *David* comes full circle by presenting killing as an explosive, chaotic, and immediate act in an unending present. Each of these masterpieces formed at the highest possible level of moral and material aspiration powerfully recalls the enduring existential reality that Rainer Maria Rilke named: "Killing is a form of our wandering mourning." The contradictoriness that animates the art of these works of art will lead anyone who would behold with them back to the universal condition of all human being—and thus back to the embodied irony of the Dream of Reason.

Let's focus on one tentative insight that flows from this contemplative beholding with four sculptures from the early modern period of Western art history. We may recall the uncompromising words of Paul Fussell, who served in the 103rd Infantry Division during World War II, from his literary masterpiece *The Great War and Modern Memory*: "Every war is ironic because every war is worse than expected."[35] To paraphrase: all killing is ironic because all "killing" is killing. Perhaps the elder King David at last knew this to be so.

(8.71) Cathedral of Chartres, *King David*, north porch

Having been a bombardier himself in 1945, the historian Howard Zinn came to the moral center of the "bomb" as the ultimate realization of "killing is a form of our wandering mourning" on the eve of his own death in 2010. He entered that void of grace so evident in the artistic ambiguity with which Michelangelo informed his youthful figure of David. For beyond all the scientific information, as well as boundless technical, political, and instrumental arguments that justified the bomb—think here as well of the authority Rusty Schweickart esteemed less than his own "sense of rightness"—Zinn saw through to the far side of incalculable complexity, to the utter impoverishment of the killing that occurred in the cities of Royan in France, and Hiroshima and Nagasaki in Japan at the very end of the war. Zinn concluded his book *The Bomb*, finalized for publication just before he died, with this compassionate challenge:

> It is the immediate victims—or tomorrow's—who have the greatest need, and the fewest wrenches. They must use their bodies (which may explain why rebellion is a rare phenomenon). This may suggest to those of us who have a bit more than our bare hands, and at least a small interest in stopping the machine, that we might play a peculiar role in breaking the social stalemate.
>
> This may require resisting a false crusade—or refusing one or another expedition in a true one. But always, it means refusing to be transfixed by the actions of other people, the truths of other times. It means acting on what we feel and think, here, now, for human flesh and sense, against the abstractions of duty and obedience."[36]

Zinn's beautiful artistic simplicity can open our eyes to the only pathway past the unspeakable progeny of killing by any means, and bring us, one by one, home to the origin of our longing. From there, now (with Vincent), we might begin to count all over again from zero. And perhaps in this way, allow us to approach the threshold of love as the only remaining "form of our wandering mourning."

> *Let us, then, allow Howard Zinn's voice to echo Marguerite Porete, who took leave of the Virtues and the "Church of the Little" as the only way to remain obedient to the "Great Church" of infinite love (amour de loin) . . . that is, to Love the noun, the beloved.*

The urgency of this challenge resonates in T. S. Eliot's lines from "Little Gidding" as we read them once more:

> Quick, now, here, now, always—
> (Costing not less than everything)
> And all shall be well and
> All manner of thing shall be well
> When the tongues of flame are in-folded
> Into the crowned knot of fire
> And the fire and the rose are one.

(Advance screen)

The "Forgotten Awareness"

On July 4, 1994, Václav Havel spoke at Constitution Hall in Philadelphia. At this "ground zero" of America's rationalized contract of social and political order, Havel acknowledged the potential fragmentation of democratic individualism into endlessly subdividing tribes, groups, and ideologies. In his related recognition that exclusive scientific rationalism was equally problematic, he alluded to a profound "forgotten awareness," which he described as:

> The awareness of our being anchored in the earth and the universe, the awareness that we are not here alone nor for ourselves alone, but that we are an integral part of higher, mysterious entities against whom it is not advisable to blaspheme.[37]

As an artist who became the first elected president of the Czech Republic following the "velvet revolution" he had guided against tyranny, Havel called for a postmodern scientific reinvigoration of our thinking that would foster non-theological "self-transcendence." Central to this transforming vision, reminiscent of the fleeting dream of *fin'amor*, is the deliberate contradictory embrace, indicated by the inconspicuous hyphen placed between "self" and "transcendence," suggesting not just transcendence beyond self, but clearly self *and* transcendence.[38]

In Prague, the capital city of the Czech Republic, there is a large mechanical clock attached to the south wall of the Old Town City Hall that rings the passing hour.[39] During the day, crowds of tourists gather to watch a stunning mechanical performance as two doors open to reveal the procession of the Apostles of Christ. One by one, each apostle moves into an open window, pauses briefly to face the people below as though engaging each spectator directly and individually. In these silent moments, everything stops. Stilled mechanical movement becomes irresistible moral presence. The doors then close. The golden cockerel just above a stone angel moves its wings and crows. The hour chimes. The gathered people go on with their busy lives, leaving behind a lingering golden light and the clock, alone again, waiting…

(8.72) Old Town Square, Prague, Czech Republic
(8.73) Astronomical Clock, 1410, restored 1948, City Hall, Old Town Prague, Procession of Apostles
(8.74) Procession of Apostles, Thaddeus and Philip
(8.75) Procession of the Apostles completed, detail of cockerel

Theodor Adorno, writing on Ludwig van Beethoven said: "We do not understand music. It understands us. When we think ourselves closest to it, it speaks to us and waits sad-eyed for us to answer."[40]

(8.76) Astronomical clock, waiting…

Just beneath the Apostles' procession in Prague, there is a complicated astronomical device that records the movement of the sun, earth, and moon. And below this level, there is a calendar dial with individual medallions representing the twelve months and astrological signs surrounded by a circle containing the names of saints identified with each day of the year.

Little more than a tourist attraction for many, this mechanical clock, first constructed at the beginning of the fifteenth century, still joins science, religion, and art in ways some who flock to see it will miss. The abrupt sound of the cockerel interrupts the silent celestial and earthly movement of the days and nights of the year with its reminder of a wholeness lost in the pressing events of the day. The crowing cockerel, of course—called a rooster in the NRSV translation of verses I quote earlier from Matthew 26—is the bird that reminds Peter how Jesus predicted he would deny him three times. Following his early morning moral awakening, Peter went outside and wept. Most visitors to Prague these days will just move on, unsuspecting, to their next activity. Within the interval of the momentary silence, however, followed by the bell ringing the hour, the sound of the inconspicuous cockerel crowing may serve as a universally human awakening to those existential questions that still fill the crowded artistic air of the Galleria dell'Accademia in Florence.

> *May we then ask, as we move on with our busy lives: Will we passively accept the empty promise of advertised "freedom of choice"—vacuous liberty—or will we deliberately assert that we are free to choose and to accept responsibility for the full consequences of this choice?*
>
> *For each of us, to choose the contemplatively active path of a Via Amoris is to enter into the living, elusive but vital and dynamic interval between two enduring realities: What will I be and what have I become relative to the beloved? Alert to the sound of the cockerel crowing, will I be prepared always to stop, "turn around," and return to the origins and condition of my being?*

We might remember here as well that Cain, the agent of the first biblical killing, chose the harvest of his labor and was rejected, not because his wheat was lacking, but for the moral emptiness of his offering.[41]

> *May I invite you to pause and reflect on four interrelated contemplative possibilities, recognizing that all four exist to some degree in each of us always? Perhaps even the frank acknowledgment of these possibilities—for each of us in our solitude—can become another reminder, like Francisco Goya's courageous print or the Prague astronomical clock, of the ever-present need to awaken to the larger reality of our increasingly busy and distracted lives . . .*

- Will I be ignorant of my shared human condition of conscious separation and longing, only to continue to walk on, reacting unknowingly to whatever befalls me, accepting life as fate, remaining irresponsible for my actions? Will I remain spiritually asleep? Conversely, to awaken now would be to acknowledge Pierre Teilhard de Chardin's remarkable reversal of an empty cliché: *We are not human beings having a spiritual experience. We are spiritual beings having a human experience.*

- Will I more or less deliberately avoid the reality of my condition of being by finding momentary strength in choosing one side or the other of every contradictory possibility? To do so means depending on the false abundance of ideology to guide my actions, and on forgetting that the absolute "order" of reason, which denies shifting "experience," is tyrannical fascism. It means also denying that absent "order," absolute "experience" is physical, intellectual, and spiritual anarchy. Will I avoid the reality of my descent into chaos by allowing distraction of every kind to provide the superficial satisfaction of imagined power or fleeting pleasure?
- Will I face the dilemma of all conscious being but, losing heart, only become unable to act, paralyzed, as though I were spiritually "as good as dead"? Will I conclude that my will and being have been taken from me, thereby recalling an earlier era when *acidia* (spiritual despair) was the worst of the "seven deadly sins"?[42]
- Will I return to the humble source of our greatest human strength by choosing to acknowledge and embrace the living contradictions in every breathing moment of our begotten existence?

The source of our greatest strength is the primal recognition of this tangled wholeness, regardless of the particular form it may assume for each of us, and of our enduring and individual effort to be in thrall to the art of works of art, with which we are encouraged to behold.

Following Rilke, we will begin to *live* this developmental, even evolutionary challenge, by returning with a different glance to those artists of the Renaissance Dream of Reason as they lived and wrestled with the question of the unalterable condition of our "wandering mourning." Their art, accomplished around the year 1500, might allow us to almost hear their voices speaking with anyone who would listen.

(Advance screen)

Redeeming the Dream

At this time, when the frailties of our lives feel more tested than ever, we are challenged to refresh what the gift of human being requires of us. The separation and longing (Milo's lament and our "wandering mourning") that began in infancy continues. The "cross" Simone Weil reminds us of remains:

> Contradiction experienced to the very depths of the being tears us heart and soul: it is the cross.... When the attention has revealed the contradiction in something on which it has been fixed, a kind of loosening takes place. By persevering in this direction, we attain detachment.[43]

Perhaps most telling during a period of chaos and confusion is the existential humility Thomas à Kempis declared as the highest wisdom:

> To see the world as it truly is, fallen and fleeting; to love the world not for its own sake, but for God's [or in my language, for the sake of wholeness] and to direct all your effort toward achieving the kingdom of heaven [intimations of this wholeness].[44]

There are, of course, many who would guide and comfort us. In our immediate moment, as I write this in summer 2020, Congressman John Lewis's posthumous letter, which he requested to have published on the day of his funeral, July 30, illuminates our path by inviting us to emulate the active nonviolent "way of love" he practiced and demonstrated during his entire life.[45] So too, Mohandas Gandhi, Martin Luther King Jr., Nelson Mandela, and Václav Havel fought the good fight of political and human aspiration. St. John of the Cross (1542–1591), a Carmelite friar and leader of the Spanish Counter-Reformation who confronted the dark night of the soul with a redeeming act, mapped out the process he imagined in the *Ascent of Mount Carmel,* his treatise documenting a way for the soul to achieve "nothing less than transformation in God."[46] And, in the face of imminent death, Socrates's "dreamless sleep" returns our conscious separation to the embrace of cosmic reunion.[47]

Given the dire circumstances that surround us, whether potential global climate collapse, pandemic devastation, economic implosion, social disintegration, or a sense of fear and anxiety, we may well pause here to look again at Goya's paradoxical print.

(8.68) Francisco Goya, *The Sleep of Reason Produces Monsters,* from *Los Caprichos,* ca. 1798

The man, plausibly exhausted by the contradiction between the "sleep" and "dream" of reason, half-consciously traces the word *nada*: nothing. Does he despair in hopelessness and nihilism? Or, may we be encouraged by the word itself—the very word of ascent used by John of the Cross—to make a first step beyond darkness into the luminous "nothing" (void) of grace-filled intimated reconciliation of even the most tragic of contradictions? By embracing the "perfect ambiguity" of reason's dream, we may rest here to gather strength in silence, not to reject our vast rational capacities, but to redeem them in the arms of humility.[48]

(Advance screen)

As a first step toward a renewed threshold of love, try to listen carefully to the three greatest masters of the Dream who along with the indomitable Marguerite Porete knew humility as few do. Let these masters of their art and practice of contemplative beholding point the way toward a redeeming vision of reconciliatory grace and promise.

Listening to Leonardo

We have already seen how Leonardo da Vinci embraced the instrumental promise and muscular strength of embodied observation and order (images 8.17–8.25). This "scientific" enthusiasm for geometry, the anatomy of the human body, machine engineering, and rational control lived together with his apparent affection for women, children, cats, and the evident gentle playfulness of direct human experience and emotion.

(8.77) Leonardo da Vinci, *Studies for a Madonna and Child with a Cat*, ca. 1478–80

In 1481, Leonardo began work on a large monastic altarpiece representing the Adoration of the Magi, the name given to artistic depictions of the nativity in which three kings, having followed a star to the manger in Bethlehem, worship the infant Jesus and bear gifts of gold, frankincense, and myrrh. Here the tender side of Leonardo's prodigious skill merges with his more cerebral engineering efforts. Unfortunately, and for reasons we may never understand, Leonardo left this *Adoration of the Magi*, now in the Uffizi in Florence, unfinished.

Fourteen years later, Leonardo received the commission for his work in the Convent of Santa Maria delle Grazie in Milan to depict an event from the end of Jesus's life: the Last Supper. Remarkably, the artistic longing of the mysterious *Adoration* anticipates the acknowledged iconic triumph of the *Last Supper* no less than the technical incompatibility of the materials involved. Whether done in ink and tempera mixed with oil and spread over a chalky gesso ground on a wood support (the *Adoration*) or fresco mixed with oil on plaster (the *Last Supper*), the works share an aggressively experimental reach. In each, Leonardo apparently pushed beyond the limits of the medium to achieve the volatile confrontation of opposites: oil and water in his *Last Supper* and the mixing of tempera and oil in a combination of preliminary under-drawing, with fully developed monochromatic form, in his *Adoration*. So too, each image resounds with energetic emotion and chaos surrounding absolute stillness and silence. While the discontinuities of form and content are clearly established and lifted up in the liturgical mystery of the *Last Supper*, they remain as yet utterly raw, exposing forever Leonardo's own artistic encounter with the experiential reality of the *Adoration of the Magi*.

(8.78) Leonardo da Vinci, *Adoration of the Magi*, 1481–82

> *First, look slowly. Two contrary figures in the picture plane prepare the way into illusory space and, just possibly, into the threshold of Leonardo's prescient, if not preconscious, understanding.*

On the left border, an older man stands lost in private contemplation. On the right border, a younger man turns outward, actively engaged by something that is outside the edge of the painting, to his left. These figures make an apparent reference to the opposition of theoretical and practical engagement with the world (respectively, *vita contemplativa* and *vita activa*). But beyond this, the acknowledgment of pictorial exterior and interior places us (as alert beholders) within the confrontational interval of objective distance and subjective implication. Mary and her child occupy both the central axis of the two-dimensional picture plane and, simultaneously, a vessel of illusory space in a vivid conflation of pictorial and sculptural realities.[49] Arcing circles of animated activity radiate from this complex "center" outward to the edges of the painting.

> *What if we imagine that the schematic effect of Leonardo's composition, combined with the affective presence of the spatial and physical movement of the many figures, offers us a direct experience of biblical epiphany in the artistic interval between finite conscious behavior and unalterable infinite discontinuity?*

Does Leonardo open the void into which grace would flow? If so, why would such an effort have gone unfinished?

Some will say Leonardo was simply too busy with other extensive projects to finish this monastic altarpiece. Others will argue that he was psychologically incapable of completing it. The most plausible immediate explanation may be that the Augustinian monks of San Donato at Scopeto in Florence, who commissioned the altarpiece, found Leonardo's preliminary work unacceptable and cancelled the project. Why the monks of San Donato and possibly even Leonardo himself might have become disenchanted remains the compelling question we dare not ignore.

Two preserved preliminary drawings for the *Adoration of the Magi* will guide us further into the origins of this most remarkable work of art made all the more important not despite, but because of, its apparent incompletion. In one preliminary drawing, Leonardo organized a complex array of active animal and human figures within a spatial context constructed according to a precise rationalized system of one-point linear perspective.

(8.79) Leonardo da Vinci, perspective study for the background of *Adoration of the Magi*, 1481

What might we take away from this study? Notice a tense unity of mathematical abstraction and organic actuality that combines the singularized monocular "order" and geometry of his Vitruvian Man with the animated visual "experience" found in the *Studies for a Madonna and Child with a Cat*. Although this latter dynamic composition may not have disturbed anyone, the gesture of the child in the drawing compared with the central figure of the Christ child in the altarpiece is a different matter.

(8.80) *Adoration of the Magi*, detail of Mary and the Christ child reaching for the offered chalice

In place of the child's enthusiastic embrace of the cat in the *Studies for a Madonna and Child with a Cat*, a very slight but real distance separates the offering made to the Christ child, who reaches toward the gift without ever touching it. By itself, this formal change would seem to have been insignificant. Another preliminary drawing for the *Adoration of the Magi* in the Louvre, however, reveals a telling iconographic transformation with especially profound implications for the monks, and perhaps for Leonardo.

(8.81) Leonardo da Vinci, *Study for the Adoration of the Magi,* 1481

The child in this drawing in the Louvre reaches out again, but this time eagerly, to grasp the king's gift, bringing it close to his body as he did the warm cat. In this context, the formally insignificant distance between the outstretched hand of the child and the proffered gift in the *Adoration of the Magi* now measures an infinite disconnection between the divinity of the Christ child—the King of Kings—and the earthly kings who have come to worship him.

(8.82) *Adoration of the Magi,* detail of the Christ child's hand reaching for the king's offering

Again, this inconspicuous detail on its own may have made no impression on the eager patrons of the new altarpiece. But another otherwise meaningless detail from the *Adoration of the Magi* moves us closer to the awakening moment that would have startled the Augustinian monks of San Donato. Among the group of onlookers at the right side of the painting, notice that the figure of a man who seemingly strains to see the action in front of him assumes new accumulative meaning in the context of this altarpiece.

(8.83) *Adoration of the Magi,* detail of blind man

For its Christian beholders the anatomically precise rendering of this blind man, comparable to other "scientific" images in Leonardo's sketchbooks, the depiction of a man literally blind to the reality of the divine epiphany directly in front of him may have appeared more like a representation of lost and groping humanity. Could it be that either of these details—the spatially estranged king or the man's blindness—signaled the crowing cockerel for the Augustinian brothers, or even for Leonardo himself?

(8.78) *Adoration of the Magi,* 1481–82

Stepping back to observe the overall composition of the *Adoration of the Magi* (image 8.78), as it was becoming an image in Leonardo's complex preparatory drawing, brings us to another potentially frightening instance of awakening. Although clearly designed with a familiar stabilizing Renaissance triangular focus at the center of the painting, another equally vivid organizational "order" emerges in the positioning of the figures around Mary and her child.

(8.84) ***Adoration of the Magi*****, with overlay of compositional triangle**

Pause for a second glance. Beyond the commonly expected rationalized geometry, an implied vertical oval shape realizes a pictorially invisible boundary, one that isolates Mary and her child from the rest of the image and, of course, from all human reach.

(8.85) ***Adoration of the Magi*****, with overlay of compositional triangle, oval, and circle**

This invisible oval of separation resembles compositionally and almost exactly the "circle of solitude" Erwin Panofsky observed in the central panel of the *Portinari Altarpiece* by Hugo van der Goes. The triptych had only recently arrived in Florence to decorate the high altar of the church of San Egidio; Leonardo must certainly have seen it.[50] Like this altarpiece, now in the Uffizi, Leonardo's tentative exploration into the collision of emotion and sense, body and mind—or as I have proposed, experience and order, not to say eros and insight—evokes a similar evolving physical state. Panofsky compares them with substances of radioactive instability, which "give off energy in the absence of any exterior stimulus; but in emitting rays they gradually destroy themselves."[51] The apparent turmoil of figures surrounding Mary and her child resemble Panofsky's inimitable description of the dynamic human activity that animates the *Nativity* of the *Portinari Altarpiece*:

(8.86) Hugo van der Goes, *Nativity* from the *Portinari Altarpiece*, ca. 1476

> In Hugo's development the position of the Portinari Altarpiece, executed about 1476, corresponds, in a sense, to that of the Ninth Symphony in Beethoven's. The rules and conventions of a "classic" form are still observed. But they are exploited, not to say strained, to the very limits of their capacity, and the irruption of the famous shepherds, carried away by an experience too powerfully subjective to be expressed without some violation of accepted iconography and "good taste," may be likened to the startling intrusion of the human voice upon the sound of instruments.[52]

In Leonardo's *Adoration,* the sound of symphonic singing has become an uncomfortably frail silence, overwhelmed by noise.

We can't be certain whether unfamiliar and challenging pictorial developments were themselves reason enough to call a halt to Leonardo's commission for the *Adoration*, but their presence remains. Given our modernized secular world of ceaseless incrementality they might now seem unremarkable. But at the end of the fifteenth century in Florence the formal and iconographic implications of this volatile preparatory drawing could have amounted to something beyond artistic bewilderment—and perhaps to have approached blasphemy. Unease with this dramatic confrontation of subjective and objective realities, let alone the explicit experiential challenge to rational order, would have been sufficient cause to stop work.

But a far deeper and more compelling problem may have begun to take shape for Leonardo and the monks of San Donato. Having Mary, the theological embodiment of the Church, alienated from humanity—as she appears to be in this image—would have been nothing less than unforgivable heresy and a challenge to the primary incarnation dogma of the Church. The unbridgeable distance between the Christ child and the kings of the world would have been worse, denying at its core the very order of the universe. Whether this visible discontinuity was the result of Leonardo's conscious thinking or an unconscious realization of doubt will obviously never be known. Nevertheless, an inchoate but real presence of deepest personal spiritual limitation, misgiving, and fear in the artist (and perhaps his patrons) would have been more than enough reason to walk away from this project.

Such powerful potential self-revelation would have left the artist and his patrons alone in the darkness of spiritual despair. Soon after work on the altarpiece stopped, Leonardo left Florence for Milan, and the monks of San Donato commissioned Filippino Lippi to paint another altarpiece featuring the *Adoration of the Magi*, now also in the Uffizi. In this altarpiece, completed in 1496, the Christ child, enveloped within a narratively coherent landscape and surrounded by adoring worshippers, clasps a golden chalice tightly in his arms.

(8.87) Filippino Lippi, a. *Adoration of the Magi*, 1496;
b. detail of the Christ child

Ironically, Leonardo's interrupted work on the *Adoration of the Magi* has sparked prodigious technical dispute concerning its authenticity.[53] Lost in the scientific and scholarly debate is an embryonic vision from some five hundred years ago of the potential for spiritual despair, emptiness, and isolation in a world dominated by technologies, which Francisco Goya, Václav Havel, and others have found in our own era. We will return to Leonardo's

Adoration of the Magi for another, more hopeful, account of why it was left not "unfinished" but "incomplete."

(Advance screen)

Listening to Michelangelo

The clearest single emblem of Renaissance optimism in the power of Man and Reason remains Michelangelo's *David* in the Galleria dell'Accademia in Florence.

(8.59) Galleria dell'Accademia, with Michelangelo's *David* and *"Slaves,"* ca. 1530–34

As we have seen, its multiple vantage points must have evoked challenges for the artist and his contemporaries. To the temporal and philosophical divide between the "before and after" questions—*What will I be?* and *What have I become?*—we may acknowledge other contradictory realities visible in the frontal and oblique views of the sculpture: rationalized (objective) muscular, intellectual strength; and emotional (subjective) vulnerability.

(8.88) Michelangelo, *David*, a. frontal view; b. oblique view from the right

But in our beholding with the art of this colossal work of art, why not be drawn into the precious interval of Michelangelo's marble embodiment of the full continuum of "experience" and "order"? Recall here the opposition of medieval *ars* and *scientia*. Now consider how Michelangelo's contemplative aspiration culminates—as an artistic sublimation of craft and theory—in an *eruditio* engaged in the deliberate and humbling embrace of contradiction, which we are invited to share as a living intimation of *sapientia*.

Two of Michelangelo's other best-known works are sculptures of the Mother and Child. One is in the Church of Our Lady in Bruges and the other is in the basilica of St. Peter in Rome. Completed before he was twenty-five years old, these marble sculptures offer another prescient signal of the young man's artistic humility and wisdom.

(8.89) Michelangelo, *Bruges Madonna*, 1501–04

The child in the *Bruges Madonna*, enveloped by his mother's body, presses his barely visible left hand against her leg. When approached obliquely from the right (as in image 8.90), this unexpectedly tender gesture transforms the objective theological iconography of the Throne of Wisdom (shown in image 8.91) into a deliberate and mutually subjective act of maternal and infantile comfort and protection.

(8.90) *Bruges Madonna*, detail with the Christ child's left hand
(8.91) Anonymous, *Throne of Wisdom* (*Sedes Sapientiae*), 1150–1200
(8.92) Onze Lieve Frau Kerke, Bruges, Belgium, with *Bruges Madonna* in situ

A sign to the left of the altar in the Bruges chapel asks visitors to remain quiet (image 8.92). To place such a request before this work of supreme understanding gives way to silence of another kind. For beholders in the chapel, the sculpture may bring to mind the evening prayer at Vespers referring to the young mother's knowledge that as she held her infant child in her lap, so too, she would one day hold him as a man.

(8.93) Anonymous, *Röttgen Pietà*, ca. 1360

Michelangelo's *Roman Pietà*—at the entrance to the monumental site of the Papal Cathedral of the Holy Roman Catholic Church, St. Peter's Basilica—will stop the busiest of tourists and soften the hardest of hearts.

(8.94) Michelangelo, *Roman Pietà*, 1498–99, St. Peter's Basilica, Rome
(8.95) *Roman Pietà*

In accepting the pain of this death with such grace, Mary has not aged a moment since she gave birth. The mother's face in the *Roman Pietà* intimates the son's claim to her eternal presence, youth, and well-being.

(8.96) a. *Roman Pietà*, detail of Mary's face;
b. *Röttgen Pietà*, detail of Mary's face

According to legend, Michelangelo added his precisely and boldly carved signature—MICHAEL • ANGELVS • BONAROTVS • FLORENT • FACIEBAT—to the sash across the mother's chest to establish his authorship of this precocious work of art.[54] In visual effect, however, the prominent presence of his name implies an acknowledgement of artistic responsibility. Yet it also conveys an expression of filial gratitude for the begotten condition of our existence. This gesture is comparable, perhaps, to what Vincent van Gogh intended in the painting where he signed his name on a vase (that is, on a vessel of solitude) holding a bouquet of sunflowers.

The *Bruges Madonna* and the *Roman Pietà*, completed during the first years of Michelangelo's work as an artist, bracket the beginning and end of life with a gentle affection that is undiminished by the sheer skill of his art. Each conjures the reach toward infinite wholeness within the reality of conscious limitation and longing. Like the reassuring hand of the child in the *Bruges Madonna*, the dangling arm of the dead son evokes heroic strength as the intimate complement of abject humility. The dazzlingly white polished marble of both sculptures is another soft echo of John O'Donohue's blessing for a child about to enter the world:

> In everything I do, think,
> Feel and say,
> May I allow the light
> Of the world I am leaving
> To shine through and carry me home.[55]

Let our own quiet contemplation with Michelangelo help us to be in thrall to the art of his nearly miraculous first steps toward the beloved.

(8.97) Michelangelo, a. *Bruges Madonna*; b. *Roman Pietà*

At the very end of his life, Michelangelo returned to the theme of Mother and Child. The result is the *Rondanini Pietà*.

(8.98) Michelangelo, *Rondanini Pietà*, ca. 1555–64, viewed from the front

This sculpture in the Sforza Castle in Milan is no less artistically confusing and mysterious than Leonardo's Uffizi *Adoration of the Magi*. More than any other single work of art by Michelangelo, however, the *Rondanini Pietà* will challenge us to remember Havel's warning of a "forgotten awareness": "that we are not here alone nor for ourselves alone."

The *Rondanini Pietà*, like Leonardo's *Adoration*, appears to be unfinished. More accurately, from the front, the sculpture has been so heavily carved as to be thematically nearly unrecognizable. The familiar polished forms of the mother and the dead Christ in the *Roman Pietà* (image 8.95), the powerful judge on the altar wall of the Sistine Chapel (image 8.49 b.), and even the dynamic assembly of figures supporting the twisted, broken body of Christ in Michelangelo's *Florentine Pietà* and his *Palestrina Pietà*, have given way to a compressed vertical mass of marble. Only Christ's feeble and bent legs, a dangling and disconnected fragment of an arm, and the roughly carved figure of Mary holding her son with her left arm remain.

(8.99) Michelangelo, a. *Florentine Pietà* (ca. 1550);
b. Michelangelo (?), *Palestrina Pietà* (ca. 1555);
c. Michelangelo, *Rondanini Pietà* (ca. 1555–64)

The ostensible "image" of the *Rondanini Pietà*, a shadow of its original form, seems to materialize from the fabric of stone and the merely suggestive marks—"brushstrokes"—left by a chisel. As a form, this sculpture recalls the oblique view of Michelangelo's youthful *David*. It closes in on itself even as it rises from a narrow, rounded base. The resulting gesture is one of utter fatigue and apparent incomprehensible disorder, a devolving dynamic transformation of component parts into an undifferentiated mass of twisted stone.

Michelangelo worked on the *Rondanini Pietà* from roughly 1555 to 1564, the year he died. Do we imagine that he died chipping away at the rational narrative of this last image, the last mother and son he would make, unable to bring it to a conclusion? Or, might we find in its art of intimated reconciliation clear evidence that he had indeed "finished" his work but left it humbly "incomplete," as Leonardo may have similarly done with his *Adoration of the Magi*?

And what if we open ourselves to the possibility that both of these works of art, often deemed unfinished in the annals of art history, speak to the profound limitations of reason and disembodied ideas when they remain independent of (and untempered by) actual immediate experience—*scientia sine ars nihil est*?

Both the *Rondanini Pietà* and the *Adoration of the Magi* acknowledge unalterable separation between finite rationality and infinite wholeness. Nicholas of Cusa had invoked "learned ignorance" as the only viable rational vision of God, but Leonardo and Michelangelo apparently came to a growing recognition of an estrangement, even weakness, in their inherent inability to embrace divine discontinuity.[56] In their doubt each heard the cockerel crow, and in their faithful embrace of the incomplete they may have sought to avoid Peter's failure. From the perspective of these two consummate artists, Jan van Eyck's motto placed across the top border of his putative *Self-Portrait* in London—*Als Ich Can*—acknowledges its own combined confidence and humility: *I did as I could, not as I would have, had I been other than the frail and mortal being I am.*

(Advance screen)

Listening to Michelangelo and Leonardo Together

Let's bring these two seemingly unfinished works of art from the very height of the artistic Dream of Reason into the same conversation. The quiet, humbling art of Leonardo's *Adoration of the Magi* and Michelangelo's *Rondanini Pietà* may be especially poignant and timely in our own era, when the inevitable and natural experience of conscious human separation and longing is for some an alienation amounting to separation without the hope of reunion.

Having come back at the end of his life to the maternal theme with which he began, Michelangelo brought the contradictoriness of living and dying into a single embrace at the most intense, personal level. The iconographic and formal fragmentation of the *Rondanini Pietà* assumes particular significance if we encounter it as seen in image 8.100. From this position, we can see two faces of the mother.

(8.100) *Rondanini Pietà*, viewed from the right front

As he carved away the bodies of the mother and the child, Michelangelo left those two faces roughly intact, thus embodying in stone the full range of emotional and intellectual experience and understanding. The face with full features turns down toward her dead son in a maternal expression of affection and intimacy. The other face—visible at an angle above the left brow with only forehead, eyes and a partial nose—turns away from the horror of his death.

(8.101) *Rondanini Pietà*, detail of Mary's two faces

In the oblique view from the left side of the *Rondanini Pietà*, we see what may well have been the first chisel marks Michelangelo made as he blocked out the base of the sculpture. They cohere as a pattern of ascending lines that both anticipate and mirror its ultimate arcing form.

(8.102) *Rondanini Pietà*, detail, viewed from the left

In artistic effect, "brushstroke" and "image" merge seamlessly as an asymptotic-like curve—rising forever toward infinity. The result is figural and abstract, material and immaterial, all self and all transcendence. Michelangelo's *Rondanini Pietà* is anchored to the earth and its stone, even as a most enduring and powerful lifting movement sweeps upward in a release of utterly inexplicable resurrection. Remarkably, even the anomalous dangling arm from the front view is integrated into this gesture as though Michelangelo had intuitively grasped its transrational presence from the start.

(8.103) *Rondanini Pietà*, viewed from the left

(Advance screen)

Now, turning to Leonardo, what if we were able to see past the apparent later additions to his *Adoration of the Magi* and view his first preparatory marks. How might we look differently at the initial emergent image that existed prior to the anticipated layers of paint? We've already seen the stabilizing compositional "triangle" and the implied oval and circle of isolation; now let's look at how the complicated array of figures, buildings, and horses follow a distinct two-dimensional circular movement surrounding the geometric center of the painting's square format.

(8.104) *Adoration of the Magi*, with overlay of concentric circles

With "new" eyes we see separately incoherent narrative details in illusory space become calmly organized two-dimensionally, resembling a framed aureole of light and recalling the structural integrity of architecture and the "sacred open secret" revealed to Johann Wolfgang von Goethe in the Cathedral of Strasbourg. The lighter values of the prepared gesso ground shine through these forms as light through a fretwork of stone.

May we imagine that Leonardo did not despair? That he was neither paralyzed nor distracted? Instead, he deliberately left this painting rationally unfinished, leaving exposed to sight and vision the very lines and tones—the "brushstrokes"—that would bring the elusive "image" to life.

Although the Augustinian brothers may have ended their commission out of confusion or fear of heresy, Leonardo may well have left his preliminary drawing as it was in order to reassert his determined effort to live and struggle within the contradictory joy and pain of our shared human condition: the "cross" of our "wandering mourning." Still visible despite the clumsy later attempts by others to "finish" this painting, the very movement of Leonardo's hand at work in an act of art remains present as a life-affirming gesture, groping like the Magi toward understanding.

(8.105) *Adoration of the Magi*, detail of Mary's face

Together, Michelangelo's *Rondanini Pietà* and Leonardo's Uffizi *Adoration of the Magi* stand as living testimony to the "forgotten awareness" in our contemporary on-rushing, head-long, and putative forward progress. Might they offer us another occasion—with Nicholas of Cusa's "learned ignorance" in mind—to look beyond the limiting materialism of our singular focus on reason to a larger vision of our "God-given" creation?

(8.106) a. *Adoration of the Magi*; b. *Rondanini Pietà*

Both obviously "unfinished" works of art are truly complete as animating artistic embodiments of the incompleteness of human longing for wholeness—a longing born from an acknowledged and unalterable condition of conscious separation with its inexorable limitations. The art of each work of art gives bodily form and substance to love the verb seeking the face of the beloved.

In its fragile embrace of a rising incompleteness, the *Rondanini Pietà* resembles nothing so much as Constantin Brancusi's soaring *Bird in Space.*

(8.107) a. *Rondanini Pietà*, viewed from the left;
b. Constantin Brancusi, *Bird in Space*, 1928

Leonardo's rejected altarpiece reveals its art most humbly and magnificently in the form of the emerging presence of an expanding "light" at the very center of his composition, precisely where he had as yet barely made a single mark, as though this artistic illumination were about to penetrate the material substance of a Gothic stained-glass window with incarnated color.

(8.108) a. *Adoration of the Magi*; b. Cathedral of Chartres,
rose window of the north transept

I am reminded of the time in Amsterdam when I saw the conductor Leonard Slatkin stand reverently in a motionless gesture of purest adoration before his orchestra, waiting patiently to allow its music to come forth. So too, I imagine, Leonardo only paused in anticipation of the epiphany of grace that would become the face of Mary. The intersecting movements of line, light, and shade that animate this emerging work of art are poised at the undying moment of a stilled and silent revelation about to occur, not for the Magi of history but (perhaps anticipating Shakespeare's words) for every "wandering bark" led by this star to the poetic interval of an artist's love.

(Advance screen)

Listening to Dürer

Albrecht Dürer, our third exemplar of the Renaissance Dream of Reason, portrayed himself in the year 1500 as a sovereign agent of creation. But later he saw himself as the "Man of Sorrows" who, like Christ, had suffered the pains of mortal existence.

(8.109) Albrecht Dürer, *Self-Portrait as the "Man of Sorrows,"* 1522

In 1525 Dürer made a quick "sketch" in watercolor and ink that brought art, science, and the "forgotten awareness" together in a singular vision. Using both word and visual image, Dürer's *Dream Landscape* apparently sought to hold fast to the most elusive of all fleeting recognitions—the intense frailty of our being.

(8.110) Albrecht Dürer, *Dream Landscape*, 1525

The painted part of this *Dream Landscape* begins spatially with loosely but precisely applied inchoate shapes that emerge as trees when seen in relation. These initial marks of raw "brushstroke" slowly become an "image" of deep space, moving from a vivid though distant foreground to a city disappearing in the mist of the middle ground, and on to a remote horizon overwhelmed by an incalculably immense form that defies definition beyond its discontinuous scale. We may see it as the apocalyptic flood at the end of biblical time, if not prophetically as an atomic "mushroom cloud."

With the methodical pace of a skilled empirical scientist, Dürer wrote down what he had seen in his dream as accurately as he could. In his journal-like revelation we find a compelling mix of rational objective precision and subjective urgency:

> In 1525, in the night between Wednesday and Thursday after Whitsunday, I saw this appearance in my sleep—how many great waters fell from heaven. The first struck the earth about four miles away from me with terrific force and tremendous noise, and it broke up and drowned the whole land. I was so sore afraid that I awoke from it. Then the other waters fell, and as they fell they were very powerful and there were many of them, some further away, some nearer. And they came down from so great a height that they all seemed to fall with an equal slowness. But when the first water that touched the earth had very nearly reached it, it fell with such

swiftness, with wind and roaring, and I was so sore afraid that when I awoke my whole body trembled and for a long while I could not recover myself. So, when I arose in the morning I painted it above here as I saw it.[57]

Perhaps Dürer as well had heard the cockerel crow. Following this description of his dream he wrote "God turn all things to the best" before simply and humbly signing his name.[58]

(Advance screen)

Moving Toward Conscious Awareness

Albrecht Dürer, Leonardo da Vinci, and Michelangelo di Buonarroti—arguably the three greatest artistic avatars of the Dream of Reason—also left behind their honest awareness of its fatal limitations. For them the path forward seems less focused on singular rational power, control, and authority than on combining both strength and profoundest existential humility—an emerging procession toward fuller conscious awareness. Dürer embraced the "Man of Sorrows" as himself, Leonardo tempered his unsurpassable gifts with doubt, and Michelangelo gave poetic voice to his awakening:

So now, from this mad passion
Which made me take art for an idol and a king
I have learned the burden of error that it bore
And what misfortune springs from man's desire.[59]

With blunt directness he lamented:

The world's frivolities have robbed me of the time
That was given for reflecting on God [wholeness].[60]

Apparently, Michelangelo sent these words to Giorgio Vasari, a fellow artist and the primary historian of the artistic triumphs that emerged from the Dream of Reason, who believed Michelangelo's accomplishments were its culmination. Along with the verse Michelangelo included a brief note:

When you are eighty, you will understand what I feel.[61]

Michelangelo was eighty-eight when he last worked on the *Rondanini Pietà*. In 2015, the sculpture was cleaned and moved from its earlier site within the Sforza castle into the Museo della Pietà, a newly renovated exhibition gallery in the converted fortress. The design and lighting of this new site have profoundly changed the way we encounter this sculpture, and perhaps works of art generally. By offering us an occasion to rediscover the value of sauntering as the means of resetting our normal hurried ways, the site allows Michelangelo's art to speak with us.[62]

> *As you approach Michelangelo's last act as an artist, allow the noise and distractions of the day to float away. Be present in the silence that pervades our common condition. Enter without thought into the thrall of one incomparable moment of hardest-won wisdom . . . and peace . . .*

(8.111) *Rondanini Pietà*, Museo Pietà Rondanini, Castello Sforzesco, Milan

Moving slowly, reverently, silently, in the space that Michelangelo animated with his art, imagine the day he completed his last work and went home to sleep. He left behind in his studio, in the complex form of the *Rondanini Pietà*, two irreconcilable obverse realities—the fullest embodied narrative of mortal lamentation and the artistic realization of eternal resurrection—poised in a deathless sculptural gesture of faith that would affirm hope embodied by love.

Here, in the quiet of this place, through our contemplative beholding with the passionate art of the *Rondanini Pietà*, Michelangelo's most telling response to the noble Renaissance Dream of Reason becomes present for us as a self-portrait of human aspiration to wholeness from our universal condition of humble longing.

(8.112) *Rondanini Pietà*, viewed from the front

This brave face offers yet another encounter with Michelangelo's terribilità. It may remind us of Thoreau's admission: "I have never yet met a man who was quite awake. How could I have looked him in the face?"

The enduring *humilitas* present in earthbound stone may invite us to reach beyond the conventional manifestos of rational superiority and power—and this time to invoke T. S. Eliot by saying softly, if not prayerfully: "Quick, now, here, now, always."

(8.113) *Rondanini Pietà*, pre-2015 installation, a. viewed from the left; b. viewed from the front

Can Michelangelo's last vision invite us to embrace the weight of mortality (image 8.113b), even as we look beyond the limits of materialist instrumentality to the transcendent wholeness of creation and our shared human being (image 8.113a)?

(Advance screen)

Reflection: Looking Back to Find Our Way Forward

At the beginning of this chapter we pondered a series of questions as we set out to consider how the Dream of Reason eclipsed the so-called medieval vision of the world. We know, of course, the transformation that ensued: how the "early modern" world that emerged in the Renaissance reemerged in the eighteenth century as the grand rationalist Enlightenment, which in turn gave way to our contemporary world of scientific certainty and technological promise.

Here we might put that historical progress aside for a moment. Let's recall instead how Thomas à Kempis characterized our relationship with each other and the world as the "medieval" spiritual vision was about to disappear.

> *Turn then, once more, to page one of Book One of Thomas's* Imitation of Christ. *As before, allow the theological vocabulary of this monastic text to give way to a universal wholeness, greater than which there is nothing.*

> This is the highest wisdom: to see the world as it truly is, fallen and fleeting; to love the world not for its own sake, but for God's [wholeness] and to direct all your effort toward achieving the kingdom of heaven [intimations of this wholeness].[63]

As we embrace the enduring human meaning of Thomas's words, with love the verb seeking the face of the beloved beyond all longing, we may want to ask more questions—different from those that started us on this particular part of our journey. Perhaps, if this "highest wisdom" summons forth Milo's lament in each of us as the origin of that longing, might it now challenge us to animate yet another historical transformation, one that might result in a "more human love"? And might that very love replace "killing" to become the only remaining form of our "wandering mourning"?

Imagine this most fragile evolution. Imagine it even though we know that such love, and its elusive goal, is nearly impossible and that, as Thomas warns, the closer we come to it the greater the pain of separation and longing will be.

Despite Thomas's warning, imagine still: if this active love were to become in vision and deed our shared path toward aspirational wholeness beyond all acquisition—our "highest wisdom"—then we might return home as that "one in a hundred millions" awakened to Thoreau's "poetic or divine life."

Arriving in Autun

Having thus turned around to find our way back to the beginning, let our first steps take us to France on the eve of the flowering of *fin'amor*, back to the ancient Roman town of Autun in Burgundy.

(8.114) Autun, France

(8.115) St. Lazarus, Autun, France, 12th century, west portal, narthex

Let's begin at the church built specifically to house the relics and the bones of Lazarus, the brother of Mary of Bethany and Martha. As the New Testament's Gospel of John tells us, Christ's last miracle before his crucifixion and resurrection, performed at the sisters' request, was to bring back Lazarus from the dead, thus offering his followers hope for spiritual rebirth and eternal life.

As we approach the entrance of the Church of St. Lazarus, and look above the doors, we come upon a semicircular wall panel, or tympanum, placed over the western entryway in the narthex of the church. The carved scene, an exemplar of a medieval "sermon in stone," represents the prophesied Last Judgment, with the weighing of the souls on Christ's left and the ascent of the saved on his right.[64] Above the horizontal base, or lintel, and below the enthroned figure of Christ surrounded by aureole of light, we see an inconspicuous, but revealing inscription directly related to progress toward our Via Amoris.

(8.116) St. Lazarus, west portal, tympanum

(8.117) St. Lazarus, west portal, inscription, *Gislebertus hoc fecit*

The inscription reads "Gislebertus hoc fecit"—Gislebertus made this. Whether Gislebertus was the artist of this tympanum or its patron is immaterial.[65] In either case, this "signature" suggests more than artistic pride or monetary support.[66] It acknowledges our individual human presence, not at a distant future biblical event, but in immediate physical relation, directly beneath the feet of the risen Christ at the moment of his "living" and eternal Judgment.

Quietly, silently, in the narrative context of Christ's Judgment, this intimate placement recalls Paul's words in 1 Corinthians 13:12: "Now I know only in part, then I will know fully, even as I am known." Standing in the narthex of the Church of St. Lazarus we have returned to the origin of our being in humble recognition, as Václav Havel reminds us, of the "forgotten awareness" that "we are not here for ourselves alone."

At the time of Gislebertus, the pilgrim to Autun would most likely have entered the church through the north portal only to discover another primal reality positioned, like the carver's inscription, directly above the doorway. The relief sculpture of Eve, now in the Musée Rolin, was then part of a complex iconography that presumably included the recumbent figure of Adam opposite Eve. In the central pillar (*trumeau*) of the doorway supporting the lintel with Adam and Eve there was a small figure of Lazarus, and in the tympanum above the door an image of the raising of Lazarus.[67]

(8.118) St. Lazarus, conjectural reconstruction of the north portal with figure of Eve (after Grivot and Zarnecky)

Pause here to reflect on the contemplative power of the figure of Eve within the general resurrectional program of this doorway and the church of St. Lazarus.

(8.119) Gislebertus (?), *Eve*, ca. 1130

Although Eve is invariably identified with the first biblical transgression, this figure of her will confound rational analysis no less than Love did in Marguerite Porete's intimate interior dialogue. For unlike other contemporaneous images of Eve, the direct formal appeal of this sculpture denies simple moralizing condemnation. Eve here is nothing if not the very fullness of visual and tactile sensuality. Rather than standing next to the Tree of Knowledge, reaching for the forbidden fruit as in the familiar narrative of the Fall, Eve moves across on the ground.[68] Conveniently positioned to preserve the beholder's post-Fall modesty, she makes no effort to cover herself.

The sculptor has carved deeply into the hard stone to reveal her breasts, rib cage, stomach, and legs with all their roundness and fleshy softness. Her combed wavy hair caresses her arms, especially the tender inner side of her right arm, echoing the curving movement of the plants in this lush and presumably aromatic garden. With one hand, she reaches back wistfully—still innocent—to pluck the fruit that would dispel wholeness and leave in its wake the burden of longing, fragmentation, and distinction between and among all things: body and mind, lust and reason, you and I, life and death. With her right hand cupped to her mouth, Eve approaches the end of her perfect waking dream with a whispered alert to her partner in Paradise—and, of course, to us. She speaks of something she can't yet comprehend: the existential reality her action anticipates.

(8.120) *Eve*, detail

Eve's wide-open eyes may then signal for us the emergent insight which she brings, through her sculptor, to this fleeting moment of physical delectation and mortal reflection. In the moment of her awakening, Eve is suspended forever in the infinite interval between two realities: the wholeness of Paradise and the endless longing of her conscious separation.[69]

Were we to imagine passing under this sculpted image of Eve at the entrance to the interior space of the Church of St. Lazarus, we might witness, and perhaps no less importantly experience, a wakening recollection of the combined beauty and sadness of our first moment of "wandering mourning." For the anxious pilgrims among us, this reassuring appeal to wholeness—as it was immediately before we were burdened with thirst, hunger, pain, loneliness, and the longing of separation—may quietly inspire faith and hope that love will indeed prevail for us, as it did for Lazarus.

For the willing beholder in Autun, the contemplative art of this figure of Eve is nothing short of the birth of solitude, as both the source of our lingering separation and the immanent means of return through Rilke's "more human love."[70] Compared to the disembodied impoverishment of mere eroticism, raw acquisition, or moralizing judgment, this figure evokes the purest innocent eros of wisdom embodied in our solitude.

Now look at image 7.36 from chapter 7, "Lust to Solitude."

(7.36) "The champagne panty. At the soda-pop price." n.d.

In the suggestive placement of a bubbling glass of champagne balanced on the hip of a reclining woman we see remarkable similarities to Eve's pose in image 8.119. But compared to Gislebertus's vivid image of Eve, the presentation of this panty-clad figure offers little more than fleeting titillation.

What we receive from Gislebertus's presentation could not be more different. Animated by the flowering plant interwoven with Eve's body (8.119), his art—joined with the overall architectural crescendo of the north transept entrance—may now trigger for us beholders the sensual insight of aspiration that will inform the threshold of love.

> *Let this artistic embodiment of a once-vital courtly* amour de loin *draw you forward, even when only traces of its presence remain.*

(8.121) St. Lazarus, present state of the north portal entrance

> *Return now to the west portal of the Church of St. Lazarus. Although small and seemingly unimportant, one figure on the right side of the lintel below the fateful "sermon in stone" stands out because of its direct subjective appeal to all willing pilgrims.*

(8.122) St. Lazarus, west portal tympanum with crouching figure indicated
(8.123) St. Lazarus, west portal lintel, detail of crouching figure

Bent over in shame, head in hand, this woeful soul turns toward us as we proceed into the church, as though imploring us not to forget "that we are not here alone nor for ourselves alone."

(Advance screen)

Learning from the Aspirations of "Fools"

Not long after Gislebertus completed his work at Autun, pilgrims on this Via Amoris might well have encountered another face of the beloved beyond the reach of finite rational calculation, acquisition, or even change, in the art of the courtly love story of Tristan and Iseult.

> *Pause here, before you proceed to the* jongleur's *tale to listen for a clear echo of the voice that began this chapter. It will come to you with these famous words, in which the bard conveys an image of transcendent beauty: "But soft? What light through yonder window breaks? It is the east and Juliet is the sun."*

Now, imagine yourself standing with Tristan and a fellow knight named Kaherdin on their return from France to Cornwall as they hid along the way of the royal procession to catch sight of Tristan's adulterous lover Iseult. In reciting the tale, the *jongleur* offers us through the men's eyes a radiant revelation of Iseult's incomparable beauty—magnitudes greater than anything we might normally experience:

> The cortege of the Queen now followed. At its head came the laundresses and chambermaids, then the wives and the daughters of the barons and counts. These passed in single file, escorted each by a young knight. Finally there advanced a palfrey carrying the loveliest woman Kaherdin had ever laid eyes on: she was beautifully made of body and face, with falling hips, well-defined eyebrows, laughing eyes and tiny teeth; a gown of red samite covered her; a string of gold and jewels bound her smooth brow.
>
> "It is the Queen," whispered Kaherdin.
>
> "The Queen?" said Tristan. "No, that is Camille, her maid."
>
> There followed on a gray palfrey another lady, whiter than snow in February, redder than roses; her bright eyes sparkled like stars reflected in a fountain.
>
> "Now I see her, there is the Queen!" said Kaherdin.
>
> "Ah, no," said Tristan, "that is Brangien the Faithful."
>
> But at once the road grew bright, as though the sun suddenly had shone out through the foliage of the great trees, and Iseult the Blonde appeared.[71]

Now, I invite you to come as a vicarious witness into King Mark's court.

Tristan, in an act of seeming madness, entered the court chamber with a specific purpose. He'd come to ask that Iseult, whom he loved, be given to him, even though she was the king's wife—indeed the queen.

Listen to how Tristan responded to the king's challenge by conveying the splendor he imagined of life with his beloved . . .

> And when he was within the courts, the serving men ran after him and cried:
>
> "The fool! The fool!"
>
> But he made play with them though they cast stones and struck him as they laughed, and in the midst of laughter and their cries, as the rout followed him, he came to that hall where, at the Queen's side, King Mark sat under his canopy.
>
> And as he neared the door with his club at his neck, the King said:

> "Here is a merry fellow, let him in."
>
> And they brought him in, his club at his neck. And the King said:
>
> "Friend, well come; what seek you here?"
>
> Tristan replied in a strangely distorted voice:
>
> "Sire, good and noble King among all, I knew that at the sight of you, my heart would melt in tenderness. God save you, fair King."
>
> "Friend, what seek you in these parts?"
>
> "Iseult," said he, "whom I love so well; I bring my sister with me, Brunehild, the beautiful. Come, take her, you are weary of the Queen. Take you my sister and give me here Iseult, and I will hold her and serve you for her love."
>
> The King said laughing:
>
> "Fool, if I gave you the Queen, where would you take her, pray?"
>
> "Oh! very high," he said, "between the clouds and heaven, into a fair chamber glazed. The beams of the sun shine through it, yet the winds do not trouble it at all. There would I bear the Queen into that crystal chamber of mine all compact of roses and the morning."[72]

Like Abbot Suger, Tristan must have known of a place "which neither exists entirely in the slime of the earth nor entirely in the purity of Heaven; and that, by the grace of God" in an act of beholding, he could be spiritually "transported from this inferior world to that higher world."[73] As the "fool," Tristan challenged the exclusive rational power, control, and authority of the King so that he might secure his love in a "crystal chamber . . . all compact of roses and the morning."

Now let one such crystal chamber unfold itself to you . . .

(8.124) Cathedral of Amiens, France, 13th century, viewed from the northwest, late afternoon

(8.125) Cathedral of Amiens, west façade

(8.126) Cathedral of Amiens, center portal of the west façade with door closed beneath the Last Judgment in the tympanum

(8.127) Cathedral of Amiens, the nave viewed from west to east

(8.128) Cathedral of Amiens, the choir, viewed from the nave through the transept

(8.129) Cathedral of Amiens, choir

(8.130) Cathedral of Amiens, looking up into vaults of the choir

Beholding in the threshold of the choir at the Cathedral of Amiens will return us to the "forgotten awareness" and Abbot Suger's experience of wholeness in the integration of earthly and celestial realities.

(8.131) Abbot Suger (1081–1151)

When and where the noisy voices of undiminished certainty disappear is immaterial. For in their place countless exemplars of wisdom, embodied compassion, and aspiration will appear to show the way forward, even when forward means turning around to recover one's first steps.

(Advance screen)

CHAPTER 9

Circles of Affection: The Origin of Love

In fact, I'm well prepared to answer your question.
—Apollodorus, in Plato's *Symposium*

LET US turn back to ancient Greece and Plato's *Symposium*, Western philosophy's foundational discussion on the nature and celebration of love.[1] As with Rembrandt's *Aristotle with a Bust of Homer*, and like the Strasbourg Cathedral that inspired Johann Wolfgang von Goethe's epiphany, it is a work of timeless art. Allow this evening of love to reveal its elusive magic directly. Let nothing distract you from the simplicity, charm, humor, and human insight it offers us.

Attend the symposium, behold with it, and then reflect. Allow yourself to be in thrall to Plato's art.

The Dream

Imagine a stilled, silent moment when the stars, like luminous platters suspended above you, seem so close you can almost touch them. Their light is unlike that of the morning or the evening; it resembles neither night nor day. The air is rich with the scent of orange blossoms. Time and space have receded. You have arrived and are present to accept an unanticipated invitation to join a small gathering conjured in the memory of someone who heard a story from someone else who heard it from someone who was there. Enter, then, the synchronic interval of love—this poetic intimation of the threshold of love—in the form of Plato's symposium on love as though everything was happening in the split second of a waking dream.[2]

(9.1) a. Socrates (ca. 470–399 BCE), marble, Roman copy of lost bronze by Lysippus, 1st century CE;
b. Plato (ca. 424–348 BCE), marble, copy by Silenion, ca. 370 BCE

(9.2) Tomb of the Diver, ca. 475 BCE, *Symposium Scene*

(9.3) Tomb of the Diver, ca. 475 BCE, *Symposium Scene*, detail

(9.4) Brygos Painter, cup (kylix), ca. 480 BCE, with *Symposium Scene*

Five young, accomplished men—Phaedrus, Pausanius, Eryximachus, Aristophanes, and Agathon—wait in Agathon's house for Socrates, who is paused en route in the entryway to a neighbor's house, characteristically lost in thought. Once he arrives, they settle in comfortably, send the "flute-girl" away, and begin to talk.[3] After exchanging gentle words of welcome, they imbibe the watered-down wine offered for their refreshment. Then Phaedrus proposes a contest in which each man is to speak in praise of Eros. And so, they speak of love.

(Advance screen)

Each speaker characterizes the love-god according to his own best awareness. In five individually focused accounts their words surround love, leaving behind circles of understanding that intersect unexpectedly, forming a lace-like palimpsest of relational integrity. Plato creates these five speeches of the *Symposium* to invite a careful and detailed engagement with their remarkable philosophical and social complexities, many of them relevant now, more than two millennia later. But here a brief summary of each speech will serve as our entry into Plato's artistic form.

Phaedrus speaks first, recalling historically that Eros, the oldest of all the gods, remains the exemplar of self-sacrifice as the highest calling of love. Pausanius then offers a legal account by distinguishing between base gratification of sexual love on the one hand and noble aspiration to wisdom on the other. Aristophanes unexpectedly interrupts the orderly proceedings with a fit of the hiccups.

Eryximachus speaks next from a physician's point of view, summarizing his understanding of love as good health grounded in harmony and balance of all things. Then, having recovered his composure, Aristophanes begins his rambling and visually detailed speech, in which he imagines love as primal longing for wholeness based on gender and what we call today sexual orientation.

In his mythical account of primordial creation, there were three human genders—male, female, and a "union of the two," the name for which, he says, is androgynous. Each of these doubled forms comprises four hands, four legs, two faces, and two sets of genitals. Aristophanes describes how Zeus, attempting to diminish the power of these humans to threaten the gods, "cut each of them into two." From then on, each "separated" being sought to reconnect with its "own other half," resulting in male and female homosexuality and, in the case of the androgynous beings, heterosexuality.

Agathon, the victorious orator and writer of dramatic tragedies, completes the five introductory speeches of the *Symposium* with a soaring, rhetorical flourish that allows him to praise love as the highest aspiration to justice, moderation, courage, wisdom, and of course, beauty, all conveniently embodied by none other than himself. Plato uses Agathon's hubris as the trigger that prompts Socrates, without hesitation, to verbally demolish the young man. After only a few fleeting moments of "Socratic dialogue," Agathon comes to a humbling awakening, saying simply, "I guess I don't know what I am talking about."

With these speeches now complete Socrates proceeds, talking not about the love-god but about what he learned from the priestess Diotima of Mantinea, whose transcendent vision of love culminated in an immutable and luminous presence of beauty. This, Socrates tells his companions, is how Diotima described love:

> First, this beauty always *is*, and doesn't come into being or cease; it doesn't increase or diminish. Second, it's not beautiful in one respect but ugly in another, or beautiful at one time but not at another, or beautiful in relation to this but ugly in relation to that; nor beautiful here and ugly there because it is beautiful for some people but ugly for others. Nor will beauty appear to him in the form of a face or hands or any part of the body; or as a specific account or piece of knowledge; or as being anywhere in something else, for instance in a living creature or earth or heaven or anything else. It will appear as in itself and by itself, always single in form; all other beautiful things share its character, but do so in such a way that, when other things come to be or cease, it is not increased or decreased in any way nor does it undergo any change.[4]

Socrates then shares an idea key to Diotima's lesson: that we move through stages from lower to higher forms of beauty—as though on a staircase—in the process of "learning what beauty really is." Diotima had continued with a series of questions, which he now poses to the guests:

> So, what should we imagine it would be like... if someone could see beauty itself, absolute, pure, unmixed, not cluttered up with

human flesh and colors and a great mass of mortal rubbish, but if he could catch sight of divine beauty itself, in its single form? Do you think ... that would be a poor life for a human being, looking in that direction and gazing at that object with the right part of himself and sharing its company? Don't you realize ... that it's only in that kind of life, when someone sees beauty with the part that can see it, that he'll be able to give birth not just to images of virtue (since it's images he's in touch with), but to true virtue (since it's true beauty he's in touch with)? It's someone who's given birth to true virtue and brought it up who has the chance of becoming loved by the gods, and immortal—if any human being can be immortal.[5]

Suddenly, awkwardly, in stumbles Alcibiades, the symposium's last guest, who shatters the purity and absolute clarity of Diotima's vision.

Until this moment the evening's conversation has focused on a varied, but relatively fixed, objective reality that was finite and yet, in Diotima's description, infinite. Plato then, as if allowing his fictional Alcibiades to echo Martin Buber across a synchronic span of two millennia—shifts the focus of the *Symposium* deliberately from a vivid "I-It" reality to a living subjective, virtually "I-You" relation: Alcibiades personalizes the dialogue, drawing on his own relationship with (and feelings for) Socrates. As each of the previous speakers has done (at least implicitly), Alcibiades describes Socrates as the very embodiment of love. And as Plato's text makes obvious, Alcibiades loves Socrates: "when asked to speak of love, he speaks of his beloved."[6]

Recall here for context the societal norms in Athens that not only sanctioned homoerotic feelings but also regulated sexual relations between older males and teenage boys, through which the younger men were assumed to learn virtue. This expectation within the culture undoubtedly shaped Plato's thinking and the way he portrayed the characters in the *Symposium*, especially Alcibiades, who admits to an astounding observation when he tells the others that Socrates has tricked him. Moreover, as Alcibiades puts it:

> I'm not the only one he's done this to; there's also Charmides the son of Glaucon, Euthydemus the son of Diocles and many others. He deceives them into thinking he's their lover and then turns out to be the loved one instead of the lover.[7]

Then, without a pause, Alcibiades goes on to say:

> I'm warning you, Agathon, not to be deceived by him, but to learn from what we've suffered and be cautious, and don't, as the proverb puts it, be the fool who only learns by his own suffering.[8]

Socrates's retort to the younger man's complaint may sound playful and seem consistent with Alcibiades's inebriated honesty. But the older man's tone turns unexpectedly curt:

> I think you're sober after all, Alcibiades. Otherwise you wouldn't have been able to conceal the motive of your entire speech by ingeniously disguising it in this way. You slipped it in at the end as though it was an afterthought—as though the point of the whole speech hadn't been to make trouble between myself and Agathon.[9]

With this brief but perplexing moment, the *Symposium* glides toward its conclusion. What happens in this narrative interlude? What is the deception that Alcibiades refers to? And what artistic gesture does Plato make to convey it?

> *Is the gesture like Robert Frost's famous "spring is the mischief in me" that animates the art of his narrative poem "Mending Wall"? Did we hear it, see it, or feel it as it passed by like a cool breeze on a hot night, present and then, with barely any effect, disappeared—overwhelmed by the onrush of events?*

In symposia hierarchy, Socrates (as the older man) was normally considered to be the "lover." Alcibiades and all the other young men were "boyfriends" who should legitimately "gratify" this most highly qualified and worthy man.[10] This same Socrates, who was the embodiment of love itself, turned Alcibiades into *his* lover. This is the sense in which Socrates tricked, deceived, or, as I prefer, encouraged Alcibiades to become a *lover* of *Love* who would forevermore aspire to approach the beloved as though he had "been bitten by a snake, . . . by something more painful still, and in the place where a bite is most painful—the heart or mind, or whatever you should call it."[11]

> *Have we come to the fullest awareness of Socrates's goal to guide not only Alcibiades, but us as well, to become lovers of Love? This moment of awakening is particularly relevant for us, the most recent "guests" at Plato's symposium.*

Is it possible that Alcibiades, in his seemingly debauched moment of sensual clarity, actually revealed to us the "more human love," the embodied love, which we set out to encounter so long ago?

What then is this embodied love? Is it, as some would have it, the uncontrollable lust of one who has lost rational restraint? Is it something to be rejected? Or is it rather pure thought unburdened by lust? Does Plato's *Symposium* challenge us to choose between Diotima and Alcibiades—in effect, to choose mind over body, lust *or* reason? Or does Plato's art suggest an entirely different response?

As in all meditative practice, don't be distracted by any prior thoughts as we proceed. If distractions creep in, let them recede . . . and return to breathing . . . in . . . out . . .

Drawing Closer

The question concerning love is the most difficult question we are challenged to live; except, perhaps, for death, that other difficulty we tend to avoid or sentimentalize. With both love and death before us, yet another implication resides in our determination, willingness, and capacity to put "childish ways" behind us. But for this we must be ready, willing, and able to distinguish between childish and childlike realities—which Plato's Alcibiades struggled to do.

Our concern is not that we won't or haven't already responded to Paul's admonition about those "childish ways," but that we have lost sight of what vital transformation such an act entails beyond normal physiological and even psychological growing up.[12] In his second letter to the Corinthians, addressed after all to adults, Paul spoke as though we are by our very nature somehow within the threshold of love, even though we often act otherwise.

As the animation of our incarnate imagination, love is the first and last question we must embrace as human beings. To accept this gift of our begotten existence we are challenged, as Rilke challenged the young poet, to *live* the question of love and, living it, to embrace that other hard question we all face, so that a "more human love" will finally redeem even death.

Shouldn't the question of love define the sacral space and character of lives at every level? The condition of our world would seem to demand it. Even our best institutions are threatened daily by the instrumental disintegration of their real purpose, which is to affirm love as the very center of our human being.[13]

Approaching the Threshold of Love

We may now return to the beginning, to the experience of ongoing change, growth, and transformation that has been our singular purpose. As abstract and bewildering as this threshold of love was when we began, our movement along a Via Amoris has offered exemplary evidence that we are not alone. Like those who have walked this way before, our deliberate effort to animate love and our willingness to be embraced by love will illuminate the daunting enormity of our awakened and conscious lives. The words of the poet T. S. Eliot, who guided us as we set out, may now resonate for us more palpably:

> Quick, now, here, now, always—
> A condition of complete simplicity
> (Costing not less than everything)
>
> And all shall be well and
> All manner of thing shall be well
> When the tongues of flame are in-folded
> Into the crowned knot of fire
> And the fire and the rose are one.[14]

The last line of "Little Gidding" presents an impossible contradiction: the all-powerful, life-giving and destructive fire and the fragile, blossoming aromatic rose—all strength and all vulnerability. This is the irreconcilable and unalterable contradiction of our awakened adult human being. It is our frail mortal existence that would seek somehow to share in the purity of Diotima's immortality, "if any human being can be immortal." Are we together? Are we walking the same path Plato and so many others have walked? Will we take the steps by which we might all share immortality in our *love*; or, at least in an ennobling vision of such *love* to which we might aspire?

During our journey we have heard Paul speak of "childish ways." Listen again to Paul as he evokes his vision of love in each one of us . . .

> When I was a child, I spoke like a child, I thought like a child, I reasoned like a child; when I became an adult, I put an end to childish ways. For now we see in a mirror, dimly, but then we will see face to face. Now I know only in part; then I will know fully, even as I have been fully known. And now faith, hope, and love

abide, these three; and the greatest of these is love (1 Corinthians 13:10–13).

What then is "love"?

Come back to Plato's Symposium. *Pause after the very first words: "In fact, I'm well prepared to answer your question."*[15]

These words belong to Apollodorus, spoken in reply to a question asked by an acquaintance he encounters in the street. Plato doesn't tell us right away what the question is, but we can imagine that he intended the reply to pique our curiosity: *What happened during the night of the famous symposium on love?*

In his capacity as author of the symposium speeches, Plato can be likened to a playful maestro who guides his repertoire of ideas, viewpoints, and styles to merge in a profound analysis, synthesis, and celebration of love. His entry into the evening's dialogue brings to mind the way Max Bruch orchestrated the adagio from his Violin Concerto no. 1 in G Minor, op. 26, which we listened to in chapter 3. As Bruch did with music, Plato situates us in what seems to be an ordinary experience and then leads us by the hand into a reverie that gently reminds us of Thoreau's departure from habit into the new world of Walden Pond.

Ironically, Plato uses the confident reply of Apollodorus as the prelude to an account several times removed from actual reality, as though the event named had been a private, inner dialogue—a fleeting dream—that took place long ago. (The symposium in question took place "when you and I were still children," Apollodorus tells the curious man, thus naming Aristodemus, an uninvited guest who tagged along with Socrates, as the original source of his information.)[16]

Even though the evening Apollodorus describes lasts only into the next day—a nanosecond of measured time—it continues from this memory into the lives of anyone seized by the endless, hence deathless, almost immortal, question into which this symposium would guide us, as its most recent uninvited guests. And that is: What is love?

The *Symposium* ends no less artistically.[17] The last lingering moments occur in a rush of confusion. Agathon changes places. He moves to the right—"on the other side"—of Socrates. By the rules of the symposium, each speaker should pass the word to his right, counter clockwise. Thus, Socrates might now eulogize Agathon, whom he had so deftly cut down earlier that night. With this change of position, the conversation that Phaedrus had begun with his primal definition of love would have continued.

But when a new group of revelers arrived "all order was abandoned," and the symposium came quickly to a chaotic and rather sudden close. After talking so respectfully, so harmoniously, so charmingly, so humorously, and so intelligently well into the night, everyone grew tired as morning approached. Most, by the end, had left or fallen asleep. Socrates's last words at the symposium were spoken with Buber's "I-You" intimacy to Agathon, Aristophanes, and perhaps to us, just as the new day broke.

What did Socrates mean to say as his words drifted into the morning mist and Plato's beautiful dream fragmented into consciousness? To sleep now is to miss the last second-hand information Apollodorus heard. It just might be the very beating heart of the *Symposium*:

> Aristodemus said he couldn't remember most of the argument, because he'd missed the start and was half-asleep anyway. But the key point, he said, was that Socrates was pressing them to agree that the same man should be capable of writing both comedy and tragedy, and that anyone who is expert in writing tragedy must also be an expert in writing comedy.[18]

Does Plato's art challenge us to find a way of knowing and being that would seek out, embrace, and sustain the irreducible contradictions of our mortal existence born in tragedy and comedy?

Can we hear Socrates, even now?

Did he encourage each one of us still listening to embody all sadness and all joy? Both together . . . to suffer love "quick, now, here, now, always" . . . as though one had been "bitten by a snake."

Just as Socrates was getting Agathon and Aristophanes to agree with him, they too fell asleep. Aristodemus, who recounted the story, may not have quite grasped the enduring significance of Socrates's final words either. Morning came and as the sun rose, "Socrates got up and went off. Aristodemus followed him as usual. Socrates went to the Lyceum, had a wash, spent the day as he did at other times, and only then in the evening went home to bed."[19]

Embracing Contradiction

What if we approach Alcibiades's sudden late arrival as the turning point in the *Symposium* that prepares us for a new—contemplative—understanding? When he says that Socrates has deceived several boyfriends into becoming *lovers of Love*, he describes precisely the sublimation of lust into eros and, presumably, reason—manifest in the five speeches and Diotima's vision—into insight. Might that jumbled, confusing, even humorous, moment anticipate for us the art, the beauty, and the love of intimated reconciliation? From this perspective, we may experience the last fleeting moments of the *Symposium* as the artistic culmination that opens the way forward to an active and purposeful love the verb: Plato's Via Amoris.

The narrative plot structure of the *Symposium* is symmetrical. It ends precisely the way it begins, in the middle of daily life. Socrates bathed in the morning, "spent the rest of the day as he did at other times and then in the evening went home to bed." But in its artistic effect, this temporal symmetry contains the raw asymmetry of human imagination as it emerges in the evening's speeches. From Phaedrus's anchoring of love in primal myth to Socrates's presentation of Diotima's immaculate vision, all of the accounts of love are explicitly objective.

But when Alcibiades arrives, this objectivity gives way to lived subjective reality: first in his emotional description of Socrates as the very embodiment of love, in his own awakening to the capacity to love within himself, and finally with Socrates's urgent attempt to persuade Agathon and Aristophanes that being writers of tragedy and comedy (respectively), they must each embody both in their work.[20] In the animated symmetry and asymmetry of its form and content, then, the *Symposium* embraces a full spectrum of psychological energy, reaching from the ordinary messiness of life to the crystalline beauty of immortal perfection.

For some who read the *Symposium* the abrupt opposition of mind and body evokes a compelling choice, with reason as the correct and even noble response, affirming the soaring vision of Diotima. Is it possible that this response misses the enduring tender wisdom of the *Symposium*? I suggest that yes, it does. Such a choice fails to heed Socrates's appeal to embrace contradiction. It remains deaf and possibly blind to Plato's masterful literary art, which reaches beyond the limitations of moralizing choice to bring us home to the immanent reality within which we all live.

A Speculative Platonic Cosmos of Color

Given Diotima's image of a staircase (or ladder) leading from lower to higher forms of beauty, we may perhaps reimagine our relationship with Plato's waking dream. Here, in relation to Socrates, he assembles those five young people—Phaedrus, Pausanius, Eryximachus, Aristophanes, and Agathon—as each presents their best individual understanding of the multiplicity of *love* the verb endlessly seeking the singularity of infinite *Love* the noun (also meaning beauty).

> *Can we imagine this group on a single flat plane intersected orthogonally by a staircase (or ladder) with Diotima at one end and Alcibiades at the other?*

In this setting, Socrates embodies not only the multiple manifestations of love that the five speakers articulate but, importantly, an irreconcilable contradiction: think of Diotima's abstract, pure ideal juxtaposed with the "human flesh and colors" (borrowing a phrase from the priestess here) of Alcibiades's emotional physical presence.

> *Keep this spatial image in mind. Socrates becomes Plato's exemplary source of love; love animated by hard-won intimations of reconciliation sought faithfully in his enduring effort to pursue humanity's highest calling: true learning.*

> *Now, imagine that the horizontal plane of this image intersected orthogonally represents the realm of color.*

As in the construction of the color-value charts we engaged in chapter 2, the five speakers and Socrates now become the chromatic equivalent of love's multiple forms in dynamic relation with the absolute values of white and black. Can this imagined setting for the *Symposium* resemble the interwoven fabric of a "more human love" seen as a cosmos of color?[21]

(9.5) A Cosmos of Color: Circles of Affection

We might also imagine that this cosmos of color finds its partner in Goethe's revelation of color at the coincidence of light and dark, even as it echoes his stained-glass "sacred open secret" that transcends distinctions between exterior and interior. In image 9.5, Socrates no longer reaches out to love. He, like Christ—and Marguerite Porete—has become the very incarnation of love. Thus, prophetically, Plato's *Symposium* remains, for anyone who would engage with it through an art and practice of contemplative beholding, a timeless reality no less vivid today than it was some twenty-five hundred years ago and will continue to be into eternity. It is another particularly luminous "cairn" guiding us along our path toward the threshold of love.

At this threshold of love, *ars* (sensory experience, observation, craft) merges with *scientia* (reflection, theory, cerebral order) to ignite *eruditio* (the process of true learning or contemplative beholding) as a Via Amoris moving inexorably in the direction of *sapientia* (wisdom). Within this cosmos of Goethean color, the enduring affective reality of Plato's *Symposium* offers a sense of wellbeing, bliss, or Johannes Kepler's "sacred ecstasy": an intimation of wholeness.

(Advance screen)

Contemplative Beholding as the Threshold of Love

In my own work as a teacher of both art and the history of art, I have seen how the apparent choice between body and mind—lust or reason—limits our ability to embrace knowledge and the ethical choices we face. This impoverishment has emerged as the very contradiction of conscious awareness lived out in relentless tension between sensual experience and cerebral order. Analogously, it emerges in works of art between material substance ("brushstroke") and content ("image").

Over time, my struggle to make sense of this ontological grounding led to an artistic awareness of intimated reconciliation that has become, for me, a literal and metaphorical threshold of beholding.[22] From the vantage point of art as a lived verb before it becomes the familiar noun that names existing works of art—that is, as an act, or art, of seeking wholeness within fragmentation—we may move from the literary art of the *Symposium* to a spatial equivalent in Greek architecture. Let me guide you as we approach this vivid exemplar of our universal human accommodation to our dilemma of conscious separation and longing.

This path will lead us from ancient Greece through the acknowledged limitations of the Renaissance Dream of Reason. And it will bring us back again into our contemporary challenge to transform "killing [as] a form of our wandering mourning" in all of its countless, often innocuous, but always destructive, incarnations, into love as the only form of our "wandering mourning."[23]

With this trajectory in mind, let us allow the artistic intensity of both eros and insight, so redolent in the divinity of the beloved, to draw us forward. The radiant faces of *Aphrodite of Milos* and *Zeus of Artemision* will help prepare us once again, but perhaps now in a new way, to enter the threshold of a "more human love."

(7.35) a. *Aphrodite of Milos*, face; b. *Zeus of Artemision*, face

> *Step forward then into your own embodied threshold of love. Imagine yourself present in the ancient theater at Epidaurus attending a dramatic presentation by Agathon or Aristophanes. Be alert to the shared human need to embrace contradiction as the foundation of the art of intimated reconciliation, ready to approach the very face of the beloved.*

(9.6) Theater at Epidaurus, Greece, ca. 350 BCE, plan

Theaters like this one at Epidaurus were performance venues for the Greek tragedies and comedies Socrates spoke of in the last moments of Plato's *Symposium*. Greek theatergoers experienced them as the training ground of love and its vital embrace of contradiction, artistically embodied for everyone to see, hear, and live. As those who would embody love, we too, like the theater at Epidaurus itself, are all center and all periphery. We too move inward and outward.[24]

To become alert to this possibility, engage the centripetal and centrifugal spatial gesture of the theater at Epidaurus. Try to embody, simultaneously, movement inward from the outer circle to the center and outward from this center to the periphery and beyond.[25]

Imagine now, in the exact center of the inner circle of the orchestra of this theater at Epidaurus, how audience members might experience their relational presence. One fact about the theater's acoustics is certain to resound: the slightest whisper from a single speaker—a single solitude—amplifies outward to those occupying the concentrically arranged seats of the theater, and further still, outward into the world, like Plato's words to us . . . and then through time to that wholeness beyond all limitation, to immortal eternity. In this way, the intimate marriage of Greek theater with Dionysian rituals and musical words (*monodies*) drew the opposed epistemologies of *logos* (logical, spoken language; *scientia,* "order") into the *pathos* (*ars,* "experience") of the lived condition of human being. This Greek image of *eruditio* (Gr., *máthisi*) embodied in theatrical "dance" resonates directly with the poetic "dance" of the *Symposium* and indirectly across time, synchronically, with the graceful pristine clarity, thinking back to chapter 5, of Mondrian's literal and pictorial "dancing" toward sapientia (*sophia*).

(9.7) Theater at Epidaurus, plan with orchestra center and concentric circles added by author

(9.8) Orchestra with figure
(9.9) View out into the surrounding landscape

(Advance screen)

The DNA of Love in Architectural Form

We now make our way to an architectural structure that will lead us to a direct encounter with the engineering—the structural DNA perhaps—of love the verb. Let us pause to reflect as we did when approaching the inner devotional space of Ryoan-ji in Kyoto and the elusive space of *ai-no-ma* generally—as well as the art of Rembrandt's *Aristotle with a Bust of Homer*, the transcendent "light" imagined into existence by Mondrian, or the humble awakening of Dürer, Leonardo, and Michelangelo.

> *Take a moment to prepare . . . to shift your attention from reading and observation to purposeful meditative action. Then return to Athens, ready to make the ascent to the Acropolis.*

(9.10) Acropolis, Athens, Greece, view from the northwest

Let us begin here, well below the summit of the Acropolis as though we were—and Goethe might have been, if given the opportunity—following the "Panathenaic way," the sacred ritual path that led from the Kerameikos cemetery and the Dipylon gate to the sanctuary of Athena and the ultimate destination of her temple, the Parthenon.

This rugged path culminates at the Propylaea, an assemblage of buildings giving shape to the entryway at this most important of all Greek spiritual sanctuaries.

(9.11) Approaching from the northwest

As we approach the Propylaea, our steps along the rocky slope bring us close to the small Temple of Athena Nike.

(9.12) Approaching from the southwest, with the Propylaea and the Temple of Athena Nike indicated
(9.13) Reconstruction of the Acropolis, with the Propylaea, the Temple of Athena Nike, along with references to Athena indicated
(9.14) Reconstruction of the Temple of Athena Nike, 427–424 BCE, Acropolis, with balustrade (red arrow) and the frieze figure of Nike (green arrow)

Recall for a moment the young Goethe standing wide-eyed and amazed in the square (parvis) of the Strasbourg Cathedral. The small temple now before us serves an analogous function, literally and figuratively, as the place of arrival, ritual acknowledgment, and preparation prior to entering the sacred ground of the sanctuary.

In passing the parapet (protective wall) that leads to the temple building, exhausted pilgrims might have been especially inspired, and even physically energized, by one of the consummate meditative works of sculpture in the entire history of art. Here, in the counterpoise of its form, as we imagine climbing the last steps of the stairway to the temple, the figure of Nike the winged Goddess of Victory, at the center of the parapet frieze on our right, realizes in a wondrous manner the merging of mortal limitation and bodily fatigue with the ineffable weightless presence of divinity.

As though she were suspended between sky and earth, just barely touching the ground with her left foot, Nike bends slightly to remove her sandal before entering the sanctuary.

(9.15) *Nike* (Victory), 410–407 BCE, from the balustrade of the Temple of Athena Nike, removing her sandal

Simultaneously stone and sensuous body ("brushstroke" and "image"), she is both anchored and weightless. Her sudden arrival infuses the wind with quiet stillness. Poised in absolute perfect balance, she is an intimated reconciliation of multiple contradictions, resolute yet demure. Her presence exudes embodied grace at the entrance to a sanctuary.[26]

You have come here to celebrate the cosmic reality of love in the combined presence of eros and insight. To engage directly with this moment and this figure of Nike, *imagine, in your own exhausted awkwardness, also reaching to remove your sandals before entering the sanctuary.*

As a form of physical meditation, try to assume Nike's *pose. Allow yourself to be drawn forward and upward by the rising "S" curve that organizes her sculpted form. Follow it from the tip of her earthbound toe to the modest tilt of her head and face framed by the gentle arc of her wings. Reach from the grounded anchor at the bottom of the architectural relief to the opened release at the top, freed from the stone cornice above her.*

(9.16) *Nike* (Victory), with the cornice of the balustrade

Having experienced the remarkably kinetic art of the Temple of Athena Nike, we'll now move through the last steps from this antechamber to the gateway (Propylaea) that leads directly into the sanctuary of Athena.

(9.17) Acropolis, steep path to the Propylaea
(9.18) Parthenon, viewed from the Propylaea

This photograph from the Propylaea (image 9.18) offers an objective descriptive view of the Parthenon. To approach the artistic reality of this entryway, imagine a reconstructed view of the Acropolis sanctuary from the Propylaea.

(9.19) Reconstruction of the Propylaea, ca. 438–432 BCE, Periclean entrance to the sanctuary of Athena, Acropolis (after Gorham P. Stevens)

Engage slowly and attentively with this gateway, leading into the sanctuary of Athena. Enter this space; allow it to acknowledge your presence.

Like the form of the theater at Epidaurus, the shape of this gateway is another gesture toward wholeness, as though it were itself one exemplar of the very threshold of love we have been approaching. The shadowed intersection of this exterior entryway with the luminous interior space of the sanctuary defines the ultimate transition along the Panathenaic way into the precinct of divinity. Like the artistic form and content of the *Symposium*, the symmetry of this gate embraces the asymmetry of the setting beyond, creating that experiential interval or *void* into which grace will flow. From here, the *Athena Promachos*, "Athena who fights in the front line," observed obliquely, stands to the left of an empty center, while the temple of the Virgin goddess, Athena Parthenos, the goal of our pilgrimage to the Acropolis, lies off to the right, in our peripheral vision.

As we move through the balanced harmony of the horizontal and vertical structure of this post and lintel gateway, we will approach the steps of the Parthenon, marked by exemplary votive plaques (image 9.20). These are the cairns that will guide our pilgrimage home to the colossal *Athena Parthenos*, the statue that once stood inside the small, sacred inner chamber (cella) of the Parthenon, and to our direct encounter with an intimation of infinite wholeness: face to face with the beloved (image 4.19).

(9.20) Reconstruction of the Parthenon, 448–432 BCE, Acropolis (after Gorham P. Stevens)

(4.19) Parthenon, inner chamber, reconstruction

(Advance screen)

Arrival: You Have Come Home to the Origin of Love

In the beginning is the relation—
—Martin Buber, *I and Thou*

(9.21) Threshold of Love I

This schematic rendering, recalling with post-and-lintel simplicity the entry to the sanctuary of Athena, generalizes its spiritual reality. It may also signal the return of a prodigal son or daughter and the freedom to begin all over again with their homecoming.

When I presented this schematic drawing to illustrate the threshold of love during "Eros and Insight" seminars, the experience affirmed my own sense of embodied presence and awakening. On such occasions my own efforts coincided with those of my students as our shared responses engaged us in common understanding. What had been remote, abstract, much too objective, and barely visible became immediate, subjectively realized, and vivid before and within us.

(9.22) Threshold of Love II: love the verb

As we began to find ourselves embodied in this form, our estrangement from the threshold of love characterized as "I/he, she, it" became Martin Buber's inclusive "I and You." Note how the two columns rising from the ground—as the contradictory realities of sensory awareness (left) and rational awareness (right)—manifest structurally in the discrete isolation of lust or reason at the base of their respective columns. Moving upward in a literal gesture of sublimation, we might imagine the transformation of this familiar alienation: Instrumental reason informed by eros will become insight. So too, lust informed by insight will become eros.

Together eros and insight are the structural capitals supporting the lintel block that joins them and constitutes the integrated reality that forms the stability of the gateway: love the verb.

Similarly, we embody two obverse capacities of awareness. Realized in their living relation, they form an integrated conscious being. In short, the so-called left and right sides of an embodied mind find their echo in the process of moving from the base of each post up to their capitals and into the lintel block that will animate their complex interweaving of multiple though contradictory potentialities.[27]

With this imagined architectural analogy before us, we come all the way home. We arrive knowing that our primal awakening to separation and longing, alive in the opposition of sensory and rational awareness, has also become the source of Rilke's "killing is a form of our wandering mourning." Now, by sublimating the opposition of lust–reason into relational eros *and* insight, we have transformed "killing" into "love." This love as an active verb is no longer the weak alternative to a more muscular "killing." It is instead the redeeming act to render "killing" not only obsolete, but over time, extinct. Remarkably, our conscious awakening—the source of our "wandering mourning"—will have become the very means of our return. Arrive with Martin Buber:

> But isn't solitude, too, a portal? Does it not happen sometimes in the stillest lonesomeness that we unexpectedly behold? Cannot intercourse with oneself change mysteriously into intercourse with mystery?[28]

In my own experience, students who find themselves in the midst of an act of beholding, immersed within their own threshold of love, usually respond simply with a smile of relief and release, no longer compelled to argue or explain.

Stepping into the Threshold of Love

Entering this threshold of love in the embrace of eros and insight as we prepare to set out on our Via Amoris will reaffirm a forgotten birthright present from the beginning. In biblical terms we may return to that fateful gate on the east side of Paradise only to rediscover in the very act of love the face of the beloved. This return need not be an imaginary reality. It is existential and prophetic.

Pause to recall Milo's lament: to be is to be separate . . . and being separate, we long to be whole. Recall as well John O'Donohue's blessing for a child entering this world: may I allow the light of the world I am leaving to shine through and carry me home.

Now, of course, we have reversed direction. Instead of reliving the primal lament at our departure from Paradise, we are, with John O'Donohue's child, returning "home" to Paradise, illuminated by its eternal light. We are no longer constrained by the burden of separation without hope of reunion. Our existential alienation has been replaced by sharing Buber's deliberately biblical recognition, that "in the beginning is the relation."[29] As the precondition of *love*, our relational embrace by both eros *and* insight allows us to take our first step into the threshold of love in the direction of this light. In this step our approach to the beloved begins.

(9.23) Threshold of Love III: entering the threshold of love

But this threshold of love will be prophetic only insofar as we realize it in each act of beholding, which in turn results in an art aspiring to wholeness from a shared condition of limitation and longing. Whether existential or prophetic, our conscious being and actions will now be informed by the implicit challenge of Plato's *Symposium* and the explicit appeal of St. Augustine, as recalled by Marguerite Porete, to "love Love and do as you will." We will have entered into our Via Amoris insofar as we will have identified, acknowledged, and embraced contradiction while forever seeking intimations of reconciliation of this and every other contradiction our conscious being entails. The rising light on the horizon is the face toward which we move.

(9.24) Threshold of Love IV: rising light

The concentric circles that expand across this schematic drawing, as though they were rays of the rising sun, echo those Greek "circles of affection"—also called circles of compassion in Confucian tradition—in which social grace would expand outward from self, to family, to city, state, the world, and beyond.[30]

(9.25) Threshold of Love V: radiance of light; Love the noun; the Beloved

These rippling circles also bring us home to the origin of our own individual Via Amoris, our individual path of love—for this origin is immanent. It is lived. It either exists within each of us, or it doesn't exist at all. It is our very being. It is the radiance of all light from dawn to the sunset that will emanate from us and affirm the comparable beauty of the darkness. Perhaps this light will echo again Thoreau's admonition: "To be awake is to be alive. I have never yet met a man who was quite awake. How could I have looked him in the face?" And yet, is it not the very softness of this radiant light with which we are invited to behold?[31]

The art of all works of art, like the Propylaea itself, will embody our beholding and will transform material limitation into intimations of wholeness beyond all limitation. The building adjacent to the Propylaea was the Pinakotheke or "picture gallery." Unlike most modern museums of acquisition and possession, the Pinakotheke at the entrance to the sanctuary of Athena was a place (borrowing Rilke's words) to "protect and border and salute" votive objects of aspiration otherwise known as living works of art: love.

(9.26) Frederick Church, *Parthenon*, 1871, viewed from the Propylaea

With the setting sun at his back, Frederick Church realized the luminous promise of his own beholding from within the shadow of the Propylaea gate. Like all such "circles of affection," the art of his painting—simply titled *Parthenon*, Temple of the Virgin Goddess—will resonate with all other works of art of all kinds, whether in paint or stone or whatever medium they appear. Although we will experience our own flood of such artistic epiphanies, we might recall here the path we have followed from the exemplary experience of Henry David Thoreau's awakening in the dawn and his evening vision while walking in an empty field, Rembrandt van Rijn's invitation to contemplate with him, Johann Wolfgang von Goethe's epiphany at Strasbourg, Piet Mondrian's transcendent "light" beyond light, the spatial mystery of *ai-no-ma*, Renaissance humility, and, perhaps most especially, a determined student's seemingly innocuous yet transforming discovery: "I saw green!" For that student (Jenny), from that moment on, "red" and "green" were no longer just two colors on an objective "color wheel." They and every other contradictory reality, present and absent, were whole again in the fleeting moment of her beholding.

In this recognition, the "circles of affection" that illuminate the schematic drawing of the threshold of love will have become the infinite silence that exists within us, within which we all exist and within which all love is born.

(9.27) Threshold of Love VI: Circles of Affection—Silence

(Advance screen)

Radiating Circles of Affection

An art and practice of contemplative beholding will animate our threshold of love in countless forms, places, and times, often with little warning. The determined and disciplined effort to articulate the compelling reality of such beholding, or to realize it for others to share, will assure the continued radiation of endless "circles of affection" of this kind. Every act informed by love embodies an art that will offer deathless occasions of beholding, encouraging others to emulate such acts as we might seek to emulate the grace of *Nike* on the balustrade of the Temple of Athena Nike, or stand with Frederick Church in the entrance to the sanctuary of Athena. These models of the threshold of love, including the post-and-lintel structure of the Propylaea itself, are, of course, only particular instances of an infinite number of possibilities that will emerge from the precondition of an awakened conscious awareness, in which love as an act of intimated reconciliation, rather than "killing," will inform our unalterable "wandering mourning."

Remembering Goethe's passionate embrace of obverse realities, we may enter another threshold of love by standing in the Gothic light of Saint-Chapelle in Paris. This royal chapel, like the Greek Pinakotheke, was erected in the thirteenth century as a reliquary, in this case to honor Christ's Crown of Thorns. To one who would behold with this artistic aspiration, Saint-Chapelle is another universally human vessel of ineffably infinite white light incarnated here as color.

(9.28) Saint-Chapelle, Paris, France, 1241–48, viewed from the southwest

(9.29) Saint-Chapelle, elevation and cross-section (after Frankl)

(9.30) Saint-Chapelle, interior

If we were completely open to the presence of the threshold of love within us, we might find another occasion of intimated wholeness in the space of the "moon viewing" platform at the seventeenth-century Imperial Detached Palace in Katsura, Japan. Here, the almost Mondrian-like irreducibility of an unadorned square bamboo platform becomes a Buddhist interval between Abbot Suger's "purity of heaven" and the "slime of the earth." Kneeling contemplatively here we will hold together the moon above and its reflection in the water.

(9.31) Imperial Detached Palace, 17th century, Katsura, Japan, aerial view with moon-viewing platform indicated

(9.32) Imperial Detached Palace, moon-viewing platform

So too, the moon-viewing platform at Ishiyamadera overlooking Lake Biwa near Kyoto may remind us of *The Tale of Genji*. It is thought that Shikibu Murasaki began writing this healing vision of love during a visit to the temple on the occasion of the full moon in August 1004.

(9.33) a. Ishiyamadera, 747, Otsu, Japan, moon-viewing platform; b. Tsukioka Yoshitoshi, *Shikibu Murasaki at Ishiyamadera* (ca. 1882)

In these and every other act of art and beholding we come face to face with the wholeness of our being from which our conscious awareness separates us, even as it provides the way of our return. All deliberate behaviors to identify and embrace contradiction will have become acts of love.

Whether in works of art or in Johannes Kepler's scientific embrace of the orbital movement of the cosmos, we will experience this incarnated love as the foundation of all "sacred ecstasy."[32] The source of Rainer Maria Rilke's "more human love," our goal from the beginning, is neither art nor science. This source lies at the very center of our enduring inner dialogue with wholeness: in Augustine's words, that infinite place "where nothing unbecoming can be found."[33] We are the living vessel of this "more human love." Science, art, religion, and everything else that will emerge from our awakened imagination will be the almost immortal offspring of this love, even as our mortal solitude remains the sacral home of this imagination.

(9.34) Ryoan-ji, Kyoto, Japan, anonymous meditation

The center and periphery of every rock and pebble, like light and shadow, reach out to us, as we do to them. Although the word *shakkei* from Japanese garden design is invariably translated into English as "borrowed landscape," consistent with Western notions of acquisition and ownership (possession, borrowing, stealing), the meaning of the phrase grounded in its *kanji* form is to give and receive assistance.[34]

(9.35) Ryoan-ji, first light

The far-off and now familiar echo we hear in the early morning silence of this place, as we move inward as well as outward, returns us to Rainer Maria Rilke's succinct definition of a "more human love... that consists in this, that two solitudes protect and border and salute each other." Quiet contemplation within the utterly *empty* center—interval—of the garden at Ryoan-ji brings us full circle to the beginning of this particular Via Amoris.

(1.1) Outer Gate I
(1.2) Outer Gate II
(1.3) Curving path
(1.4) East Gate
(1.5) Pond with moored boat
(1.6) Pond with two rocks
(1.7) Pond with two rocks and still water
(1.8) Pond with ripples
(1.9) Matsuo Bashō, text, "Breaking the silence..."

From within the threshold of love, a primal reality illuminates our being: the contemplative knowledge of the very infinity of our solitude assures us we are never alone and, therefore, can never be forsaken by Love.

(9.36) Circles of Affection

(Advance screen)

IV

VIA AMORIS

CHAPTER 10

Homecoming and Departure

So we saunter toward the Holy Land; till one day the sun shall shine more brightly than ever he has done, shall perchance shine into our minds and hearts, and light up our whole lives with a great awakening light, so warm and serene and golden as on a bank-side in autumn.
—Henry David Thoreau, *Walking*

"Via Amoris" (part IV of our journey together) brings us not to a final destination but to a welcoming place of arrival, from which we may continue on our individual paths toward a way of love where love is the means. This chapter, paired with chapter 11, will guide us to a place of potential renewal. Will you return with me for a moment to Kyoto, where our journey began?

(0.2) Bamboo Path, Kyoto, Japan

Now imagine a path, any path, where there is neither beginning nor end (finite but framed before and after by infinity) . . .
and where both sides are simultaneously open and closed,
embracing free but deliberate choices and their consequences . . .
a movement into time and space beyond reckoning that will bring us home . . .

Our Shared Reawakening at the Cathedral of Chartres

(10.1) Cathedral of Chartres, France, 12th–16th century, viewed from the southwest

Having come back to this Gothic monument of earthbound transcendence, pause to contemplate a particular detail in the north tower you may have never before noticed.

(10.2) North tower, location of the "frightened cat" indicated

(10.3) North tower archivolts with the "frightened cat"

(10.4) "Frightened cat," detail

(10.5) "Frightened cat's" view from the north tower to the *parvis* below

The arrow in image 10.2 points to an inconspicuous place in the archivolts of the north tower of the cathedral. As we focus on that spot in images 10.3 and 10.4, notice how a figure of a frightened cat invokes a sense of vertigo (image 10.5) as a compelling equivalent of our human condition. The art and love immanent in the particular elevating lift of the cathedral structure, its sculptural program, stained glass windows, and liturgical rituals echo our human aspiration to wholeness from our condition, described by Simone Weil, as gravity and grace.

Now approach the Cathedral of Chartres from the west. Behold with the art of this threshold as one exemplar of an uncountable number of occasions born in our shared awakening.

At this point on our path, pause to ask: Have we put childish ways behind us? Have we chosen to pursue intimated reconciliations of the contradictoriness that our conscious being entails?

If so, we may now celebrate a second birth in the healing arms of *artistic* embodiment.[1]

Be present with the cathedral. Allow its cosmic scale to resonate with the asymmetry of your human face, mirrored in the asymmetry of its stone façade.

Here, recall also the twelfth-century troubadour Jaufré Rudel, who wrote of reaching the threshold [of love] when we see ourselves reflected in the eyes of the beloved.[2]

(10.6) Cathedral of Chartres, viewed from the west

Prepare to embrace and be embraced by the western rose window as it quietly occupies two places simultaneously.

Seen from a distance, this stone and glass flower remains suspended well below the median point between the ground and the disappearing tips of the towers—comparatively "close by," poised, and stable.

(10.7) Schematic location of the rose window within the façade rectangle

Move closer to the threshold of the cathedral façade.
As you approach the triple portal entryway, the western rose,
still suspended, will also soar upward . . .
beyond reach, remote . . . grand . . .

(10.8) Approaching the soaring presence of the rose window

Like Mary herself, this rose window is both mother and queen, the very paradoxical embodiment of intimacy and monumental transcendence, present to our awakened experience.

(10.9) Schematic rendering of the soaring presence of the western rose window within the façade
(10.10) Schematic rendering of the perceptual relativity of the western rose window within the façade
(10.11) Detail of the west façade with the asymmetrical relation of the lancet and rose windows indicated

The western rose window is placed just slightly to the left of the central axis of the façade (by roughly 5 inches). This barely visible positioning may affirm the vulnerability and longing embodied in the façade's overall asymmetry. Stone, lead, and crucible-fired glass, at once solid and fragile, exterior and interior, join in the irreconcilable interval of contradiction.

(10.12) Western rose window, a. exterior; b. interior

By raising the location of the rose window just slightly within the rectangle and blending forms generally, one artistic encounter with the cathedral façade, a pastel by Robert Sweeney (10.13), intimates the gentle reconciliation of its contradictory realities.[3] Two other images of the cathedral (10.14, a. and b.), bracket Sweeney's blended image. Chaim Soutine responds subjectively to the contradictory energy between experience and order (*ars/scientia*; eros/insight), whereas Jean-Baptiste-Camille Corot seeks to stabilize their relationship. Corot's effort may be confirmed in the knowledge that he added the seated figure in the lower left corner of the painting at a later date, fixing the scale of the cathedral as an objective measure compared to Soutine's vividly felt one. Sweeney's Chartres seeks balance within the contradiction.

(10.13) Robert Sweeney, *Chartres*, 1974
(10.14) a. Chaim Soutine, *Cathedral of Chartres*, 1933;
b. Jean-Baptiste-Camille Corot, *Cathedral of Chartres*, 1830–72

Once inside the cathedral, white exterior light incarnated as color changes almost imperceptibly with the movement of the sun to soften the hardest asymmetry of passionate embrace, inviting us home to the very origins of our most intimate being. Arrival here may recall nothing so much as Henry Adams's admission: "One becomes, sometimes, a little incoherent in talking about it; one is ashamed to be as extravagant as one wants to be; one has no business to labor painfully to explain and prove to oneself what is as clear as the sun in the sky; one loses temper in reasoning about what can only be felt."[4]

(10.15) Cathedral of Chartres, view of the nave from the east
(10.16) Western rose and lancet windows in late afternoon light

Return to the parvis *before the western gateway. As though sharing Henry David Thoreau's path of aspiration to "poetic or divine life," now stand within the thrall of the royal portal (image 10.17). Be as present as possible, here in this late afternoon light.*

(10.17) Royal portal of the west façade in late afternoon light

Reminiscent of Roman imperial triumphal arches, this threshold to a "higher life than we fell asleep from" reverses the vertigo embodied by the "frightened cat," far above but not forgotten, as it clings terrified to the archivolts of the north tower. Below, at ground level, lifted above the foundation stones of the cathedral building, are sculpted figures of the biblical kings and queens of Judah. They provide the human genealogy and column-like structural support for an array of carved capitals portraying the narrative of Christ's earthly life from infancy to death and resurrection. The capitals in turn support the elevated lintels above the three entrances and the three grand tympana of the façade, framed by ascending archivolts.[5]

Pause to allow this architectural conflation of solid stone, structural weight, and artistic suspension to emerge in your experience. Be in its fleeting interval.

Let the informing asymmetry of the whole façade now ripple outward from each detail, including the remarkable fusion of idealized royalty and individual humanity apparent in the bodies and faces of the royal entourage greeting you. Be present with them and their longing.

Having embraced them and been embraced by them, look up to the storied events. First, note the narrative of Christ's life in the historiated (figured) capitals moving from left to right. Then, one by one, turn to the three timeless images from this life that will sublimate all gravity-bound transience and vertigo into timeless reality.

On our right, above the southern doorway, the enthroned mother and child—the Throne of Holy Wisdom, flanked by two kneeling angels—crowns the narrative moments of the nativity and the presentation of Christ in the temple, and serves as an exterior anticipation of sacramental ritual. Personifications of the seven liberal arts (grammar, logic, rhetoric, arithmetic, geometry, astronomy, and music) animate and tutor our multiple human capacities to help us comprehend this place of physical incarnation as well as the mysterious epiphany of interior awakening that lies beyond this façade.

As instruments of learning, these particular skills were never understood to be ends in themselves. Their overarching purpose—easily forgotten in our increasingly rationalized and materialist world—was to define, encourage, and model our human journey as mortal beings, held in the grip of gravity, but lifted up by our spiritual aspiration for wholeness beyond limitation. Along the path toward Thoreau's "poetic or divine life," these Seven Liberal Arts, joined together in their embrace of the contradictory *trivium* (arithmetic, music, and geometry) and *quadrivium* (astronomy, grammar, rhetoric, logic), offer an exemplary guide to our "wandering mourning" and the abundant "higher" education toward which we seek to move, whether individually or as part of an institution's curriculum.

On our left, the tympanum of the northern doorway unfolds its image to the sound of trumpets, signaling the moment of return to a celestial empyrean, embodied here in the biblical ascension of Christ.[6]

In the center, flanked by prophets, the twelve apostles arrayed across the lintel block are divided into four groups of three—who, going forth, would spread this wisdom to the four corners of the "flat" earth that the cathedral architects and stone carvers perceived. Above the apostles we come face to face with the sun-like presence of eternity in the form of the enthroned figure of the risen Christ, surrounded by an aureole of undying light and the four beasts of the prophetic apocalypse, all poised in stillness and silence.

(10.18) Royal portal with central doorway opened

Be with the celestial and earthbound figures who greet you; especially, perhaps, with the gracefully tall woman on the right-side jamb.

To enter the illuminated darkness beyond this doorway (image 10.18) is to return home into a waiting embrace. Here the intimation of reconciliation of all contradictory realities—including the asymmetry of conscious being—will occur as a most gentle awakening, felt as the softest, most intimate possible brush with all infinity.

Allow the tears of infantile departure to become here new tears of joyful arrival in the threshold of love—as though a prodigal son or daughter had at last come home.

(Advance screen)

To Be Is to Be Separate . . . and Being Separate, We Long to Be Whole

In one rapidly sketched drawing by Rembrandt van Rijn, the intimacy of monumental transcendence embodied by the Cathedral of Chartres gives way to the monumental transcendence of intimacy itself.

(10.19) Rembrandt van Rijn, *Two Women Teaching a Child to Walk,* ca. 1635–37

Coming forth into the light, a child leaves behind the passive comfort in familiarity to enter the turbulence of life's separation and longing, living and dying, joy and sadness—each forever tied to the other. From Rembrandt's grounded, if not literally kneeling, vantage point while creating the art of this work of art, he measures for us beholders the impossible truth of our "wandering mourning." It reaches from the confident imploring gesture of the mother's hand "touching" the left border of the drawing as if pointing the way, to the bent-over muffled lamentation of the elderly grandmother, and then back again to the focused determination of the child learning to walk.

Imagine holding this drawing, preserved on a tiny piece of paper no larger than your hand, as close to you as Rembrandt may have been to the child. As you did when the "frightened cat" became a conscious presence in your awareness, allow the implication of the crown-like "crash helmet" the child wears to acknowledge this poignant moment and its reference to human affliction.

As exemplars, the Cathedral of Chartres and Rembrandt's diminutive drawing are helpful guides to anyone who, in beholding with them, would move toward a path of love. Walking this path, the contentious and asymmetric partners of active and contemplative being merge, forming a singularly syzygetic whole, fraught and heavy with gravity. This path of love attempts to reconcile difference, ambiguity, and contradiction. It redeems the limitations of clear theory and tangled practicality, aging, mortality, and all the tribulations that loving invites and inevitably requires.

On this path, living aspiration to wholeness within our acknowledged condition of human longing will have become the enduring presence of immanent grace and resurrection. Like the stone structure of the cathedral or the fragile scrap of inked paper, each occasion of this loving will appear before us as another "cairn." Each will guide us beyond the lingering, but now virtually imploring, question ("So what?") into the fullest poetic implications of an endlessly open and optimistic potential: Will you see green?

Recall the challenge we set out to embrace on our path: the elusive mutuality of a "more human love." Rainer Maria Rilke responded to this longing in a poem suffused with wistful hopefulness:

> You who never arrived
> in my arms, Beloved, who were lost
> from the start,
> I don't even know what songs
> would please you. I have given up trying
> to recognize you in the surging wave of
> the next moment. All the immense
> images in me—the far-off, deeply-felt
> landscape, cities, towers, and bridges, and
> unsuspected turns in the path,
> and those powerful lands that were once
> pulsing with the life of the gods—
> all rise within me to mean
> you, who forever elude me.

You, Beloved, who are all
the gardens I have ever gazed at,
longing. An open window
in a country house—and you almost
stepped out, pensive, to meet me.
Streets that I chanced upon—
you had just walked down them and vanished.
And sometimes, in a shop, the mirrors
were still dizzy with your presence and,
startled, gave back my too-sudden image.
Who knows? Perhaps the same
bird echoed through both of us
yesterday, separate, in the evening . . .[7]

Pause, now, to reflect in the light of two water-bound plants, entirely separate but implicated one with the other across an immeasurable void, floating above unknowable depths . . .

(0.1) Two water lily blossoms, Ryoan-ji, Kyoto, Japan

(Advance screen)

Self-Transcendence and the Evolutionary Spiral

"Wandering mourning" is the conscious condition of our begotten existence. This condition will not change. And yet within us we hold the potential to change the particular form of wandering mourning Rilke identified as "killing," and aspire instead to a way of loving that would animate a universal behavioral ethic, independent of cultural difference, even as it fosters abundant diversity in the embrace of all *otherness.*

In this evolutionary transformation—from an epistemology of killing to an epistemology of loving—multiple visions of wholeness beyond limitation will slowly take shape, not by any exterior transcendent force, but from within the very "DNA" of our human being. Instead of tracing our footsteps back in time, let them now proceed from this moment, not as the culmination of an evolutionary process, but as a forward spiral into the millions of years to come.

(10.20) Cécil Baboulène: a. *L'histoire de la terre*, evolutionary spiral; b. indicated detail

Beginning at this moment, this emerging evolutionary spiral will expand upward and forever through time, outward through developmental periods comparable to those that preceded them, and toward wholeness greater than which there is nothing.[8] Over time perhaps, each individually lived Via Amoris will become another of Henry David Thoreau's "one in a hundred millions [awake] to a poetic or divine life." We might then even evolve with the passing of every morning and evening "till one day the sun shall shine more brightly than ever he has done, shall perchance shine into our minds and hearts, and light up our whole lives with a great awakening light, so warm and serene and golden as on a bank-side in autumn."[9]

We can experience the plausibility of a self-generating Via Amoris as vivid as the rising sun each morning—even as the setting sun anticipates the next inexorable cosmic rotation—when we travel again to Japan, to Uji, to behold with the art and love of the Phoenix Hall (Hōōdō) in the Buddhist temple named Byōdō-in.[10]

Imagine now turning toward the morning . . . [11]

(10.21) Uji River Bridge, Uji, Japan, early morning
(10.22) Byōdō-in, Uji, Japan, north gate in early morning light
(10.23) Byōdō-in, Phoenix Hall (Hōōdō), 1053, morning light
(10.24) Full light
(10.25) Afternoon light
(10.26) Evening light
(10.27) Lingering light

Allow the night to pass and approach the Phoenix Hall once again in the morning light.

(10.28) Center bay in morning light

The golden glow of the renowned sculpture of Amida Buddha by the artist Jōchō will merge with the light of the early morning sun as it penetrates this darkened Phoenix Hall. As Thoreau might have responded had he been at Phoenix Hall rather than in the woods at Concord, "and thus the darkness bear its fruit, and prove itself to be good no less than the light."[12]

By simply and silently positioning ourselves on the near bank (image 10.28), we beholders may experience the transrational presence of infinite reality on the far side, across the interval of water. The actual distance to the island representing the Pure Land where Amida Buddha is enthroned in eternity is barely fifty feet. But drawing from a concept of time in multiple Eastern wisdom traditions, its artistic distance conceptually approaches the discontinuous wholeness we might achieve by converting the Western icon of approximate infinity ($E = mc^2$) into multiple *kalpas* or roughly 1.28 trillion years: in the Buddhist imagination, our "speed of light" has become, perhaps, the task of measuring a single *kalpa* by filling a cube sixteen miles high, deep, and wide with one mustard seed every one hundred years.

(10.29) Center bay in morning light, detail
(10.30) Amida Buddha in first light
(10.31) Phoenix Hall, Amida Buddha by Jōchō, ca. 1053

Those of us beholding with this incomparable figure of meditative release may well experience its own intimated reconciliation as the obverse of Rembrandt's contentious "brushstroke" and "image." With the Amida Buddha, the artist Jōchō opens an interval of contemplative simultaneity where actual gold leaf becomes transcendently illuminated flesh.

To engage the silent "still point" of this beholding, try to mimic the kinetic balance embodied in the figure of Amida Buddha. Assume the pose of horizontal grounding and vertical suspension as though you also were floating in eternity on the lotus blossom prepared for you there.

Let your arms, hands, and fingers mirror those of Amida Buddha. Hold fast to the disciplined corporeal gesture: back straight, shoulders squared. Soften your face, eyes, and mouth as you simulate the welcome repose of cosmic arrival.

Repeat this invocation: Namu Amida Butsu (Buddha I beseech thee).

(Advance screen)

Via Amoris: A Way of Love, Where Love Is the Means

The change, growth, and transformation we might now imagine will occur in every action, whether inconspicuous or obvious, of individual people. Long before institutions and social behavior generalize love the verb, its living presence will emerge in the determined choices (and their consequences) that shape and order our conscious awareness. In this sense the famously activist saying falsely attributed to Mohandas Gandhi—"Be the change you want to see in the world"—fails to engage first with the begotten condition of our individual human being: the contradiction of separation and longing.

What if we embrace Parker Palmer's powerful observation that epistemology is ethics, by which he means that we can enlarge the way we know by acknowledging the paradoxical nature of our being? The dynamic reality of our being will then be centered in each one of us before it radiates outward. Our every effort to embrace contradiction, therefore, will add, first in ourselves and then the world, another "circle of affection" reaching in endless movement toward the infinite mutuality of all being. The first step—the precondition—will be the sublimation of "killing" into "loving" until "killing" as an act of instrumental reason or unthinking lust will have been rendered obsolete in the short run and extinct within the span of time. Without our knowing its end, we may nonetheless track an evolutionary trajectory toward wholeness through countless acts aimed toward reconciliation. Whether dramatically large and public or small and intimately private, each act will reaffirm our ability and willingness to say—"I saw green!"

Let two paths "embedded" in works of art from the medieval European world amplify the full breadth of the way forward: the first is a page from an illuminated manuscript; the second is a stone labyrinth in a cathedral's nave.

The seventh-century illuminated Book of Durrow, predating the more well-known Book of Kells by nearly a hundred years, includes all four gospels (as well as prefatory material) and six elaborately designed carpet pages.[13] Images 10.32 and 10.33 show the carpet page that appears opposite the opening words of the gospel of John the Evangelist: "In the beginning was the Word, and the Word was with God, and Word was God."

(10.32) Book of Durrow, 7th century, carpet page and *In Principio Verbum* (John 1:1)
(10.33) Book of Durrow, carpet page

This carpet page, inscribed on calfskin (vellum), is a vertical rectangle framed by six smaller rectangles containing animals interlaced mouth to tail. In the center, a gold-bordered white square encloses a gold-rimmed circle with two overlapping red, green, and gold lines on a black ground surrounding another circle with a Celtic cross. Three additional white circles with interwoven geometric patterns form an implied inverted triangle opening upward.

For a moment allow quiet meditation with the whole carpet page . . . then focus on the centralized square and circle . . . and in time . . . try to follow the two lines fully . . . then rest with the stillness of the Celtic cross . . .

(10.34) Carpet page, detail

Now, let multiple contradictories merge in intimated reconciliation: horizontality with verticality and the diagonality of the open trinitarian triangle . . . the square with the circle . . . white and black with the colors and gold of Christ's overlapping humanity and divinity . . . centered stillness and peripheral movement . . .

Imagine the monastic beholder, for whom this image will have become in contemplation a visual equivalent of the Christian logos: divine incarnation. . . . In the beginning was the Word . . .

Emerging from our focused meditation with the carpet page circle and its interwoven colored lines, we might reflect on a passage from the biblical book of the Apocalypse (as interpreted by the composer Olivier Messiaen), which describes "Someone" seated on a throne in heaven: "One will note here," Messiaen says, "that the Divinity is not named, and the bedazzlement received produces a resonance of complementary colors: jasper and carnelian are red, the rainbow that flashes around this red is green, like an emerald."[14]

Now approach the second path. A stone labyrinth from the first half of the thirteenth century in the nave of the Cathedral of Chartres follows a looping trajectory toward a central floral pattern.

(10.35) Cathedral of Chartres, the labyrinth viewed from above

Although both the carpet page and the labyrinth are "Christian" works of art, I suggest we set aside the complicated symbolic associations of both and respond to them only as circular pathways moving inexorably between an outer periphery and a center. Despite this similarity, they are fundamentally different. The manuscript path offers a conceptual pilgrimage meant to be engaged visually without actually moving, while the architectural path invites the act of walking toward a center of unchanging silence that is mirrored in the stillness of the manuscript.

These two particular paths return us to the universal human contradictoriness of our conscious existence. Taken together, these medieval works of art remarkably resemble the two images of Earth from space that we encountered in chapter 2 (image 2.12) as contemporary emblems of "experience" and "order": elusive, shifting, subjective, sensual realities as opposed to fixed, objective, abstract, conceptual, cerebral realities.

(2.12) a. William Anders, *Earthrise*, 1968;
b. NASA, *Earth from Space*, 2002

With these two views of Earth—as with the tension between practice and theory—wisdom (*sapientia*) resides in our capacity of true learning through contemplative beholding (*eruditio*) to embrace and be embraced by the very contradictoriness of their respective paths (*ars sine scientia nihil est . . . scientia sine ars nihil est*).

(2.32) *Sapientia* (wisdom)

Now approach the paths in the illuminated manuscript (with the detailed view) and the cathedral (from an eye-level view of the labyrinth) shown side by side in image 10.36.

(10.36) a. Book of Durrow, detail of carpet page;
b. Cathedral of Chartres, the labyrinth at eye level

As precisely constructed invitations to contemplative arrival, each path embodies intelligible and sensible movement toward deliberate change, growth, and transformation. Independent of their presumed devotional or ritual functions, each work of art is an exemplar of intimated reconciliation, including the asymmetry of exterior and interior, movement and stillness, stability and change. If we engage directly with each path, we might experience for ourselves their shared wisdom of contemplative reconciliation.[15]

By allowing our eyes to follow the overlapping nonintersecting lines of the carpet page or to imagine actually walking the labyrinth at Chartres, we might reposition ourselves within an unalterable human procession of obverse possibilities. Imagine, as we did with the coming of the new millennium in the twenty-first century, being ready to approach the first year of a New Era—now, today. We might then start out from this reimagined "beginning." Although anchored in the past, the world, and our universal ontological embrace of self and transcendence, we will be on a new path. Four cairns of relational awareness will help us avoid our previous histories of ignorance, bias, and ideology which have so often led to "killing" rather than "loving" as the form of our "wandering mourning."

1. Awareness of "I" and "self." Include the interrelated realities of "experience" and "order" within each of us in equal measure as the very foundation of our human capacity not only for knowing and acting, but also for living within the contradiction of our given condition of conscious being and our awakening to the birth of longing.
2. Awareness of "I" and known *others*. Include human and nonhuman creatures, objects, ideas, and all of nature familiar to each of us (that is, to the "me" that I know and appreciate).
3. Awareness of "I" and unknown *others*. Include human and nonhuman creatures, objects, ideas, and all of nature unfamiliar to each of us (that is, to the "me" that I do not know or yet appreciate, but to whom and to which I remain open).
4. Awareness of "I" and the "wholeness" of all reality.

These four *relational* circumstances exist at all times in the conscious presence of our being. But to foster the fourth aspiration of "I" and the "wholeness" of all reality—self and transcendence—we will have to pay special attention: first, to the weight of ego; second, to the easy temptation of tribalism and ideology; third, to the estrangement of xenophobic fear or hatred of foreigners and foreignness.

Movement along any Via Amoris thus challenges our ability to see our familiar selves, as we really are, in the face of an unfamiliar *other*, as well as to seek out the unknown parts of ourselves, perhaps even our enemies—and to look beyond human life to embrace all of nature: open to infinite and finite possibilities, to see "green" where once there was only "red."

(Advance screen)

CHAPTER 11

A Point of Renewal

It's as though the world has simply become too much for us to deal with. There is no way back. Only a dreamer can believe that the solution lies in curtailing the progress of civilization. The main task in the coming era is something else: a radical renewal of our sense of responsibility.... We must discover a new respect for what transcends us: for the universe, for the earth, for nature, for life, and for reality.

—Václav Havel, "Radical Renewal of Human Responsibility," 1995

IN THE long history of killing, the atomic bombings of Hiroshima and Nagasaki on August 6 and 9, 1945, remain unique as singularly efficient acts of death—one bomb for each city. The use of those two weapons—till now unsurpassed—defines the awful clarity that renders the paradoxical sleep-dream of reason beyond "monsters," beyond calculation. And yet, nuclear proliferation and development of hydrogen bombs, orders of magnitude greater that the Hiroshima and Nagasaki bombs, extend their potential for repeating this horror beyond all thinking.

> *Was Václav Havel right? Has the world "become too much for us to deal with?" Are we challenged to "discover a new respect for what transcends us: for the universe, for the earth, for nature, for life, and for reality?"*
>
> *Have we reached a point of reckoning, a point of turning, renewal, and restoration of faith, hope, and love?*

Given recent and ongoing circumstances—a pandemic, economic, social, and environmental collapse—we may indeed find ourselves saying quietly, *we are lost... time to change direction... to return home... to continue on by starting again*... even as we remember Shakespeare's timeless guiding wisdom: "This is an art which does mend Nature, change it rather, but the art itself is Nature." And so too are beauty and love. Now may be the time for each of us to decide... to choose: Will killing be the enduring form of our wandering mourning? Or... will it be love? We are free to choose, knowing the consequences are ours alone.

> *Our future is in our hands, minds, and hearts. Do we hear the cockerel crowing?*

(2.1) Vincent van Gogh, *Wheatfield with Crows*, 1890

> *Be with Vincent on his Via Amoris. Contemplate with him and with the art of one of the large landscapes about which he wrote to his brother: the painting "will tell you what I can't say in words."*
>
> *May we also imagine that the art of* Wheatfield with Crows *resides in our beholding . . . in the silence that lies beneath raucous cawing . . . the silence and solitude in which love is born.*
>
> *Was this the moment of Vincent's turning from unmanageable complexity to start over again at the beginning, counting from zero . . . one . . . two . . . three . . .*
>
> *Might it be ours . . .*

The tragic circumstances of Vincent's death shortly after completing this painting may offer a vivid cairn on our path toward renewal. I can imagine that to stop the killing, he chose not to accuse his assailant. Instead, he may well have diverted attention from what most likely was a careless accident.[1] I can also imagine the compassion, forgiveness, and longing that informs the human condition lingering in Vincent's words—"*la tristesse durera toujours*" (the sadness will last forever)—as reported by his brother Theo in a letter to their sister Elizabeth.[2] Within the complexity of Vincent's life, and despite the conjecture that has expanded since his final moments, a quiet, beautiful simplicity remains. Recalling Vincent's cheerful letter to his mother and sister in July, acknowledging "the sadness of extreme solitude," I can also re-imagine that as he lay dying, Vincent committed an act of art.[3] Rather than either the pathos of suicide or the martyrdom of despair, may we behold with one last loving gift from the artist, Vincent van Gogh, marking the path forward: art as love the verb seeking wholeness...

As we look toward renewal, a primal human aspiration on an emerging Via Amoris, remember the ancient city of Kyoto—the setting for Murasaki Shikibu's eleventh-century tale of the Shining Prince Genji. Remember

Genji's endless longing in the face of irreparable loss as we revisit the modern city—and that horrific event of our recent past.[4]

Return to Kyoto and Wonder *What If . . .*

(6.3) Kyoto, Japan, looking west toward Hiroshima

At the end of World War II, Kyoto was selected as the original target for the first atomic bomb until a strategic "choice" sacrificed Hiroshima and Nagasaki in its place. Kyoto was spared because of its position as the intellectual and cultural capital of Japan—and very possibly for personal reasons by the US secretary of war, Henry L. Stimson, who had traveled to Kyoto during the 1920s and celebrated his honeymoon there.[5]

Be present in the spared city of Kyoto. From here, prepare to approach Hiroshima alert to the universal "ground zero" of our human being with the lens of history and the potential for change, growth, and transformation—Vincent's art and love.

Share the possibility of an awakening moment with Albrecht Dürer, Leonardo da VInci, and Michelangelo di Buonarroti who experienced their own awakenings at the very origin of the Dream of Reason. Share it with Rusty Schweickart, who in 1959 faced his moment of choice as a bomber pilot on duty at an airbase in Taiwan, ready to deliver the bomb. And be with him in 1985, following his own growth and transformation, when he decided he could no longer accept bombing as a reasonable choice.

(Advance screen)

Freedom to Choose

For many, August 6, 1945, is a distant memory, overwhelmed by time and endless subsequent disasters (natural and human). For others it is not a memory at all, but rather a date they have been taught to "remember." Before continuing along this Via Amoris and encountering the images I offer along the way, might I invite you to reflect on the events of that day not so long ago? It may be that we are faced here with a reality well beyond our rational capacities. Even so, it is vital that we try with the fullness of our being.

On the first anniversary of the first atomic bombing, John Hersey offered a compassionate effort to measure the human dimension of that day with his book *Hiroshima.* He wrote about meeting a woman named Nakamura-san who tried to grasp for him the event and its effects. Nakamura-san is known as a hibakusha (literally, a person affected by a bomb, but specifically applied to a survivor of the atomic bombings of Hiroshima and Nagasaki).

> "The atom bomb," she would say when asked about it, "is the size of a matchbox. The heat of it was six thousand times that of the sun. It exploded in the air. There is some radium in it. I don't know just how it works, but when the radium is put together, it explodes." As for the use of the bomb, she would say, "It was war and we had to expect it." And then she would add, "*Shikata ga nai,*" a Japanese expression as common as, and corresponding to, the Russian word "*nichevo*": "It can't be helped. Oh, well. Too bad."[6]

At the end of his four-part, extended and detailed essay Hersey quotes an excerpt from the essay of a schoolboy who described his own memory of the bombing. The child's charming innocence makes unarguably clear that all the adult rationality surrounding this reality can't touch its full scope other than with deepest humility, remorse, sadness:

> It would be impossible to say what horrors were embedded in the minds of the children who lived through the day of the bombing in Hiroshima. On the surface their recollections, months after the disaster, were of an exhilarating adventure. Toshio Nakamura, who was ten at the time of the bombing, was soon able to talk freely, even gaily, about the experience, and a few weeks before the anniversary he wrote the following matter-of-fact essay for his teacher at Nobori-cho Primary School: "The day before the bomb, I went for a swim. In the morning, I was eating peanuts. I saw a light. I was knocked to little sister's sleeping place. When we were saved, I could only see as far as the tram. My mother and I started to pack our things. The neighbors were walking around burned and bleeding. Hataya-san told me to run away with her. I said I wanted to wait for my mother. We went to the park. A whirlwind came. At night a gas tank burned and I saw the reflection in the river. We stayed in the park one night. Next day I went to Taiko Bridge and met my girl friends Kikuki and Murakami. They were looking for their mothers. But Kikuki's mother was wounded and Murakami's mother, alas, was dead."[7]

The searing reality of Hiroshima in 1945 remains beyond all grasping. The vast scientific reporting and analysis, the literary and artistic struggle to capture it, and, of course, the effort of anyone who has been to Hiroshima, can only approach its incalculable immensity from the outside.[8] We remain remote from the infinite truth. At best, our understanding must resemble Nicholas of Cusa's "learned ignorance" echoed by Albert Einstein: "As our circle of knowledge expands, so does the circumference of darkness surrounding it." The somber sound of a bell rung randomly by visitors to the Peace Park Memorial and a stark inscription—"On August 6, 1945, the United States of America dropped an atomic bomb on Hiroshima"—are the two enduring truths. They fix in our memory the reality of the cosmic wholeness and finite being we all share.

Recall here once more Rilke's haunting observation that "killing is a form of our wandering mourning." Must it be so? Or one by one will we return to our begotten origins to start all over again? Will we be prepared this time to "border and protect and salute" each other's divine solitude in the evolution of a "more human love" as the only remaining form of our wandering mourning? Hersey concluded *Hiroshima* with a schoolboy's innocence. Picasso followed the ruthless bombing of another town with a large, complex mural-like image of fragmenting destruction simply named *Guernica* (chapter 8, image 8.67), for which the first rudimentary sketches by this most sophisticated artist resemble those of a young child—as though he too had to start all over again.

> *Similarly prepared to begin again, come back to August 6, 1945.*
>
> *Now imagine what might have been the view from the cockpit of the aircraft, named* Enola Gay *after the pilot's mother, as you approach Hiroshima.*

The military mission time is 08:15:45: "T-minus 15 seconds and counting…" In Hiroshima, it is a little after 8:15 in the morning.[9]

(11.1) Rebuilt Hiroshima, Japan, aerial view with Peace Memorial Park (white sign on the left) and hypocenter (white sign on the right), the location of the explosion of the bomb at "air zero," 1,968 feet above Shima hospital: "T minus 15 seconds and counting…"

(11.2) Aioi Bridge, 2007, Hiroshima, site of planned "ground-zero"

The Aioi Bridge was the center of the original Hiroshima bombing target: "ground zero." The woman on the bicycle in image 11.2, taken in 2007, uses the umbrella to shield herself from the hot sun.

(11.3) Model of the Nakajima area of Hiroshima before bombing, with the target bridge and the Hiroshima Prefectural Industrial Promotion Hall indicated

As you examine this model of Hiroshima, imagine the time is now "T-minus 5 seconds and counting . . . "

(11.4) Model of the Nakajima area of Hiroshima, after bombing, Peace Memorial Park Museum

The time is now "T-plus forever . . . and counting . . . "

The first atomic bomb missed its target by about 200 yards. The effect was nevertheless the same: Near total devastation. Some 70,000 to 80,000 people died instantly. Roughly 180,000 casualties. The collateral damage? Incalculable.[10]

(11.5) Actual "ground-zero," (hypocenter), Hiroshima Prefectural Industrial Promotion Hall indicated

Kenzaburo Oe, winner of the 1994 Nobel Peace Prize, accepted an assignment in 1965 to report on a nuclear arms conference in Hiroshima, held in conjunction with the twentieth anniversary of the bombing. In *Hiroshima Notes*, the book he wrote in response to his experience there, he chose not to focus on the abstraction of endless instrumental debate about nuclear technology, military strategic efficacy, and political positioning, polarized at the time as a result of the Cold War arms race. Instead, like John Hersey before him, Oe turned to the face of human devastation—and actually looked directly into it. His embrace of human affliction, exemplified in the congenital impairment of his son, Hitari, brought him to the recognition of a humbling "ground zero" in each one of us. *Hiroshima Notes* makes clear that discussion of the calculable and extensively documented physical destruction must give way to the utterly incalculable physical, psychological, and spiritual devastation of the "Hiroshima people" and their neighbors in Nagasaki.[11] Their metastasizing pain, endured with such courage and nobility, implicates us all, however far from the physical "ground zero" we may be.[12] The horror is no longer measurable by images of "it" or "them."

This human reality is indivisible. It reaches infinitely far beyond the once acceptable rationalized increments of 1.0 to 1.5 to 2.0 to 2.5 to 3.0 kilometers into that "darkness" that surrounds our knowing. It is the "you" we see before us. Human compassion alone will comprehend and transcend this killing. Reflecting on the book in a 2005 interview, Oe explained, "I found through my research and through my involvements with various movements, that it was necessary to begin again and to keep beginning again, *to start from zero at Hiroshima,* facing the worst situation possible and then creating a new way to live."[13]

Oe ends *Hiroshima Notes* by naming Dr. Fumio Shigeto, a survivor of the bombing and director of the A-bomb Hospital in Hiroshima. His admiration for the doctor's combined restraint and determination in the face of contradiction and trauma recalls the mysterious poetry of *ai-no-ma,* if not love: "And if we would also be authentic human beings, then we already have impressive models in the Hiroshima people, such as Dr. Shigeto, who have neither too little nor too much hope, who never surrender to any situation but courageously carry on with their day-to-day tasks."[14]

(Advance screen)

During a recent autumn gathering of friends, my neighbor Patty Kimura placed herself in the expanding circumference of this most fragile understanding as she read one of her poems to the group.[15]

Sixteen minutes
07:59, 6 August 1945

in sixteen minutes
a beautiful bright clear light
will fill your eyes
sparks will fly and shimmer
all around you

in sixteen minutes
the floor will slip
beneath your feet
your toes will feel
the sudden coolness of earth

in sixteen minutes
a wonderful wind
will rush through you
sweeping by bits and pieces of sky

so you comb your thick white hair
and smile at the worn picture

in the corner of your dresser
three little faces
staring shyly back
waiting for your return

in sixteen minutes
you will turn in the middle of the street
and look in a shop window
you will see a bolt of soft cotton
red flowers and bright yellow bees
just right
for a little girl
for the granddaughter
you hope to meet someday

in sixteen minutes
near the center of town
the overcast will clear
for just a second
you will feel the air
turn hot, electric
buzzing
shearing off your skin

Listening afterward to her comments about writing the poem, we realized that Patty is the granddaughter referred to in the poem: with that reading, a feeling of reconciliation transformed a very ordinary living room into another threshold of love, illuminating ever so gently the surrounding darkness.

In Hiroshima with an A-Bomb Survivor

In 2007 I visited Hiroshima with my class as part of the Associated Kyoto Program. There we met a woman who was one of the few remaining hibakusha, an A-bomb survivor named Miyoko Matsubara.[16] During her brief presentation at the Peace Memorial Park Museum, she spoke about her anger toward the people who had bombed her city. Although she was then only a young girl, she sensed that her life had been changed forever. It had been catastrophically diminished—and yet enhanced in ways she could not yet comprehend.

(11.6) Hiroshima Prefectural Industrial Promotion Hall, opened August 5, 1915

In 1945, the Hiroshima Prefectural Industrial Promotion Hall was an emblem of civic pride, collective success, and prosperity designed by the Czech architect Jan Letzl (1880–1925). Its unusual three-storied concrete structure and domed silhouette served to affirm Japanese mastery of Western industrial engineering and manufacturing. In a city of ground-hugging wooden buildings, this monument for the promotion of local industry was a literal Asian embrace of the Dream of Reason.[17] The hall opened to the public on August 5, 1915, and it was destroyed precisely thirty years and one day later.

(11.7) Hiroshima Prefectural Industrial Promotion Hall, after bombing, August 6, 1945

What's left of the structure is now called, simply and hauntingly, the A-Bomb Dome.

(11.8) Peace Memorial Park, with visitors, 2007

My wife and I met a young girl in Hiroshima's Peace Memorial Park, who in image 11.8 is teasing me to take her picture while her friend asks my wife in nervous school-boy English for an American autograph. The girl is about the same age Miyoko Matsubara was when the bomb exploded over her city during her early morning walk to school. The building in the background is the A-Bomb Dome.

(11.9) A-Bomb Dome, Hiroshima, early evening, 2007
(11.10) At sunset, 2007

In image 11.10 the setting sun illuminates the skeletal remains of the A-Bomb Dome in the late evening. The photo is reminiscent of a verse from Hindu scripture that came to J. Robert Oppenheimer's mind as he witnessed the detonation of the bomb at the Trinity testing site in New Mexico in July 1945. "If the radiance of a thousand suns were to burst at once into the sky, that would be like the splendour of the mighty one." The learned quotation Oppenheimer recalled from the Bhagavad Gita is all the more powerful when we remember that he also gave voice to the declaration of the Hindu god Vishnu, which follows in the sacred text: "Now I am become Death, the Destroyer of Worlds." This transforming reality becomes more disturbing when we hear Nakamura-san tell Hersey that "the heat of [the bomb] was six thousand times that of the sun." And it is more disturbing still when seen through the schoolboy's innocent eyes: "I saw a light. I was knocked to little sister's sleeping place."

Here I return to Miyoko Matsubara, on the day she spoke to me and the students in the AKP class. Her gentle acceptance, despite knowledge and experience, all but belies two bluntly stated comments she made, which stand out in my memory.

First, she described how much, in the beginning, she had hated all Americans for what they had done. Then she told us how, over time, she had come slowly to know that in order to live her life, which had been spared, she would have to learn everything about America, including how to love Americans and to be loved by them. Since this awakening, she has lived her entire life struggling to embody the *ai-no-ma* of this "more human love."

Second, she said with startling honesty: "If we had invented the bomb first, we would have used it."[18]

(Advance screen)

Reflection: Learning How to Be

Might it all have been otherwise? Recall (from chapter 6) the words of the author Jun'ichirō Tanizaki: "I always think how different everything would be if we in the Orient had developed our own science.... In fact, our conception of physics itself, and even the principles of chemistry, would probably differ from that of Westerners; and the facts we are now taught concerning the nature and function of light, electricity and atoms might well have presented themselves in different form."[19]

What if he were right, and the Japanese had indeed invented their own physics and even their atoms? Might there have been, as he surmised, a different kind of "physics"?

Is it possible that this other kind of "physics" already exists and has for a long time? That it resembles *ai-no-ma* as a place of mysterious meeting? That it is present in the cosmic structure of the Phoenix Hall at Byōdō-in, as well as in the no less elusive mystery of quantum mechanics? If such an integrative *ai-no-ma* had prevailed, is it also possible that the chain of events might have been different—that Japan would not have felt the need to attack Pearl Harbor, and we would not have decided to incinerate Miyoko Matsubara's home?[20]

An August 2017 article by James Temperton in *Wired* magazine may bring us back to reconsider the responsibility of our freedom to choose (while accepting the consequences of our choices). Citing a scholar of the Sanskrit language and Hindu religion, Temperton has proposed that Oppenheimer sought to reconcile or make sense of his actions: in reviewing Oppenheimer's knowledge of Hindu theology, he recalled the physicist's humbling understanding that life's events were not, as professed, "illusory" and therefore without cosmic meaning or weight. This personal belief by Oppenheimer, the very man who directed the Los Alamos laboratory that developed the atomic bomb, may reveal itself in a comment he made two years after the Trinity test: "In some sort of crude sense which no vulgarity, no humor, no overstatements can quite extinguish, the physicists have known sin; and this is a knowledge which they cannot lose."[21] With this bluntly honest admission—this mea culpa—perhaps it is time to shift our attention away from the endless arguments about making and using the atomic bomb; time to move beyond the moral, religious, political, strategic, and even technological frames to a new frame. Oppenheimer and the other scientists are not alone. We are all together as wandering mourners for whom killing, at last, must become loving.

Have we arrived at the point of renewal?[22] The lingering challange offered by Václav Havel in 1994 to choose "a radical renewal of our sense of responsibility...for the universe, for the earth, for nature, for life, and reality" calls out to our human capacity to replace killing with loving. Blame for killing, after all, depends on where you choose to start. Might we begin, each of us, by coming home to our immanent being? Might it even be simply a friend speaking quietly, as when I traveled to Hiroshima and Hideo Higuchi said to me, "Remember, it's zero for zero."

By facing humbly the incomprehensible reality of such destruction, might we come home to the beginning—the question of what it is *to be*—by which I mean acknowledging and embracing our enduring universal human reality—as portrayed in the pages of this book as Milo's lament? From here we will be prepared to move forward by seeking in every imaginable way to *intimate* reconciliation of the very contradictoriness—the existential paradox—of our conscious being. *To be is to be separate... and being separate, we long to be whole.* This is the wandering mourning within which we all live. In this threshold, a new awakening will inform all our knowing with learning *how to be* at the center, rippling outward to embrace and transform all other learning—whether institutional or private: including learning *how to know* (humanities), *how to relate* with others (social sciences), *how to do* (natural sciences), and all other acts of our free imagination.[23]

If epistemology is ethics, then our very survival resides in a vibrant epistemology of love. Thus, given the unchanging condition of our mortal being, our efforts will reconcile contradiction and conflict as we embrace our ever-expanding capacity to engage an art and practice of contemplative beholding. They will allow us to replace tendencies toward transactional, finite "solutions" with the evolutionary energy of productive ambiguity in our aspirations toward wholeness.

Returning to the story of Cain and Abel in chapter 1, the lesson we take from it is neither about the value of wheat or of lambs; both are equally worthy. Nor is the story a mere condemnation of Cain's self-serving intention. His sin was translating cosmic "failure" into a victimhood animated by resentment rather than an acceptance with deepest remorse and humility. Self-assured malice led to Cain's killing of Abel—and leads to all "killing." As with *ars* and *scientia*, the skillful and the priestly, or work and prayer, the lesson is about devotion to acts of intimated reconciliation.

Beholding with these biblical brothers invites us to avoid deadly tantrum and instead aspire endlessly to *eruditio*—higher learning. Doing so will help us make the "leap" from enmity to wisdom, from "killing" to "loving," and the moment-by-moment creation of a place, as St. Augustine envisioned, "where nothing unbecoming can be found." Our evolution depends on a "more human love" that will "protect and border and salute" another's solitude—not split it asunder into destructive fragmentation.[24]

If we were to return to this existentially anchored epistemology—this ground zero of our being—we might come back once more to Kyoto where we began, ready to set out on a way of love along which love is the means.

On this path, art that had once been a mere bystander to events, whether as critic, interpreter, revealer, or even soothing entertainer, will become instead an agent committing acts of healing between ourselves and the world we inhabit; acts of beauty and love that animate our shared evolutionary change, growth, and transformation.

In the Lingering Light

> *Return now to Kyoto, the city spared by reason and a young couple's honeymoon, to rediscover the ground zero of our begotten being. Be ready to set out all over again toward the beloved.*

On leaving the temple of Manshu-in one early spring evening in 2007, I came upon this flowering cherry tree and saw the obverse of Nakamura-san's heat "six thousand times that of the sun."

(11.11) Blossoming cherry tree, Kyoto, 2007

From one perspective, this image is nothing other than a blossoming cherry tree in the early spring. From the vantage point of syzygetic implication, however, this evening moment is remarkably provocative. The blossoms appear to hold the light of the day, as if to suggest a fragile endurance at the center of the dwindling brightness, a deliberate holding on to the fading light. The word *zanshō*, I am told by friends in Kyoto, evokes hope in the midst of the melancholy of change and disappearance.[25] As such, this *zanshō*—this "lingering light"— realizes a delicate recognition that our passage through darkness will be carried by the promise of a luminous dawn, animated by our capacity to reach across the infinite gap of discontinuity. Seen from the shadow of the setting sun, this dazzling tree is a place of mysterious meeting between night and day. In Nichiren Buddhism, *zanshō shima* refers to the "fundamental darkness" of our human condition and its "obstacles" to enlightenment (greed, anger, foolishness). We might find them reminiscent of the apostle Paul's singular pleading with the citizens of Corinth: if we were to put behind us the childish ways that prevent us from coming face to face with wholeness, and to "know even as we are known," love, buttressed by confidence (faith) and optimism (hope), will prevail.[26]

(11.12) Kamo River, Kyoto, 2007

The Kamo River runs through the center of Kyoto. Within the drama of late afternoon light along the river, the barely visible imminent greening of early spring grass measures chromatically the reddish and greenish color of the toy rackets held by children at play—as though this utterly innocent pairing might intimate the complementary unity between the living and the dead. A determined, rational choice spared the ancient yet still vibrant city of Kyoto and obliterated Hiroshima and Nagasaki instead. Had there been another way of knowing and being in the world, we might have made a different choice—one that didn't incinerate in a matter of seconds either of those cities and so many of their innocent inhabitants. In Hiroshima, that meant mostly mothers and children on their way to school: by 8:20 it was all over. Had there been another way of knowing and being in the world, there might have been another form of our "wandering mourning."

(11.13) Imadegawa Bridge, Kyoto, 2007

The Imadegawa Bridge joins the east and west banks of the Kamo River along the broad boulevard that leads past the imperial palace in northern

Kyoto. This is plainly a bridge made for moving cars, trucks, and people around the city with ease. Just beneath the lower border of this photograph there is another, as yet invisible, bridge.

(11.14) Bird and Turtle Bridge, Kyoto, 2007

With the sacred Mt. Hiei in the background, we can observe and compare the utilitarian link between riverbanks to a bridge that invites random interactions among turtles, birds, and children. One bridge is relentlessly practical. The other is open, free, charming. One bridge is limited to its material function while the other invites childlike behavior as well as physical connection. One bridge is a work of engineering that facilitates commerce and traffic. The other is a work of art that allows for the miraculous coexistence of all things continuous and discontinuous; all things mortal and immortal. One bridge provides incremental efficiency. The other offers hope through a veil of playfulness that animates a shared condition of separation and longing, as implied by two randomly placed birds existing within their solitude.

(11.15) Two birds, Kyoto, 2007
(11.16) Two bridges in evening light, Kyoto, 2007

One bridge is all power, control, and authority, the very embodiment of conscious utilitarian, instrumental purpose. The other offers joyful, laughing encouragement; even for adults. In the late evening light, just after a storm, these two bridges hold before us the paradoxical claims of our lives, challenging us to seek their reconciliation.

(Advance screen)

Two Solitudes That "Protect and Border and Salute Each Other"

Given the premise that space and time do not exist until we construct them, we are free to embrace contradiction, rather than reject or demolish it—and so begin to return to a shared human aspiration toward wholeness beyond contradiction in those of our free and humble acts that would, by some means, begin to approach that wholeness.

Once, when visiting in Kyoto with Goshima-san and his wife, I asked if they would kneel in the *engawa* of their traditional Japanese home. My purpose was to make an image that would illustrate the structural *ai-no-ma* between "interior" space, where the family altar and *tokonoma* are located, and the "exterior" space of their garden with its lantern. They kindly agreed; and dressed in formal attire, they knelt patiently while I prepared to photograph them.

(11.17) Goshima-san and his wife kneeling in the engawa of their home, Kyoto, 2007

I took the picture and was satisfied that it would serve one day to inform students far from Kyoto that *ai-no-ma* was clear architectural evidence of an alternative to the rational dualities we take for granted.

Then, without comment from me, Goshima-san, or his wife, something happened.

(11.18) Goshima-san and his wife bowing in the *engawa*

Quietly, everything changed. The objective image for my classroom presentation of a spatial construction in Japan had become instead two people bowing into the space between them, closing the infinite gap of their conscious separation: a physical version of Frost's "Mending Wall." With absolute simplicity on the farthest side of complexity, two people entered a place of mysterious meeting, as in the fateful encounter of lovers. In the blink of an eye, this quiet gesture had revealed the profoundest integrative potential of *ai-no-ma*.

When the couple resumed their upright kneeling position, they remained motionless for several lingering seconds. A different knowing awareness now illuminated the space and the day. It filled the enduring interval where "two solitudes protect and border and salute each other." Here, now—in the passing stillness of the moment—the graceful eros of visionary ethical insight emerged, summoned by our endless longing for wholeness from an acknowledged and unalterable condition of limitation. The silence of the mutual gaze between these two people brought an epistemology of love home to the body where it is born. Although this small epiphany had occurred unexpectedly, it nonetheless radiated moral possibility. This gentle intimation of reconciliation, felt as the very experience of change, growth, and transformation, had become the embodiment of all beauty, art, and, of course, Rainer Maria Rilke's "more human love." This is the love that will diminish the meanness that weighs so heavily on us all.

At this threshold of love my Western "I" came face to face with a foreign "You," even as two people had silently acknowledged their own individual longing in a reverent act of bowing.

(Advance screen)

We might now recall the decidedly embodied formation of love that concluded Plato's *Symposium*. We may also come back to Paul's letter to the Corinthians. From the beginning of our journey I have interspersed passages from this letter like cairns along our way. Here I offer this passage, with its remarkably physical characterization of love:

> Love is patient; love is kind; love is not envious or boastful or arrogant or rude. It does not insist on its own way; it is not irritable or resentful; it does not rejoice in wrong-doing, but rejoices in the truth. It bears all things, believes all things, hopes all things, endures all things. (1 Corinthians 13:4–7)

Allow Georgia O'Keeffe, at the beginning of her glorious career as an artist, to show us in one simple image the long reach of such love.

(11.19) Georgia O'Keeffe, *Blue Lines X*, 1916

Made with the unmediated directness of unmixed ultramarine blue, these "brushstokes" of watercolor paint on paper, which she tinged with a wash of pale orange, evoke an "image" of celestial totality: all blue, all complement; all dark, all light; all figure, all ground; all symmetry, all asymmetry; all horizontality, all verticality; gravity and grace—the slime of the earth and the purity of heaven—measured tenuously by that one spare, barely visible, diagonal line as if hinting at the frailest but vital reconciliation that would embrace all longing, all pre-ecclesiastical, pre-scientific, entirely human spirituality, reaching out to grasp the ungraspable in an undying act of *loving Love*...

> Love—thou art high—
> I cannot climb thee—
> But, were it Two—
> Who knows but we—
> Taking turns—at the Chimborazo—
> Ducal—at last—stand up by thee—
>
> Love—thou art deep—
> I cannot cross thee—
> But, were there Two
> Instead of One—
> Rower, and Yacht—some sovereign Summer—
> Who knows—we'd reach the Sun?

Love—thou art Veiled—
A few—behold thee—
Smile—and alter—and prattle—and die—
Bliss—were an Oddity—without thee—
Nicknamed by God—
Eternity—

Emily Dickinson wrote this poem in 1862 in Amherst, Massachusetts, far from the noise of the American Civil War that had begun in spring of the preceding year. Three-quarters of a million soldiers and uncounted numbers of noncombatants were killed.[27] When we seek our Via Amoris, we are not making a choice to simply stop "killing" in every form. We are seeking the evolutionary transformation of lesser to higher human being.

(Advance screen)

Evolution Uninterrupted

From the long perspective of geologic and prehistoric time, the reawakening of *fin'amor*, and its brief soaring path (like that of a shooting star) in twelfth century Aquitaine, will be an eternally contemporary event, arcing forward as a "more human love." The art we choose to realize in every act of love—whether as a newborn child who unconsciously reaches *toward* something, or in a sorrowful lamenting of precognitive awakening, or as an adult in endless longing—will resemble that of our earliest human entry into the mysterious interval between "brushstroke" and "image" preserved in the forgotten caves along the Vézère River in southwestern France. There we will remember the endless wonder and reverence for the human animation of the night sky.

Interpretation of this cave wall imagery varies. Even so, the irreducible fact that unites the material fabric of our conscious existence with the unchanging mystery of infinite reality remains a constant beacon for our human aspiration to wholeness—beyond all effort and calculation, and forever present within us as our shared "poetic or divine life." We too may respond synchronically to the stately procession of these images painted on limestone surfaces as though they were luminous constellations inviting us as always to move, to breathe, to be alone and whole together.

Imagine you are present in the caves at Lascaux. Soft flickering light from oil lamps animates the images barely ten feet above you. Listen to the welcoming sound of a rudimentary flute. Prepare to enter the "Hall of the Bulls."

(11.20) "Hall of the Bulls," Lascaux (Montignac, Dordogne, France), 15,000–10,000 BCE

(11.21) "Hall of the Bulls," with visitors, 1984

Along our chosen Via Amoris, putting behind our "childish ways" to break through fundamental darkness will come to mean that living deliberately challenges us to understand as "adults" that we are not led by external things: not by authorities, virtues, churches, institutions, science, or religion. These are only the offspring of our acts of a "more human love" born in our living *sacral* imagination and behavior. From within this threshold of love the contradictions that now divide and torment us are also the very origin of our reconciliation with each other and that wholeness—greater than which there is nothing—within which we live.

In 1862, Stephen Foster echoed Dickinson's poetic "Love—thou art high" with song and the plaintive question, "Why, no one to love?" This is the music that we set out with at the start of our path.

> 1. Why, no one to love in this beautiful world,
> Full of warm hearts and bright beaming eyes!
> Where is the lone heart that nothing can find
> That is lovely beneath the blue skies...
>
> *Chorus:*
> *No one to love:*
> *Why, no one to love?*
> *What have you done in this beautiful world,*
> *That you're sighing of no one to love?*
>
> 2. Dark is the soul that has nothing to dwell on!
> How sad must its brightest hours prove!
> Lonely the dull brooding spirit must be
> That has no one to cherish and love...
>
> *Repeat chorus:*
>
> 3. Many a fair one that dwells on the earth
> Who would greet you with kind words of cheer.
> Many who would gladly join in your pleasures
> or share in your grief with a tear.

No one to love:
Why, no one to love?
Where have you roamed in this beautiful world
That you're sighing of no one to love?

(Advance screen)

(*) **Stephen Foster, "Why, No One to Love:"**

You may never take a course in the history or practice of art. Even so, imagine waking up each morning with a work of art in some form in your memory, so that you might hear again and again the sound of the cockerel crowing for you as you live out your own glorious procession of the obverse, committing acts of art wherever you are. Henry David Thoreau, who guided us away from habit to live deliberately, may now set us on our way again: imagine moving beyond our own threshold of love toward the resurrection light of every morning and the dawning of a living love that will inexorably render extinct all "killing." In parting from his experiment at Walden, Thoreau said: "I left the woods for as good a reason as I went there."[28] So too, every deliberate act of intimating reconciliation will become another new cairn along an abundant Via Amoris until that day when each of us will be mirrored in the unalterable perfection of the beloved.

In the meantime, with St. Augustine, Marguerite Porete, and every other guiding exemplar of human aspiration: *love Love* and do as you will . . .

(Advance screen)

Rembrandt van Rijn, *Return of the Prodigal Son*, ca. 1669,
The State Hermitage Museum, St. Petersburg

Coda: Returning Home

REMBRANDT painted *Return of the Prodigal Son* in the last months of his life. He died at the age of sixty-three. As a vivid emblem of forgiveness and unconditional compassion, we may well associate it with his own humility and honest contrition at the end of his life.

> *As an occasion of contemplative beholding rather than analysis, interpretation, or even heartfelt self-reflection, this majestic work of art may also offer you an unexpected homecoming.*

The well-known narrative of the prodigal son, his brother, and the two paths they follow is told in Luke 15:11–32. Here is the basic story:

The younger of a man's two sons leaves home and squanders his inheritance in "dissolute living." The oldest son stays behind, remaining loyal to his domestic duties. In time, the prodigal son—hungry, disgraced, and filled with remorse—returns to his father saying, "I have sinned against heaven and before you" (Luke 15:18). Upon seeing him, the father rejoices and orders him to be clothed in the best robe and given a ring for his finger and new sandals for his feet. The fatted calf, he says, will be killed in celebration. When the elder son comes back from the field and learns of these plans, he speaks angrily to his father:

> "Listen! For all these years I have been working like a slave for you, and I have never disobeyed your command; yet you have never given me even a young goat so that I might celebrate with my friends. But when this son of yours came back, who has devoured your property with prostitutes, you killed the fatted calf for him!" The father answered, saying, "Son, you are always with me, and all that is mine is yours. But we had to celebrate and rejoice, because this brother of yours was dead and has come to life; he was lost and has been found." (Luke 15:29–32)

How, then, might your contemplative beholding respond to Rembrandt's version of this biblical parable?

(12.1) Rembrandt van Rijn, *Return of the Prodigal Son*, ca. 1669

Looking carefully, we see that Rembrandt himself is concerned with a deeply humble awakening to a forgotten wholeness ("I have sinned against heaven and before you"). He shows less interest in the joy, excitement, and emotion of the son's return to material abundance and familial virtue, including the rage of the brother. Note the prodigal's still-scuffed sandals, his one bare foot, his ragged clothes, and the unexpectedly reverent expression the older brother directs toward his younger sibling. This now respectful gesture—and those of everyone else in the painting, especially the seated man in the hat—models the look and posture of deepest contemplative understanding.

The noise of celebratory "music and dancing" in the parable gives way in Rembrandt's painting to the soft quieting of sound, to an exquisite stillness that relieves the turmoil of our longing. And, importantly, the father's enfolding compassion visually anticipates the pictorial embrace of the willing beholder—whether prodigal son or daughter—who would contemplate slowly with the art of this most tender work of art.

> *To approach this existential epiphany, go to St. Petersburg. Walk to the wide and long gallery in the Hermitage where you will find the painting waiting for you, suspended alone on a green-velvet-covered wall that is placed at a right angle to the gallery to interrupt the normal flow of movement.*
>
> *Like a cairn along a woodland trail, this presentation invites you to stop there—to tarry a moment—and allow an art and practice of contemplative beholding, rather than the customary hurried movement of museum consumption, to guide you.*

Return of the Prodigal Son is large, a roughly life-sized vertical rectangle that mirrors our presence as we stand before it. Compare Rembrandt's youthful print of the son's return from 1636, which shows the father and son in profile separated from us by two steps and a cane.

(12.2) a. *Return of the Prodigal Son*, print (1636);
b. *Return of the Prodigal Son* (ca. 1669)

In his "last" painting, however, he places us within the narrative space.

(12.3) *Return of the Prodigal Son*, ca. 1669

Surely Rembrandt intended this direct appeal to us as an invitation. At the center of the lower border, the golden light that falls on the stone threshold creates an illuminated empty place just to the right of the kneeling son. From here, our glance rises toward the two-dimensional center of the picture plane that coincides precisely with the middle ground of the painting's illusory space, and the face of a woman looking forward as if also to engage us. This centered place—suspended within perfectly balanced compositional asymmetry, both horizontal and vertical—gathers the generally somber darkness of the painting before us.

> *Focus on this area of the painting until you feel the figures momentarily freed from their role in the verbal narrative of the parable. Let them serve a complementary pictorial function, revealing a delicate ratio of relation that joins the visible still point at the center of the painting with the luminous "empty" place of arrival on the stone threshold.*

In this place of humility and embodied longing (thirst, hunger...) Rembrandt's art, present in his *Return of the Prodigal Son*, may emerge before us. This is an occasion—*waiting*—for our own return home, redolent of Simone Weil's "loosening," release, peace, and resurrection.

> *Be still, here, now. Listen. For all the noise, movement, and celebratory excitement of the biblical narrative, there is no sound here... except perhaps the welcoming voice of one who was able to love and be loved...*

Reflecting on the lives of Henry David Thoreau, Marguerite Porete, and the arc of the preceding chapters, we might now imagine that the prodigal son, by leaving home, also took leave of unthinking habit and external virtues, only to discover within himself the spiritual realization of love's virtue in an ever-expanding capacity for self and transcendence animated by moral reconciliation on his return. May we all...

(Advance screen)

Expressions of Gratitude

BEHOLDING is the result of mutuality between and among people, objects, all of nature, and the vastness of being beyond any reckoning. *Contemplative Beholding: A Way of Life and Love* is my attempt to share my effort to be such a beholder along a path of love, where love is the means—a Via Amoris. Rather than listing acknowledgements of support, I have chosen to express unbounded gratitude for the life beholding has given me and for the uncountable sources of its joy, beginning with the light of the star Venus shining in the eastern sky.

Although I have been critical of two important realities that have defined and animated my path—the discipline of art history and museums, large and small—I know well that they have been the "necessary angel[s] of earth" that have guided me home. At their best, they inform the "cathedrals" of aspiration we seek to build with all the energy and imagination we possess. Their vitality is the measure of any doubt. The works of art they preserve and protect are among the stars of my firmament.

This book results from the intersection of two professional efforts. The first is my classroom attempt to enter into the thrall of works of art by engaging with their art. To do this I have not only tried to define what such art might be, but also to engage its particular presence in the work of artists both known and anonymous. My exemplars range from Rembrandt's hand-sized drawing of the monumental reality present in a child's first steps, *Two Women Teaching a Child to Walk*, to the amazing intimacy of the colossal Cathedral of Our Lady in Chartres (images of both appear in chapter 10).

The second sustained effort informing this work has been my long collaboration with Arthur Zajonc to discover the human interval between art and science. Our work has taken shape in several courses, which we planned and then taught together in a single classroom. We began with an upper-level seminar called "Re-imagining the Human in a Technological Age," in which we attempted to discover an enduring reality, untouched by the rapid and continuous transformation of the machines that surround us. In time, this original effort evolved into the seminar for first-year students called "Eros and Insight." Our conversation and work together, one of the profoundest joys of my professional life, remains a continued source of incomparable inspiration for which I am forever grateful. As will become clear to anyone familiar with our teaching, what I have written draws on our shared work, even as it seeks to complement that of Professor Zajonc. In addition to my colleague, I owe sincerest thanks to all the students who participated over many years in these and in other courses I have offered in the history of art. Their passion and intelligence assure me that they will be the ones to carry our efforts into the larger symposium on love we all share. I am especially grateful to Blair Kamin, a student and friend whose continuing support means so much.

My path to an art and practice of contemplative beholding has been long and slow. Along the way, many institutions have provided just the right help and guidance at just the right time. I am forever grateful to Bill Ward and Prosser Gifford, President and Dean of the Faculty at Amherst College, who opened the way to my life as a teacher, and to President Julian Gibbs and his wife Cora Lee for their artistic sensibilities. I am grateful as well to many friends and colleagues who shared the joys and pains of the academic world: Rowland Abiodun, Linda Caron, Betsey Garand, Carol Keller, Sam Morse, Paul Rockwell, Dick and Do Schmalz, Becky and Dale Sinos, Natasha Staller, Robert Sweeney, Wako Tawa, and Geoffrey Woglom. My gratitude also goes to Ray Moore, the director of the Associated Kyoto Program (AKP), who invited me to teach in Kyoto, and his wife, Ilga, who made living there a paradise; and to Tom Rohlich at Smith College, who invited me twice more to teach with the AKP and enriched my experience and understanding of life and art in Japan. Mirabai Bush, the founder and first director of the far-reaching Center for Contemplative Mind in Society and the Association for Contemplative Mind in Higher Education, has been a continuing source of inspiration and encouragement. So to, Tessa Bielecki and Fr. Dave Denny of the Desert Foundation have informed my sense of the spiritual dimension of contemplative beholding.

From this center, my gratitude expands to include the educational support provided by the following institutions, teachers, and grants: Rutgers University (Warren Sussman and Robert Rough); Bryn Mawr College (Charles Mitchell and Jim Snyder); Princeton University (Robert Koch); the National Gallery of Art (directors John Walker, J. Carter Brown, and visiting scholar René Huyghe gave me the opportunity to be in residence as a Chester Dale Fellow and the generous subvention for travel in Europe to visit museums and architectural sites from Scotland to Greece); and to John Hand, curator of Northern Renaissance Painting. A Fulbright-Hays Fellowship allowed me to work at the Centre national de recherches "Primitifs flamands" in the Institut royale du patrimoine artistique in Brussels, Belgium. The long list of museums and architectural sites from east to west have been the ground of all my exploring.

My deepest gratitude is for lifelong friends who have sustained me and taught me. They are forever at the center of my thoughts: David Hubner, my dear friend from fourth grade on; George Kolt, and Guy and Moira Monseu, who gave me everything French, including the rolling "r"; and F. X. Grondin as spiritual mentor. In Japan, with extended periods of living in Kyoto, I awoke to all that is *other*—to fullness. Hideo and Fusako Higuchi, whom I met in Amherst on their first trip to America in 1972, opened their hearts and home to me and my wife Sara; Yoshitada Uda was the perfect cicerone who led us to Saigyo's poetry and his distant "hut" of absolute solitude high in the mountains above Yoshino, and to the burial sites of Matsuo Bashō and Jun'ichirō Tanizaki; Miyamoto-sensei and his wife shared the unique warmth of their eternal city with us.

I am grateful to Christopher Bamford for his acceptance of my manuscript for publication by Lindisfarne Books. His enormous learning and subtle editorial guidance made it possible to bring together the printed word with independent digital images of works of art as a source of true beholding, recalling medieval Books of Hours. I am also grateful to John-Scott Legg, executive director of Lindisfarne Books, and to Mary Giddens and Curran Giddens for guiding *Contemplative Beholding* toward publication. Roberta Diehl and Willa Jarnagin in the Department of Digital Communications at Amherst College constructed the companion website of images with the technical skill and artistic vision that provided the essential bridge between word and image.

Thank you as well to Henry Lyman for permission to open *Contemplative Beholding* with his poem "The Cairn," which sets the tone for what follows.

I am also especially grateful to several generous readers for their support and insight, and for suggestions that pushed me to focus and amplify my thinking. Rowland Abiodun, Susan Burggraf, Mirabai Bush, Diana Chapman Walsh, Mohammed Hamid Mohammed, and Parker Palmer offered me substantive encouragement that brightened the silence of solitude with love.

Mary Bagg turned a manuscript into this book. Her tremendous skill, learning, attention to everything from largest thematic coherence to comma-level detail, along with her poetic sensibilities and empathy, helped to infuse the text with the conversationality that echoes the warmth and trust of the classroom. Readers who would be beholders owe Mary a large debt of gratitude, as do I.

Finally, my enduring gratitude is for the generous love of my family: my parents, Mimi and Kelly; my sister and brother, Jennifer and Peter; my beloved Sara; our two daughters, Amy and Meg; and their families including Ed, Grady, Hazel, Kal, and Milo. They are the north star of my life, the true source of all beholding.

Audio and Image List

Audio (available on the website)

Thoughts About Word and Image

Stephen Foster (1826–1864), "Why, No One to Love," sung by Arleen Auger, Delos International, Inc. 1992

Chapter 2

Erich Korngold, *Die tote Stadt* "Marietta's Song," sung by Renée Fleming, "The Beautiful Voice," with the English Chamber Orchestra, Jeffrey Tate, audio CD, Decca 2018

Chapter 3

Max Bruch (1838–1920), Violin Concerto no. 1 in G Minor, op. 26: second movement, Adagio, performed by Joshua Bell, *The Romantic Violin*, audio CD, Decca 2004

Chapter 11

Stephen Foster (1826–1864), "Why, No One to Love," sung by Arleen Auger, Delos International, Inc. 1992

Images (appearing in the book)

Cover and Opening Invitation to Behold

Katsushika Hokusai (1760–1849), *Boy Viewing Mount Fuji*, ca. 1839, ink and color on silk, Freer Gallery of Art and Arthur M. Sackler Gallery, Washington, DC, Gift of Charles Lang Freer (1853–1908)

Coda: Returning Home

12.1 Rembrandt van Rijn, *Return of the Prodigal Son*, ca. 1669, State Hermitage Museum, St. Petersburg, Russia

Images (appearing on the website)

The images listed below include photographs and schematics by the author, works of art in the public domain, images drawn from online sources, and slides scanned from the Amherst Collection Visual Resources teaching collection. The date, medium, dimensions, and location of works of art are given in full on their first mention.

Front Matter:

Thoughts About Word and Image

Jan van Eyck (ca. 1390–1441), *Madonna of Chancellor Rolin*, 1430–34, oil on panel, Musée du Louvre, Paris, France

An Opening Invitation to Behold

Katsushika Hokusai (1760–1849), *Boy Viewing Mount Fuji*, ca. 1839, hanging scroll, Japanese paper, wood, ink and color on silk, Freer Gallery of Art and Arthur M. Sackler Gallery, Washington, DC, Gift of Charles Lang Freer (1853–1908)

Introduction

0.1 Two water lily blossoms, Ryoan-ji, Kyoto, Japan (author)
0.2 Bamboo path, Kyoto, Japan (author)
0.3 Milo Kalambokis, *Autumn Light*, 2020, tempera on panel, private collection

I: Preparation

Chapter 1: Beginning—In Silence and Solitude

1.1 Outer Gate I, Ryoan-ji, Kyoto, Japan (author)
1.2 Outer Gate II (author)
1.3 Curving path (author)
1.4 East Gate (author)
1.5 Pond with moored boat (author)
1.6 Pond with two rocks (author)
1.7 Pond with two rocks and still water (author)
1.8 Pond with ripples (author)
1.9 Matsuo Bashō, text, “Breaking the silence …”

Chapter 2:
Reconciliatory Longing—A Condition of Our Human Being

II. Setting Out

Chapter 3: Focused Attention and Open Awareness—Rembrandt van Rijn

Chapter 4:
Embracing the Obverse—Johann Wolfgang von Goethe

Chapter 5:
Measuring Contradiction—Piet Mondrian

Chapter 6: Breaking the Law of the Excluded Middle—*Ai-no-ma*

III. Heading Home

Chapter 7: From Lust to Solitude—From Grasping to Acceptance

7.8 *Esquiline Aphrodite*, 2nd century BCE, marble, Palazzo dei Conservatori, Rome, Italy

7.9 *Esquiline Aphrodite*, 2nd century BCE, marble, Musée du Louvre, Paris, France

7.10 *Aphrodite with Flowing Gown*; Roman copy of Greek original, 2nd century BCE, marble, Museo Nazionale Romano, Palazzo Massimo alle Terme, Rome, Italy

7.11 Rembrandt van Rijn, *Woman Bathing in a Stream*, ca. 1655, oil on canvas, National Gallery, London, United Kingdom

7.12 *Aphrodite Bathing*, 3rd–2nd century BCE, marble, British Museum, London, United Kingdom

7.13 Praxiteles, *Knidian Aphrodite*, 2nd-century Roman copy of 4th-century BCE original, marble, Roman copy, Glyptothek, Munich, Germany

7.14 *Eros Asleep*, 3rd–2nd century BCE, bronze, Metropolitan Museum of Art, New York, New York

7.15 *Crouching Aphrodite*, 3rd-century BCE, marble, Museo Archeologico Nazionale di Napoli, Naples, Italy

7.16 *Capitoline Aphrodite*, Roman copy of 3rd-century BCE original, marble, Capitoline Museums (Museii Capitolini), Rome, Italy

7.17 Masaccio, *Expulsion*, 1427, fresco, Brancacci Chapel, Florence, Italy

7.18 Hugo van der Goes, *Adam and Eve*, ca. 1470, oil on wood, Gallerie degli Uffizi, Florence, Italy

7.19 Albrecht Dürer, *Adam and Eve*, 1504, engraving, Metropolitan Museum of Art, New York, New York

7.20 Titian, *Adam and Eve*, ca.1550, oil on canvas, Museo Nacional del Prado, Madrid, Spain

7.21 Rembrandt van Rijn, *Adam and Eve*, 1638, etching, The Art Institute of Chicago, Chicago, Illinois

7.22 Diane Arbus, *A husband and wife in the woods at a nudist camp, N.J.*, 1963, gelatin silver print, The Art Institute of Chicago, Chicago, Illinois

7.23 *Medici Venus*, 1st-century BCE, Roman copy of 4th-century BCE original, marble, Gallerie degli Uffizi, Florence, Italy

7.24 a. *Aphrodite Bathing*; b. *Medici Venus*

7.25 *Kallipygos Aphrodite*, 1st century BCE, marble, front and back, Museo Archeologico Nazionale di Napoli, Naples, Italy

7.26 *Kouros* (male youth), ca. 6th century BCE, marble, Metropolitan Museum of Art, New York, New York

7.27 *Kritios Boy*, 5th century BCE, marble, Acropolis Museum, Athens, Greece

7.28 *Young Athlete*, 4th century BCE, marble, Staatliche Kunstsammlungen, Dresden, Germany

7.29 *Hermes with the Infant Dionysos*, marble, copy after Praxiteles, ca. 340 BCE, Olympia, Greece

7.30 *Charioteer of Delphi*, 470 BCE, bronze, Delphi Museum, Delphi, Greece

7.31 *Apollo (Apollo Belvedere)*, 2nd century, Roman marble copy of 4th-century-BCE Greek bronze, Vatican Museums, Pio Clementino Museum, Vatican, Rome, Italy

7.32 *Aphrodite of Melos*, ca. 150–125 BCE, marble, Musée du Louvre, Paris, France

7.33 *Zeus of Artemision* (Zeus or Poseidon), 5th century BCE, bronze, National Archeological Museum, Athens, Greece

7.34 a. *Aphrodite of Melos*, torso; b. *Zeus of Artemision*, torso

7.35 a. *Aphrodite of Melos*, face; b. *Zeus of Artemision*, face

7.36 "The champagne panty. At the soda-pop price," n.d., advertisement, *New York Times*

Chapter 8: Dream of Reason—Redeemed by Humility

8.1 Sunset at Chartres, France

8.2 Jan van Eyck, *Madonna in the Church*, ca. 1440, oil on wood, Gemäldegalerie, Berlin, Germany

8.3 Albrecht Dürer (?), *Madonna and Child* ("The Madonna with the Iris"), ca. 1500–10, oil on wood, National Gallery, London, United Kingdom

8.4 Albrecht Dürer, a. *Iris*,1503, watercolor, Kunsthalle, Bremen, Germany; b. *Tuft of Cowslips*, 1526, gouache on vellum, National Gallery, Washington, DC

8.5 Albrecht Dürer, a. *Portrait of His Father* (attributed), oil on canvas, 1497, National Gallery, London, United Kingdom; b. *Portrait of His Mother*, drawing, 1514, Stiftung Preussischer Kunstbesitz, Berlin, Germany

8.6 Albrecht Dürer, *Pope Julius II* (?), 1506, drawing, study for *Feast of the Rose Garlands*, Stiftung Preussischer Kulturbesitz, Gemäldegalerie, Berlin, Germany

8.7 Albrecht Dürer, *Self-Portrait*, 1484, silver point, Graphische Sammlung Albertina, Vienna, Austria

8.8 Albrecht Dürer, *Hare*, 1502, watercolor, Graphische Sammlung Albertina, Vienna, Austria

8.9 Albrecht Dürer, *The Little Owl*, 1506, watercolor, Graphische Sammlung Albertina, Vienna, Austria

8.10 Albrecht Dürer, *View of Nuremberg*, 1496–97, watercolor, Kunsthalle, Bremen, Germany

8.11 Albrecht Dürer, *View of Antwerp*, drawing, 1520, Graphische Sammlung Albertina, Vienna, Austria

8.12 Albrecht Dürer, *Draftsman Drawing a Lute*, 1525, woodcut in *The Painter's Manual*, translation Walter S. Strauss (New York: Abaris Books, 1977)

8.13 Chuck Close, Working photograph for *Phil*, 1969, gelatin silver print, ink and masking tape, George Eastman Museum, Rochester, New York

8.14 Albrecht Dürer, *Draftsman Drawing a Recumbent Woman* (Aphrodite and Hephaestus?), 1525, woodcut in *The Painter's Manual*, translation Walter S. Strauss (New York: Abaris Books, 1977)

8.15 Albrecht Dürer, *Self-Portrait in a Fur Cloak*, 1500, oil on wood panel, Alte Pinakothek, Munich, Germany

8.16 a. Albrecht Dürer, *Self-Portrait in a Fur Cloak*; b. Jan van Eyck, *God the Father* from the *Altarpiece of the Mystic Lamb*, 1432, oil on panel, St. Bavo, Ghent, Belgium

8.17 a. Villard de Honnecourt, *Geometric Man*, ca. 1230, drawing, (H. Hahnloser); b. Leonardo da Vinci, *Study of a Male Nude*, ca. 1503–09, drawing, Royal Library, Windsor Castle, Windsor, United Kingdom, Royal Collection Trust/ copyright Her Royal Majesty Queen Elizabeth II, 2018

8.18 Leonardo da Vinci, *The Proportions of the Human Figure* (after Vitruvius), ca. 1490, drawing, Galleria dell'Accademia, Venice, Italy

8.19 Leonardo da Vinci, *Studies of the Human Hand*, ca. 1490, drawing, Royal Library, Windsor Castle, Windsor, United Kingdom

8.20 Leonardo da Vinci, *The Sexual Act in Vertical Section* ("genito-urinary system"), ca. 1490, drawing, Royal Library, Windsor Castle, Windsor, United Kingdom

8.21 Leonardo da Vinci, *Embryo in the Womb*, ca. 1510, drawing, Royal Library, Windsor Castle, Windsor, United Kingdom

8.22 a. Textbook image of fetus in utero, D. Stabler and J. Rankin, *Physiology in Childbearing*, 3rd edition (Edinburgh: Baillière Tindall, 2010); b. Limbourg Brothers, Paradise from the *Très Riches Heures du Duc de Berry*, 1416, manuscript, Musée Condé, Chantilly, France

8.23 Leonardo da Vinci, *The Brain* (of an ox?), injected to demonstrate the shape of the cerebral ventricles, ca. 1490, drawing, Royal Library, Windsor Castle, Windsor, United Kingdom

8.24 Leonardo da Vinci, *Study of the Human Skull in Sagittal Section*, from front, 1489, drawing, Royal Library, Windsor Castle, Windsor, United Kingdom

8.25 Leonardo da Vinci, *Giant Wisk*, ca. 1490, drawing, Royal Library, Windsor Castle, Windsor, United Kingdom

8.26 Leonardo da Vinci, *Last Supper*, 1495–98, fresco (oil and tempera on plaster), Convent of Santa Maria delle Grazie, Milan, Italy

8.27 Refectory wall, 15th century, Convent of Santa Maria delle Grazie, Milan, Italy

8.28 Leonardo da Vinci, *Last Supper*, a. detail of disciples to Christ's right; b. detail of disciples to Christ's left

8.29 Leonardo da Vinci, *Last Supper*, linear perspective indicated in white, central axis of figures indicated in red (author)

8.30 Leonardo da Vinci, *Last Supper*, detail of the figure of Jesus

8.31 Refectory, Convent of Santa Maria delle Grazie, 15th century, Milan, Italy

8.32 Refectory with visitors, 20th century

8.33 Refectory, Mont St. Michel, 13th century, Normandy, France

8.34 Antoine Lafrery, *Seven Pilgrimage Churches of Rome*, 1575, ("old" basilica of St. Peter indicated), engraving, Metropolitan Museum of Art, New York, New York

8.35 Old basilica of St. Peter, conjectural reconstruction, ca. 1450, Rome, Italy (H. W. Brewer, 1891)

8.36 Old basilica of St. Peter, 4th century, Rome; a. conjectural reconstruction of the interior program; b. conjectural reconstruction of the apse mosaic (after Maffeo Vegio, 1407–1455)

8.37 a. Old basilica of St. Peter, plan showing longitudinal movement east to west; b. Michelangelo, plan for the crossing of the new basilica of St. Peter, 1546–64

8.38 a. Old basilica of St. Peter, conjectural reconstruction of the nave, transept and apse; b. New basilica of St. Peter, 16th century, Vatican, Rome, Italy, view of the chancel beyond the dome from the nave, centered on the *baldichino* of Gian Lorenzo Bernini, 1624–32

8.39 Sistine Chapel, Vatican, Rome, Italy, a. before 1508; b. after 1512

8.40 Michelangelo, *Drunkenness of Noah*, 1508–12, fresco, ceiling of the Sistine Chapel, Vatican, Rome, Italy

8.41 Michelangelo, ceiling of the Sistine Chapel, 1508–12, viewed from east to west, *Drunkenness of Noah* indicated

8.42 Michelangelo, ceiling of the Sistine Chapel, 1508–12, fresco, viewed from west to east (lower to upper), *Separation of Light from Darkness* indicated

8.43 Michelangelo, *Separation of Light from Darkness*, 1508–12, fresco, ceiling of the Sistine Chapel, Vatican, Rome, Italy

8.44 Michelangelo, *Creation of the Sun, Moon, and Planets*, 1508–12, fresco, ceiling of the Sistine Chapel, 1508–12, Vatican, Rome, Italy

8.45 Michelangelo, *Gathering of the Waters*, 1508–12, fresco, ceiling of the Sistine Chapel, Vatican, Rome, Italy

8.46 Michelangelo, *The Creation of Adam*, 1508–12, fresco, ceiling of the Sistine Chapel, Vatican, Rome, Italy

8.47 a. Cathedral of Chartres, France, 12th–16th century, north porch, location of sculpture indicated; b. detail, *Creation of Adam* (author)

8.48 Michelangelo, *Last Judgment*, 1534–41, fresco, altar wall of the Sistine Chapel, Vatican, Rome, Italy

8.49 a. Cathedral of Reims, France, 13th century, west façade, *Coronation*; b. Michelangelo, *Last Judgment*, 1534–41, fresco, figures of Christ and Mary, altar wall of the Sistine Chapel

8.50 Cathedral of Reims, France, 13th century, center portal of west façade

8.51 a. Cathedral of Reims, France, 13th century, west façade; b. Sistine Chapel, 16th century, Vatican, Rome, Italy

8.52 Galleria dell'Accademia, Florence, Italy, with Michelangelo's *David* and visitors

8.53 a. Donatello, *David*, 1408–09, marble (6' 2''), Museo Nazionale del Bargello, Florence, Italy; b. Michelangelo, *David*, 1501–04, marble (17'), Galleria dell'Accademia, Florence, Italy

8.54 Donatello, *David*, 1408–09, marble (6' 2''), Museo Nazionale del Bargello, Florence, Italy

8.55 Donatello, *David*, c. 1425–30, bronze (5' 2 ¼''), Museo Nazionale del Bargello, Florence, Italy

8.56 Polykleitos, *Doryphorus* (spear-bearer), Roman marble copy (6' 6''), after a bronze original, c. 450–440 BCE, Museo Nazionale di Napoli, Naples, Italy

8.57 Donatello, *David*, c. 1425–30, bronze (5' 2 ¼''), Museo Nazionale del Bargello, Florence, Italy; a. detail of feather against David's leg; b. detail of Goliath's beard between David's toes

8.58 Donatello, *David*, ca. 1440, bronze (5' 2 ¼''), viewed from front, side, and back, Museo Nazionale del Bargello, Florence, Italy

8.59 Galleria dell'Accademia, Florence, Italy with Michelangelo's *David*, 1501–04, and *"Slaves,"* ca. 1530–34

8.60 Michelangelo, *David*, 1501–04, marble (17'), viewed from below center, Galleria dell'Accademia, Florence, Italy

8.61 Michelangelo, *Captive Atlas*, ca. 1530–34, marble, Galleria dell'Accademia, Florence, Italy

8.62 Michelangelo, *David*, raised view

8.63 Michelangelo, *David*, viewed from the right

8.64 Michelangelo, *David*, detail of face viewed from the right

8.65 a. Donatello, *David*, 1408–09, head and face in shadow; b. Michelangelo, *David*, head and face

8.66 Francisco Goya, *The Third of May 1808*, 1814, oil on canvas, Museo del Prado, Madrid, Spain

8.67 Elliot Erwitt, *Boy Viewing Guernica*, 1995, Museo Nacional Centro de Arte Reina Sofia

8.68 Francisco Goya, *The Sleep of Reason Produces Monsters*, from *Los Caprichos*, ca. 1798, Etching and aquatint, The Metropolitan Museum of Art, New York, New York

8.69 Gian Lorenzo Bernini, *David*, 1623–24, marble, Galleria Borghese, Rome, Italy

8.70 a. Donatello, *David*, 1408–09; b. Donatello, *David*, ca. 1425–30; c. Michelangelo, *David*, 1501–04; d. Gian Lorenzo Bernini, *David*, 1623–24

8.71 Cathedral of Chartres, France, 12th–16th century, *King David*, north porch

8.72 Old Town Square, Prague, Czech Republic (author)

8.73 Astronomical Clock, 1410, restored 1948, City Hall, Old Town, Prague, Czech Republic, people gathering (author)

8.74 Astronomical Clock, City Hall, Old Town, Prague, Czech Republic, Procession of Apostles Thaddeus and Philip (author)

8.75 Astronomical Clock, City Hall, Old Town, Prague, Czech Republic, Procession of Apostles completed (author)

8.76 Astronomical Clock, City Hall, Old Town, Prague, Czech Republic, waiting … (author)

8.77 Leonardo da Vinci, *Studies for a Madonna and Child with a Cat*, c. 1478–80, pen and ink, British Museum, London, United Kingdom

8.78 Leonardo da Vinci, *Adoration of the Magi*, 1481–82, drawing in charcoal, watercolor ink, oil on wood, Gallerie degli Uffizi, Florence, Italy

8.79 Leonardo da Vinci, Perspective study for the background of *Adoration of the Magi*, 1481, pen and ink, Gallerie degli Uffizi, Gabinetto dei Disegni e delle Stampe, Florence, Italy

8.80 Leonardo da Vinci, *Adoration of the Magi*, detail of Mary with the Christ child reaching for the offered chalice

8.81 Leonardo da Vinci, *Study for the Adoration of the Magi*, 1481, pen and ink, Musée du Louvre, Cabinet des Dessins, Paris, France

8.82 Leonardo da Vinci, *Adoration of the Magi*, detail of the child's hand and the king's offering

8.83 Leonardo da Vinci, *Adoration of the Magi*, detail of blind man

8.84 Leonardo da Vinci, *Adoration of the Magi*, with overlay of compositional triangle (author)

8.107 a. Michelangelo, *Rondanini Pietà*, viewed from the left; b. Constantin Brancusi, *Bird in Space*, 1928, bronze, Museum of Modern Art, New York, New York

8.108 a. Leonardo da Vinci, *Adoration of the Magi*; b. Cathedral of Chartres, France, 13th century, rose window of the north transept, stained glass, iron, lead, and stone tracery

8.109 Albrecht Dürer, *Self-Portrait as the "Man of Sorrows,"* 1522, drawing with lead pencil on blue-green primed paper, Kunsthalle, Bremen, Germany

8.110 Albrecht Dürer, *Dream Landscape*, 1525, watercolor, pen and ink, Kunsthistorisches Museum, Vienna, Austria

8.111 Michelangelo, *Rondanini Pietà*, Museo Pietà Rondanini, Castello Sforzesco, Milan, Italy

8.112 Michelangelo, *Rondanini Pietà*, viewed from the front

8.113 Michelangelo, *Rondanini Pietà*, pre-2015 installation; a. viewed from the left; b. viewed from the front (author)

8.114 Autun, France

8.115 St. Lazarus, Autun, France, 12th century, west portal, narthex

8.116 St. Lazarus, Autun, France, 12th century, west portal, tympanum

8.117 St. Lazarus, Autun, France, 12th century, west portal, inscription, *Gislebertus hoc fecit*

8.118 St. Lazarus, Autun, France, 12th century, conjectural reconstruction of the north portal with the figure of Eve (after Grivot and Zarnecky)

8.119 Gislebertus (?), *Eve*, ca. 1130, Musée Rolin, Autun, France

8.120 Gislebertus (?), *Eve*, ca. 1130, detail, Musée Rolin, Autun, France

8.121 St. Lazarus, Autun, France, 12th century, present state of the north portal entrance (author)

8.122 St. Lazarus, Autun, France, 12th century, west portal tympanum with crouching figure indicated

8.123 St. Lazarus, Autun, France, 12th century, west portal lintel, detail of crouching figure

8.124 Cathedral of Amiens, France, 13th century, viewed from the northwest, late afternoon (author)

8.125 Cathedral of Amiens, west façade (author)

8.126 Cathedral of Amiens, center portal of the west façade, with door closed beneath the Last Judgment in the tympanum (author)

8.127 Cathedral of Amiens, the nave viewed from west to east

8.128 Cathedral of Amiens, viewed from the nave through the transept to choir

Chapter 9: Circles of Affection—The Origin of Love

IV. Via Amoris

Chapter 10: Homecoming and Departure

Chapter 11: A Point of Renewal

Coda: Returning Home

12.1 Rembrandt van Rijn, *Return of the Prodigal Son*, ca. 1669, oil on canvas, State Hermitage Museum, St. Petersburg, Russia

12.2 a. Rembrandt van Rijn, *Return of the Prodigal Son*, 1636, etching, pen and ink; b. Rembrandt van Rijn, *Return of the Prodigal Son*, ca. 1669

12.3 Rembrandt van Rijn, *Return of the Prodigal Son*

Selected Reading

The primary source for *Contemplative Beholding: A Way of Life and Love* is the *art* of works of art, including painting, sculpture, and architecture. The following books have informed my thinking and assured me that as beholders in solitude, we are not alone. Further references are included in the endnotes.

Ackerman, Diane. *A Natural History of Love*. New York: Vintage, 1995.

Adams, Henry. *Mont Saint Michel and Chartres* [1904]. New York: Viking, 1986.

Armstrong, Karen. *Twelve Steps to a Compassionate Life*. New York: Anchor, 2011.

Bachelard, Gaston. *The Poetics of Space*. Trans. by Maria Jolas. Boston: Beacon Press, 1969.

Barbezat, Daniel P., and Mirabai Bush. *Contemplative Practices in Higher Education: Powerful Methods to Transform Teaching and Learning*. San Francisco: Jossey-Bass, 2014.

Bly, Robert. *The Soul Is Here for Its Own Joy: Sacred Poems from Many Cultures*. New York: HarperCollins, 1995.

Buber, Martin. *I and Thou*. Trans. by Walter Kaufmann, New York: Simon & Shuster, 1970.

Cheng, François. *The Way of Beauty: Five Meditations for Spiritual Transformation*. Trans. by Jody Gladding. Rochester, VT: Inner Traditions, 2009.

Collingwood, R. G. *Essays in the Philosophy of Art*. Bloomington: Indiana University Press, 1964.

De Rougemont, Denis. *Love in the Western World*. Trans. by Montgomery Belgion. Princeton, NJ: Princeton University Press, 1983.

Dustin, Christopher, and Joanna Ziegler. *Practicing Mortality: Art, Philosophy and Contemplation*. New York: Palgrave Macmillan, 2005.

Eco, Umberto. *Art and Beauty in the Middle Ages*. New Haven, CT: Yale University Press, 1986.

Fliegel, S. *A Higher Contemplation: Sacred Meaning in Christian Art of the Middle Ages*. Kent, OH: Kent State University Press, 2012.

Fromm, Eric. *On Being Human*. New York: Continuum, 1994.

Goethe, Johann Wolfgang, von. *Goethe on Art*. Selected, ed., and trans. by John Gage. Berkeley: University of California Press, 1980.

Heidegger, Martin. *The Question Concerning Technology*. Trans. by W. Lovitt. New York: Harper & Row, 1977.

———. "Building Dwelling Thinking." In Po*etry, Language, Thought*. Trans. by Albert Hofstadter. New York: Harper & Row, 1971.

Holly, Michael Ann, and Keith Moxey, eds. *Art History, Aesthetics, Visual Studies*. Williamstown, MA: Sterling and Francine Clark Art Institute, 2002.

Kabat-Zinn, Jon, *Full Catastrophe Living: Using the Wisdom of Your Body and Mind to Face Stress, Pain, and Illness*. New York: Dell Publishing, 1991.

———. *Wherever You Go, There You Are: Mindfulness Meditation in Everyday Life*. New York: Hyperion, 2005.

Keating, T. *The Human Condition: Contemplation and Transformation*. New York: Paulist Press, 1999.

Kegan, R. *The Emerging Self: Problem and Process in Human Development*. Cambridge, MA: Harvard University Press, 1982.

———. *In Over Our Heads*. Cambridge, MA: Harvard University Press, 1994.

Keller, Evelyn Fox. *A Feeling for the Organism: The Life and Work of Barbara McClintock*. New York: Henry Holt, 2003.

Lao-tzu. *Tao Te Ching*. Trans. by Stephen Mitchell. New York: Harper & Row, 1988.

Merton, Thomas. *The Seven Story Mountain*. New York: Harcourt, Brace, 1948.

———. *The Asian Journal*. New York: New Directions, 1975.

———. *Love and Living*. New York: Harcourt, 1979.

———. *New Seeds of Contemplation*. New York: New Directions, 1972.

———. *Learning to Love: Exploring Solitude and Freedom*. New York: HarperCollins, 1997.

Miles, Margaret. *Image as Insight: Visual Understanding in Western Christianity and Secular Culture*. Boston: Beacon Press, 1985.

Mood, John J. L., *Rilke On Love and Other Difficulties: Translations and Considerations of Rainer Maria Rilke*. New York: Norton, 1975.

Nouwen, Henri, J. M. *The Return of the Prodigal Son: A Story of Homecoming*. New York: Image Books, 1994.

O'Donohue, John. *To Bless the Space Between Us*. New York: Doubleday, 2008.

Palmer, Parker. *To Know as We Are Known: Education as a Spiritual Journey*. San Francisco: Harper & Row, 1983.

———. *The Courage to Teach: Exploring the Inner Landscape of a Teacher's Life*. San Francisco: Jossey-Bass, 1998.

Palmer, Parker, and Arthur Zajonc. *The Heart of Higher Education: A Call to Renewal.* San Francisco: Jossey-Bass, 2010.

Panofsky, Erwin. "Art History as a Humanistic Discipline." In *Meaning in the Visual Arts: Papers In and On Art History.* Woodstock, NY: Overlook Press, 1974.

Pieper, Josef. *Only the Lover Sings: Art and Contemplation.* Trans. by Lothar Krauth, San Francisco: Ignatius Press, 1990.

Plato. *The Symposium.* Trans. by Christopher Gill. New York: Penguin, 1999.

Porete, Marguerite (1250–1310). *The Mirror of Simple Souls.* Trans. by Ellen L. Babinsky. New York: Paulist Press, 1993.

Rilke, Rainer Maria. *The Poetry of Rilke.* Trans. by Edward Snow. New York: North Point Press, 2009.

———. *Letters to a Young Poet.* Trans. by M. D. Herter Norton. New York: Norton, 1962.

———. *Sonnets to Orpheus.* In *The Poetry of Rilke.* Trans. by Edward Snow. New York: North Point, 2009.

Schiller, Friedrich (1759–1805). *On the Aesthetic Education of Man.* Trans. by Reginald Snell. Mineola, NY: Dover, 2004.

Solovyov, Vladimir. *The Meaning of Love.* Trans. by Thomas R. Beyer Jr. Great Barrington, MA: Lindisfarne Books, 1985.

Springsted, Eric, O. *Simone Weil and the Suffering of Love.* Cambridge, MA: Cowley, 1986.

Taylor, Harold. *Art and the Intellect.* New York: Museum of Modern Art, 1960.

Teilhard de Chardin, Pierre. *The Phenomenon of Man.* Trans. by Bernard Wall. New York: Harper & Row, 1959.

Thomas à Kempis (ca. 1379–1471). *The Imitation of Christ.* Trans. by William C. Creasy. Notre Dame, IN: Ave Maria Press, 2004.

Thoreau, Henry David. *Walden and Other Writings.* New York: Modern Library, 1992.

Weil, Simone. *Gravity and Grace.* Trans. by Arthur Wills. Lincoln: University of Nebraska Press, 1997.

Zajonc, Arthur. *Catching the Light: The Entwined History of Light and the Mind.* New York: Bantam, 1993.

———. *Meditation as Contemplative Inquiry: When Knowing Becomes Love.* Great Barrington, MA: Lindisfarne Books, 2009.

Notes

Introduction: Contemplative Beholding with the Art of Works of Art

1 For art as *techne* and *poesis*, see Martin Heidegger, chapter 7, note 10. I understand that the word "*Bauhaus*" (literally, construction house; colloquially, workshop) was created by its founders in Germany to represent an explicit effort to combine both active craft and conceptual theory (medieval *ars* and *scientia*; see note 9 below). Importantly, the verb *bauen* stems from the Old High German word *būan*, which for Heidegger meant "to dwell" (i.e., holding "earth and sky, divinities and mortals" in relation; see chapter 2, note 22). In Yoruba language and culture, the word *oríkì* conflates verb and noun in the spiritual activity of "divination" that, on reflection, echoes the act, attitude, and result identified in this book as "beholding." See Rowland Abiodun, *Yoruba Art and Language: Seeking the African in African Art* (New York: Cambridge University Press, 2014), 5 passim. I remain grateful for his generous guidance expanding my understanding.

2 John Keats, *The Letters of John Keats*, ed. by H. E. Rollins, 2 vols. (Cambridge: Cambridge University Press, 1958), vol. 1, 193–194. See chapter 8 to compare Nicholas of Cusa's "learned ignorance."

3 William Wordsworth's famous "Intimations of Immortality from Recollections of Early Childhood" is one explicit exemplar of discomfort, sadness, and loss as the birth of art. Note here that my use of italics for the word *artist* (and in the next paragraph, *artistic*) is meant to stress the significance of *art* the verb. Wordsworth, "Intimations of Immortality..." in *The Oxford Book of English Verse*, chosen and edited by Sir Arthur Quiller-Couch (Oxford: Clarendon, 1939), 626–633. See chapter 2 for my definition of the "ontological perspective" as the precondition for art and beholding.

4 See Parker Palmer and Arthur Zajonc, with Megan Scribner, *The Heart of Higher Education: A Call to Renewal* (San Francisco: Jossey-Bass, 2010), especially 19–33. Parker Palmer's stark observation connecting epistemology and ethics draws on his life's involvement with renewal in education, community development, and spiritual well-being. His wide ranging contributions focus his conviction that the way we know informs directly how we behave. His recent publication with Arthur Zajonc, along with his *Courage to Teach* (1997, 2007) offer compelling

inspiration and guidance for anyone concerned with the fullest potential of our shared human journey.

5 William Shakespeare, *The Winter's Tale*, scene IV, act IV, "The Shepherd's Cottage." See Frederick Turner, "The Art of Nature," *Lapham's Quarterly*: "Human art, fiction, invention, and technology are not unnatural forces that have suddenly erupted into nature, but rather the natural continuation of nature's own evolutionary processes," https://www.laphamsquarterly.org/book-nature/art-nature (accessed Nov. 20, 2020).

6 See chapter 4 for an account of Goethe's artistic and spiritual awakening at the Strasbourg Cathedral.

7 Joel M. Upton, *Petrus Christus: His Place in Fifteenth-Century Flemish Painting* (University Park: Pennsylvania State University, 1990).

8 Ibid., 76–77. One painting in the Metropolitan Museum of Art in New York, the *Friedsam Annunciation*, reasonably attributed to Petrus Christus, includes the Annunciate standing in the portal of a church. Although described by one writer as resembling an anxious cat unable to decide whether to come in or go out, this positioning is vividly and literally within the threshold of love between the interior and exterior, public and private realities of our lives. The pictorial inscription reads: REGINA C[O]ELI LET[ARE] (Queen of Heaven, Rejoice), taken from the antiphon hymn replacing the Angelus at Eastertime to invoke Christ's resurrection.

9 This reference to *ars* and *scientia* is not arcane. It will remind us of a time before our modern separation of "Art" and "Science" when *ars* and *scientia* together integrated sensory experience, observation, craft, and practice with cerebral reflection, theory, and conceptual order. A third term, *eruditio*, saw "learning" as distinct from *scientia*, leading to *sapientia* (wisdom of the divine; infinite wholeness). Erwin Panofsky, in "The History of Art as a Humanistic Discipline," the introduction to *Meaning in the Visual Arts* (Garden City, NY: Doubleday, 1955), 25, identified *scientia* with "knowledge" and the natural sciences; and *eruditio* with the humanities as the "process of learning." For the integration of *ars* and *scientia,* see chapter 2, note 30. Although Charles Morgan, the founding director of the Mead Art Museum (originally the Mead Art Building), didn't use the terms *ars* and *scientia*, his plan for the building exemplifies his intention. He also gave many works of art from his private collection to the College. For more on the Mead Art Museum, see Blair Kamin, *Amherst College: An Architectural Tour by Blair Kamin* (New York: Princeton Architectural Press, 2020), 58–63.

10 This phrase captures St. Augustine's concluding vision in his *City of God*, trans. by G. G. Walsh et al. (Garden City, NY: Doubleday, 1958), 541.

11 Leanna James, "Eros and Insight," *Amherst Magazine* (Spring 2004); Arthur Zajonc, "Human Endogenous Development," *Moving World Views: Reshaping*

Sciences, Policies and Practices for Endogenous Sustainable Development, ed. by B. Haverkort and C. Reijntjes (Leusden, Netherlands: Compas, 2006).

12 In this context, the word "sacral" means to locate human imagination within the embrace of finite and infinite reality.

13 There is considerable reason to be optimistic about fundamental pedagogical change in the academic community toward "higher," if not non-ecclesiastical "spiritual" education. At the turn of the twenty-first century, the publication of Parker Palmer's *The Courage to Teach: Exploring the Inner Landscape of A Teacher's Life* (San Francisco: Jossey-Bass, 1998) was a morning bell to renewal; Palmer and Zajonc, *The Heart of Higher Education* offered another compelling pathway forward. Arthur Zajonc, as president of the Mind and Life organization, started important initiatives for expanding contemplative ways of knowing and being generally. For a broad discussion of contemplative education in the United States see Mirabai Bush and Rob Lehman, *Contemplation Nation: How Ancient Practices Are Changing the Way We Live* (Kalamazoo, MI: Fetzer Institute, 2011); Daniel Barbezat and Mirabai Bush, *Contemplative Practices in Higher Education: Powerful Methods to Transform Teaching and Learning* (San Francisco: Jossey-Bass, 2013). The extensive academic activities and reach of The Association for Contemplative Mind in Higher Education, Northampton, MA, offers further reason for optimism. For other advances, see L. A. Sanders (ed.), *Contemplative Studies,* New Directions of Teaching and Learning, no. 134 (San Francisco: Wiley Periodicals, summer 2013); D. Rechtschaffen, *The Way of Mindful Education: Cultivating Well-Being in Teachers and Students* (London: Norton, 2014).

14 Henry David Thoreau, *Natural History of Massachusetts,* quoted in C. Dustin and J. Zeigler, *Practicing Mortality: Art, Philosophy and Contemplative Seeing* (New York: St. Martin's, 2005, 17).

15 Christopher A. Dustin, "The Liturgy of Theory: Lessons on Beauty and Craft," *The Tangeman Lecture,* delivered at Yale University, April 27, 2003, https://ism.yale.edu/sites/default/files/files/The%20Liturgy%20of%20Theory.pdf (accessed Nov. 20, 2020). See also Dustin and Zeigler, *Practicing Mortality.*

16 Martin Luther (1483–1546), *Against the Heavenly Prophets in the Matter of Images and Sacraments,* in H. W. Janson, *History of Art,* 5th ed. (New York: Harry N. Abrams, 1995), 626.

17 Václav Havel, Acceptance speech on receiving The Liberty Medal at Independence Hall, Philadelphia, July 4, 1994, "The New Measure of Man," *New York Times,* July 8, 1994, 27; also as "The Need for Transcendence in the Postmodern World," http://www.worldtrans.org/whole/havelspeech.html, 2; republished with small changes in Havel, *The Art of the Impossible: Politics as Morality in Practice—Speeches and Writings, 1990–1996* (New York: Fromm, 1998).

18 My language is a variation of the comment by A. Coomaraswamy (1877–1947), *The Transformation of Nature in Art* (New Delhi: Indira Gandhi National Centre for the Arts, Sterling, 1995): "The artist is not a special kind of man, but every man is a special kind of artist"; so too Eric Gill, "The artist is not a different kind of person but every person is a different kind of artist," and Meister Eckhart, "An artist is not a special kind of person. Rather every person is a special kind of artist."

19 In the current academic world the apparent pedagogical and democratic efficiencies of digital Mass-Online-Open-Courses (MOOCs) threaten the value of retaining the embodied reality of genuine "higher" education.

20 Martin Buber, *I and Thou*, trans. by W. Kaufmann (New York: Simon & Shuster, 1970 [1923].)

21 Henry David Thoreau, *Walden*, in *Walden and Other Writings,* ed. by B. Atkinson (New York: Modern Library, 1992), 85–86.

22 Arthur Zajonc, *Meditation as Contemplative Inquiry: When Knowing Becomes Love* (Great Barrington, MA: Lindesfarne Books, 2009).

23 Martin Heidegger, "The Question Concerning Technology" [1962], in *The Question Concerning Technology and Other Essays*, trans. by W. Lovitt (New York: Harper & Row, 1977), 4.

24 Johannes Kepler, "Let nothing confine me: I will indulge my sacred ecstasy," *Harmony of the World* (1619), in G. Holton and S. G. Brush, *Physics, the Human Adventure: From Copernicus to Einstein and Beyond*, 2nd edition (New Brunswick, NJ: Rutgers University, 2001), 158. Johann Wolfgang von Goethe, "... the experience of a higher kind," in D. L. Sepper, *Goethe contra Newton: Polemics and the Project for a New Science of Color* (Cambridge: Cambridge University Press, 1988), 186.

25 David Foster Wallace, *This is Water: Some Thoughts Delivered on a Significant Occasion about Living a Compassionate Life* (New York: Little, Brown, 2009). Of the many notes and letters from students, the one David Wallace sent to me shortly after his graduation from Amherst College in 1985 is especially rewarding: "This is just a quick note to thank you for Art 11, which was (and I sure hope you know it was) a really phenomenal course. You have opened a door for me as a student and as a sensuous entity, and that is no small gift. Maybe this makes up for some of the obnoxious people in the class who talked and burped and turned in one-sentence papers and opened the rear doors of the hall even though you asked them not to. Your patience with them was not of this earth. Anyway, you've been involved in a teaching capacity with two of the five best courses I had at Amherst College. You've earned yourself a fan."

26 Henry David Thoreau, "Walking" (lecture in the Concord Lyceum, April 23, 1851; published in *Atlantic Monthly* in 1862 after his death), in Thoreau, *Walden and Other Writings*, 627.

27 It is important to note here that the images that accompany this text are in no way equivalent to direct experience with the works of art, sites, and music they record. In an era of disappearing books in favor of LED lighted screens and electronically reproduced sound, embodied contemplation requires a deliberate and purposeful sensual presence. Consequently, I encourage you to acknowledge that your own engaged experience is essential to the fullest encounter with the themes of this book. Matsuo Bashō (1644–1694) invoked relational presence as vital to the art of haiku poetry with the blunt admonition: "Go to the pine if you want to learn about the pine, or to the bamboo [*bashō*] if you want to learn about the bamboo. And in so doing you must leave your subjective preoccupation with yourself." *The Narrow Road to the Deep North and Other Travel Sketches*, trans. by N. Yuasa (New York: Penguin, 1966).

28 Thoreau, "Walking," 662–663.

Chapter 1: Beginning: In Silence and Solitude

1 Rainer Maria Rilke, *Letters to a Young Poet*, trans. by M. D. Herter Norton (New York: Norton, 1993 [1934]), 45. See also Stephen Mitchell, *Rainer Maria Rilke: Letters to a Young Poet*, trans. and with a forward by S. Mitchell, New York: Vintage, 1986, 77–78; Rainer Maria Rilke, *Letters to a Young Poet: A New Translation and Commentary*, trans. by Anita Barrows and Joanna Macy (Boulder, CO: Shambhala), 2021, "Letter 7." Although the two latter, more recent translations reverberate in the modern ear, for my purposes, Herter Norton's translation echoes the early 20th-century context of Rilke and the young poet Franz Kappus, both of whom had been military academy cadets. For me, Norton's language captures not only the urgency of Rilke's liberation from the pains of patriarchy (especially power, control, and authority) but also his vision beyond the limitations of gender, male or female. His phrase "the feminine human being" (Mitchell, "the female human being" / Barrows and Macy, "female humans") intimates a universal humanity vivid in Rilke's poetic integration of "masculine" language with military connotations (*protect*, *border*, and *salute*) preceded by "feminine" qualities associated with nurturing (*infinitely considerate and gentle, and kind and clear in binding and releasing*). So too, Norton's translation of the German *grüßen* as "salute" or salutation, rather than Mitchell's or Barrows and Macy's "greet," may suggest honoring as well as greeting another solitude in the three components of a "more human love," following "protect" as preserving and "border" as affirming another's agency independent of gender. Historically, the act of military saluting appears to have begun between chivalric knights who raised their armored visors in a friendly gesture of acceptance, vulnerability, and honor.

On the other hand, two segments of the Mitchell translation resonate strongly with a divine and human origin of love grounded in solitude that I have exemplified in chapter 2 as "Milo's lament" in the experience of separation and longing: (1) "the great love which was once *granted* to you when you were a boy" (my italics, rather than Norton's "enjoined upon you"); and (2) the concluding sentence, "I believe that *that* love remains so strong and intense in your memory because it was your first deep *aloneness* (my italics) and the first inner work that you did on your life."

2 Rainer Maria Rilke, *Sonnets to Orpheus*, II, 11 (Rilke's italics: "*Töten ist eine Gestalt unseres Trauern...*"), trans. by J. J. L. Mood, in *Rilke on Love and Other Difficulties* (New York: Norton, 2004 [1975]), 135–138.

3 See Joel M. Upton, *Petrus Christus: His Place in Fifteenth-Century Flemish Painting* (University Park: Pennsylvania State University, 1990). 60–64.

4 Ta-Nehisi Coates, "Letter to My Son," *The Atlantic*, September 2015, 82–89. Coates's "Letter to My Son" is an excerpt from his book *Between the World and Me* (New York: Spiegel & Grau, 2015). As one of the epigraphs in his essay Coates used the following quote from James Baldwin: "And have brought humanity to the edge of oblivion: because they think they are white." Baldwin, "On Being White... and Other Lies," (*Essence*, April 1984) in David R. Roediger, *Black on White: Black Writers on What It Means to Be White* (New York: Schocken, 1998), 177–180:

> By deciding that they were white. By opting for safety instead of life. By persuading themselves that a Black child's life meant nothing compared with a white child's life. By abandoning their children to the things white men could buy. By informing their children that Black women, Black men and Black children had no human integrity that those who call themselves white were bound to respect. And in this debasement and definition of Black people, they debased and defamed themselves.
>
> *And have brought humanity to the edge of oblivion: because they think they are white.* (italics mine) Because they think they are white, they do not dare confront the ravage and the lie of their history. Because they think they are white, they cannot allow themselves to be tormented by the suspicion that all men are brothers. Because they think they are white, they are looking for, or bombing into existence, stable populations, cheerful natives and cheap labor. Because they think they are white, they believe, as no child believes, in the dream of safety. Because they are white, however vociferous they may be and however multitudinous, they are as speechless as Lot's wife—looking backward, changed into a pillar of salt.... It is a terrible paradox, but those who believed that they could control and define Black people divested themselves of the power to control and define themselves.

5 "Killing" of course takes many forms, from the most brutal to the apparently gentle, even humorous. On the occasion of my marriage, my father urged me: "Never,

ever, make a joke about Sara. However funny it may appear at the moment, neither you nor she will quite know how much or how deeply it hurt her."

6 T. S. Eliot, "Little Gidding" [from *Four Quartets*], in *Collected Poems 1909–1962* (New York: Harcourt Brace, 1991), 208–209.

7 Henry David Thoreau, *Walden*, in *Walden and Other Writings,* ed. by B. Atkinson (New York: Modern Library, 1992), 84–85.

8 Ibid., 85.

9 Ibid., 86.

10 Ibid., 85.

11 Nobuyuki Yuasa translated the Bashō poem shown in image 1.9. I include here the original Japanese and, for comparison, a translation by Lafcadio Hearn: *furu ike ya / kanawazu tobikomu / mizu no oto* ("old pond / frog jumped in / sound of water")

12 Thoreau, *Walden*, 77.

13 Quoted in Erwin Panofsky, *Abbot Suger on the Abbey Church of St.-Denis and its Art Treasures* (Princeton, NJ: Princeton University, 1946), 63, 65; Umberto Eco, *Art and the Middle Ages*, trans. by H. Bredin (New Haven, CT: Yale University Press, 1986), 14.

Chapter 2: Reconciliatory Longing: A Condition of Our Human Being

1 The conversion of Saul (d. Rome ca. 67 CE) to Paul occurred on the road to Damascus in the Roman Empire. See Acts 9:3–18. Paul and Peter were the primary apostles to Christ and the founders of the Christian Church.

2 Meyer Schapiro, "On a Painting of Van Gogh," in *Modern Art: 19th and 20th Centuries* (New York: George Braziller, 1979), 89–90.

3 Michael Hubner's clinical social work for the department of social service at Boston's Beth Israel Hospital resonates with my definition of the existential reality of intimated reconciliation grounded in the very separation and longing I witnessed in what I've called Milo's lament. For a lucid account of her clinical application of D. W. Winnicott's theory of transitional objects and phenomena ("Transitional Objects and Transitional Phenomena: A Study of the First Not-Me Possession," *The International Journal of Psychoanalysis* 34 (1953): 89–97), see her "Pain and Potential Space: Toward a Clinical Theory of Meaning," *Bulletin of the Menninger Clinic* 48, no. 5 (1984) 443–454: "I have suggested that pain—specifically, the pain of separation—is at the nexus of self and object and that each human being seeks return to a primordial state of given meaning in which self and object were one.... A variety of human activities and states... may be understood as acts of meaning. What these acts have in common is illusory reunion [intimations of reconciliation] with the primary object, a form of separation that is, paradoxically, a form of reunion."

4 Martin Buber, *I and Thou* [*Ich und Du* in the original German, 1923], trans. with prologue by Walter Kaufmann (New York: Simon & Shuster, 1970 [1923]), 77.

5 For C. S. Lewis this lifelong yearning is *Sehnsucht*, "Joy," "the inconsolable longing," St. Augustine's "restless heart" (*Confessions*, I,1), in P. Kreeft, *C. S. Lewis for the Third Millennium—Six Essays on* The Abolition of Man (San Francisco: Ignatius Press, 1994), 26. For a poetic account of an infant's coming to consciousness reconstructed by an adult in retracing memory to the "beginning" and expanding in a spiral to the periphery of awareness, echoing the creation story of Genesis from chaos to form, see Andrei Bely, *Kotik Letaev*, trans. by G. J. Janecek (Evanston, IL: Northwestern University, 1999), especially pp. 5–14 in which Milo's lament takes particular form. Gabriel Gonzalez, a student in the "Eros and Insight" seminar, pointed me to this text. Another seminar student, Richard Altieri, imagined "Separation" several years later:

> For the first few months after his birth,
> The watery blue of my son's eyes
> Was hollow. I could almost peer through it;
> I could almost see what he saw.
>
> He'd cry. Sometimes for milk or to be changed.
> But most often he wanted to be held.
> I'd feel the patter of his faint pulse
> As his tears gave way to warm, wet breathing.
> One night, as I held him tight against me,
> My son began to cry. I looked down
> And saw new eyes. The transparent blue was gone.
> In its place was a darker, more solid hue.
>
> And as his eyes beheld mine for the first time,
> Some part of him—some part of me—now knew
> That I was I; that he was he; and that loneliness
> Was the yearning to lose the self in others.

6 The plot summary of *Die tote Stadt* follows a synopsis that appears on the Erich Wolfgang Korngold website, which cites the New York Opera website. Based on the novel *Bruges-la-Morte*, written by Georges Rodenbach in 1892, and first performed in 1920, the opera surely embodies in sound and word the hopeful yearning following the devastation of World War I. Johan Huizinga's contemporary *Herbst des Mittelalters*, unfortunately translated not as the "harvest" but *The Waning of the Middle Ages*, found similar optimism is his rediscovery of the art of the fifteenth-century Flemish painters, most especially Jan van Eyck.

7 Henry David Thoreau, *Walden*, in *Walden and Other Writings,* ed. by B. Atkinson (New York: Modern Library, 1992), 84–85.

8 John O'Donohue, *To Bless the Space Between Us: A Book of Blessings* (New York: Doubleday, 2008), 83–84.

9 Rainer Maria Rilke, *Letters to a Young Poet*, trans. by M. D. Herter Norton (New York: Norton, 1993 [1934]), 27; John J. L. Mood, *Rilke on Love and Other Difficulties* (New York: Norton, 1975), 25.

10 All quoted verses from the Bible come from the New Revised Standard Version unless otherwise cited.

11 Raymond Carver, in the title work of *Cathedral: Stories* (New York: Vintage, 1989) brings cathedral building home to the embodied imagination: when a blind man asks the narrator to help him draw a cathedral so that he may envision its physical shape and properties in his mind's eye, the narrator experiences a catharsis to change his understanding of what it means to "see."

12 Simone Weil, *Gravity and Grace*, trans. by A. Wills (Lincoln: University of Nebraska Press, 1952), 45 (italics in original).

13 Ibid., 45, 55.

14 Robert Kegan, *The Evolving Self: Problem and Process in Human Development* (Cambridge, MA: Harvard University Press, 1982) and *In Over Our Head: The Mental Demands of Modern Life* (Cambridge, MA: Harvard University Press, 1994).

15 Rilke, *Letters to a Young Poet*, 50.

16 See Francesco J. Varella, Eleanor Rosch, and Evan T. Thompson, *The Embodied Mind* (Cambridge, MA: MIT Press, 1992). Recent neuroscientific understanding (Lisa Feldman Barrett, "Your Brain Is Not For Thinking," *New York Times*, Nov. 23, 2020) appears to confirm Shakespeare's poetry, "the art itself is Nature" as well as my corresponding "reconciliatory longing," which results in deliberate and purposeful acts of contemplative art, beauty, and love that seek wholeness from a lived condition of limitation. Barrett describes in simple terms the neurological process of body budgeting, or allostasis, in which activities like walking and running deplete our bodies of energy while activities like eating and sleeping serve as deposit to replenish that energy. She offers exemplary evidence with thirst: the brain recognizes from past experience drinking water hydrates the body—and thus allows us to feel less thirsty in seconds, even though the water takes some twenty minutes to move into the blood stream. To Barrett's thirst I would add, hunger, fatigue, cold, heat, confusion, fear, loneliness, and grief. In this light, our body, brain and mind may assume their natural syzygetic relationship.

17 Wallace Stevens, quoted from "Angel Surrounded by Paysans," *The Collected Poems of Wallace Stevens* (New York: Vintage, 1990), 496.

18 Wallace Stevens, "Final Soliloquy of the Interior Paramour," in Stevens, *Collected Poems*, 524.

19 Christopher A. Dustin, "The Liturgy of Theory: Lessons on Beauty and Craft," *The Tangeman Lecture*, delivered April 27, 2003; Christopher A. Dustin and Joanne E. Zeigler, *Practicing Mortality: Art, Philosophy, and Contemplative Seeing* (New York: Palgrave Macmillan, 2005).

20 My colleague Rowland Abiodun made this rich connection for me. See his recent comprehensive study, *Yoruba Art and Language: Seeking the African in African Art* (New York: Cambridge University Press, 2014), 88–120. In a presentation to the colloquium "Re-Imagining the Human in a Technological Age," offered by Professor Zajonc and me, Professor Abiodun began with a sustained Yoruba invocation to Osun. After nearly ten minutes of uninterrupted oral poetry, Professor Abiodun said simply, "Now that Osun is present with us, we may begin."

21 Buber, *I and Thou* [*Ich und Du*, original in 1923]. See Walter Kaufman's prologue, 14 and 35. Kaufmann justifies his reasons—and I offer here a simplified summary—for choosing to translate the German words "Ich" and "Du" within the text as "I and You." (The word *Thou* nevertheless remains in the title.) In German the second-person singular pronoun "Du" is not even similar to "Thou": As Kaufmann explains, "German lovers say *Du* to one another, and so do friends. *Du* is spontaneous and unpretentious, remote from formality, pomp and dignity." And if "Thou immediately brings to mind God," writes Kaufmann, it makes us think not of "the God to whom one might cry out in gratitude, despair, or agony" but rather "the God of the pulpits, the God of the holy tone.... *Thou* is a preachers' word, but also dear to anticlerical romantic poets... but it has no place whatever in the language of direct, nonliterary, and spontaneous human relationships."

22 Martin Heidegger, "Building Dwelling Thinking," in *Poetry, Language, Thought* (New York: Harper Collins, 1971), 147–148: "By a *primal* oneness the four—earth and sky, divinities and mortals—belong together in one." "This simple oneness of the four we call *the fourfold*. Mortals *are* in the fourfold by *dwelling*. But the basic character of dwelling is to spare, to preserve. Mortals dwell in the way they preserve the fourfold in its essential being, its presencing. Accordingly, the preserving that dwells is the fourfold."

23 Thoreau, *Walden*, 85–86.

24 Carl G. Jung, *The Undiscovered Self* [original 1958], trans. by R. F. C. Hull (New York: Penguin, 2006).

25 Thoreau, *Walden*, 77.

26 Marguerite Porete (1250–1310), *The Mirror of Simple Souls*, trans. by E. L. Babinsky (New York: Paulist Press, 1993).

27 Although it is obviously impossible to determine precisely *what* an infant perceives visually and aurally, infantile perception and cognition have become a focused

subject of developmental psychology. See L. B. Cohen, "Our Developing Knowledge of Infant Perception and Cognition," *American Psychologist*, 34, no. 10 (Oct. 1979): 894–899; *Infant Vision*, ed. by F. Vital-Durand, J. Atkinson, and O. J. Braddick (Oxford: Oxford University, 1996); *Perceptual Development: Visual, Auditory, and Speech Perception in Infancy*, ed. by A. Slater (East Sussex, UK: Psychology Press, 1998). Post-cognitive experience, reported in near-death episodes, may recapitulate the infantile reality of precognitive sensory response to the world, especially in the realm of sound—"celestial" music—"white" light and, perhaps, weight.

28 See chapter 10, note 14.

29 William James, *The Principles of Psychology*, 2 vols. (New York: Henry Holt, 1890), 488, quoted in M. T. Swanston and N. J. Wade, *Visual Perception: An Introduction* (Philadelphia: Taylor and Francis, 2001), 23–24.

30 James Ackerman, "'*Ars Sine Scientia Nihil Est*': Gothic Theory of Architecture at the Cathedral of Milan," *The Art Bulletin* 31, no. 2 (June 1949): 84–111: "The medieval builder is evidently concerned with the problem of balancing theory (or *scientia*) and practice (or *ars*). In no sense is this equivalent to the distinction between structure and form. Structure and form are intimately related and interconnected in every step of the creative process" (107). Ackerman's conclusion points toward an intimation of reconciliation between *ars* and *scientia*: "The modern argument for form versus structure is as meaningless as the medieval argument of *ars* versus *scientia*, for it likewise disrupts a partnership which can function only in happy union" (107–108). P. Frankl, *The Gothic: Literary Sources and Interpretations through Eight Centuries* (Princeton, NJ: Princeton University Press, 1960), 57–86. See also note 44 below.

31 Charles de Tolnay, *Hieronymous Bosch* (New York: Reynal with William Morrow, 1966), 360–363; Stefan Fischer, *Hieronymous Bosch: The Complete Works*, trans. by K. Williams (Cologne: Taschen, 2013).

32 William Shakespeare, "[Sonnet] 116," *Shakespeare's Sonnets and Poems*, The Folger Shakespeare Library (New York: Washington Square, 2004), 251.

33 William Shakespeare, "[Sonnet] 146," *Shakespeare's Sonnets and Poems*, 313.

> Poor soul, the centre of my sinful earth,
> Feeding these rebel powers that thee array,
> Why dost thou pine within, and suffer dearth,
> Painting thy outward walls so costly gay?
> Why so large cost, having so short a lease,
> Dost thou upon thy fading mansion spend?
> Shall worms, inheritors of this excess,
> Eat up thy charge? Is this thy body's end?
> Then soul, live thou upon thy servant's loss,

And let that pine to aggravate thy store;
Buy terms divine in selling hours of dross;
Within be fed, without be rich no more:
So shalt thou feed on Death, that feeds on men,
And, Death once dead, there's no more dying then.

34 Thoreau, *Walden*, 85.

35 Hans Morevec, *Mind Children: The Future of Robot and Human Intelligence* (Boston: Harvard University, 1990).

36 Václav Havel, acceptance speech on receiving The Liberty Medal at Independence Hall, Philadelphia, on July 4, 1994, "The New Measure of Man," *New York Times*, July 8, 1994, 27; also, as "The Need for Transcendence in the Postmodern World," http://www.worldtrans.org/whole/havelspeech.html, 2; republished with small changes in Havel, *The Art of the Impossible: Politics as Morality in Practice—Speeches and Writings, 1990–1996* (New York: Fromm, 1998).

37 Hesiod, *The Homeric Hymns and Homerica*, trans. by H. G. Evelyn-White (Cambridge, MA: Harvard University Press, 1914).

38 Wallace Stevens may have echoed a lingering danger of such hubris. Compare his line "Yet I am the necessary angel of earth," in "Angel Surrounded by Paysans," *The Collected Poems of Wallace Stevens*, 496.

39 Thoreau, *Walden*, 20: "I have thought that Walden Pond would be a good place for business, not solely on account of the railroad and the ice trade; it offers advantages which it may not be good policy to divulge; it is a good port and a good foundation. No Neva marshes to be filled; though you must everywhere build on piles of your own driving. It is said that a flood-tide, with a westerly wind, and ice in the Neva, would sweep St. Petersburg from the face of the earth."

40 Stephen J. Gould, "Nonoverlapping Magisteria," *Natural History* 106 (March 1997): 16–22. For a contemplative alternative to NOMA, see chapter 10 in the section titled "Via Amoris: A Way of Love, Where Love is the Means" and the carpet page of the Book of Durrow.

41 Although isolated in darkness, the Earth in the photograph from space, taken in 1968 from Apollo 8, is apparently less than a complete circle. The famous image called the "Blue Marble" was made by the crew of Apollo 11 in 1972. Image 2.10, *Earth from Space*, is a composite photograph made by NASA in 2002.

42 Archibald MacLeish, "Riders on the Earth, Brothers in Eternal Cold," *The New York Times*, Dec. 25, 1968; later published in *Riders on the Earth: Essays and Recollections* (Boston: Houghton Mifflin, 1978), xvi.

43 Ironically, contemporary digitalization of reality only extends this observational "distance" even as it refines optical precision.

44 So too, the randomness of Jackson Pollock's "disembodied" paintings is contained within carefully organized rectangles.

45 Looking ahead to chapter 8: Leonardo da Vinci may have confirmed the reality of collaborating epistemologies as the path to *eruditio*, leading to *sapientia* (wisdom) in his famous "notebook" phrase, "Two weaknesses leaning against one another add up to one strength." Quoted in Panofsky, *Meaning in the Visual Arts*, 19. Walter Isaacson's stunning 2017 account of Leonardo's life and work, grounded in extensive scholarly research, makes no mention of the relation of *ars* and *scientia* even though examples of their integration appear in Leonardo's hand and voice. Isaacson, *Leonardo da Vinci* (New York: Simon & Schuster, 2017). Isaacson's recommendation to "avoid [epistemological] silos," drawing on the conclusion that Leonardo "knew that art was a science and science was an art" (522–523) does not identify this overlap of art and science with the premodern human capacity for *ars* and *scientia* with which Leonardo was surely familiar since the great debate about their role in architecture took place in Milan. They were different, even contradictory—as "experience" and "order"—but not opposed. Together, they inform human imagination and learning (*eruditio*) reaching toward infinite wholeness (*sapientia*). Perhaps Isaacson's closing words—"be open to mystery"—do. See also note 30 above.

46 See chapter 9; see also, Plato, *The Symposium*, trans. by Christopher Gill (London: Penguin, 1999), 50.

47 Thomas à Kempis, *The Imitation of Christ*, trans. by William Creasy (Notre Dame, IN: Ave Maria, 2004), 30. Creasy's translation is particularly effective for those wishing to behold with this enduring masterpiece of spiritual aspiration, but I have added the bracketed word and phrase to identify my own non-ecclesiastical understanding.

Chapter 3: Focused Attention and Open Awareness: Rembrandt van Rijn

1 Japanese tea ceremonies I've attended end with the tea master pouring cold water to extinguish the sound of boiling water with which it began, resulting in a distinct and palpable awareness of silence.

2 In Catholic worship, the sound of three bells opens the liturgical *interval* of the Canon of the Holy Mass in which the mystical "presence" of Christ occurs.

3 Robert Frost, *Collected Poems, Prose, and Plays* (New York: The Library of America, 1995), 39–40.

4 Frost's intentional involvement of the reader (beholder) in "Mending Wall" may be suggested in the publication of *North of Boston* (New York: Henry Holt, 1914), where "Mending Wall" follows the poetic invitation to the reader that opens the book—"you come too"—titled "The Pasture."

> I'm going out to clear the pasture spring;
> I'll only stop to rake the leaves away

(And wait to watch the water clear, I may):
I sha'n't be gone long. — You come too.
I'm going out to fetch the little calf
That's standing by the mother. It's so young,
It totters when she licks it with her tongue.
I sha'n't be gone long. — You come too.

5 Perhaps synesthesia, like poetry, opens multiple intervals of interrelated cognition fostering the experience of intimated reconciliation, in this case between sound and space.

6 Václav Havel, Acceptance speech on receiving The Liberty Medal at Independence Hall, Philadelphia, on July 4, 1994, "The New Measure of Man," *New York Times*, July 8, 1994; also as "The Need for Transcendence in the Postmodern World," http://www.worldtrans.org/whole/havelspeech.html; republished with small changes in *The Art of the Impossible: Politics as Morality in Practice—Speeches and Writings, 1990–1996*, Fromm International, New York, 1998.

7 Martin Luther (1483–1546), *Against the Heavenly Prophets in the Matter of Images and Sacraments*, in H. W. Janson, *History of Art*, 5th edition (New York: Abrams, 1995), 626.

8 John Keats, *The Letters of John Keats*, ed. by H. E. Rollins, 2 vols. (Cambridge: Cambridge University Press, 1958), vol. 1, 193–194. See chapter 8 to compare Nicholas of Cusa's "learned ignorance."

9 Quoted in Erwin Panofsky, *Abbot Suger on the Abbey Church of St.-Denis and its Art Treasures* (Princeton, NJ: Princeton University Press, 1946), 63, 65.

10 Johann Wolfgang von Goethe, *Faust,* Part One, A Norton Critical Edition, trans. by W. Arndt, ed. by C. Hamlin (New York: Norton, 2001), lines 1692, 1695, and 1700 (lines 1699–1706, quoted below).

If the swift moment I entreat:
Tarry a while! You are so fair!
Then forge the shackles to my feet,
Then I will gladly perish there!
Then let them toll the passing-bell,
Then of your servitude be free,
The clock may stop, its hands fall still,
And time be over then for me!

In concluding Part Two, Goethe has his redeemed, now-blind Faust imagine a beneficent and loving world as he repeats his fateful declaration with entirely new visionary meaning and urgency (lines 11578–11586, quoted below).

And so, ringed all about by peril, here
Youth, manhood, age will spend their strenuous year.
Such teeming would I see upon this land,
On acres free among free people stand.
Oh tarry yet, though art so fair!
My path on earth, the trace I leave within it
Eons untold cannot impair.
Foretasting such high happiness to come,
I savor now my striving's crown and sum.

11 Simone Weil (1909–1943), "Contradiction," in *Simone Weil, An Anthology*, ed. by S. Miles (New York: Grove, 2000), 240–241: "Man's great affliction, which begins with infancy and accompanies him till death, is that looking and eating are two different operations. Eternal beatitude is a state where to look is to eat."

12 Museum professionals may want to reimagine their function to include the creation of explicit circumstances for contemplative beholding with the art of works of art. See chapter 2, where I describe an installation I have imagined for Bosch's *Garden of Earthly Delights.*

13 Walter Liedtke, *Dutch Painting in The Metropolitan Museum of Art*, vol. 2 (New York: The Metropolitan Museum of Art, 2007), 629–659.

14 The current title, *Aristotle with a Bust of Homer*, replaced *Aristotle Contemplating a Bust of Homer* as recently as 2013. See Simon Schama, *Rembrandt's Eyes* (New York: Knopf, 1999), 582–591. Schama has suggested that the figure should be identified as Apelles rather than Aristotle. Don Antonio Ruffo's own inventory identified the figure as either Aristotle or Albertus Magnus.

15 Julius S. Held, *Rembrandt's Aristotle, and other Rembrandt Studies* (Princeton, NJ: Princeton University, 1969).

16 See chapter 10, note 14.

17 At the time of this painting, Rembrandt made many images that challenge a similar experience of self-conscious separation and involvement. For two examples see images 3.43 and 3.44.

18 Schama, *Rembrandt's Eyes*, 18. Here Schama may have been referring to this fundamental artistic reality in his description of this painting as "a compact grammar; an account of painting as both noun and verb; the calling and the labor; the machinery and the magic; the elbow grease and the magic."

19 Rembrandt's self-portraits at this time suggest as much, especially his *Self Portrait* in Edinburg; see image 3.46.

20 *Aristotle with a Bust of Homer* was once the most expensive painting sold in America.

21 Weil, *Gravity and Grace*, 151.

22 Rainer Maria Rilke, *Letters to a Young Poet*, trans. by M. D. Herter Norton (New York: Norton, 1993 [1934]), 27.

23 Weil, *Gravity and Grace*, 151.

24 My suggestion of Rembrandt's use of dark neutral blue-violet across the upper border of *Aristotle with a Bust of Homer* draws on my perception of the apparently deliberate relationship of color values—red to green, neutral yellow to neutral blue-violet—in his pictorial construction of illusory space combined with the two-dimensional counterpoint of rising movement and poised suspension that runs along the central axis to foster a moment of contemplative release in the beholder.

Color ranging from purple to violet and red-violet occurs in several of Rembrandt's well-known paintings from early to late in his career, including as examples: *History Painting*, 1629, Stedelijk Museum De Lakenhal; *Raising of Lazarus*, 1630/31, Los Angeles County Museum; *Belshazzar's Feast*, 1635, National Gallery, London; *The Syndics*, 1663, Rijksmuseum, Amsterdam; *The Jewish Bride*, 1665, Rijksmuseum, Amsterdam. In *The Jewish Bride* there is a sublime chromatic blending in the shadow of the man's right sleeve of neutral purple and violet with red-violet and red of the woman's dress across the central axis of the composition; *Self-Portrait*, 1669, National Gallery, London, UK. For a detailed and completely comprehensible account of Rembrandt's working techniques based on both associated theory and direct practice, see Ernst van de Wetering, *Rembrandt: The Painter at Work* (Amsterdam: Amsterdam University, 1997), especially chapters, 6, 7, 9, and 10.

25 For examples, see Millard Meiss, *French Painting in the Time of Jean de Berry: The Boucicaut Master* (New York: G. Braziller, 1968); *French Painting in the Time of Jean de Berry: The Limbourg Brothers and Their Contemporaries* (New York: G. Braziller, 1974); and *The Belle Heures of Jean, Duke de Berry* (New York: The Cloisters, The Metropolitan Museum of Art, G. Braziller, 1974). Compare Rainer Maria Rilke's poetic *Book of Hours*: *Love Poems to God*, trans. by A. Barrows and J. Macy (New York: Riverhead, 1996).

26 Mark Rothko (1903–1970) rejected the notion that he was an abstract (disembodied?) painter interested only in "color." In his words, he was engaged "only in expressing basic human emotions—tragedy, ecstasy, doom, and so on. And the fact that a lot of people break down and cry when confronted with my pictures shows that I can communicate those basic human emotions.... The people who weep before my pictures are having the same religious experience I had when I painted them. And if you, as you say, are moved only by their color relationship, then you miss the point." Rothko, quoted in J. Baal-Teshuva, *Mark Rothko, 1903–1970: Pictures as Drama* (New York: Taschen, 2003), 50. I recall somewhere Rothko saying simply: "These are my tears."

27 To imagine Rembrandt's *Aristotle with a Bust of Homer* as no more than an oily rag may be a comfortable conclusion for materialist scientific reductionism.

28 Weil, "Contradictions," in *Simone Weil, An Anthology*, 240–241.

29 See chapter 2, note 21, where I explain why, like Kaufmann, I prefer to use "You" rather than "Thou" to translate the German second-person-singular pronoun when referring directly or in reference to Martin Buber *I and Thou*, [*Ich und Du* in the original German], trans. by W. Kaufmann (New York: Scribner's, 1996).

30 Rembrandt's artistic embrace of blindness may or may not have come from his own concern with cataracts or blindness in his family. In his detailed discussion of Rembrandt's sustained interest in the story of Tobit and Tobias, based on the apocryphal Book of Tobit, included in the Dutch Bible in 1618, Julius S. Held suggested the possibility that Rembrandt's father was blind. See Julius S. Held, *Rembrandt and the Book of Tobit* (Northampton, MA: Gehenna, 1964), 27–28. From my perspective, Rembrandt's more than fifty paintings, drawings, and prints of the story of a son's curing the blindness of his father offer artistic testimony of new insight occasioned by equally sustained contemplative beholding with the art of works of art, including, of course, the consummate exemplar of *Aristotle with a Bust of Homer.*

31 Aristotle, *Problemata*, XXX.1, 953a10–14, trans. by E. S. Forster (Oxford, UK: Clarendon, 1927).

32 My observation here draws on the experience of a 2001 exhibition of Willem de Kooning's late paintings in the Corcoran Gallery in Washington, DC. For a broad discussion of artistic process, mental acuity, and aging, see T. J. Clark, Caroline Tanner, and Laurens Park White, "Painting from Memory: Aging, Dementia, and the Art of Willem de Koonig," Occasional Papers of the Doreen B. Townsend Center for Humanities, no. 5 (Berkeley, CA: Doreen B. Townsend Center for Humanities, 1996), 1–39.

33 See relevant sections in chapter 9 for Plato's *Symposium.*

34 Josef Pieper, *Only the Lover Sings: Art and Contemplation* (San Francisco: Ignatius, 1990), 25 and 33 (epigraph); 25 (here): "An activity which is meaningful in itself, first, cannot be accomplished except with an attitude of receptive openness and attentive silence—which, indeed, is the exact opposite of the worker's attitude marked by concentrated exertion. One of the fundamental human experiences is the realization that the truly great and uplifting things in life come about perhaps not without our own efforts but nonetheless not through those efforts. Rather, we will obtain them only if we can accept them as gifts."

Chapter 4: Embracing the Obverse: Johann Wolfgang von Goethe

1 In 1809, at age sixty, Goethe (1749–1832) began to reflect on the youthful origins of the artistic path his life had taken; he completed writing a year before his death. His published reflections contain vivid memories of his arrival in Strasbourg and chronicle the transforming effect of his encounters

with the cathedral. Johann Wolfgang von Goethe, *Poetry and Truth from My Own Life*, vol. 1, trans. by M. Steele Smith (London: G. Bell and Sons, 1930), 316–354.

2 Goethe's recollections of his architectural experiences in Strasbourg echo Frederick Schiller's (1759–1805) contending "impulses" seeking reconciliation in the form of a "play impulse" (intimations of reconciliation, perhaps), identified by Schiller as "Beauty." Frederick Schiller, *On the Aesthetic Education of Man*, trans. by R. Snell (Mineola, NY: Dover, 2004), see especially "Letters" 12–16, pp. 64–84). From another perspective, they embody an early experience of the Goethean *aperçu*. *Goethe's Way of Science: A Phenomenology of Nature*, ed. by D. Seamon and A. Zajonc (Albany: SUNY, 1998).

3 Goethe, *Poetry and Truth*, 318–320: "And from the summit [tower], I saw before me the beautiful country which was to be my home for some time: the noble city, the wide meadows around it, thickly set with spreading trees, that striking richness of vegetation which follows the windings of the Rhine, and marks its banks and its islands, large and small. Nor is the lowland, stretching from the south, and watered by the Iller, less rich in varied green. Even westward, towards the mountains, there is much low-lying ground, which affords quite as charming a view of wood and meadow-growth, whilst the northern and more hilly part is intersected by innumerable little brooks, which induce a rapid vegetation everywhere. Added to these luxuriant meadows, to this prodigal wealth of scattered groves, let the imagination picture green ripening tracts of highly cultivated arable land, where hamlets and farmsteads mark the most fertile spots, and all this vast immeasurable plain, prepared for man like a new paradise, bounded far and nearby mountains partly cultivated, partly overgrown with woods; it will then be possible to conceive the rapture with which I blessed the kind of fate that has appointed me, for some time to come, so beautiful a dwelling-place." And later (334): "It was exactly like being carried up into the air by a balloon."

4 Ibid., 319–320: "After my descent to the square, I still tarried awhile in front of the venerable pile; but what I could not quite clearly explain to myself, either on this or subsequent occasions, was that I looked upon this stone miracle as a monster, which would have struck terror into me, if its regularity had not made it possible to grasp the whole conception, whilst its finish gave pleasure to the eye. Yet I did not trouble myself with meditating on this contradiction, but suffered this astonishing monument quietly to work upon me by its presence."

5 Johann Wolfgang von Goethe, "On German Architecture," trans. by E. G. Holt, in *A Documentary History of Art* (New York: Doubleday, 1958), 364–365. This first youthful response may be compared with Goethe's memory of the occasion nearly forty years later. See Goethe, *Poetry and Truth*, 341–345.

6 Goethe, "On German Architecture," 365.

7 Ibid., 361–363. For clarity I have substituted the word "fortune" in brackets to replace "possession." These "ants" are presumably the biased French and Italian aesthetes who do not comprehend Steinbach's vision any more than secularized Enlightenment thinking preserves the divinity of wholeness.

8 Ibid., 362–363.

9 Ibid., 364.

10 Ibid., 365–366.

11 Johann Wolfgang von Goethe, "Epirrhema," in *Goethe's Werke,* Hamburgischer Ausgabe, vol. 1, ed. E. Tunz (Munich: C. H. Beck, rev. ed, 1981), 358; translation by A. Zajonc, who gave me this vital reference.

12 Goethe, "On German Architecture," My italics for emphasis.

13 Ibid., 369.

14 Compare, in Martin Buber, *I and Thou,* trans. by W. Kaufmann (New York: Simon & Shuster, 1970), 62: "The You encounters me by grace—it cannot be found by seeking. But that I speak the basic word to it is a deed of my whole being, is my essential deed."

15 See Edward Snow, *The Poetry of Rilke* (New York: North Point, 2009), 425.

16 Rainer Maria Rilke, *Sonnets to Orpheus*, II, 11 (italics Rilke's: "*Töten ist eine Gestalt unseres wandernden Trauern . . .*"), trans. by J. J. L. Mood, in *Rilke on Love and Other Difficulties* (New York: Norton, 2004 [1975]), 135–138.

17 Rainer Maria Rilke, *Letters to a Young Poet*, trans. by M. D. Herter Norton (New York: Norton, 1993 [1934]), 27; John J. L. Mood, *Rilke on Love and Other Difficulties* (New York: Norton, 1975), 25.

18 Johann Wolfgang von Goethe, *Theory of Colours* [1810], originally trans. into English by C. L. Eastlake in 1840 (Cambridge, MA: MIT Press, 1970); David Seamon, "Goethe's Way of Science as a Phenomenon of Nature," *Janus Head* 8, no. 1 (2005): 86–101. Throughout the Middles Ages theologians often described the Virgin Mary as a spotless glass penetrated by a beam of sunlight. Goethe would surely have known Mary as both the "mediatrix" and the rose window that inspired Bernard of Clairvaux (St. Bernard) in the twelfth century to write the following explanation of the simile. "Just as the brilliance of the sun fills and penetrates a glass window without damaging it, and pierces its solid form with imperceptible subtlety, neither hurting it when entering nor destroying it when emerging: thus the Word of God, the splendor of the Father, entered the Virgin chamber and then came forth from the closed womb." Millard Meiss, "Light as Form and Symbol in Some Fifteenth-Century Paintings," *The Art Bulletin* 27, no. 3 (1945): 5–6.

19 Snow, *The Poetry of Rilke,* 425. Although to my ear the phrase "*wandering mourning*" in J. J. L. Mood's translation (see note 16 above) captures more directly Rilke's "*wandernden Trauerns*" in the final stanza of the sonnet than

Snow's "wandering sorrow," his translation of the concluding words hint at the fragile relation between killing and loving as the primal character of that *wandering mourning*, even as the poet's animation of those fateful curtains as "you" may recenter our moral imagination.

20 Goethe, *Poetry and Truth*, 348–354.

21 Ibid., 354.

22 Arthur Zajonc, "Every Object Well Contemplated, Changes Who You Are," *Ideas on the Nature of Science*, ed. D. Cayley (Fredericton, NB, Canada: Goose Lane Editions, 2009), 129–148.

23 Johann Wolfgang von Goethe, *Goethe: Scientific Studies,* ed. and trans. by D. Miller, New York: Suhrkamp, 1988), 55–56. Quoted in Johann Wolfgang von Goethe, *The Metamorphosis of Plants*, Introduction and Photography by G. L. Miller (Cambridge, MA: MIT Press, 2000), xxi.

Chapter 5: Measuring Contradiction: Piet Mondrian

1 Henry David Thoreau, "Walden," in *Walden and Other Writings,* ed. by Brooks Atkinson (New York: Modern Library, 1992), 85. You may of course repeat this experience using the full intensity equivalent of any other primary or secondary color, even as subtle pictorial variations of neutralized complementaries may whisper their meaning. Goethe's experience with color complementaries led to his articulation of the "Law of Required Change," described by Arthur Zajonc in "Goethe's Theory of Color and Scientific Intuition," *American Journal of Physics* 44, no. 4 (April 1976): 327–333. "This law states that as a strong impression is received its complement is produced by the individual, so that when the external stimulus is removed the complementary inner gesture becomes expressed—thus the appearance of an afterimage, tears when joyful, and so on. The eye then is *not* a passive device but rather a creative organ, one which 'demands completeness and seeks to complete the color circle in itself.'"

2 Jennifer Fitzpatrick (Jenny), Amherst College, Amherst, MA, Oct. 2011. Rumi's affectionate "Mouse and Frog" story may be read as an interior dialogue mirrored in Jenny's experience of intimated wholeness in color presence and absence; see Jalāl ad-Dīn Muhammad Rūmī (1207–1273), in *The Essential Rumi*, trans. by C. Barks (San Francisco: Harper, 1995), 79.

3 Compare Olivier Messiaen, *Lecture at Notre Dame,* trans. by T. J. Tikker (Alphonse Leduc, 2001), 12–13 [originally published 1978]: "'God bedazzles us by excess of Truth,' said Saint Thomas. 'Contemplation sees something, but what does it see? An excellence above all, which is not one thing, nor another.'"

4 Thomas Merton (1915–1968), "A Mid-summer Diary for M," in *Learning to Love: Exploring Solitude and Freedom (The Journals of Thomas Merton, Volume*

Six 1966–1967), ed. by Christine Bochen (San Francisco: Harper, 1998), 347–348.

5 Ibid., 320.

6 Ibid., 348.

7 Rainer Maria Rilke, *Letters to a Young Poet*, trans. by M. D. Herter Norton (New York: Norton, 2004 [1934]), 41. This quotation opens an eloquent account of the romantic relationship between Merton and M by a female Anglican priest with a similar experience. (See Cynthia Bourgeault, "Merton in Love," originally presented as a lecture to the Vancouver Chapter of the International Thomas Merton Society, Nov. 2000, http://merton.org/ITMS/Seasonal/27/27-2Bourgeault.pdf). Bourgeault concludes with the recognition that "the real vocation is to bear the paradox; to open one's heart and consciousness so deeply that one pierces through the apparent contraries of the surface—the great "either/ors" that give shape and definition to life at this level [*gravity*]—and sinks down into the underlying wholeness, the root of unity, allowing it to be restored and mirrored in the stillness of one's own being thus consecrated [*grace*]."

8 So too, love is the faithful entry into the mystical "cloud of unknowing." See Anonymous, *The Cloud of Unknowing* (14th century), ed. by E. Underhill (Charleston, SC: BiblioBazaar, 2007 [1922]).

9 Simone Weil, *Gravity and Grace*, trans. by A. Wills (Lincoln: University of Nebraska Press, 1952), 151.

10 See (in note 1) other references to Goethe. Also: "[The eye is] compelled to a form of opposition: setting extreme against extreme and intermediate against intermediate, it quickly merges opposites and strives to achieve a whole, both successively and simultaneously in time and space." (Quoted and trans. by A. O. Tantillo, "The Subjective Eye: Goethe's *Farbenlehre and Faust*," in *The Enlightened Eye: Goethe and Visual Culture*, ed. by E. K. Moore and P. A. Simpson (Amsterdam and New York: Editions Rodopi, 2007), 271. See also Johann Wolfgang von Goethe, *Theory of Colour* (1810), trans. by C. L. Eastlake (Cambridge, MA: MIT Press, 1970; David Seamon, "Goethe's Way of Science as a Phenomenon of Nature," *Janus Head* 8, no. 1 (2005): 86–101, n. 2; David Seamon and A. Zajonc, (eds.), *Goethe's Way of Science: A Phenomenology of Nature* (Albany: SUNY, 1998); Arthur Zajonc, *Catching the Light: The Entwined History of Light and Mind* (New York: Bantam, 1993).

11 David Bohm, *The Special Theory of Relativity* (New York: W. A. Benjamin, 1965), 148, quoted in Parker J. Palmer and Arthur Zajonc, with Megan Scribner, *The Heart of Higher Education: A Call to Renewal* (San Francisco: Jossey-Bass, 2010), 67.

12 Ernst Mach, *The Analysis of Sensations, and the Relation of the Physical to the Psychical* (1897), trans. by C. M. Williams (London: Dover, 1959). Scott

Edgar, "The Limits of Experience and Explanation: F. A. Lange and Ernst Mach on Things in Themselves," *British Journal for the History of Philosophy* 21, no. 1 (2013): 100–121.

13 This is not to say Courbet never painted "angels" as realized in the art of his own unique beholding.

14 See Joop M. Joosten, *Catalogue Raisonné of the Work of 1911–1944*, vol. 2 (New York: Abrams, 1998), 323, n. 3.03).

15 I understand that Einstein's formula $E = mc^2$ acknowledges the need for a conversion factor in the mathematical squaring of the speed of light.

16 Albert Einstein, *The World as I See It* (New York: Philosophical Library/Open Road, 2015), 5. Italics mine, for emphasis.

17 Charmion von Wiegand, quoted in David Sylvester, *About Modern Art*, 2nd edition (New Haven, CT: Yale University Press, 2014), 132.

18 Ibid.

19 Unlike natural light, the harsh artificial illumination of the museum setting diminishes the very quiet effect of applied paint and the most subtle variations of color.

20 Mondrian sought to articulate his artistic aspiration verbally in his commentaries on Neo-Plasticism in the periodical *De Stijl*. For Mondrian's profound and enduring encounter with Madame H. P. Blavatsky, Rudolf Steiner, and theosophy in general, and their influence on his art, see Robert P. Welch, "Mondrian and Theosophy," in *Piet Mondrian: 1872–1944*, Centennial Exhibition (New York: Guggenheim Foundation, 1971), 35–51; John Milner, *Mondrian* (New York: Abbeville, 1992).

21 T. S. Eliot, "Burnt Norton," Four Quartets, in *Collected Poems, 1909–1962* (New York: Harcourt Brace Jovanovich, 1991), 177. "Burnt Norton" was first published in 1935.

22 Unfortunately, in my opinion, the white wall in the museum installation for both works obscures Mondrian's "white light," seriously diminishing their artistic presence.

Chapter 6: Breaking the Law of the Excluded Middle: *Ai-no-ma*

1 Bertrand Russell, writing in 1912 and quoted in *The Problems of Philosophy* (New York: Oxford University Press, 1997), 72–73, suggests there are traditionally three "Laws of Thought" that correspond to the "fact that things behave in accordance with them": (1) "*The law of identity*: 'Whatever is, is.' (2) *The law of contradiction*: 'Nothing can both be and not be.' (3) *The law of the excluded middle*: 'Everything must either be or not be.'" For Aristotle, in Metaphysics, Book IV, Part 7, trans. by W. D. Ross, 2nd edition (Oxford, Clarendon, 1928): "But on the other hand there cannot be an intermediate between contradictories, but of

one subject we must either affirm or deny any one predicate. This is clear, in the first place, if we define what the true and the false are. To say of what is that it is not, or of what is not that it is, is false, while to say of what is that it is, and of what is not that it is not, is true; so that he who says of anything that it is, or that it is not, will say either what is true or what is false." See also, *Great Books of the Western World*, ed. by R. M. Hutchins (Chicago: Encyclopedia Britannica, 1952), vol. 8, 525–526.

2 Contemplatively, we might imagine ourselves, like Rilke's famous panther, in a place where the observed becomes the observer. See Rainer Maria Rilke, "The Panther," in *The Selected Poetry of Rainer Maria Rilke*, ed. and trans. by S. Mitchell (New York: Vintage, 1989), 25.

3 Traditionally the Japanese, like the Chinese, present their family names first and their given names last. The author's name has been Westernized; his family name is Tanizaki.

4 Jun'ichirō Tanizaki, *In Praise of Shadows*, trans. by T. J. Harper and E. G. Seidensticker (Sedgwick, ME: Leete's Island Books, 1977), 7.

5 Amaterasu, daughter of the dieties Izanagi and Izanami, serves as the celestial progenitor of the human-divine emperor. See the reference later in this chapter to Heidegger's use of the word "dwelling," which comprises "earth and sky, divinities and mortals" (also see chapter 2, note 22).

6 Günter Nitschke, "Ma: Place, Space, Void," *Kyoto Journal* (Fall, 1988): 33–39; Richard B. Pilgrim, "Intervals (Ma) in Space and Time: Foundations for a Religio-Aesthetic Paradigm in Japan," *History of Religions* 24–25 (1984–1986): 255–277.

7 For an extensive glossary of Japanese terms, see *Japanese Architecture and Art Net Users System* (JAANUS, http://www.aisf.or.jp/~jaanus/, number 1). For the adaptation of a connecting *ai-no-ma* in a Shinto Hachiman shrine to Buddhist architecture joining the inner sanctuary (*naijin*) with the outer sanctuary (*gaijin*), see Kakichi Suzuki, *Early Buddhist Architecture in Japan*, trans. by M. N. Parent and N. S. Steinhardt (Tokyo: Kodansha International, 1980), 35; Mitsuo Inoue, *Space in Japanese Architecture*, trans. by Hiroshi Watanabe (New York: Weatherhill, 1981).

8 These additional *kanji* for *ai-no-ma* include 相の間 and 合の間 in which "*ai*" on the left may be trans. as "opponent," "other side," "mutual," "together," and on the right as "meet," "match," "coming together, "agreeing with." I am grateful to Professor Wako Tawa, Fusako Higuchi, and Thomas Rohlich for their translations.

9 Professor Thomas S. Rohlich kindly suggested to me one example of a similar sentiment in a Shinto poem (Imperial Collections # 1855 in the Shin-kokinshu): "Is it the cold night or my thin robes that make it seem so cold? Frost seems to have settled between the snow upon the shrine beams." (夜や寒き 衣

やうすき かたそぎの ゆきあひのまより 霜やをくらん—yo ya samuki/ koromo ya usuki/ katasogi no/ yuki-ahinoma yori/ shimo ya okuran—translation Rohlich). What is ***frost*** that settles ***between*** the snow upon the shrine beams? Is it two related truths: objective and subjective realities held together by something that is and is not snow? For general commentary on love in the Heian court, see Ivan Morris, *The World of the Shining Prince: Court Life in Ancient Japan* (New York: Vintage, 2013); "The Heian Period," in *The Cambridge Encyclopedia of Japan*, ed. by R. Bowring and P. Kornicki (New York: Cambridge University Press, 1993).

10 Murasaki Shikibu, *The Tale of Genji*, trans. by E. G. Seidensticker (New York: Knopf, 1992). See also the recent translation by Rynall Tyler (New York: Penguin, 2003) and Sei Shōnagon, *The Pillow Book: The Diary of a Courtesan in Tenth Century Japan*, trans. by A. Waley (North Clarendon, VT: Tuttle, 2011). Poetic versions of this *ai-no-ma* occur throughout *The Tale of Genji*. Genji's own words concerning a fragile moment with Murasaki capture the sense of a place of mysterious meeting, as in the fateful encounter of lovers reminiscent of Abbot Suger's "strange region of the universe": "People make a great deal of the flowers of spring and the leaves of autumn, but for me a night like this, with a clear moon shining on snow, is the best—and there is not a trace of color in it. I cannot describe the effect it has on me, weird and unearthly somehow. I do not understand people who find a winter evening forbidding" (*Tale of Genji*, 357). Genji's wistful reflection is also remarkably reminiscent of Robert Frost's "spring mischief" in his "Mending Wall," interpreted in my reading from chapter 3, as the inspiration of poetry that opens the void of new understanding at the core of contradiction into which grace will flow. Illustrated scrolls of the *Tale of Genji* are another abundant pictorial source of *ai-no-ma* (see *Reading the Tale of Genji: Its Picture-Scrolls, Text and Romance*, ed. by R. Stanley-Baker, M. Fuminobu, and J. Tambling (Folkestone, Kent: Global Oriental, 2009).

11 Murasaki Shikibu, *The Tale of Genji*, 6.

12 In 1959 Jun'ichirō Tanizaki published his novella *Bridge of Floating Dreams*, in which he develops and unites themes of searching: for the lost culture of Japan and for a lost mother. The book's title is a direct reference to "The Floating Bridge of Dreams," the last chapter of *The Tale of Genji* and a metaphoric reference to the dream-like quality of life and falling in love; the entire book draws heavily on the story of Genji and those who carry the plot forward after he dies. The atmospheric power conveyed in descriptions of the house gardens comes from the fact that Jun'ichirō Tanizaki based the physical setting in the novella on his own home in Kyoto, called Sekison-tei.

Motoko Rich's recent thoughts (*New York Times*, April 15, 2023) about *The Tale of Genji* that address a woman's perspective—hers and Murasaki Shikibu's—are sobering, especially those concerning the at times brutish behavior of the Radiant Prince. But focusing on Rich's admittedly contemporary rather than contemporaneous view may obscure the universal reality of separation and loss seeking solace that seems to have animated so much of the long story as it follows the sadness of Genji's dying mother and grieving father. Would that a contemplative Via Amoris might assure the syzygetic reality of mortal frailty, joy, and longing for wholeness beyond death from a humbly human perspective for us all.

13 I refer here as I did in the introduction (see the section titled "Toward a Living Reality") to David Foster Wallace, *This Is Water: Some Thoughts Delivered on a Significant Occasion about Living a Compassionate Life* (New York: Little, Brown, 2009).

14 See chapter 9 in this book for Plato's *Symposium* and the conflict between multiple and contradictory visions of love.

15 Murasaki Shikibu, *The Tale of Genji*, 18, 20.

16 Ibid., 102.

17 The author of *The Tale of Genji*, a woman whose real name has been lost or perhaps never preserved for posterity to protect her reputation, adhered to Heian court tradition in which fictional characters were referred to only by social class or rank (Shikibu is the rank of the author's father). Murasaki was adopted as the name of the heroine (Genji's beloved) to avoid confusion in commentaries and translations, as were other names used in lieu of rank and status.

18 So too, *murasaki* as color and the scent of lavender embodies life's unending melancholy reminiscent of Milo's infantile lament. In chapter 38, "The Bell Cricket," the sound of the bell cricket evokes an ever-present passage from "here" to "there" and back, most vivid in the autumn air of evening beneath a full moon.

19 *The Romance of Tristan and Iseult* (as retold by Joseph Bedier), trans. by H. Belloc (New York: Vintage/Random House, 1994), 41–45.

20 The Kyoto International Conference Center (Kokusaikaikan) was designed by Sachio Otani (1924–2013) who assisted Kenzō Tange (1913–2005) in designing the Hiroshima Peace Memorial Museum.

21 Simone Weil, *Gravity and Grace*, trans. by A. Wills (Lincoln: University of Nebraska Press, 1952), 151.

22 For Messiaen, see chapter 10, note 14. Kenneth Rexroth, *One Hundred Poems from the Japanese* (New York: New Directions, 1955), x and passim for numerous examples of this "poetry of sensibility" resonant with a poetic *ai-no-ma*. From the dedication page, an exchange between Murasaki and Genji:

MURASAKI:

The troubled waters
Are frozen fast.
Under clear heaven

Moonlight and shadow
Ebb and flow.

GENJI:

The memories of long love
Gather like drifting snow,
Poignant as the mandarin ducks,
Who float side by side in sleep.

23 The philosopher, poet, and mystic Friedrich von Hardenberg (1772–1801), who went by the pseudonym Novalis, sought the relation between a conscious "I" and infinite wholeness ("absolute I"). See "Fichte Studies, 1795–96," ed. by J. Kneller, in *Cambridge Texts in the History of Philosophy* (Cambridge: Cambridge University Press, 2003). The following explanation of how he pursued this search comes from Elizabeth Mittman and Mary R. Strand, "Introductory Essay: Representing Self and Other in Early German Romanticism," in *Theory and Practice: A Critical Anthology of Early German Romantic Writings*, Jochen Schulte-Sassa, General Editor (Minneapolis: University of Minnesota Press, 1997), 51–52: "Novalis's notion of the 'Non-I' leads to his concept of the 'You,' another being that is different from as well as independent of the self. Otherness as 'You' is not merely the opposite of the self. For Novalis, the 'absolute I,' then, is the paradoxical simultaneity of wholeness and division, sameness and otherness.... It is neither real nor ideal, but both at once....What Novalis calls 'absolute beginning' which is a retroactive 'construction' of a *subject who longs to return to the starting point of his/her consciousness*; the subject presupposes an originary 'act of freedom' that occurs outside of structures of differentiation, beyond the world of opposition." My italics for emphasis here may remind us of Milo's lament.

24 See chapter 2, note 22.

25 Utagawa Hiroshige is the artist's professional name (he was also known professionally as Ichiyūsai Hiroshige; his original name was Andō Tokutarō). For a similar feeling of conflated realities, compare Rilke's poem, "Before Summer Rain," in *The Selected Poetry of Rainer Maria Rilke*, 35.

26 The city of Kyoto itself is a richly organized spatial construction. Originally known as Heian-Kyō, the site of *The Tale of Genji*, Kyoto was the imperial capital of Japan for a thousand years. Kyoto was selected as the original target for the first atomic bomb, but was spared at the expense of Hiroshima and Nagasaki. See chapter 11, note 5.

27 For general information concerning the following Buddhist temples, see Gouvenor Mosher, *Kyoto: A Contemplative Guide* (Rutland, VT: Tuttle, 1978). Although now out of print, Mosher's guide is sensitive to the need for contemplation as well as information. For Sanzen-in see Mosher, 51–61.

28 For a still more animated version of this spiritual welcome, one might visit the temple called Eikan-do on the eastern border of Kyoto. Here a standing figure of the Amida Buddha is shown turning his head, according to legend, to greet the monk Eikan who, having lost track of time in his garden meditation, arrived late to the scheduled services, saying gently to him, "Eikan, you're late."

29 Pure Land Buddhism is one of the most widely practiced traditions of Buddhism in East Asia. In Japan it exists with Zen Buddhism under the large umbrella of the Mayahana sect, which has split from the other main sect, Theravada. The basis of the Pure Land practice is prayer and chanting to what the tradition names the Amida Buddha, which as I have suggested in this chapter, will guarantee a devotee to a place in the Pure Land (the equivalent of Western-conceived heaven). The Amida Buddha ("Celestial Buddha") should not be confused with the Buddha we traditionally know as a prince called Siddhartha, who promised no afterlife, paradise, or heaven. See David Watts Barton, "Zen Buddhism vs. Pure Land Buddhism," *Japanology*, May 15, 2017, https://japanology.org/2017/05/zen-buddhism-v-pure-land-buddhism/.

30 Rilke, "Buddha in Glory," *The Selected Poetry of Rainer Maria Rilke*, 69.

31 Zen Buddhism, also under the Mayahana umbrella (see note 29 above), is a more austere practice focused on meditation and inward probing, through which students of Zen endeavor to seek their true nature instead of expressing devotion to a deity.

32 For Shinju-an see Mosher, *Kyoto: A Contemplative Guide*, 256–266. Shinju-an (the Pearl Temple) was built by the priest Ikkyū at the end of the 15th century after Daitoku-ji was destroyed by fire during the Onin wars.

33 Sanskrit origin: *vahir*—outside; *awndar*—inside.

34 Mosher, *Kyoto: A Contemplative Guide*, 272–278.

35 Matsuo Bashō (1644–1694), *The Narrow Road to the Deep North and Other Travel Sketches*, translation N. Yuasa (New York: Penguin, 1966), 13.

36 Genji: "'And so here we are, rushing into monkish ceremonies side by side. Who would have expected it? Let us pray that we will share blossom-strewn lodgings in the next world.' Borrowing her inkstone, he wrote a poem on her cloves-dyed fan: 'Separate drops of dew on the leaf of the lotus, / We vow that we will be one, on the lotus to come.'" (Murasaki Shikibu, *The Tale of Genji*, 669).

37 Multiple rational "interpretations" of this garden all too easily distract our contemplative awakening here in favor of objectifying explanation and hence estrangement from the garden, the moment, and ourselves.

38 For Daisen-in see Mosher, *Kyoto: A Contemplative Guide*, 262–263.

39 Suffering from "Minamata disease," these people were afflicted by damage to the nervous system or congenital deformation caused by high levels of mercury deposited in the soil and water by a fertilizer factory in the town of Minamata, Japan.

Chapter 7: Lust to Solitude: From Grasping to Acceptance

1 See relevant comments in chapter 2, note 30, from James Ackerman on medieval architecture.

2 Friedrich Hölderlin, quoted in Martin Heidegger, "The Question Concerning Technology and Other Essays," trans. with introduction by William Lovitt (New York: Harper & Row, 1977), also available at https://mediatheoryart.wordpress.com/2016/02/03/the-question-concerning-technology-2/. See also note 10 below.

3 C. S. Lewis, *The Allegory of Love: A Study in Medieval Tradition* (New York: Oxford University, 1958), 1–23. See also, Francis X. Newman, *The Meaning of Courtly Love* (Albany: SUNY, 1968). For the tragic association of courtly love and the Cathars of Languedoc, see Denis de Rougemont, *Love in the Western World* (Princeton, NJ: Princeton University Press, 1983). The iconic story of the fatefully triangulated "love" of Tristan, Iseult, and King Mark assumes its artistic intimation of reconciliation at the moment in the Wood of Morois when the king reveals to the contemplative beholder the wisdom of sublimated love by "marrying" the adulterous lovers rather than killing them. See Joseph Bédier, *The Romance of Tristan and Iseult* (New York: Random House, 1965), 98–99 (also, the original 1900 text is available at Project Gutenberg, https://www.gutenberg.org/files/14244/14244-h/14244-h.htm#link2H_4_0010).

4 Eleanor of Aquitaine (1122/24–1204), a shining embodiment of the ideals of courtly love, animated the expanding presence of those ideals from France to England. See Ralph Turner, *Eleanor of Aquitaine: Queen of France, Queen of England* (New Haven, CT: Yale University Press, 2009), and Fiona Swabey, *Eleanor of Aquitaine, Courtly Love, and the Troubadours* (Westport, CT: Greenwood, 2004).

5 For biographical information, see Elizabeth Spearing, ed., *Medieval Writings on Female Spirituality*, with an introduction and notes by Elizabeth Spearing, and with extracts from *The Mirror of Simple Souls*, trans. by A. C. Spearing (New York: Penguin, 2002), xvi–xxi and 120–144. For extensive biography and the full text, see *Marguerite Porete: The Mirror of Simple Souls* trans. and introduced by Ellen L. Babinsky (New York: Paulist Press, 1993).

6 Spearing, *Medieval Writings on Female Spirituality*, xix.

7 Porete, quoted in Spearing, *Medieval Writings on Female Spirituality*, 124–125. Compare with St. Augustine "Love, and do what you will," see note 21.

8 Ibid., 121–122.

9 Rainer Maria Rilke, *Letters to a Young Poet,* translation M. D. Herter Norton (New York: Norton, 2004), 45. Italics mine, for emphasis. Rilke's definition of a "more human love" echoes precisely the behavioral aspiration of *fin'amor.*

10 Encouraged by Marguerite Porete, Arthur Zajonc and I tried this meditation exercise during a class meeting of our seminar "Eros and Insight." The first part of naming our current "values" went easily and quickly, resulting in a long

list eagerly and confidently shared by everyone. The second part of "taking leave" of these "virtues" was remarkably difficult. Students acknowledged feelings of disorientation, confusion, betrayal, and especially estrangement, fear, and a lurking danger. Nevertheless, slowly, hesitantly, several in the class began to articulate a new awareness in which a direct but unfamiliar experience of solitude rather than loneliness began to emerge. Is it possible that we had ventured into that extraordinary realm of art, if not love, that culminated Martin Heidegger's "Question Concerning Technology" (*Question Concerning Technology and Other Writings*, 34) in which art was no longer "a sector of cultural activity"?

> In Greece, at the outset of the destining of the West, the arts soared to the supreme height of the revealing granted them. They brought the presence [*Gegenwart*] of the gods, brought the dialogue of divine and human destining, to radiance. And art was simply called *technē* [my translation: beholding]. It was a single, manifold revealing. It was pious, *promos*, i.e., yielding to the holding-sway and the safekeeping of truth.
>
> The arts were not derived from the artistic. Art works were not enjoyed aesthetically. Art was not a sector of cultural activity.
>
> What, then was art—perhaps only for that brief but magnificent time? Why did art bear the modest name *technē*? Because it was a revealing that brought forth and hither, and therefore belonged with *poēsis*. It was finally that revealing which holds sway in all the fine arts, in poetry, and in everything poetical that obtained *poēsis* as its proper name.

The same poet [Friedrich Hölderlin, 1770–1843] from whom we heard the words:

But where danger is, grows
The saving power also.

says to us:

. . . poetically dwells man upon this earth.

11 Vincent van Gogh, *Letters: The Complete Illustrated and Annotated Edition*, ed. by L. Jansen, H. Luijten, and N. Bakker (New York: Thames and Hudson, 2009), vol. 5, 287–289 and vol. 6, in attached CD Rom.

12 *Van Gogh's Letters: Unabridged and Annotated* (web exhibit, in French), "Letter from Vincent Van Gogh to Theo van Gogh, Auvers-sur-Oise, c. July 10, 1890," accessed July 16, 2020, http://www.webexhibits.org/vangogh/letter/21/649-fr.htm?qp=feelings.apprehension. Note that the English translation provided by the website is somewhat more literal than the Jansen, Luitjen, and Bakker edition—"and I did not have to go out of my way very much in order to try to express sadness and extreme loneliness"—but still embellished.

13 Vincent van Gogh, *Letters: The Complete Illustrated and Annotated Edition*, 287.

14 Ibid., 289.

15 In addition to several other images of sunflowers, *Sunflowers in a Vase* (1888, oil on canvas, National Gallery, London, UK), is one of nine versions of this composition.

16 See chapter 2, note 2.

17 Robert Kegan, *The Evolving Self: Problem and Process in Human Development* (Cambridge, MA: Harvard University Press, 1982); Robert Kegan, *In over Our Heads: The Mental Demands of Modern Life* (Cambridge, MA: Harvard University Press, 1994). Thomas Merton associated love and solitude directly with true maturity. See Thomas Merton, *Learning to Love: Exploring Solitude and Freedom*, ed. by Christine M. Bochen (San Francisco: Harper, 1997); see entry under "April 14, 1966": "One thing suddenly hit me—that nothing counts except love and that solitude that is not simply the wide-openness of love and freedom is nothing. Love and solitude are the one ground of true maturity and freedom.... True solitude embraces everything, for it is the fullness of love that rejects nothing and no one, is open to All in All."

18 In completing the color value exercise earlier in the seminar, the students encountered directly the unavoidable presence of an infinite interval between black/white and red/green, not to mention that between "experience" and "order." Their effort to "take leave" of their "virtues" brought them further home as adults to that enduring reality of separation and longing first experienced as Milo's lament and then forgotten. Both occasions marked the change, growth, and transformation "Eros and Insight" sought to foster. The solitude that now informed them echoes the awareness of the Japanese poet and Buddhist priest, Saigyo (1118–1190) who found a similar kind of *dwelling* in his remote hut high in the mountains above Yoshino:

> A mountain village / where there is not even the hope / of a visitor – / if not for the loneliness, / how painful life here would be! (Trans. by D. Keene, *Seeds in the Heart*: *Japanese Literature from Earliest Times to the Late Sixteenth Century* ([New York: Columbia University, 1999]).
>
> I have given up / all hope of having visitors / in my home. / If not for solitude, / how dismal my life would be. (Trans. by S. D. Carter, *Traditional Japanese Poetry: An Anthology* [Stanford, CA: Stanford University Press, 1991], 167).

19 Porete, quoted in Spearing, *Medieval Writings on Female Spirituality*, 120. I've italicized *along with other observances* to emphasize that the beholding described here was more than mere observation of a painting.

20 *Lyrics of the Troubadours and Trouvères*: *An Anthology and a History*, translation and introduction by Frederick Goldin (Garden City, NY: Anchor/Doubleday, 1973), 100–101.

21 Porete, quoted in *Medieval Writings on Female Spirituality*, 125: "And yet, says Reason, I say this much, that he who has these two strings in his heart, the light of Faith and the power of Love, has permission to do what pleases him, by witness of God himself, who says to the Soul, 'Love Love, and do what you will.'" St. Augustine: "Once for all, then, a short precept is given you: Love, and do what you will: whether you hold your peace, through love hold your peace; whether you cry out, through love cry out; whether you correct, through love correct; whether you spare, through love do you spare: let the root of love be within, of this root can nothing spring but what is good." See Homily 7 on 1 John 4:4–12, trans. by H. Browne, in *Nicene and Post-Nicene Fathers,* First Series, vol. 7, ed. by P. Schaff (Buffalo, NY: Christian Literature, 1888), rev. and ed. for New Advent by Kevin Knight (reissued by Hendrickson, 2004).

22 *The Letters of Abelard and Heloise,* trans. by B. Radice (New York: Penguin, 1974), 51, 53, 55. Is it possible that *The Letters* might be read as Peter Abelard's own interior dialogue in which he, like Marguerite Porete, occupied multiple roles, including the integrative feminine one of Heloise?

23 Defining "sin" all too often invites retributive sinning. Defining "evil" invites the evil of "justifiable" killing. See chapter 8.

24 Rilke, *Letters to a Young Poet,* 50.

25 Jaufré Rudel, "When the Days Grow Long in May," in *The Soul Is Here For Its Own Joy*: *Sacred Poems from Many Cultures*, ed. by Robert Bly (New York: HarperCollins, 1995), 143; italics mine for emphasis.

26 The head and right forearm of this particular "crouching Aphrodite," housed in Naples, are modern restorations.

27 Kenneth Clark, *The Nude: A Study in Ideal Form* (Garden City, NY: Doubleday, 1956), 109–174.

28 *Kallipygos*, from the Greek *kalli* (beautiful) and *pygē* (buttocks).

29 Porete, quoted in Spearing, *Medieval Writings on Female Spirituality*, 128.

30 Bédier, *The Romance of Tristan and Iseult*, 151. Béroul (a 12th-century Norman poet), Thomas of Built (Thomas of Britain, living in England at the court of Henry II and Eleanor of Aquitaine), and Gottfried von Strassburg (early 13th century) all wrote versions of the romance.

Chapter 8: Dream of Reason: Redeemed by Humility

1 William Shakespeare, "[Sonnet] 116," *Shakespeare's Sonnets and Poems*, The Folger Shakespeare Library (New York: Washington Square, 2004), 251.

2 Dante Alighieri, "The Woman I Adore," in Robert Bly, *The Soul is Here for Its Own Joy: Sacred Poems from Many Cultures* (New York: HarperCollins, 1995), 145.

3 For a review of the wide range of literary disparagement of "Gothic," see Paul Frankl, *The Gothic: Literary Sources and Interpretation through Eight Centuries* (Princeton, NJ: Princeton University Press), 235–414.

4 C. S. Lewis, *The Allegory of Love: A Study in Medieval Tradition* (Cambridge: Cambridge University Press, 2013), 1–23.

5 Nicholas of Cusa, *On Learned Ignorance*, trans. by J. Hopkins (Minneapolis, MN: A. J. Banning, 1981).

6 Millard Meiss, "Light as Form and Symbol in Some Fifteenth-Century Paintings," *The Art Bulletin* 27, no. 3 (1945); Erwin Panofsky, *Early Netherlandish Painting: Its Origins and Character* (Cambridge: Cambridge University Press, 1953), 148. This text, from the "Little Chapter for Lauds on the Feast of the Assumption," is in the Book of Wisdom, VII, 29 and 26.

7 Meiss, "Light as Form and Symbol," and Panofsky, *Early Netherlandish Painting*, 148.

8 Panofsky, *Early Netherlandish Painting*, 147.

9 Meiss, "Light as Form and Symbol," 179. The modern trompe l'oeil frame around this painting replaces the lost original frame, which was apparently inscribed with words from a hymn that compares the miracle of the Incarnation of Christ to light passing through stained glass without shattering it, just as the Mother gave birth to the Child while remaining a virgin. Across the bottom of the frame, the words *Flos Floriolorum Appellaris* identified Mary as the flower of flowers. See also: Panofsky, *Early Netherlandish Painting*, 147–148; Elizabeth Dhanens, *Hubert and Jan Van Eyck* (New York: The Alpine Fine Arts Collection, 1980), 316–328, 390.

10 Abbot Suger, quoted in Erwin Panofsky, *Abbot Suger on the Abbey Church of St.-Denis and its Art Treasures* (Princeton, NJ: Princeton University Press, 1946), 63, 65; Umberto Eco, *Art and the Middle Ages*, trans. by H. Bredin (New Haven, CT: Yale University Press, 1986), 14.

11 For a recent survey of the long history that culminated in the Renaissance Dream of Reason, see Anthony Gottlieb, *The Dream of Reason: A History of Western Philosophy from the Greeks to the Renaissance* (New York: Norton, 2000).

12 One modern example of this new practical "wisdom" might be exemplified by Walter Lippmann in *A Preface to Morals* (Boston: Beacon, 1960 [1929]). The cultural historian Johan Huizinga quoted admiringly Michelangelo's famous putative dismissal of late medieval art exemplified by Jan van Eyck: "Flemish painting pleases all the devout better than Italian. The latter evokes no tears, the former makes them weep copiously. This is not a result of the merits of this art; the only cause is the extreme sensibility of the devout spectators. The Flemish pictures please women, especially the old and very young ones, and also monks and nuns, and lastly men of the world who are not capable of understanding true harmony. In Flanders they paint, before all things, to render exactly and deceptively the outward appearance of things.... Though the eye is agreeably impressed, *these pictures have neither art nor reason; neither symmetry nor proportion; neither choice of values nor grandeur. In short, this art is without power and without distinction*

[my italics]; it aims at rendering minutely many things at the same time, of which a single one would have sufficed to call forth a man's whole application." Huizinga followed his "quotation" of Michelangelo with the observation: "It was the medieval spirit itself which Michelangelo judged here." Huizinga, *Waning of the Middle Ages* (Mineola, NY: Dover, 1999 [1924]), 244. For Michelangelo's assessment of his own artistic accomplishments, see quotations in this chapter, cited in notes 59–61 below.

13 Marguerite Porete, *The Mirror of Simple Souls*, trans. and introduced by Ellen Babinsky (New York: Paulist Press, 1993), 79.

14 For some, technical analysis of this painting suggests the presence of artists other than or in collaboration with Albrecht Dürer. See P. Ackroyd, et al., "A Virgin and Child from the Workshop of Albrecht Dürer?" (London: The National Gallery Technical Bulletin 21, 2000), 28–42.

15 For an account of Dürer's travels to Antwerp and Ghent, see Erwin Panofsky, *The Life and Art of Albrecht Dürer* (Princeton, NJ: Princeton University Press, 1943), 205–210.

16 For a comprehensive account of the place of this singular self-portrait in the history of German art see Joseph Leo Koerner, *The Moment of Self-Portraiture in German Renaissance Art* (Chicago: University of Chicago Press, 1993).

17 Kenneth Clark, *A Catalog of the Drawings of Leonardo da Vinci in the Collection of His Majesty the King: At Windsor Castle* (New York: Macmillan, 1935); Kenneth Keele and Jane Roberts, *Leonardo da Vinci Anatomical Drawings from the Royal Library Windsor Castle* (New York: The Metropolitan Museum of Art, 1983); Frank Zöllner, *Leonardo da Vinci: Paintings, Sketches and Drawings* (London: Barnes & Noble, 2006); Martin Cleyton and Ron Philo, *Leonardo the Anatomist* (London: Royal Collection Publications, 2012).

18 Leonardo's particular classical conceptual understandings may have included Hippocrates, Avicenna, and Galen; see C. G. Gross, "Leonardo da Vinci on the Brain and Eye," *The Neuroscientist* 3, no. 5 (1997): 347–354.

19 See Keele and Roberts, *Leonardo da Vinci Anatomical Drawings*, 55 (no. 10).

20 See Michelle Legro, "Top Chef, Old Master: Leonardo in the Kitchen," *Lapham's Quarterly*, September 14, 2001, https://www.laphamsquarterly.org/roundtable/top-chef-old-master.

21 This arrangement of four groups of three, as in the central tympanum of the royal portal of the Cathedral of Chartres, may also refer symbolically to the "mystery" of the Trinity spread to the four corners of the world.

22 Hugo van der Goes's *Portinari Altarpiece* (oil on panel) came to the church of Santa Maria Nuova in Florence, Italy, in 1483.

23 Ernst Mach, *The Analysis of Sensations, and the Relation of the Physical to the Psychical* (1897), trans. by C. M. Williams (London: Dover, 1959). Compare this

association of Mach's with the *Last Supper* to one with Mondrian in chapter 5, image 5.11.

24 The debate among the disciples may be about more than a general reaction to Jesus's words warning of betrayal. It may also point to contemporaneous Dominican views concerning the nature of the liturgy of transubstantiation.

25 The *Last Supper* was apparently commissioned by Ludovico Sforza on the occasion of the death of his beloved wife. Would that the *Last Supper* might be offered as a devotional occasion of contemplative beholding, comparable to that suggested in chapter 2, for Hieronymous Bosch's *Garden of Earthly Delights* in the Prado, Madrid (images 2.7, 2.8.).

26 Bernard of Clairvaux, 7.5, from Cistercian Fathers' Series, *On the Songs of Songs*, 75.5, trans. by I. Edmunds (Kalamazoo: Cistercian Publications, 1980).

27 For a summary of the original iconography of the basilica of St. Peter, see James Snyder, *Medieval Art: Painting-Sculpture-Architecture, 4th–14th Century* (Upper Saddle River, NJ: Prentice Hall, 2006), 27–64.

28 The exceptionally rich iconographic program for the Sistine Chapel ceiling appears to have been largely that of Michelangelo himself. The preexisting decoration of the north, south, and east walls of the chapel includes images of the lives of Moses and Christ along with portraits of the popes.

29 In the context of the renewal of the basilica *The Delivery of the Keys* (1482) may be the most important of the preexisting wall frescoes, artistically and symbolically. In giving the keys to St. Peter, Christ established divine papal authority through the continuous succession of future apostolic popes.

30 David's unusual hat with its crown of laurel may even speak silently of a synchronic, if not learned, joining of contemporaneous Florence and ancient Greece in the form of a modern-day Socratic youth.

31 Emily Dickinson, "Tell All the Truth but Tell It Slant," in *The Complete Poems of Emily Dickinson*, ed. by T. H. Johnson (Boston: Little, Brown, 1960), 506–509.

32 Recalling the occasion of the atomic weapon test at the Trinity site, J. Robert Oppenheimer was quoted as saying in a television documentary on NBC recorded in 1965: "We knew the world would not be the same. A few people laughed, a few people cried, most people were silent. I remembered the line from the Hindu scripture, the Bhagavad Gita. Vishnu is trying to persuade the Prince that he should do his duty and to impress him takes on his multi-armed form and says, 'Now, I am become Death, the destroyer of worlds.' I suppose we all thought that one way or another." Quoted in James Grebey, "Why Did Oppenheimer Say, 'Now I Am Death, the Destroyer of the Worlds,' and What Did It Mean?", *SYFY Wire*, July 24, 2023, and Robert Jungk, *Brighter than a Thousand Suns: A Personal History of the Atomic Scientists* (New York: Harcourt Brace, 1958), 201.

33 See Gar Alperovitz, *Atomic Diplomacy: Hiroshima and Potsdam* (New York: Vintage Books, 1996) and *The Decision to Use the Atomic Bomb and the Architecture of an American Myth* (New York: Vintage Books, 1995); Herbert Feis, *The Atomic*

Bomb and the End of World War II (Princeton, NJ: Princeton University, 1966); Howard Zinn, *The Bomb* (San Francisco: City Lights, 2010).

34 Russell "Rusty" Schweickart (1935–), a retired Apollo astronaut, made this acknowledgment at a conference at Amherst College in 1995, echoing an address he gave to philosophers and theologians in Kyoto in 1987 and published as "Reflections: Our Backs Against the Bomb, Our Eyes on the Stars," *Discover*, July 1987, https://static1.squarespace.com/static/5c59cd6d7980b31c02d8a8fd/t/5c5b723724a69477fa2554ff/1549496888071/Backs_Against_the_Bomb.pdf.

35 Paul Fussell, *The Great War and Modern Memory* (Oxford: Oxford University Press, 1975), 7.

36 Zinn, *The Bomb*, 87.

37 Václav Havel, "The Need for Transcendence in the Postmodern World," http://www.worldtrans.org/whole/havelspeech.html.

38 Ibid.

39 Malina Jakub, *Prague Horloge: A Guide to the History and Esoteric Concept of the Astronomical Clock in Prague* (Czech Republic: Eminent, 2005).

40 Lois Schapiro, a musician and fellow beholder at Wellesley College, referred me to Theodor Adorno's words.

41 Saint Ambrose, The Sacrament of the Incarnation of Our Lord, in *Theological and Dogmatic Works*, trans. by R. J. Deferrari (Washington, DC: Catholic University of America, 1963), 44, 219–220.

42 The Seven Deadly Sins: Pride, Envy, Gluttony, Lust, Anger, Greed, Sloth (*acidia*). Hieronymous Bosch's *Table Top of the Seven Deadly Sins,* ca. 1500, in the Prado in Madrid, offers the human incarnation of these sins at precisely the time of the emerging Dream of Reason. Although this work of art is currently displayed as a painting hung on a museum wall, its art must include its presence as a table for a sacral meal.

43 Simone Weil, *Gravity and Grace*, trans. by A. Wills (Lincoln: University of Nebraska Press, 1952), 151.

44 Thomas à Kempis, *The Imitation of Christ*, trans. by W. Creasy (Notre Dame, IN: Ave Maria Press, 2004), 3. I have added the bracketed word and phrase to connect it to my own non-ecclesiastical understanding.

45 John Lewis, "Together, You Can Redeem the Soul of Our Nation," *New York Times*, July 30, 2020.

46 St. John of the Cross, *Dark Night of the Soul* and *Ascent of Mount Carmel*, trans. by Kieran Kavanaugh and Otilio Rodriguez (Washington, DC: Institute of Carmelite, 2017); a sketch of Mt. Carmel appears in Book I, chapter 13, p. 110, in which the word *nada* ("nothing") appears multiple times along the path of the "perfect spirit," including one on the mountain itself.

47 See Plato, *Apology*, trans. by Benjamin Jowett, in *Dialogues* (Oxford: Clarendon, 1953). Socrates' dreamless sleep (40cd) echoes this eternal *nada*: "Let us reflect in another way, and we shall see that there is great reason to hope that death is

a good, for one of two things: either death is a state of nothingness and utter unconsciousness, or, as men say, there is a change and migration of the soul from this world to another. Now if you suppose that there is no consciousness, but a sleep like the sleep of him who is undisturbed even by the sight of dreams, death will be an unspeakable gain. For, if a person were to select the night in which his sleep was undisturbed even by dreams, and were to compare with this the other days and nights of his life, and then were to tell us how many days and nights he had passed in the course of his life better and more pleasantly than this one, I think that any man, I will not say a private man, but even the great king, will not find many such days or nights, when compared with the others. Now if death is like this, I say that to die is gain; for eternity is then only a single night."

48 Arthur Zajonc, *Beyond Materialism*, chapter 10, 13–29.

49 The figure of Mary is remarkably similar to Michelangelo's *Bruges Madonna* completed twenty years later; see image 8.89.

50 Panofsky, *Early Netherlandish Painting*, 332.

51 Ibid.

52 Ibid.

53 Maurizio Saracini, "Diagnostic Investigations on the *Adoration of the Magi* by Leonardo da Vinci," in *The Mind of Leonardo—The Universal Genius at Work*, exhibition catalogue ed. by P. Gauluzzi (Florence, Italy: Giunti, 2006), 94–101. In 2012–2013, the painting was under restoration at the Opificio delle Pietre Dure in Florence. See also Frank Zöllner, *Leonardo da Vinci 1452–1519: Paintings, Sketches and Drawings* (Cologne, Germany: Taschen, 2000), 50–55, 180.

54 See Frederick Hartt, *Michelangelo: The Complete Sculpture* (New York: Abrams, 1968), 80. Incredulity before this youthful work of art may remind the reader of Albrecht Dürer's *Self Portrait* at age 13, see image 8.7.

55 John O'Donohue, *To Bless the Space Between Us: A Book of Blessings* (New York: Doubleday, 2008), 83–84.

56 Nicholas of Cusa distinguished between the rational instrumentality of *ratio* and the visionary capacity of *intellectus*; see Jasper Hopkins, "Nicolas of Cusa (1401–1464): First Modern Philosopher?" in *Midwest Studies in Philosophy* 26 (2002), also in *Renaissance and Early Modern Philosophy*, ed. by P. French and H. Wettstein (Malden, MA: Blackwell, 2002), 15.

57 Text transcribed and trans. by Otto Benesch in *the Art of The Renaissance in Northern Europe: Its Relation to the Contemporary Spiritual and Intellectual Movements*, revised edition (Leicester, UK: Phaidon, 1965), 7.

58 Panofsky, *The Life and Art of Dürer*, 12. Panofsky noted Dürer's essential humility in his own words: "For, the lie is inherent in our very cognition."

59 Michelangelo, quoted in Simone de Beauvoir, *The Coming of Age*, trans. by P. O'Brian (New York: Norton, 1996 [1970]), 514.

60 Ibid.

61 Ibid.

62 This new site, which so powerfully transforms the materialist objectification of works of art into an occasion of life-altering beholding, was designed by Michelle de Lucchi. The lighting is by Artimede. Cleaned, the *Rondanini Pietà* reminds us of John O'Donohue's blessing. It is my sense that the art of this sculpture is best encountered from the front in an arc from the oblique left to the oblique right, and not from the full 360 degrees provided.

63 Thomas à Kempis, *The Imitation of Christ*, 30.

64 "Sermon in stone" is commonly used to describe medieval churches, and most especially their relief sculptures, which spoke to literate and illiterate pilgrims alike. Although the phrase is often attributed to Bernard of Clairvaux, the founder of the Cistercian Order of the Church, I have not yet found a reliable source to confirm that attribution. But according to John LeClercq, a medieval historian, Benedictine monk, and author of the introduction to Bernard's sermons, we can imagine that among Bernard's many visits to churches in France, he would have certainly come to Autun and the Church of St. Lazarus. LeClerqc tells us that Bernard "saw the ascension [of Christ] as the fulfillment of the mystery of love in which the Incarnate Word returned to the glory of the Father," and because of that wrote more sermons on "the brilliance of the ascension" than on any other "mystery" of Christ. He quotes a section from one such sermon, relevant to our imagining of Bernard at Autun, in which Bernard addresses Christ directly: "I read that at the resurrection of Lazarus, your spirit groaned and writhed in distress. Yet this happened not because it was forced on you, but because you consented to it out of kindness." See John LeClerqc, "Introduction," in Gillian R. Evans, ed. and trans, *Bernard of Clairvaux: Selected Works* (Mahwah, NJ: Pauline Press, 1987), 45. Bernard also warned forcefully against the potential for misuse, material excess, and spiritual distraction of art. See Conrad Rudolph, *The "Things of Greater Importance": Bernard of Clairvaux's Apologia and the Medieval Attitude toward Art* (Philadelphia: University of Pennsylvania Press, 1990).

65 See Denis Grivot and George Zarnecki, *Gislebertus: Sculptor of Autun* (New York: Hacker Art Books, 1985); Linda Seidel, *Legends in Limestone: Lazarus, Gislebertus, and the Cathedral of Autun* (Chicago: University of Chicago Press, 1999).

66 Another contemporary artist "signed" his work with the words, "Gilabertus, who is not unknown made this." See Linda Seidel, "A Romantic Forgery: The Romanesque 'Portal' of Saint Etienne of Toulouse," *Art Bulletin* 50 (1968): 33–41.

67 Grivot and Zarnecki, *Gislebertus: Sculptor of Autun*, 150.

68 Compare images 7.17–7.22 in chapter 7.

69 Compare the contemporaneous image of the Fall of Man at the Abbey of St. Pierre in Moissac. Although the painting of *Adam and Eve* by Titian in the Prado in Madrid (7.20) is similar in its portrayal of physical beauty, the apparent

deliberate classicizing form of this image suggests an emblem of rectitude (i.e., a "beauty" about to be lost) rather than insight in the embodied eros of sensuality.

70 Contrasting the powerful message that Rilke has brought to our journey thus far by defining a "more human love . . . that consists in this, that two solitudes protect and border and salute each other," and in our "close reading" (*lectio divina*) of the Dream of Reason, we might look at John Milton's epic 17th-century poem *Paradise Lost*. In his grand expansion of the Temptation and Fall of Mankind, from one chapter in one book of the Bible (Genesis) into twelve books of blank verse, Milton creates an Eve whose desire for solitude directly leads to her Fall—and later to Adam's. In Book 9, Milton sees in his Eve a rebelliousness and desire for independence from Adam, which prompts her to suggest that they spend time alone in separate parts of the garden (ll. 214–219). Against Adam's protests, which he bases on the necessity for him to protect her, she argues more forcefully for their separation (ll. 322–326). The fallen angel Satan, disguised as a serpent, then encounters Eve not by chance but in a calculated effort to take advantage of her solitude. Despite her resistance when she realizes that the serpent has led her to the very fruit God has prohibited her to eat, she succumbs to his convincing personal endorsements of what the forbidden fruit provides. He tells her that upon eating it, he experienced a "Strange alteration," a "Reason in my inward Powers, and Speech" (ll. 599 and 600). He goes on to further sing the praises the fruit: "O Sacred, Wise, and Wisdom-giving Plant, / Mother of Science, Now I feel thy Power / Within me clear" (ll. 679–681). See Sandra M. Gilbert, "Eve in Milton's *Paradise Lost*: Poignancy and Paradox, published June 21, 2018, on the website for the British Library's "Discovering Literature: Restoration and the 18th Century" project, https://www.bl.uk/restoration-18th-century-literature/articles/eve-in-miltons-paradise-lost-poignancy-and-paradox.

71 Joseph Bédier, *The Romance of Tristan and Iseult* (New York: Random House, 1965), 124–125.

72 Ibid., 133–134.

73 Abbot Suger, quoted in Panofsky, *Abbot Suger on the Abbey Church of St.-Denis and its Art Treasures*, 63, 65.

Chapter 9: Circles of Affection: The Origin of Love

1 Plato, *The Symposium*, trans. by Christopher Gill (London: Penguin, 1999). For an extensive narrative synopsis of *The Symposium* and its scholarly commentary see D. Naugle, "The Platonic Concept of Love: The *Symposium*," www.docs-archive.com/The-Platonic-Concept-of-Love-pdf.

2 The *Symposium* begins and ends in the ordinariness of the day bracketing a dream-like interlude comparable to the *adagio* of Max Bruch's Violin Concerto, no. 1, in C. See chapter 3 for the aural interlude.

3 In the *Symposium,* sending away the "flute-girl" may signal not only a seriousness of purpose, but also a focus on a distinction between lust and eros. Flute girls (*aulêtrides*, more accurately, "female aulos players") were often slaves, and just as often stereotypically thought to be prostitutes. Three factors contribute to this simplistic view: their suggestive dress, as portrayed in painted red clay vases of the seventh to fifth centuries BCE; their significant presence at symposia, where drunken excesses were known to occur; and the likelihood that as slaves they were subject to unwanted sexual advances. Recent scholarship in classics and musicology shows flute girls to be more complex and nuanced than mere entertainer / call girls. See M. Goldman, "Associating the Aulêtris: Flute Girls and Prostitutes in the Classical Greek Symposium," *Helios* 42 (2015): 29–60.

4 Plato, *Symposium*, 48–49. Diotima's description of love echoes Shakespeare's "love is not love that alters when it alteration finds."

5 Ibid., 49–50.

6 See C. D. C. Reeve, "Plato on Friendship and Eros," in *Stanford Encyclopedia of Philosophy*, last revised 2016, https://plato.stanford.edu/entries/plato-friendship/#SocArtLov.

7 Ibid., 62.

8 Ibid.

9 Ibid.

10 Greek word *eromenos* is translated as "boyfriend" in Gill's and other versions of the *Symposium.* A brief excerpt from the speech of Pausanius brings context to the other quoted words in in this paragraph: "These two rules must be combined (the one governing the love of boys and the one governing the love of wisdom and other kinds of virtue), to create the conditions in which it is right for a boy to gratify his lover. These conditions are realized when lover and boyfriend come together, each observing the appropriate rule: that the lover is justified in any service he performs for the boyfriend who gratifies him, and that the boyfriend is justified in any favor he does for someone who is making him wise and good. Also the lover must be able to develop the boyfriend's understanding and virtue in general, and the boyfriend must want to acquire education and wisdom in general. When all these conditions are met, then and then alone is it right for a boyfriend to gratify his lover, but not otherwise." Plato, *Symposium*, 17.

11 Plato, *Symposium*, 57. Leading up to the line quoted, Alcibiades says: "Also, I think it would be wrong of me to let Socrates' proud action pass into oblivion now that I've embarked on his eulogy. Besides, my experience is that of someone bitten by a snake. They say that someone who's had this experience is only prepared to say what it's like to those who've been bitten themselves, because they're the only ones who'll understand and make allowances if the pain drives you to do and say shocking things."

12 See chapter 2, note 14, citing Robert Kegan, *The Evolving Self: Problem and Process in Human Development*, and *In Over Our Head: The Mental Demands of Modern Life*.

13 According to a 1972 UNESCO Commission report, there are four pillars for reshaping worldwide education. The first pillar, "learning to live together," requires three additional pillars, including "learning how to know" and "learning how to do." The fourth pillar of reimagined education is "learning how to be." (See Edgar Faure, *Learning to Be: The World of Education Today and Tomorrow,* UNESCO, 1972); Maren Elfert, "Revisiting the Faure Report and the Delors Report," *Power and Possibility*, http://doi.org/10.1163/9789004413320_002). From the perspective of *Contemplative Beholding: A Way of Life and Love*, learning how to be human is the precondition for the remaining three pillars. It is the threshold act of ontological awakening that forms the epistemological foundation of a new ethic of love.

14 T. S. Eliot, "Little Gidding" (from *Four Quartets*) in *Collected Poems* 1909–1962 (New York: Harcourt Brace, 1991), 208–209.

15 Plato, *Symposium*, 3. Imagine, as silent symposium beholders, our pleasure when we hear the punning wordplay in Plato's use of the noun *erôs* ("love") and the verb *erôtan* ("to ask questions").

16 Ibid., 4.

17 My colleague Rebecca Sinos integrates the beginning and ending of the *Symposium* as parts of a coherent poetic whole.

18 Plato, *Symposium*, 63.

19 Ibid., 64.

20 Alcibiades's description of Socrates as the embodiment of love poetically echoes the earlier characterizations of love in each of the five speeches.

21 This imagined "cosmos of color" emerged during many conversations with Arthur Zajonc.

22 See chapter 2, where I explain intimations of reconcilation in detail.

23 As one companion in this enduring challenge, compare John J. L. Mood, *Rilke on Love and Other Difficulties: Translations and Considerations of Rainer Maria Rilke* (New York: Norton, 1975), xii, epilogue, 115–117.

24 Recall Goethe's "sacred open secret"; see chapter 4.

25 In art, science, and life, we are often asked to sustain what appear to be impossible polarities. In art, with brushstroke and image, and in quantum physics, wave-particle duality is such a case. Much of the drama of life arises through the coincidence of opposites. For the "Eros and Insight" seminar I co-taught with Arthur, he proposed a Point and Circle exercise #7 as a way to illustrate sustaining contradictions:

(1) Begin by mentally visualizing a blue circle. This in itself may take some practice. With it vividly before your mind's eye, reduce the size

of the blue circle until it becomes a point, and then expand the point again until it becomes a circle of the original size. Repeat this until the transformation from circle to point and back again is fluid.

(2) Now replace the blue circle with a circle of the opposite color (yellow). Repeat by reducing and increasing the size of the yellow circle until, as for the blue circle, the movement between point and circle is fluid.

(3) Now bring the two elements together and practice "sustaining contradictions" or what Nicolas of Cusa called the "coincidence of opposites." Visualize a yellow point at the center of the blue circle. Simultaneously expand the yellow point into a large yellow circle and decrease the size of the blue circle until it becomes a blue point. Expand and contract the oppositely colored circles, and then describe the experience.

This exercise was by far the most difficult for the students of the seminar. The suggestion to "animate" the exercise with choreographed "dancers" wearing blue and yellow jackets helped. Student responses noted intersecting abstract and physical realities reminiscent of Diotima's vision and Alcibiades's physical presence.

26 Reminiscent of Martin Heidegger's "four-fold: earth and sky, mortals and divinities;" see chapter 2, note 18.

27 For left-handedness as a function of our embodied mind, see *Neuropsychology of Left-Handedness,* ed. by Jeannine Herron (New York: Academic Press, 1980). Jill Bolte Taylor, in *My Stroke of Insight* (New York: Penguin, 2006), describes the dramatic awakening of the overlooked potential of right-brain openness during her experience of a cerebral stroke.

28 Martin Buber, *I and Thou,* trans. by W. Kaufmann (New York: Simon & Shuster, 1970), 151.

29 Buber, *I and Thou,* 78: "Rather, the longing for relation is primary, the cupped hand into which the being that confronts us nestles; and the relation to that, which is a wordless anticipation of saying You, comes second. But the genesis of the thing is a late product that develops out of the split of the primal encounters (*Urerlebnisse*), out of the separation of the associated partners—as does the genesis of the I. In the beginning is the relation—as the category of being, as the readiness, as a form that reaches out to be filled, as a model of the soul; the *a priori* of relation; *the innate You.*"

30 Arthur Zajonc, "Human Endogenous Development" in *Moving Worldviews: Reshaping Sciences, Policies and Practices for Endogenous Sustainable Development,* ed. by B. Haverkort and C. Reijntjes, (Leusden, Netherlands: Compas, 2006); see also Karen Armstrong, *Twelve Steps to a Compassionate Life* (New York: Random House, 2011).

31 Compare Rembrandt van Rijn's *Aristotle with a Bust of Homer* (image 3.7) and Lao-tzu, *Tao Te Ching,* trans. by Stephen Mitchell (New York: Harper & Row,

1988), no. 58, "She is pointed, but doesn't pierce. Straightforward, but supple. Radiant, but easy on the eyes."

32 For Johannes Kepler, see the introduction. Where Simone Weil called contradiction the "cross," we might be encouraged to embrace the universally human impulse embedded in Thomas à Kempis's challenge to the pilgrim: "Listen closely. Everything is founded on the cross [conscious awareness—Milo's lament], and everything consists in dying on it, and there is no other road to life and to true inner peace than the road of the holy cross and of our daily dying to ourselves. Walk where you will, seek where you will, and you will find no loftier way above nor safer way below than the way of the holy cross." Thomas à Kempis, *Imitation of Christ*, trans. by W. Creasy (Notre Dame, IN: Ave Maria Press, 2004), 78–81, 155–156.

33 Saint Augustine, *City of God*, Books 17–22, in *Fathers of the Church,* Volume 24, trans. by G. G. Walsh and D. J. Honan (Washington DC: Catholic University of America, 1954), 506. Augustine described this goal as a place where: "There will be such poise, such grace, such beauty as become a place where nothing unbecoming can be found. Wherever the spirit wills, there in a flash, will the body be. Nor will the spirit ever will anything unbecoming either to itself or to the body."

34 I am grateful to Professor Wako Tawa for this interpretation of the *kanji* for the word *shakkei*.

Chapter 10: Homecoming and Departure

1 The italics here emphasize that I use the word *artistic* not as a mere adjective synonymous with "creative" but rather to signify the animating force of art as a verb: the *artist* is one who commits acts that fix the experience of intimated reconciliation by which others, when they behold, will be *artists* themselves.

2 See chapter 7, note 25, for Jaufré Rudel. Here I suggest an experiment if you doubt the "beauty" in the asymmetry of your face. Try using the digital power of Adobe Photoshop to create its opposite. Copy one-half of a frontal photograph of someone you cherish, flip it left to right and join the two parts in a new image: behold!

3 Robert Sweeney, who made this pastel during a visit to Chartres with me in 1974, is the artist who transformed an old carburetor into a cosmos of saturated color as a demonstration of artistic beholding for my class (see Introduction, Finding a Path to a Via Amoris). His vantage point for this pastel is identical to that of my photograph (image 10.6).

4 Henry Adams, *Mont Saint Michel and Chartres* [1904] (New York: Penguin, 1986), 123.

5 Adolf Katzenellenbogen, *The Sculptural Program of Chartres Cathedral: Christ, Mary, Ecclesia* (Baltimore: John Hopkins University), 1961.

6 There is continuing debate about the precise definition of this iconography.

7 R. M. Rilke, "You Who Never Arrived," *The Selected Poetry of Rainer Maria Rilke*, trans. by Stephen Mitchell (New York: Penguin, 1989), 131.

8 The direction of such deliberate self-transcendent being shares the evolutionary emergence of Pierre Teilhard de Chardin's visionary "noosphere," or the expanding synchronicity of the Global Consciousness Project. Pierre Teilhard de Chardin, *The Phenomenon of Man*, trans. by B. Wall (New York: Harper, 1959). See also Global Consciousness Project, Princeton, NJ, and Institute of Noetic Sciences, Petaluma, CA.

9 Thoreau, "Walking" [lecture in the Concord Lyceum, April 23, 1851; published in *Atlantic Monthly* in 1862 after his death], in *Walden and Other Writings*, ed. by Brooks Atkinson (New York: Modern Library, 1992), 662–663.

10 The final chapters of *The Tale of Genji* occur in the area of Uji, Japan. The final chapter is titled "The Floating Bridge of Dreams." See Murasaki Shikibu, *The Tale of Genji*, trans. by E. G. Seidensticker (New York: Knopf, 1992).

11 For those unfamiliar with Gordon Bok's beautiful 1974 song of forbearance in hard times, titled "Turning Toward the Morning," I share this refrain:

> Oh, Joannie, don't you know
> That the stars are swinging slow,
> And the seas are rolling easy
> As they did so long ago?
> If I had a thing to give you,
> I would tell you one more time
> That the world is always turning
> Toward the morning.

12 Thoreau, *Walden and Other Writings*, 85.

13 Carpet pages were a regular feature of illuminated manuscripts from early Christianity (the oldest dating to the seventh century). Some art historians believe their design may have been influenced by oriental rugs or other textiles. They are nearly always symmetrical and devoted almost exclusively to brilliantly colored, elaborate ornamental design motifs with geometric patterns that may include interlacing lines and repeated animal forms. Similar decorative pages appear in early Hebrew and Islamic illuminated manuscripts, although "carpet pages" may not be the term used to describe them.

14 Olivier Messiaen, "Lecture at Notre-Dame" [Notre-Dame Cathedral, Paris], trans. by T. J. Tikker (Paris: Alphonse Leduc, 2000), 14. In this lecture the composer explains two sensory experiments to describe two phenomena, complementary colors and the natural resonance of sounding bodies, which he believes are crucial to fully understanding music. As a further reflection on his assertion, as well as on the nature of bedazzlement, he quotes the fourteenth-century

mystic John of Ruusbroec: "Contemplation sees something, but what does it see? An excellence above all, which is not one thing, nor another."

15 In addition to subjective "experience" and objective "order" (*ars* and *scientia*), contemplative engagement with the carpet page as an image compared to contemplative physical movement within the labyrinth may for some resemble the alternative paths of kataphatic and apophatic prayer (i.e., with thought and image or without, by transcending thought and image). For a comparison of kataphatic and apophatic contemplation or prayer see: http://opcentral.org/resources/2015/01/13/frederick-g-mcleod-apophatic-or-kataphatic-prayer/.

Chapter 11: A Point of Renewal

1 Steven Naifeh and Gregory Smith, *Van Gogh: The Life* (New York: Random House, 2011), Appendix: A Note on Vincent's Fatal Wounding. Since this publication, two movies made by artist-painters have doubted suicide as the cause of death: *Loving Vincent* (2017, written and directed by Dorota Kobiela and Hugh Welchman) and *At Eternity's Gate* (2018, written and directed by Julian Schnabel).

2 Letter from Theo to Elizabeth, Aug. 5, 1890, trans. and ed. by Robert Harrison, http://webexhibits.org/vangogh/letter/21etc-Theo-Lies.htm.

3 See notes 11–14 in chapter 7 regarding differences in translation.

4 One stunning synchronic echo of Genji's ceaseless journey may be Walt Whitman's "Out of the Cradle Endlessly Rocking" included in *Complete Poetry and Collected Prose*: *Literary Classics of the United States* (New York: Viking, 1982). The poem conveys a young boy's first encounter with longing in the aftermath of death—as expressed in the song of a mockingbird mourning his mate—while standing on the shore *between* sea and land, named Paumanok by Native Americans. Coming back to this shore as a grown man, he is haunted by memories of what the "he-bird" sang—forever longing amidst the tears and waves on the sand. A few excerpts follow:

> Out of the cradle endlessly rocking,
> Out of the mocking-bird's throat, the musical shuttle,
> Out of the Ninth-month midnight,
> Over the sterile sands and the fields beyond,
> where the child leaving his bed wander'd alone,
> bareheaded, barefoot...
>
> A man, yet by these tears a little boy again,
> Throwing myself on the sand, confronting the waves,
> I, chanter of pains and joys, uniter of here and hereafter,
> Taking all hints to use them, but swiftly leaping beyond them,
> A reminiscence sing...

He call'd on his mate,
He pour'd forth the meanings which I of all men know...

Hither my love!
Here I am! here!
With this just-sustain'd note I announce myself to you,
This gentle call is for you my love, for you...

5 See Otis Cary, *Mr. Stimson's "Pet City"—The Sparing of Kyoto, 1945* (Kyoto, Japan: Amherst House, Doshisha University, 1987). See also Barton J. Bernstein, "Truman at Potsdam: His Secret Diary," *Foreign Service Journal*, July/Aug. 1980; Edwin O. Reischauer, in *My Life between Japan and America* (New York: Harper & Row, 1986), 101, identified Otis Cary as the one who credited Stimson with the recommendation to spare Kyoto.

6 John Hersey, *Hiroshima* (New York: Knopf, 1946); "Hiroshima," *New Yorker*, August 31, 1946; see also a memorial edition, "Sunday Reading: Hiroshima," *New Yorker*, August 2, 2020).

7 Ibid.

8 Gabrielle Decamus, *Invisible Colors: The Arts of the Atomic Age* (Cambridge, MA: MIT Press, 2017) provides a comprehensive account of the ways the arts (literary, dramatic, pictorial) have responded to the atomic age, ranging from Marie Curie to Hiroshima and Nagasaki to Fukushima. Her study is especially valuable for bringing together views from West to East as witnesses or, as she puts it, "global Hibakusha" (persons affected by the atomic bombings) to the events of our nuclear era.

9 The bomb bay doors of the B-29 bomber, "Enola Gay," opened at about 08:15:15. After dropping roughly six miles, the atomic bomb named "Little Boy" exploded around 08:16 at about 580 meters (1,900 feet) above the Shima Hospital (https: //www.atomicheritage.org/history/hiroshima-and-nagasaki-bombing-timeline). For the altitude see R. H. Minear, *Hiroshima: Three Witnesses*, ed. and trans. by R. H. Minear (Princeton NJ: Princeton University Press, 1990), 3.

10 For the immediate physical and human toll, see Hersey, "Hiroshima," and *Hiroshima* (New York: Knopf, 1946), with a new Knopf edition (1985), with a final chapter written forty years after the explosion. *The United States Strategic Bombing Surveys: European War, Pacific War* (Maxwell Air Force Base, Alabama: Air University Press, 1987); ("ground zero" is the term used in this report to designate the location on the ground directly beneath the bomb's actual place of detonation above ground known as "air zero."). See also: The Committee for the Compilation of Materials on Damage Caused by the Atomic Bombs in Hiroshima and Nagasaki, ed., *Hiroshima and Nagasaki: The Physical, Medical, and Social Effects of the Atomic Bombings*, trans. Eisei Ishikawa and David L. Swain (New York: Basic Books, 1981). Drawing on this report, Richard Minear records

"118,661 dead, 30,524 severely injured, 48,606 slightly injured, 3,677 missing, and 118,613 uninjured." Minear, *Hiroshima: Three Witmesses*, 3.

11 Kenzaburo Oe, *Hiroshima Notes*, trans. by D. Swain and T. Yonezawa (New York: Grove, 1995). See Minear, *Hiroshima: Three Witnesses*, for detailed personal accounts of the lived experience of the Hiroshima bombing by Tamiki Hara, Yōko Ōta, and Sankichi Tōge, including a series of poems by Tōge preceded by the following dedication (on page 304): "Dedicated to those whose lives were taken by the atomic bombs dropped August 6, 1945, on Hiroshima and August 9, 1945, on Nagasaki, to those who have continued down to the present to be tormented by the terror of death and by pain, to those who as long as they live have no way of extinguishing their agony and grief, and finally to those throughout the world who abhor atomic bombs." The first of the poems is "Prelude" (page 305).

> Bring back the fathers!
> Bring back the old people!
> Bring back the children!
> Bring me back!
> Bring back the human beings I had contact with!
> For as long as there are human beings,
> a world of human beings,
> bring back peace,
> unbroken peace.

12 For a selected photographic record of the bombing of Hiroshima, see John W. Dower, *Ground Zero 1945*, with Adam Harrison Levy, David Monteyne, et al. (Göttingen, Germany: Steidl, 2011); John W. Dower and Shigeru Miyagawa, "Ground Zero 1945: Pictures by Atomic Bomb Survivors," Visualizing Cultures website, MIT, 2008, https://visualizingcultures.mit.edu/groundzero1945/index.html.

13 Lindsley Cameron, "Starting from Zero at Hiroshima: An Interview with Kenzaburo Oe," June 24, 2005, 3–4 (italics mine). Accessed March 9, 2021, https://www.vqronline.org/web-exclusive/starting-zero-hiroshima-interview-kenzaburo-oe.

14 Kenzaburo Oe, *Hiroshima Notes*, 183.

15 Patty Kimura, born in Honolulu, Hawaii, thirteen years after the Hiroshima bombing, imagined poetically what might have been.

16 The Associated Kyoto Program (AKP) was created as a multi-college consortium organized to provide American students a year's educational experience living in Kyoto, Japan.

17 Jun'ichirō Tanazaki articulates poetically the tense ambiguity of this cultural accomplishment in his book *In Praise of Shadows*, trans. by T. J. Harper and E. G. Seidensticker (Sedgwick, ME: Leete's Island Books, 1977).

18 Under the leadership of Norman Cousins, *The Saturday Review* in 1949 created a Moral Adoptions Program in Hiroshima for 400 children orphaned by the atomic explosion of August 6, 1945. In 1951 Reverend Kiyoshi Tanimoto, John Hersey (*Hiroshima*, 1946), along with Pearl S. Buck, Norman Cousins, and Reverend Marvin Green, sought further to bring Japan and the United States together in their determination to redeem the recent past of Hiroshima and "explore ways of peace" in the creation of the Hiroshima Peace Center Foundation. In 1953 the "Hiroshima Maidens" program brought 25 young girls who had been badly wounded, disfigured, or crippled in the bomb blast to the United States for medical care, including numerous surgeries. One of these Hiroshima Maidens named Shigeko Sasamori has spent her life traveling and speaking as the living embodiment of horror and compassionate promise. See: Norman Cousins, *The Present Tense: An American Editor's Odyssey* (New York: McGraw-Hill, 1967), 324 ff.

Although Miyoko Matsubara was one of the Hiroshima Maidens who received surgeries in Tokyo and Osaka, she did not travel to America. Her recollection, written in 1999, is both moving and frank (Wikipedia.org/wiki/Hiroshima_Maidens; Miyoko Matsubara; "The Spirit of Hiroshima," https://web.archive.org/web/20130420074231/http:/www.wagingpeace.org/articles/1999/00/00_matsubara_spirit-hiroshima.php:

> With the warm help of these people and many others, I became one of sixteen young women known as the "Hiroshima Maidens" who traveled to Tokyo and Osaka for hospital treatment. Eight years after the bombing, when I was 20, in May 1953, I found myself in Osaka where I eventually underwent more than ten operations over a seven-month period. These operations were quite successful and, as a result, I was able to open and close my dysfunctional eyelid and to straighten out my crooked fingers. I was filled with gratitude towards those people who reached out with warm, loving hands and softly stroked my eyelid that wouldn't shut. I returned to Hiroshima, wishing for a way to express my thanks.... I and two other "Hiroshima Maidens" began work there as live-in caretakers. From morning until night, we were mothers to these children, helping them with homework, meals, going to the bathroom, and changing and washing clothes. Exactly one year later, in May 1955, my two companions left this job to travel to Mt. Sinai Hospital in New York to undergo more cosmetic surgery. For myself, I just didn't feel right about traveling to the U.S., the country which had dropped the atomic bomb. I was left behind alone.

19 Jun'ichirō Tanazaki, *In Praise of Shadows*, 7.

20 For comments by Miyako Matsubara, see "The Americans Are Not the Enemy," *Christian Social Action* 7, no. 8 (July–August, Japan, 1995): 9–11.

21 J. Robert Oppenheimer, quoted in James Temperton, "'Now I Am Become Death; the Destroyer of Worlds.' The Story of Oppenheimer's Infamous Quote," *Wired*, Aug. 9, 2017 (https://www.wired.co.uk/article/manhattan-project-robert-oppenheimer).

22 Having recently experienced the 75th anniversary of the bombings of Hiroshima and Nagasaki (August 2020), now might be a fitting time to reframe our thinking and behavior. In 1945 Paul Fussell was a 21-year-old army lieutenant about to be positioned for an allied assault on Japan to end the war. His "Thank God for the Atom Bomb," *The New Republic*, August 1981, written for the 40th anniversary of the bombings, is a compellingly detailed and thoughtful description of the direct experience of killing and dying at the center of the logic for targeting Hiroshima and Nagasaki from the Allied perspective. It can help to clarify our way forward, but for all of its passion and expansive references, it leaves unaddressed the tangled human source and horror of all killing. So too, the summer 2023 "blockbuster" film *Oppenheimer* avoids this universal origin by focusing the burden of destruction on J. Robert Oppenheimer. Oppenheimer's own haunting mea culpa may have implicated his colleagues in physics and even science, but not the human condition itself. Hiroshima and Nagasaki are only the most lethal episode of universal human killing. Whether limited or catastrophic, killing remains, in Rainer Maria Rilke's poetic summary, a "form of our wandering mourning."

23 My point here refers back to the UNESCO "four pillars" of education; see chapter 9, note 13.

24 On reflection, the science of nuclear physics appears to offer an unexpected insight in our search for a "more human love." Where the intimations of reconciliation of irreconcilable contradiction we have pursued embody the finite experience of infinite reunion, the dynamic activity of both fission and fusion reactions accelerates disintegration. Although the poetic energy of Einstein's $E = mc^2$ reaches for the relativity of finiteness and infinite wholeness, its material counterpart—unleashed (uncontained)—causes unfathomable destruction. Is it possible that metastasizing disintegration, fostered by the negative potential of digital technology no less than the personal reality of collapsing tribal isolation, mirrors nuclear fragmentation even as it translates the instantaneous physical devastation of Hiroshima and Nagasaki into a vividly perceptible social, intellectual, and spiritual devolution we dare not ignore?

25 Professor Wako Tawa agrees with this interpretation of *zanshō*. To Western ears, the sound of Buddhist temple bells in Kyoto may be unfamiliar. In place of a ringing tone, there is a muffled and somber sound felt as much in the reverberations of "lingering sound" as it is heard. The memorial bell rung randomly by visitors to the Peace Park in Hiroshima produces a similarly haunting "lingering sound."

26 My improvised encounter with 1 Corinthians 13:8–12.

27 Emily Dickinson, "Love Thou Art High," in *The Complete Poems of Emily Dickinson*, ed. by T. H. Johnson (Boston: Little, Brown, 1976), 217–218.

28 Thoreau, "Walden," in *Walden and Other Writings* (New York: Modern Library, 1992), 303.

Index

The entries in this index are meant to point readers not only to the people, places, and things that an index normally includes, but also—and more importantly, for their deeper reflection—to the interrelated and recurring themes of this book.

For some entries I provide pages to locate only their initial references and definition, such as for Via Amoris, or Rilke's "more human love" and his "killing is a form of our wandering morning." Others appear with multiple page numbers, if not comprehensive ranges, so that readers can follow the threads throughout, such as Milo's lament; Simone Weil's "gravity and grace"; and the relationship of brushstroke and image. For example, my student Jenny's sudden awakening to seeing "green" where there was only "red" offers several occasions for self-change, growth, and transformation that culminate in the coda's final moment of contemplative beholding with Rembrandt's *Return of the Prodigal Son*. Page numbers followed by "n" indicate notes that continue a discussion from the text or branch off into a related topic.

I list paintings and drawings, sculptures, music, books, essays, poems, and frequently cited quotations under the names of their respective artists, composers, performers, and authors only, instead of double-listing them under their titles as well—with the occasional exception: Rembrandt's *Aristotle with a Bust of Homer*, being the focus of chapter 3, and Leonardo da Vinci's *Adoration of the Magi* and *Last Supper*, the subjects of detailed analyses, deserve main entries with their own subheadings; also, several works by unknown artists appear in alphabetical order by title.

B

D

E

I

J

K

L

Endorsements for

Contemplative Beholding: A Way of Life and Love

Diana Chapman Walsh, president emerita, Wellesley College; trustee emerita, Amherst College; life member emerita, MIT Corporation

Contemplative Beholding: A Way of Life and Love is an inspiring journey into the art of beholding, of recognizing and of fully savoring the moments given to us in our brief lives to behold in such way that those moments will remain with us as sacred endowments. Upton extends this invitation "to anyone interested in discovering or rediscovering those enduring joys that will redeem the necessary sadness of human being." How could anyone resist the enormity of what's on offer here?

Here is just one of Upton's many heart-stopping observations: "Our human trajectory since the turn of the fifteenth century seems to have brought us to a point of shared desolation, which the superficial charisma of our dazzling accomplishments only partially obscures."

This is an amazing book, a unique book (and I don't use that word lightly), a book filled with erudition, insight, and, yes, *eros,* a great abundance of love. I loved the book.

I am deeply grateful for this active integration of embodied contemplative beholding, art, and love — which, as Upton says, is "our best alternative to the destructive meanness that weighs upon us all." Nothing could be more important at this perilous time in our history.

Mirabai Bush, founder and senior fellow, Center for Contemplative Mind in Society

This is an important book! Most contemplative scholars have favored working with text over image. Joel Upton has developed a form of contemplative engagement with images based on ancient methods of learning from art fused with contemporary technology to guide us in the act of "beholding." Challenged by the visual limits of the printed page, in *Contemplative Beholding: A Way of Life and Love* he takes us beyond the confines of the book to the illuminated digital presence of a painting, helping us learn to behold, to bring a painting to life. Using the beholding practice with the digitally illuminated image, we can form a relationship with a painting or other work of art leading to an intimate form of understanding: direct perception or insight. It makes beholding relevant outside the museum, even outside the classroom. With the book and the images, we can engage with the painting and its truth anywhere. Upton's work along with that of Arthur Zajonc, Steven Rockefeller (Middlebury), Barbara Dilley (Naropa), Linda Susan Beard (Bryn Mawr), Marilyn Nelson (UConn), Brad Grant (Howard) and so many others, is creating an academic environment in which students can understand their subjects more deeply while discovering meaning in their own lives.

Mohammed Hamid Mohammed, senior program officer, Fetzer Institute

Reading *Contemplative Beholding: A Way of Life and Love* is a thoroughly engaging and satisfying endeavor. Dr. Upton elegantly weaves his deeply personal experience with his knowledge of art history and a range of disciplines. He presents his argument not so forcefully as to unsettle — but rather as a generous sharing of his wisdom that sedimented and percolated over decades — by inviting the reader into a contemplative beholding of the many art works and literary jewels he includes in the book. Most of all, what I found compelling is that love is the energy and the center of that intimacy, the ground zero of knowledge and relationships.

Parker Palmer, author, educator, activist; founder and senior partner emeritus of the Center for Courage and Renewal

Author of *The Courage to Teach: Exploring the Inner Landscape of a Teacher* (1997), 2007; *A Hidden Wholeness: The Journey Toward and Undivided Life,* 2004; *The Heart of Higher Education: A Call to Renewal,* 2010 (coauthored with Arthur Zajonc)

From where I sit, *Contemplative Beholding: A Way of Life and Love* speaks to one of the most challenging and important goals for American higher education. In my own words, that goal is to open the classroom and the academic enterprise generally to a range of excluded epistemologies or modes of knowing. To call Upton's book "creative" and "original" is to understate the case, I think. I regard his approach as extraordinary, unlike anything I have seen during my forty years of engagement with these issues.

The "objectivist" epistemology that has dominated American higher education has either marginalized or driven out the epistemological challenges posed by traditional disciplines such as art and music; by contemporary reformulations such as quantum mechanics; and by upstart disciplines such as black studies and women's studies. And because there is a "trickle-down" effect from epistemology to pedagogy to ethics, the dominance of "objectivism" has had unfortunate implications for the latter two fields—resulting in pedagogies that distance students from the worlds they study, and an ethic (or anti-ethic) among parts of the educated class that relieves them from responsibility for those worlds.

This, in brief, is why I enthusiastically support Upton's effort to "animate human imagination of all kinds in the deliberate act of contemplative reconciliation of contradictory realities." Implicit in his approach, I believe, is a demonstration—rooted in both scholarly and pedagogical practice—that these "contradictory realities" are, in fact, paradoxical, with "the sensual" and "the cerebral" (as Upton names them) complementing each other and leading to a fuller form of knowing, teaching, learning, and living. *Contemplative Beholding* is, in my experience, unique (or nearly so), and kindred books may be hard to find.

Rowland Abiodun, John C. Newton Professor of the History of Art and Black Studies, Amherst College

Author of *Yoruba Art and Language: Seeking the African in African Art,* Cambridge University Press, 2014

Contemplative Beholding: A Way of Life and Love invites the reader to ask the very difficult question: What really preceded the word and the image? How do we make sense of that energetic substance that has eluded most scholars, especially when they become all too entangled and entwined with traditional art historical methodologies?

Contemplative Beholding challenges the reader but also lifts them to confront the "art" of art. Therein lies the imperative — to embark on a "spiritual journey." We experience a transformation in the way we behold art and see ourselves in it.

This is a fresh vision of the works of art with which we may already be familiar.

I laud this effort in piecing together the very fabric of notable artworks in all their constituent parts to remind us that their inherent power lies within their response to human experience.

Susan Burggraf, chief academic officer, Naropa University

I experienced Joel Upton's *Contemplative Beholding: A Way of Life and Love* as an invitation into the vast potential found when we cultivate a gaze that is soft, open, and precise, the gaze of love. This is the child-like gaze of the mature meditator. Upton leads the patient novice and expert alike to realize the grand, sweet, entirely accessible world-within-this-one of profound spirituality. With the speed and degradation of awareness that come from saturation in the disembodied and unkind superficiality of many of the offerings of popular culture, Upton's work restores appreciation of and access to our human capacity to understand and to see fully as leading surprisingly to love, the key to living whole.

This book unlocks the lifetime of discovery that the marriage of arts and humanities with contemplative practice heralds. Reading it and practicing the lectio divina that it encourages might best take place over a lifetime. As we behold the images, the text carefully walks through the literary, historical, and philosophical perspectives that invite us to a more complete appreciation all the way through, to a turn that stops the mind and leaves us again and again in a place of awe.

Since I don't have the eloquence to express the fullness of the experience, my eyes soften with tears as I feel the unlikely joy and humor and just-so completeness of *seeing* that developed and somehow didn't leave me as I engaged with Joel Upton's *Contemplative Beholding: A Way of Life and Love.*

I will recommend this book widely among my colleagues at Naropa, a contemplative university. While there are now many articles and books about contemplative education, Upton's is unique in offering complete access to the heart of liberal education to the genuine student in all of us.